# MAKING SENSE
# OF MANAGEMENT

# MAKING SENSE
# OF MANAGEMENT

## A Critical Introduction

*Mats Alvesson*
and
*Hugh Willmott*

This book belongs to:

Chris Hewitt
Tel; 0113 2716175

**SAGE** Publications
London • Thousand Oaks • New Delhi

SAGE Publications Ltd
6 Bonhill Street
London EC2A 4PU

SAGE Publications Inc
2455 Teller Road
Thousand Oaks, California 91320

SAGE Publications India Pvt Ltd
32, M-Block Market
Greater Kailash – I
New Delhi 110 048

**British Library Cataloguing in Publication data**

A catalogue record for this book is
available from the British Library

ISBN 0 8039 8388 3
     0 8039 8389 1 (pbk)

**Library of Congress catalog card number 96–068525**

Typeset by Mayhew Typesetting, Rhayader, Powys
Printed in Great Britain by Redwood Books,
Trowbridge, Wiltshire

*For Yvonne and Miha, and for Irena, Sasha, Anna and Chloe*

# Contents

# Preface

Why *Making Sense of Management?* Principally, because we believe that management is too important to be left to management gurus and the recyclers of the received wisdoms distilled in standard textbooks. The purpose of this book is to provide a fresh perspective on management that is at once broad and critical. *Broad* in the sense that the theory and practice of management is examined in relation to the emergence of modern capitalist society; and *critical* because assumptions underpinning the world of management are subjected to scrutiny rather that unacknowledged or disregarded.

We hope that this book will be of interest and relevance to practitioners working in different specialisms of management. Partly for this reason, we have included substantial sections on the major specialisms of management in addition to providing more general discussions of established ideas about management and organization. The book is also intended to be of value to students and teachers of management who remain unconvinced by, or who have become disillusioned with, more established ways of making sense of management.

To this end, we have brought together, for the first time in a single text, literatures that are scattered and buried in numerous journals across diverse specialisms. In addition to providing a useful sourcebook and pointers for further reading and research, this text is intended to stimulate further the development of an alternative approach to management theory and practice – an approach in which a preparedness to subject received wisdom to penetrating critical scrutiny is valued as a practical quality rather than dismissed as irrelevant or treated as heresy.

The book is the culmination of a project that can be traced back over the past ten years. An initial exploration of shared interests occurred in 1985 at a conference on Critical Perspectives on Organizational Analysis held in New York at Baruch College. These were pursued through the convening of a workshop in 1989. The positive reception given the publication of a selection of papers from that workshop (Alvesson and Willmott, 1992) sustained us in the preparation of the present book. Chapter 7 is a substantially revised and expanded version of an article originally published in *Academy of Management Review*, vol. 17, no. 2. Writing this book has been very much a joint project, with each of us being involved in the preparation of all the chapters. In a number of cases, alternative drafts were prepared and revised before we settled on a preferred approach. However, inevitably, the balance of contribution differs between the chapters. Chapters 1, 2 and 6 bear a stronger imprint from Hugh Willmott whereas Mats Alvesson has the stronger influence in Chapter 4, with the remaining chapters being more equal in their balance of contributions.

It has to be admitted that we underestimated the ambitiousness of the current undertaking and the time that it would take to complete. We are most grateful to Sue Jones at Sage for accommodating and indulging a project that has been juggled around other more or less expected events, including arrivals of children and changes of institution. We would also like to express our thanks to colleagues, friends and students for the continuing stimulation and encouragement, even – and perhaps especially – when their intellectual orientations have not been unequivocally sympathetic to those privileged in this book.

Since so many colleagues have helped us in diverse ways with this project, it is perilous to single out individuals for acknowledgement. Nonetheless, we would like to extend particular thanks to Stan Deetz, John Forester, David Knights, Bjørn Kjønstad, Richard Laughlin, John Mingers, Glenn Morgan, Jenny Owen, Michael Power, Richard Whittington and Edward Wray-Bliss, a number of whom provided us with comments on draft chapters. We are also grateful to the facilities provided by Copenhagen Business School during Hugh Willmott's appointment as a Guest Professor during 1989 when we had an opportunity to share ideas at some leisure, and to the Swedish Research Council for the Humanities and Social Sciences for a grant that made it possible to supplement telephone conversations and postal exchanges of drafts and disks with a number of face-to-face meetings in Copenhagen, Shrewsbury and Paris. We are also heavily indebted to our secretaries – Ann MacKinnon, Margareta Samuelsson and especially Mary O'Brien who carried the main burden of what, at times, must have seemed an endless redrafting process. However, our greatest debt is to our immediate family and especially to our respective partners, Yvonne and Irena, who have assisted this collaboration with great patience and good humour.

*Mats Alvesson and Hugh Willmott*
January, 1996

# Introduction

Management as a function, management as a distinct work, management as a discipline and area of study – these are all products of this century. (Drucker, 1977: 11)

The irrationality of domination, which today has become a collective peril to life, could be mastered only by the development of a political decision-making process tied to the principle of general discussion free from domination. (Habermas, 1971: 61)

During the last ten to fifteen years or so, old certainties about 'how' to manage have been unsettled by a number of developments. These have included increased concerns about the 'ethics' of business and management, the social and ecological consequences of economic activity, the widening application of information and communication technologies and, not least, the commercial success of 'new' (e.g. Japanese) philosophies and practices.

Contemporary disaffection with established management theory and practice is evident in the scale and recurrence of the change programmes taking place in so many organizations and also in the massive sales of books by the new 'gurus' – such as Peters and Waterman's *In Search of Excellence* (1982), Kanter's *When Giants Learn to Dance* (1989) and Hammer and Champy's *Reengineering the Corporation* (1993). Leaving aside the capacity of these books to generate substantial fortunes for their authors, their espoused purpose is to provide managers with fresh perspectives on management and innovative techniques for addressing emergent challenges.

But how fresh and incisive are these ideas? Do they indeed make connections between the major social and ecological problems of the modern world and the role of management in producing and addressing such problems? 'Guru' books can open a space for more critical thinking about established management theory and practice, but do they provide a new or especially challenging way of making sense of management? All too often, ideas presented as radical and revolutionary (e.g. Peters, 1992; Hammer and Champy, 1993) are actually preoccupied with preserving established priorities and privileges (e.g. profitable growth; managerial rule). They are dressed up in the language of innovation and liberation, yet they are more firmly wedded to refurbishing the status quo, with all its attendant social and ecological problems, than they are to processes of emancipatory change.

We believe that the theory and practice of management is poorly served by books that lack a *critical* perspective on the challenges and dilemmas

currently confronting those working and managing in modern organizations. As social and ecological problems pile up in the global economy,
there is an eerie sound of deckchairs being rearranged and repaired on the
*Titanic.* Instead of addressing more fundamental questions about the
defensibility and sustainability of this wasteful and divisive economy,
attention is focused upon ostensibly novel ways of regenerating management practice – such as Total Quality Management (TQM) and Business
Process Reengineering (BPR).[1] Commercial concerns about the inflexibility
and poor responsiveness of established organizational practices have
resonated with expressions of disillusionment about the effectiveness of
supposedly rational (e.g. bureaucratic) means of organizing. But very little
consideration has been given to the rationality of contemporary management theory and practice with regards to fundamental values and goals.

Where, then, do we turn for ideas that can provide a different and
challenging understanding of management theory and practice? Traditions
of social philosophy and social science – especially those that have questioned received wisdoms – can provide an important, yet largely neglected,
source of guidance and inspiration. In particular, the tradition of Critical
Theory and associated currents of thought have relevance for such a project.
Why Critical Theory? Because it is interdisciplinary and not doctrinaire; and
because it has been wrestling for decades with issues concerning management that are now increasingly acknowledged to be problematical for
human well-being – such as the mindless equation of scientific development
with social progress, the destructive effects of consumerism and commercialization, and the tendency of the modern state to equate policies (e.g.
deregulation) intended to enhance and/or legitimize capitalist accumulation
with the development of a more civilized, caring and just society.

In drawing upon the tradition of Critical Theory, we do not claim to
provide comprehensive coverage of all issues relevant for making sense
of management. We have not sought to offer a more wide-ranging view of
understanding of the political and economic contexts of management
which, in any case, has been developed by those who are better equipped to
produce such an account (e.g. Kellner, 1989). Our more modest ambition
has been to offer a preliminary and tentative sketch of management which,
we hope, may assist in the process of questioning and transforming
practices that are needlessly wasteful, harmful and divisive.

## Knowledges of Management – Conventional and Critical

Doubts about the value of established management ideas and practices have
coincided with an acceptance and expansion of management as a subject of
academic study. In combination, these developments have supported the
emergence of innovative ways of making sense of management that depart
from conventional assumptions and prescriptions, often by drawing selectively upon ideas developed within the social sciences.[2]

Scientific thinking has been venerated in modern societies. It is also widely accepted that the most taxing and recurrent problems of management are people-centred rather than technical in character.[3] It is not surprising, therefore, to find social scientific ideas being used to diagnose and address problems of management.[4] But the role of reason, in the guise of social science, in renovating managerial practice raises an interesting question. Namely, does reason have relevance for interrogating and transforming management practice in ways that extend *beyond* its established function of providing consultants and managers with a swirling pool of ideas and findings for addressing *only* those problems that are defined or predefined by managers and consultants?

In this book, we answer such questions in the affirmative. Yes, reason can, and should, have a broader role that extends beyond its use as a resource for identifying and legitimizing technologies of management control. Instead of being irrationally restricted to the task of refining the means of accomplishing existing ends (e.g. by eliminating needless effort and waste from current organizational practices), reason can also make a contribution in questioning whether *the existing ends routinely generate needless waste and divisiveness* (see Chapter 2).[5] Not only can reason be mobilized to refine the means of pursuing established ends; it can also be deployed to scrutinize the rationality of the processes through which the ends themselves are determined.

A basic problem with current theory and practice is that a narrow, instrumental conception of reason has largely eclipsed a broader critical appreciation of the emancipatory power of reason, with the – often irrational – consequence that what have appeared to be effective solutions to managerial problems have actually produced even bigger social and ecological problems (see Chapter 1). Only by standing back from immediate pressures to produce a technical fix to pressing problems is it possible to appreciate, *inter alia*, how a problem comes to be understood in a particular way and that, potentially, it could be diagnosed differently; why particular kinds of goals and solutions are routinely favoured when other goals and solutions could be pursued; and what changes are necessary if we are to confront, rather than merely displace, pressing social and ecological problems. As Thomas (1993: 12) has recently suggested, when contemplating the role of critical reflection in problematizing established management theory and practice, the value of such reflection 'lies ultimately in its ability to enhance our freedom, even to increase our chances of survival'. Critical reason cannot be equated with, or reduced to its contribution to, social engineering, troubleshooting or empire-building.

That the vast majority of textbooks and guru handbooks on management pay little or no attention to the relevance of *critical reason* to understanding and diagnosing the theory and practice of management is, in our view, a lost opportunity and a matter of much regret.[6] A preoccupation with the acquisition of techniques and ideologies of problem-solving is reflected in the view that management is exclusively about current 'practice' or prevailing ways of 'getting things done'. From this perspective on management, the development of understanding and theory is largely an irrelevance except insofar as it may contribute technical refinements to established practices. As Thompson and McHugh (1990: 28) have ruefully observed, in most literature on management, consideration of 'many deep-seated features of organizational life – inequality, conflict, domination, subordination and manipulation' is neglected or suppressed in favour of 'behaviourial questions associated with efficiency and motivation'. There is a reluctance to question the 'sacred' role and prerogative of management – a position that is routinely protected by the defensive understanding that the purpose of such questioning is to 'knock' management rather than to stimulate debate about its role and legitimacy.

An interest in developing *critical* knowledge of management, it is worth stressing, does not imply that a technical problem-solving orientation is worthless or bogus, or that it becomes irrelevant when a broader view of management is developed. On the contrary, both technical and critical orientations are legitimate, and we welcome the forging of closer links between them (Willmott, 1994b). Technical problem solving is an integral aspect of managing complex organizations; it does not become redundant – though it is likely to be transformed – with the development of less irrational, socially divisive forms of management theory and practice. But, reflection upon conventional wisdom can and should extend beyond the technical role of providing more effective diagnoses and 'fixes' for managerial problems, as managers commonsensically define them. Our intention in this book is to make the insights of critical thinking more accessible to, and hopefully thought-and-action-provoking for, a wide audience of management teachers and practitioners without trivializing their contents or patronizing our readers. It is our hope that the following chapters will provide a timely resource for making sense of management in ways that help to challenge received wisdoms and practices rather than uncritically reproduce or elaborate them.

## Plan of the Book

Chapter 1 clears the ground for the rest of the book. It introduces various themes that are expanded in the later chapters. Its basic purpose is to suggest that management is very much a *social and organizational* activity, in the sense that it involves unstable and unpredictable interactions between people. To represent management as something akin to engineering, as is frequently done, is highly misleading as the process of managing necessarily is a medium and outcome of a complex field of politico-economic, cultural and moral relations. Accordingly, *social theory* provides a relevant resource for understanding and reflecting critically upon the organization and dynamics of management practice. Critical Theory, we argue, is sufficiently open, broad and self-questioning both to address issues spawned by social and economic change and to accommodate the contributions of other strands of critical thought.

Chapters 2 and 3 are concerned with setting our overview of management in its intellectual context. Chapter 2 directly confronts the argument that management can be, or should be, 'scientific' – in the sense of the claim that basing management upon objective, scientific knowledge would remove subjectivity and politics from management practice. We challenge the view propounded by Weber and followers that knowledge of society, including knowledge of management, is – or ever can be – value-free. Taking the side of Critical Theory, we argue that the role of scientific knowledge is to expose dogmas and domination, not to replace them with seemingly unassailable scientific knowledge. Burrell and Morgan's model of different paradigms of knowledge generation is used to illustrate the diversity of social scientific knowledges and also to locate Critical Theory in relation to studies of management inspired or influenced by other critical traditions. Chapter 3 presents a brief history of the emergence and development of the Critical Theory of the Frankfurt School, the principal intellectual inspiration for this book. In this chapter, we also give some indications of limitations in Critical Theory – a concern to which we return in Chapters 7 and 8.

In Chapters 4–6, we examine the study of management and its subdisciplines, drawing upon Critical Theory as our primary source of guidance. Chapter 4 considers and illustrates a number of alternative conceptualizations of management and organization. Among other things, we explore the ways in which management can be understood as a form of technocracy, as a process of mystification and as a colonizing power (as management thinking and techniques are introduced into more realms that previously were considered to be strictly 'personal' or 'cultural'). In Chapters 5 and 6, we turn our attention to the various subdisciplines of management. In Chapter 5, we consider the 'soft' or 'qualitative' specialisms of organization theory, marketing and strategic management.[7] We present a brief overview of the focus and variety of perspectives within each specialism. We then explore the contribution of studies that challenge or overturn conventional wisdom within each specialism, especially those studies that are directly indebted to Critical Theory. Chapter 6 considers the specialisms of accounting, operational research and information systems – the 'hard' or 'quantitative' disciplines. Following a similar pattern to Chapter 5, it shares the same purpose of reviewing and illustrating the contribution of critical studies to making sense of the existence and application of these specialisms.

Chapters 7 and 8 present a series of reflections upon the relevance and value of the broad approach to understanding management introduced in the previous chapters. Chapter 7 explores the scope for bringing together elements of conventional understandings of management with insights drawn from its critical study. This entails some questioning of the practical relevance and accessibility of Critical Theory – something which, in principle, is

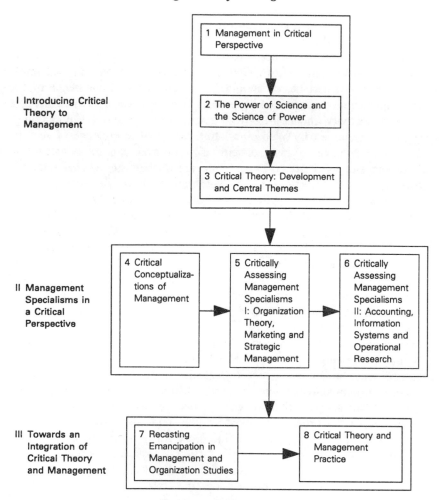

Figure i.1 *Overview of Chapters*

consistent with its commitment to self-reflection and autocritique. In particular, we suggest the need to concretize the abstractions, and indeed pollute the purism of Critical Theory, if it is applied in organizational contexts or is used to inform non-esoteric management research. To this end, we sketch some ideas for the fruitful merging of the insights of Critical Theory and the recurrent preoccupations of management and organization studies. Chapter 8 is more directly concerned with management practice as we consider the relevance of Critical Theory for the development of management practice that, arguably, is more defensible ethically and politically.

Overall, then, the chapters are structured in a way that allows our approach to making sense of management to be introduced and elaborated in Chapters 1–3, illustrated in Chapters 4–6 and reflected and developed upon in Chapters 7–8 (see Figure i.1).

To benefit from this structure, the book is probably best read in chapter order. Nonetheless, we anticipate that some, perhaps most, readers will prefer to look first at sections that are of most immediate interest to them. Partly because we anticipate a readership with varied backgrounds, knowledge and concerns, it is possible to read each chapter without reference to the others. To assist non-linear readings, we have provided many cross-references to indicate where related arguments are expanded and have resisted the temptation to remove minor repetitions.

Precisely because it steers away from recycling the cliches and recipes found in most textbooks prepared for management students and handbooks written for practising managers, we would like the book to be read by practitioners as well as by students; and it is not just the hope of royalty cheques that stimulates this desire! We firmly believe that forms of analysis developed within the critical traditions of social theory are actually more pertinent and insightful for making sense of the everyday tensions, irrationalities and dilemmas encountered by practising managers than the tired ideas and superficial prescriptions contained in most management textbooks and guru handbooks.

Unlike most management texts, we make no promises that the following chapters provide recipes for the solution of everyday managerial problems, or even that their contents will directly advance the reader's career as a manager (though it is by no means incompatible with such an outcome). Rather, our hope is that the book will contribute to the development of less superficial and destructive forms of management theory and organizational practice. Through processes of critical reflection and discussion, it is to be hoped that ways will be found, individually and collectively, to identify and reduce the needless waste and divisiveness in modern organizations over which mainstream theory and practice of management presides.

## Notes

1 See, for example, Oakland (1989) and Hammer and Champy (1993). For critical discussions of TQM, see Wilkinson and Willmott (1995a) and for a critique of Business Process Reengineering, see Willmott, 1994c, 1995e; Willmott and Wray-Bliss, 1995).

2 In *Search of Excellence* (Peters and Waterman, 1982: Chapter 4), for example, the work of the social psychologists and organization analysts James March and Karl Weick is heavily cited to advance and legitimize the authors' alternative approach.

3 In recent years, there has been an especially keen interest in the effectiveness of clans (Ouchi, 1981) and corporate cultures (Deal and Kennedy, 1982) as alternatives, or supplements, to the 'iron cage' of bureaucracy and the 'whip' of the market.

4 Earlier examples include Chris Argyris's *The Applicability of Organizational Sociology* (1972) and Tom Lupton's *Management and the Social Sciences* (1971). The knowledge of management and organization generated by 'open systems' theory, Lupton claimed, can transform management practice, as what previously had occupied 'the sphere of ideology and guesswork will be raised to the level of scientific discourse and technological know-how' (Lupton, 1971: 141).

5 In this process, reason can also be mobilized to reflect critically upon its own limits, and

particularly the modern tendency to privilege a scientistic ethos that devalues the concerns and virtues of mundane, common-sense reasoning (Habermas, 1971).

6 That books written by management gurus will be targeted at the 'professionalism' and material self-interest of their readers is perhaps to be expected. Routinely, their contents seek to combine light entertainment with the aggrandizment of managerial work and hints for the advancement of individual careers. Unfortunately, most academic textbooks and research monographs are swept along by parallel concerns. All too often, they seem preoccupied with a concern to make management a respectable area of study rather than to raise challenging questions about its foundations or to subject management theory to critical examination.

7 Of course, much work in these areas is quantitative, but these specialisms are more behaviourially oriented.

# PART I

# INTRODUCING CRITICAL THEORY TO MANAGEMENT

---

## 1

## Management in Critical Perspective

In all societies, people are involved in the complex and demanding business of organizing their everyday lives. Each of us engages in a daily struggle to accomplish ordinary tasks and maintain normal routines. This management of routines is something that we all contribute to, and are knowledgeable about – it is 'second nature'. But, in modern societies, responsibility for the management of everyday tasks, routines and identities increasingly has become the preserve and monopoly of experts, including managers, who are trained and employed to shape, organize and regulate so many aspects of our lives. The phenomenal growth of leisure and personal services industries in recent years is symptomatic of this trend.

Experts have assumed the role of 'improving upon' the custom and practice of established traditions, habits and routines (Scott and Hart, 1989; Deetz, 1992a). Managers now exert a secular influence over forms and spheres of activity that previously were organized by sacred or military authorities and/or, locally or domestically, within communities and households. Government, education, health, consumption, the arts, leisure and, of course, work have all become objects of management knowledge and control (Luke and White, 1985).

Managers are employed in diverse organizations. They perform a wide variety of roles and tasks; they are trained and located within different specialisms; and they work at different levels in organizational hierarchies. They also work in uncertain conditions, are in possession of imperfect information and are under pressure to be responsive to a plurality of demands. This diversity makes it far from easy to generalize about what managers do (Whitley, 1984a), or indeed to make any coherent sense of management – a problem that is compounded by the variety of meanings ascribed to the term 'management' (see Child, 1977).

Amid the confusion and uncertainty about what management is, there has been a tendency to privilege one meaning: management as a universal process that comprises a number of technical functions. Central to this formulation is the understanding that management is a distinctive component of all complex systems, and that it is rational to allocate this activity to those who are deemed to be experts. However, a moment's reflection makes it obvious that the technical functions of management do not exist, and indeed can never exist, in a social or historical vacuum. As Child (1969: 16) has noted, the meaning and activity of management is 'intimately bound up with the *social* situation of the managing group' (emphasis added). If this is so, then technical conceptions of management, which are blind to this 'situation', are actually expressions of the particular circumstances in which the theory and practice of management develops.

Hales (1993) situates the development of management in the context of the guardians of private capital and the growth of the modern state. He observes how 'the separation of management is an outgrowth of disparities in socio-economic power, the acquisition or initiation of work processes by private capital or the state, and the desire for control which flows from that: hence the contested nature of that separation' (ibid.: 6 and 8). Management is thus understood, or theorized, as a product of the historical context in which it emerges, takes shape and then increasingly gives shape to its context. Hales relates the separation of management, as a function and status group, to its role in maintaining, developing and controlling forms of work organization that pre-serve disparities of socio-economic power within the private and public sectors. In practice, the work of managers, Hales suggests, is not a neutral, technical activity precisely because disparities of ownership, income and opportunity demand, as a precondition of the coordination of employee effort, the exercise of control to stimulate effort and contain dissent.

In all societies, whether primitive or advanced, capitalist or socialist, productive processes are coordinated or 'managed'. The issue, then, is not whether management will continue to exist as an activity. Rather, the critical issue is the *kind* of management there will be; and, most crucially, whether the theory and practice of management will continue to normalize and exploit social divisions and be driven by the priorities of élites, or whether it will become more democratically accountable to a majority of citizens, producers and consumers.

## Beyond the Understanding of Management as a Technical Activity

When management is represented as a *technical activity*, a blind eye is turned to the *social relations* through which managerial work is accomplished and upon which it ultimately depends (Whittington, 1992). This blindness reflects and reinforces the understanding that problems of management can be adequately diagnosed and remedied by developing more efficient and effective means of technical control. Problems (e.g.

unemployment, pollution) that are fundamentally *social* and *political* in organization come to be interpreted as amenable to *technical* solutions. However, when instrumental forms of reasoning alone are deemed to be relevant and legitimate resources for advancing the science of management (Willmott, 1995b), our understanding of management is unnecessarily and dangerously restricted in its capacity to address the escalating social and ecological problems of the modern world (see Lipietz, 1992). What Burris (1993: 179) has argued in relation to the use of new communication technologies is equally applicable to other areas and specialisms of management. Namely, that if the design and implementation of new systems is to become more democratic 'with the social and political factors receiving as much attention as technical ones' (ibid.), it cannot be assumed that all problems are amenable to a 'technical fix' within the status quo or that technical experts alone possess the expertise to devise and implement effective solutions.

Blindness to the social media of management also restricts awareness of how the human difficulties and challenges associated with organizing everyday tasks are compounded whenever major divisions – manifest in differences of values, objectives and resources – exist between those involved in accomplishing such tasks. Where there are divisions – of class, gender, ethnicity, etc. – between managers and managed, everyday difficulties of securing cooperation are magnified. Whenever communication between managers and managed is impeded and distorted by institutionalized forms of domination (e.g. patriarchy), cooperation is conditional and precarious.

Managers are not unaware of the pressures and contradictions of their work. They frequently feel frustrated and abused by the systems which they supposedly control, and they frequently bemoan the difficulties encountered in gaining unequivocal cooperation and commitment from their colleagues as well as from their staff (Watson, 1994). However, received wisdom provides them with minimal insight into these problems. Management education and training routinely encourages managers to privilege the claims of technical, instrumental reason (see above) though it excludes exposure to ideas that, potentially, are highly relevant for making sense of the pressures and contradictions of their work. Conventional representations of management may furnish managers with a comforting sense of their own 'impartiality', 'professionalism' and functional importance. But conventional wisdom marginalizes, or trivializes, the politics of managerial work. Managers are thus prevented from gaining a more critical perspective on their involvement, as key players (and victims), in the development of 'a continually refined administration of human beings [in which] science, technology, industry and administration interlock in a circular process' (Habermas, 1974: 254).

Once an exclusively technical image of management is abandoned, managers are seen to juggle competing demands for resources and recognition, demands that come from other managers as much as from their subordinates (Burns, 1977; Kotter, 1982). However, a narrow focus upon intergroup politics can itself deflect attention from more fundamental conflicts of interest that are rooted in deeper social divisions – divisions which include those of gender and ethnicity, as well as those between employers and employees as buyers and sellers of labour. It therefore makes little sense to abstract the technical, universal functions of management from the social media of their operation. Or, rather, it makes only ideological sense to spare from critical scrutiny the claim that managerial authority is firmly based upon objective expertise uncoloured by sectional values and objectives.

Representing management as a predominantly technical activity creates an illusion of neutrality. Management theory is sanitized and management practice is seemingly distanced from the structures of power and interest that, inescapably, are a condition and consequence of its emergence and development (Willmott, 1984a, 1987). In the context of capitalist societies, economic and political risks associated with ownership have been met and spread by the development of management as a distinct (and comparatively privileged) social group who are primarily accountable to owners, not employees or consumers. The rise of management has institutionalized the lack of democratic control over the allocation of resources within, and by, work organizations. This lack of accountability increases the social and ecological risks for employees, customers and citizens (Deetz, 1992a). Once management becomes a separate social group, the idea of a community of interest becomes problematical, especially where there is little or no accountability of managers to the managed. Even where women and ethnic minorities join the ranks of management, a condition of entry and promotion is adherence to established values and preoccupations that are predominantly those of white, middle-class males – the group that has been identified and socialized as most likely to pursue the objectives of owners and respect their property. Before expanding upon this understanding, we outline briefly the main theoretical inspiration for this way of making sense of management.

## Critical Theory and Modern Society

Since time immemorial, and certainly since the Enlightenment, human beings have mobilized their powers of critical reasoning to doubt and change established customs, ideologies and institutions – such as the practice of witchcraft, slavery and, more recently, patriarchal ideas that have denied universal suffrage. In common with the other strands of critical thinking,[1] Critical Theory (CT) builds upon this legacy to scrutinize contemporary practices and institutions. For example, it challenges the rationality of the acquisitiveness, divisiveness and destructiveness that accompanies the relentless expansion of globalizing capitalism as nation states compete with each other to produce the most favourable conditions for investment. Insofar as management theory and practice are implicated in these developments, they are clearly relevant targets of critical analysis.

## The Capacity for Critical Reflection

Our cultural separation from nature enables human beings to construct a meaningful world, and to question and change our values and institutions. In the contemporary era, the Enlightenment tradition of critical self-reflection continues to support a questioning attitude towards the claims of authorities (Schroyer, 1973), including the claims of management experts and gurus. But this critical spirit has to be actively nurtured if it is not to be suppressed or diluted – as, for example, when power and control becomes concentrated in the hands of an élite that successfully mobilizes their privileged access to material and symbolic resources to secure control through terror and/or propaganda.

The intent of CT is to challenge the legitimacy and counter the development of oppressive institutions and practices. For example, in the field of management, phallocentric values and practices are widely revered, institutionalized and appear to be normal. Conversely, alternative (e.g. feminist) values and practices are frequently marginalized and devalued (Ferguson, 1984). A glaring, yet largely unnoticed, form of oppression is the virtual exclusion of women from processes of managerial knowledge development and dissemination (Calas and Smircich, 1992; see also Chapter 2). Critical Theory seeks to highlight, nurture and promote the potential of human consciousness to reflect critically upon such oppressive practices, and thereby facilitate the extension of domains of autonomy and responsibility. By autonomy, CT means the capability of human beings to make informed judgements that are not impeded and distorted by socially unnecessary dependencies associated with subordination to inequalities of wealth, power and knowledge. By responsibility is meant a developed awareness of our social interconnectedness and, thus, a realization of our collective responsibility for each other.

In modern Western societies, the ideology of individualism encourages us to assume that we are each sovereign, self-determining beings. This ideology is routinely reinforced whenever, for example, 'success' in gaining grades at school, 'winning' jobs in the labour market or even 'acquiring' sexual partners, is routinely attributed to the qualities that individuals are deemed to possess. Without denying that human beings differ, critical reflection upon such manifestations of the ideology of individualism reveals the identification and valuing of specific attributes to be a product of culturally specific processes and practices (in the family, in the school, etc.). Processes that are currently dominant encourage us to understand and identify ourselves as self-determining beings. Critical reflection upon the ideology that sustains such processes is difficult, however, precisely because the ideology operates to impede or dull the understanding that our sense of sovereignty is not integral to human nature but, rather, is socially generated and reproduced.

In this context, 'autonomy' is not simplistically equated with increased opportunities to get better grades or jobs. Such ideas simply reflect and reinforce the ideology of individualism as they ascribe 'achievement' to the individual rather than to the social processes that make possible the gaining of grades and/or the ascription of attributes to individuals. Instead, the idea of autonomy anticipates the possibility of developing a society in which critical reflection upon prevailing ideologies is actively promoted, including the ideology of individualism, as a means of securing emancipation from the sufferings associated with confused thinking and oppressive social relations. To put this another way, the idea of autonomy anticipates the development of social relations that exemplify 'responsibility'. Instead of assuming the illusion of independence, a critical understanding of autonomy acknowledges the everyday reality of interdependence. In practical terms, this means that the attribution of any achievement, or quality, to individuals is fully recognized to be the outcome of social processes to which each human being contributes. In turn, critical examination of such established ideologies encourages a transformation of institutions that preserve the social relations that nurture and legitimize such thinking.

Democracy is viewed as a condition and a consequence of autonomy and responsibility. Decision making that is unequivocally democratic can occur only when individuals are able to think and act autonomously and responsibly. Committed to applying critical reason to expose and overcome domination, Critical Theory (CT), Habermas argues,

> takes up a partisan position in the controversy between critique and dogmatism, and with each new stage of emancipation it wins a further victory. In this kind of practical reason (as contrasted with technical reason), insight and the explicit interest in liberation by means of reflection converge. The higher level of reflection coincides with a step forward in the progress toward the autonomy of the individual, with the elimination of suffering and the furthering of concrete happiness. (Habermas, 1974: 254)

Some forms of critical thinking are sceptical, if not dismissive, about the possibilities of emancipation – on the grounds, for example, that it is not possible to adjudicate rationally between two competing ideologies. In contrast, CT contends that emancipatory progress has been made in the past and, potentially, can be made in the future. The abolition of slavery, for example, is identified as an emancipatory step, as are struggles to develop more democratic forms of government – even though these advances are often compromised and precarious. While critical reflection is rarely a sufficient condition of such change, it is generally a necessary element in discrediting ideas and practices that legitimize and sustain diverse, institutionalized forms of oppression.

CT has always been a broad church (see Chapter 3) but it does not have a monopoly over critical thinking. The tradition of CT has been concerned to stimulate and support diverse processes of critical reflection rather than to present itself as providing a definitive formulation of the nature, content and dynamics of these processes. This reflection comprises abstract and concrete elements or moments – sometimes described, respectively, as 'reconstruction' and 'critique'.

Reconstruction mobilizes critical reason to diagnose prevailing conditions. For example, reconstruction identifies and analyses the presence of social elements (e.g. class, patriarchy) within the formulation and application of the functional rationality that supposedly governs the disciplines and techniques of management. Relatedly, reconstruction suggests that problems of management are frequently mystified – for example by denying or naturalizing the presence of these social elements. Critique goes beyond reconstruction as critical *self-reflection* occurs. When engaging in reconstruction, the individual acts as a *surveyor* of problems in a way that assumes a separation of the observer from the observed. Critique, in contrast, takes responsibility for the problems that are identified and involves a commitment to *participating* in changing the conditions that are diagnosed as fostering and legitimizing mystification and associated practices of domination – such as views of management which, in presenting it as a neutral or technical activity, deny or distort its fundamentally social elements. Reconstruction can inform critique but it is not necessarily productive of it. Reconstruction, Connerton (1976: 20) notes, may lead to 'a greater sophistication in the possession of our theoretical knowledge . . . without necessarily changing our practical conduct'. In contrast, critique entails 'a process of self-reflection, in individuals or groups, designed to achieve liberation from the domination of past constraints' (ibid.). Critique goes beyond diagnosis. This it does by showing how, for example, an effective solution to seemingly technical problems demands a change in the conditions (e.g. structured social inequality, prevailing forms of business school education) that must be actively struggled for.

When at work or in education, it is not unusual for practitioners or students of management to experience some twinges of discomfort about some aspect of the theory and/or practice of management. What or how they are being told, or are being required to do, may be disquieting or mildly offensive because it violates their sense of propriety or reasonable conduct. For instance, Watson (1994) studied a group of senior managers who, following interviews with their new managing director, Paul Syston, suspected of being hired as an axeman, feared for their jobs.[2] In principle, such unnerving occasions can stimulate a process of reflection on the structures that make such episodes possible. However, for this to occur, there must be access to some form of theory that provides a different way of making sense of such experiences of managerial work. It is understandable, in the light of our earlier discussion of the ideology of individualism, that the managers studied by Watson were preoccupied with Syston's motives, his personal style and his inclinations. But their experience could have prompted them to reflect upon the conditions that make it possible for bosses to treat their subordinates in such a distant, intimidating and unendearing way. Had they pursued this process of reflection, these managers might have understood or 'reconstructed' their treatment by Syston as symptomatic of the contradictory positioning of managers within capitalist organizations – a position in which they are simultaneously rendered responsible for organizational performance and, as sellers of labour, are in fear of losing their jobs.

Instead of personalizing the problem in terms of Syston's personal style or his appearance as 'a bit of a miserable sod' (ibid.: 103), these managers could have been prompted to reflect upon how the hierarchical relationship (and associated social distance) between managing directors and senior managers operates as a potent mechanism of control over managers as well as other employees. Arguably, it was this structural arrangement of subordination, and not Syston's personality *per se*, that made it difficult for the senior managers to ask him directly what his plans were. Indeed, the temptation for those in power to develop this non-communicative style can itself be interpreted as a response to the pressures that *they* experience. By refusing to enter into any kind of personal relationship with his senior managers, Syston effectively denied any moral relationship to them, and was therefore more easily able to treat them as commodities to be hired and fired at will.

To move from reconstructive diagnosis to critique would require the senior managers to reinterpret the anxieties and paranoia fuelled by Syston's silence about his plans for the company (ibid.: 103) as symptomatic of the structural arrangements, rather than as self-indicative of their personal inadequacies. In turn, a process of critical self-reflection could have reduced their anxiety and, as a consequence, enabled them to deal more effectively with their new boss. Instead of simply deciding to 'wait and see' or even agreeing to work on the assumption that Syston was listening and willing to be persuaded (ibid.: 104–5), their interviews with him could have prompted a process of critique. For example, they could have resolved individually and collectively to work towards the development of more democratic structures of corporate governance so that those occupying managerial positions (e.g. managing directors) become more accountable to fellow employees – a shift that, logically, requires managers to seek out, challenge and change diverse anti-democratic industrial structures and practices, including their own dealings with each other and their subordinates. Such a shift, it is worth stressing, would involve not only procedural changes in the structure of corporate governance but substantive, embodied changes in how managers make sense of their responsibilities and undertake their work. Changes of this kind, however slight or fumbling, can and do occur as people realize, through a process of critical self-reflection, that an emancipatory change in structures is a condition as well as a consequence of the transformation of self. In general, people who are inclined to 'wait and see' rather than to 'reflect and act' are simultaneously the victims and the perpetrators of the situations from which they desire to escape.

In sum, the intent of CT is to foster a rational, democratic development of modern institutions in which self-reflective, autonomous and responsible citizens become progressively less dependent upon received understandings of their needs, and are less entranced by the apparent naturalness or inevitability of the prevailing politico-economic order. To this end, CT encourages the questioning of ends (e.g. growth, profitability, productivity) as well as their preferred means, such as dependence upon expert rule and bureaucratic control, the contrivance of charismatic corporate leadership, gendered and deskilled work, marketing of lifestyles, etc.

## Critical Theory and Management Practice

As we have noted, much received wisdom represents management as a neutral technology of goal achievement that carries with it no implicit moral commitments and consequences (Macintyre, 1981). Whenever managers devise or adopt methods (e.g. of job or organizational design) on the 'rational' grounds that they are more effective or efficient, they implicitly endorse and legitimize a society in which it is acceptable to treat human beings as means rather than ends (Roberts, 1984). In textbooks and in training courses, management disciplines and skills (e.g. the skills of selection and appraisal that are ascribed to Human Resource Management) are presented as neutral techniques that guide and empower individual employees to work more effectively.

A major problem for making sense of management is that 'whether a given manager is effective or not is on the dominant view a different question from that of the morality of the ends which his [*sic*] effectiveness serves or fails to serve' (Macintyre, 1981: 71). The authority ascribed to managerial techniques and skills operates ideologically to legitimize the treatment of individuals as objects of managerial decision making who are excluded from participating fully in decisions that directly or indirectly affect their working lives (Steffy and Grimes, 1992). And yet beneath, and often obscured by, the operation of the systems established by management is the everyday working life, or lifeworld, of employees. In this world, moral evaluations (e.g. about the trustworthiness of managers' promises) motivate and condition behaviour, as we noted in the earlier example of Syston's treatment of his senior managers. Moral judgements are repeatedly made about the acceptability or reasonableness of others' behaviour or expectations. As Anthony (1986: 198) has observed, the practice of management inescapably 'rests upon a moral base'. Even when this moral basis is denied or mystified by the functional rhetoric of technical rationality, both managers and managed make more or less explicit reference to moral notions of 'fairness' and 'reasonableness' in order to gain a measure of unforced agreement as they strive 'to get things done through other people' (Fox, 1974).

Whether deliberately or inadvertently, management practices invariably assume, promote and reward certain values and behaviours as they frustrate and punish the pursuit of competing agendas. For example, when managers assume the moral virtue and/or effectiveness of motivation techniques that are based upon individual performance (e.g. performance related pay), competitive and egoistic forms of behaviour are implicitly sanctioned (Perrow, 1986) that are frequently pregnant with unintended consequences. Techniques that stimulate individualistic behaviour perversely fuel the desire for ever more potent ways of satisfying the egoism that they breed; and, in this process, the application of such techniques tends to undermine any efficiency gains that they initially produce (Roberts, 1984). Moreover, and of considerable historical consequence, the widespread use of such techniques *deflects attention* from moral-practical concerns about how individuals might cooperate to develop organizations, societies and a world system, that is more rational in terms of its collective husbanding and allocation of scarce resources in ways that address basic social demands for education, housing, health care, etc.

> We shrink back from the truth if we believe that the destructive forces of the modern world can be 'brought under control' simply by mobilising more resources – of wealth, education, and research – to fight pollution, to preserve wildlife, to discover new sources of energy, and to arrive at more effective agreements on peaceful coexistence. Needless to say, wealth, education, research, and many other things are needed for any civilisation, but *what is most needed today is a revision of the ends which these means are meant to serve.* (Schumacher, 1974: 247, emphasis added)

For CT, 'best management practice' is not simply a matter of identifying the most technically rational means of achieving current ends (e.g. profitable growth); rather, 'best practice' is evaluated in terms of its contribution to the realization of the progressive objectives of autonomy, responsibility, democracy and ecologically sustainable development. In countering apathy and fatalism, CT envisions the possibility of societal development that is guided by the emancipatory power of critical reason rather than by the self-serving efforts of dominant élites. Relatedly, the responsibility of management is not equated with sustaining the status quo by developing new techniques (e.g. TQM and BPR) to 'manage' the contradictions of modern organizations. Rather the responsibility for management is understood as a collective task concerned with the identification and realization, through processes of critical self-reflection, of alternative values and practices that are humanly (and ecologically) more fulfilling and less degrading.

Since CT unsettles many received wisdoms about management, it is worth stressing that it is not inherently or relentlessly 'anti-management'. The intent of CT is not to indulge in the Utopian project of eliminating hierarchy, removing specialist divisions of labour or even abolishing the separation of management from other forms of work.[3] Rather, its aspiration is to foster the development of organizations in which communications (and productive potentials) are progressively less distorted by socially oppressive, asymmetrical relations of power. It is possible and likely that the democratization of managerial activity will result in the replacement of divisive work organizations by collectives or cooperatives in which there is minimal vertical division of labour. Still it is perhaps more likely that some vertical as well as horizontal divisions will be retained, but will be more the product of rational, democratic choice, than an outcome of autocratic decisions made by an élite supported by an unexamined belief in the naturalness or justice of their rule.

As it champions ideas about 'autonomy', 'responsibility', 'democracy' and even 'ecological balance', critical thinking must sink or swim through an ongoing struggle with competing views that are hostile to its claims and aspirations. It is only by struggling to mobilize the emancipatory potential of human reason, CT argues, that barriers to human cooperation and communication can be brought to consciousness, rationally debated and collectively transformed. Whether or not people, organizations and societies are responsive to the claims of critical thinking is partly a test of the eloquence of its advocates. But, from the perspective of CT, the translation of these claims into practice is also a test of the extent to which the dominance of means–ends rationality in modern societies has disabled and deafened the audience to their appeal.

When set in this context, this book can be interpreted as an expression of hope. While it makes the assumption that change of the kind desired by CT is possible, we favour a more eclectic orientation in which a range of critical thinking – including the ideas of Foucault, feminists, labour process analysts and poststructuralists – can be helpful in reflecting critically upon contemporary management theory and practice. We certainly do not believe that CT has all the answers, though we suggest that it has been rather neglected by students of management in comparison to other strands of critical thinking. We see this book as a way of remedying this neglect without, we hope, slipping into an imperialistic approach where CT displaces the contributions of other approaches, or where immodest claims are made about its capacity to guide reconstruction and critique or to provide a blueprint for the future. Incidentally, the absence of such a blueprint is perhaps frustrating or disappointing but it is not accidental; it reflects an emphasis upon the self-determination of ends rather than reliance upon an 'authority' (i.e. our authority) to identify them.

Finally, while we are in overtly reflective mode, it is worth stressing that this book is not intended to offer a definitive statement of critical management studies as a 'field' or distinctive 'approach'. This field is not only contested but, we hope, will remain so. By bringing together and discussing elements that have been highly dispersed, the aim of this book is to make a small contribution – a step on the road – to the development of management theory and practice that is emancipatory in intent.

As we noted earlier, CT has been a major inspiration. But since we are not persuaded that CT has all the answers (see Chapters 3 and 7, especially), we have not been inclined to confine our analysis within it. Unlike students of philosophy, who seem destined to become devotees of a particular Master or school of thought, the fate of critical students of management seems to be an eclectic borrowing from diverse critical traditions. Accordingly, we have drawn upon traditions other than CT where these have seemed to enrich, qualify or be of more direct relevance for our analysis. In doing so, we have no doubt sacrificed theoretical rigour and consistency on the altar of practical relevance.

Partly as a consequence of our tendency towards theoretical promiscuity, many questions remain unanswered – such as the issue of whether a coherent formulation of 'critical reasoning' is consistent with such an eclectic approach. And much requires further clarification – such as how the ideas presented here can have practical relevance, in the classroom and beyond, for the everyday working lives of managers. In short, much additional work needs to be done. It is our hope that the lacunae and limitations of this initial attempt to sketch a possible way of making critical sense of management makes this need for additional work more apparent; and that, when diagnosing these shortcomings, others are inspired to develop more compelling remedies for this need.

### The Seduction of Capitalism and the Limits of 'Progress'

When contemplating the achievements of the modern, Western era, it is comforting to believe that the enlightening advance of science has swept away much dogma and prejudice. Certainly, the dogmas of religion and superstition have been widely challenged and debunked as capitalism and science have delivered unparalleled improvements in material standards of living. But ancient dogmas have been intertwined with and/or superseded by modern, secular myths – such as the understanding that science guarantees progress, that markets ensure freedom and efficiency, that affluent consumption is the route to happiness, and that experts know best.

In modern capitalist economies, values and practices other than those that contribute directly to economic growth and consumption have been progressively marginalized and neutralized, though there have been repeated expressions of disenchantment with capitalism's fruits and recurrent efforts to fashion new values and practices. Nonetheless, capitalism has extended its domain to encompass the production and provision of every conceivable product and service, relentlessly transforming them into commodities to be supplied for a profit. But, at the same time, organized capitalism has absorbed and even supported pressures to provide a basic level of public goods, in the form of housing, health care and education – a provision that has facilitated an important measure of economic and political stability, and with it a degree of commitment to mass consumption. As Bauman has commented in relation to the power of consumption to integrate people into the mass production world of advanced capitalism:

> Seduction is the paramount tool of integration (of the reproduction of domination) in a consumer society. It is made possible once the market succeeds in making the consumers dependent on itself. ... Market-dependency is guaranteed and self-perpetuating once men and women, now consumers, cannot

proceed with the business of life without tuning themselves to the logic of the
market . . . rationality comes to mean the ability to make right purchasing
decisions. . . . (1988: 221–2)

With technological progress and wealth creation has come the creeping
commercialization and commodification of everyday life. Most recently, its
advance has developed the 'new' markets of entertainment, leisure and
images of ecological correctness. And as the purpose and meaning of life
become progressively identified with the pleasures gained from consumption, the governance of modern economic and political institutions increasingly 'becomes less a matter of determining the appropriate direction for
society than one of adjusting its institutions and policies to the flows of
economic and technological development. Politics in short is increasingly
reduced to the technically oriented task of "keeping the machine running"'
(Fischer, 1990: 15–16; see also Heydebrand, 1985).

In the sphere of consumption, the discipline of marketing oils the wheels
of the machine by representing consumer needs as 'givens' that can be
quantified and satisfied by applying its specialist expertise (see Chapter 5).
There is scant reflection upon how these needs are socially produced or
upon how marketing techniques play a central role in the development
or reproduction of consumer needs. Leading marketing textbooks (e.g.
Kotler, 1976) exclude consideration of how demand for products is constituted by exploiting anxieties and by fuelling aspirations. In the world of
marketing, as in other management specialisms, 'the environment' is
referred to as if it were something 'out there' rather than an integral part of
our lives (Naess and Rothenberg, 1991): it becomes yet another sphere or
object of management knowledge and control – equivalent to the markets
for entertainment, health and leisure – ripe for colonization (Deetz, 1992a).
Growing environmental anxiety among consumers is then seized upon as a
new opportunity for product differentiation and achieving competitive
advantage (e.g. through the so-called greening of products or the building
of 'environmentally friendly' corporate images).

The strength of psychological and material attachment to capitalist
values (e.g. individualism) and priorities (e.g. private accumulation) means
that responsibility for social and ecological destruction is more likely to be
attributed to industrialization, science, weak regulation, irresponsible companies or some combination of such factors, than to the logic of a politico-
economic system founded upon domination and exploitation.[4] From a
critical perspective, in contrast, the discourses and practices of marketing,
for example, are seen to be as much a propagator and seducer of consumer
desire as they are an articulation of, or response to, human need (Morgan,
1992). In the face of mounting problems, politicians and industrial leaders
are increasingly preoccupied with 'managing' the survival and growth of
their (capitalist) economies or businesses – at the expense of renewing and
debating the meaning of the modern values of freedom, community and
democracy, and facing up to the question of debating how an espoused
commitment to these values can be translated into substantive action

(Habermas, 1971; O'Connor, 1994). Refusing to recognize the interconnectedness of social and ecological problems, remedial measures are so often directed at the margins where improvements can be painlessly made: for example, to areas where regulations might be introduced to curb the worst excesses of capitalist development or to fields where state provision might be extended or redistributed to relieve the grossest, most embarrassing, delegitimating manifestations of social deprivation and neglect. However, in the search for a 'balanced budget' in conditions of low growth and global competition between nations to attract capital investment, even core welfare programmes are being redefined as breeding grounds for the culture of dependency.

## *The Challenge of Change and the Vision of Democracy*

Despite burgeoning evidence of the irrationality and destructiveness of modern societies, capitalist values and priorities continue to fill and expand the moral vacuum produced by the displacement of traditional institutions and religious beliefs. The priority of wealth accumulation and the acquisition of commodities continues to marginalize and override the relevance and potency of other modern ideals, such as those of autonomy and democracy, that were so critical for the rational and cultural ascent out of the Dark Ages and the dawning of the Enlightenment. And yet, the disorientation and destruction visited upon the planet by the dynamism and instability of capitalism also stimulates critical thinking. For example, the globalization of communications has been instrumental in heightening and spreading awareness of the increasing division between North and South and the deteriorating ecological situation.[5] More generally, as Giddens (1991: 28) has observed, in the most technologically advanced of modern societies there is a growing 'recognition that science and technology are double-edged, creating new parameters of risk and danger as well as offering beneficent possibilities for humankind'. In other words, there is a growing sense of unease about the avowed rationality of scientific and technical fixes to human problems, and a greater openness – and associated perils – to other, diverse sources of authority, including the claims of Critical Theory.

It is when the experience of daily living, including media images, contradicts – or is perceived to contradict – the sense of values and identity acquired by individuals that individual and collective efforts to question inequalities, injustices and irrationalities are stimulated. In Habermasian terms, values nurtured in the lifeworld are mobilized to problematize and transform aspects of a system that are sensed to pose an intolerable threat to a valued sense of self-identity. It is through social movements that individuals become collectively mobilized and engaged in struggles to exert control over the future of society and organizations.

> Social movements . . . are the principle agents in the contemporary struggle for participatory democracy. The emergence of these movements – ecological or

'Green' movements, feminist movements, progressive trade union movements, neighbourhood control movements, consumer cooperatives and worker ownership movements, and so on – represent an uncompromising call in contemporary society for democratic participation and self-management. As alternative movements, they have identified the technocratic system and its apolitical decision-making strategies as primary targets of their countercultural opposition. (Fischer, 1990: 355–6)

Despite the difficulties and obstacles encountered in fostering emancipatory change, social movements demonstrate possibilities for promoting moral and political renewal. At the centre of this process is the understanding that a free, democratic society is not the same as a society that boasts nominally democratic political institutions. Rather, a democratic society is properly known by the strength of its members' everyday commitments to, and the upholding of, democratic values in all its institutions, including its corporations where goods and services are produced and distributed. As Deetz (1992a: 350–1) has observed, 'Workplace democracy is a moral political issue, not one of greater productivity and satisfaction . . . We know something of civic responsibilities, and we need to take them to work . . . The moral foundation for democracy is in the daily practices of communication . . . The recovery of democracy must start in these practices.' In this process, managers can play their part. It is too simplistic or convenient to exclude them on the grounds that managers are the architects of oppressive, undemocratic practices and/or that they are responsible only to the owners. As we argue below and later in this chapter, the position and subjectivity of many managers is much more complex and open than is suggested by such black-and-white formulations of their work. Certainly, managers are hired to ensure that work processes are designed and controlled in ways that realize a profit for shareholders. But, as employees, they are also people who experience the oppression as well as the privileges associated with the controls to which they are subjected (e.g. budgets, appraisals, targets, etc.).

Managers are not mere functionaries. They can experience pain when laying people off or disappointing their aspirations. However, when faced with such experiences, what managers lack – and do not find in conventional management textbooks – is a way of making sense of such experiences. As a consequence, they can become hardened, find rationalizations for their actions or become bewildered in the face of employee reactions to them. Consider the example of a plant manager at a major chemicals company described by Nichols and Beynon (1977: 40–3) who, after reading a leaflet in which managers were called 'pigs', responded, '"*Us* they mean", he said to a fellow manager: "It's *us* they're talking about. I'm no pig. I bloody well *care* about what I'm doing."' What this manager found hard to bear was being required, as a consequence of a decision made in Head Office, to make a number of workers redundant. He found this difficult – not only because he knew 'that redundancy can be "fucking awful"' (ibid.: 43), but because it led, or forced, him to think of employees as numbers who had to be cajoled or subtly pressured to leave voluntarily. '"You see you find yourself counting: 'That's fourteen gone. That'll give a bit of space in the system. One of them's changed his mind – the bastard!'. I don't think I'm like *that* – but you certainly find yourself doing it"' (ibid.).

This manager experienced his work, or at least this aspect of it, as 'a moral problem'. He was confused about the extent of the personal responsibility that he bore for 'counting numbers'. In an effort to answer this question, he asked himself what those being made redundant thought. Did they think that he was responsible? '"The thing is I don't think they think it's *me*. I don't think it's *my boss*. They think it's '*them*'. But we're 'them'. But it's not *us*. It's something *above us*. Something up there."' Nichols and Beynon report that this manager concluded this soliloquy by gazing up at the ceiling. He was at a loss to understand his actions and the extent to which he should take personal responsibility for them. The problem with conventional management textbooks is not so much that they fail to provide managers with an answer to such issues but that, for the most part, they *studiously avoid* addressing such issues. In effect, the existence of such problems and dilemmas is denied. Management is represented as a set of techniques that are functionally necessary for the smooth running of systems. Instead of confronting the positioning of management with capitalist relations of production, the focus is upon the *design* of systems rather than their effects, and upon the *techniques* that professional managers should acquire to ensure their smooth operation. Or, to put this another way, these texts represent and make sense of management as a technology, not as a social relation. When confronted directly with his work as a social relation, this manager was at a loss to make sense of it.

Currently, managerial work is itself being intensified and/or rendered increasingly insecure as hierarchies are flattened. Career paths are becoming more uncertain as the comparative safety of specialist, functional 'chimneys' is being eroded by moves to increased teamworking. In this context, it becomes more apparent that many managers are the victims (in terms of additional stress and job loss), and not just the perpetrators, of control systems that they design, operate and police. In many cases, insecurity may be productive of increased compliance, although pressures for innovation render such a passive response rather risky; but, equally, there is a potential for the experience of internal conflict to promote critical reflection that, in turn, can be productive of more or less proactive support for moves that are conducive to processes of democratization at work (see Deetz, 1992a, Chapter 12). As Rosen (1987) has argued, contradictions are forces in conflict that are productive of transformation. To the extent that managers are able to exercise discretion, they cannot realize *any* future that they may dream about. But they can use their influence and the opportunities that are presented to them to make it more likely that a possible reality (e.g. of greater democratization), currently in the process of becoming, will actually emerge.

A commitment to democracy is most clearly fulfilled in the practical process of placing under more democratic control the corporations that shape so many aspects of our everyday lives – a democratic process that has less to do with the introduction of formal systems of voting than with the effective channels of accountability through which different groups and interests are able to participate fully in decisions that affect their daily lives.

## Making Sense of Management: Unpacking the Received Wisdom

The spokespersons of modern societies take pride in being rational, educated and even enlightened. It might therefore be expected that management knowledge would be subjected to critical scrutiny and debate. Management textbooks, it might be imagined, would encourage the development of a reflective, critical understanding commensurate with its modern character and rational aspirations. However, even the most cursory consideration of management textbooks, and most journals, rapidly confounds such an expectation. Instead of a commitment to encourage critical scrutiny, we find a continuous recycling of ideas that permit very limited reflection upon the conditions and consequences of established theory and practice.

### Dominant Images of Management and the Aura of Science

Received wisdom assures us that, as a consequence of processes of rationalization and modernization, organizations are now managed on a more rational basis. Managers are portrayed as the heroes of modern society: 'No job is more vital to our society than that of the manager. It is the manager who determines whether our social institutions serve us well or whether they squander our talents and resources' (Mintzberg, 1975: 737). The expertise of managers, this soothing doctrine continues, establishes them as competent and trusted mediators between the claims of a plurality of stakeholders and interest groups – consumers, suppliers and employees as well as employers. Their specialist expertise enables managers to make decisions that ensure the efficient and effective fulfilment of the needs of organizations and society. As professionals, managers ensure that the claims of all groups are effectively acknowledged, rationalized and satisficed. Professional management thus provides the key to the good society.

> Our society has in this century become a society of organizations. Organizations depend on managers, are built by managers, directed and held together by managers and made to perform by managers. Once an organization grows beyond a very small size, it needs managers who practice professional management. This means management grounded in a discipline and informed by the objective needs of the organization and of its people, rather than management based upon ownership or political appointment. (Drucker, 1977: 32–3)

Such views assume that integrating the needs of the organization with the needs of its employees is a matter of applying the 'correct' techniques. It simply requires the replacement of amateurs by 'professional management' who are in possession of the requisite expertise. This view is widely echoed and reinforced in the majority of textbooks where we find variations on the following definition of management as the art or science of 'getting things done through other people'.[6] Daft, for example, asserts that 'Getting things done through people and resources and providing direction and leadership are what managers do' (1988: 5). Such textbook definitions of management take for granted the distinction between managers and managed, while simultaneously emphasizing the idea that management is a technical, universal, politically neutral process of 'getting things done'. The objectives of management are portrayed as *given* and *unproblematical*; and the division between managers and managed is presented as something that is either 'natural' or functionally necessary for achieving the requisite results.'

The idea that managerial work is guided by the rational calculus of management theory is most powerfully expressed in the representation of management knowledge as 'science' (Willmott, 1995b).[7] The linking of management to science implies its neutrality and authority, and thereby assists in securing the exercise of managerial prerogative without any wider social accountability. When the so-called science(s) of management are abstracted from the cultural and historical contexts of its conception and application, teachers and practitioners of management are spared the unsettling realization that the very formulation of 'scientific' management theories, as well as their implementation, occurs within politically-charged, value-laden contexts (see Chapter 2). Since managers possess, or have access to, the relevant 'scientific' body of knowledge for managing complex systems, the argument implies, they must be allowed to proceed without let or hinderance. Conversely, any form of knowledge that fails to exhibit the relevant scientific credentials is, by implication, deemed to be suspect or subjective, if not subversive. In short, this belief in science legitimizes a technocratic understanding of management.

Yet, paradoxically, it is precisely the more inexact and scientifically unsupported forms of knowledge that are most often valued and celebrated by practising managers. In particular, texts that are attentive to the politics of management are often deemed to be most 'realistic' by practitioners. As Susman and Evered (1978: 584) have observed, 'Many of the findings in our scholarly management journals are only remotely related to the real world of practising managers and to the actual issues with which members of organizations are concerned, *especially when research has been carried out by the most rigorous methods of the prevailing conception of science*' (emphasis added). In a similar vein, Bedeian (1989), when speaking as the President of the American Academy of Management,[8] has referred to the mountain of 'mindless research' that 'often restates the obvious'. If management academics persist in being mindless, he concludes, they 'will continue to deserve the criticism so commonly sent our way by the popular press' (ibid.: 14). If, as the observations of Bedeian suggest, much academic research on management has little immediate practical relevance for managers, it is relevant to ask why such 'mindless' research continues to be funded by government and business.

Perhaps the sponsors of such research believe that, eventually, its findings will justify the investment. Alternatively, resistance to scientific knowledge by 'prescientific' or 'unprofessional' managers may be viewed as the problem, for which additional research is identified as a part of the solution. A rather different, more sceptical interpretation of the puzzle is that scientific research continues to attract support because it makes a valuable, even magical, contribution in creating and legitimizing an *image and ideal of managers as impartial experts* whose prerogative is associated with, if not founded upon, *scientifically respectable bodies of knowledge*, and not because there is any realistic prospect of this research addressing, let alone solving, the problems or deficiencies of management (Cleverley, 1971; Willmott, 1984a; Thomas, 1993). As Pfeffer has commented:

> It is certainly much more noble to think of oneself as developing skills toward the more efficient allocation and use of resources – implicitly for the greater good of society as a whole – than to think of oneself as engaged with other organizational participants in a political struggle over values, preferences and definitions of technology. (1981a: 12)

Although frequently ignored or rejected as useless mumbo-jumbo by practitioners, 'mindless' conventional academic research is often supported, we suspect, because the association of management with science provides a valuable veneer of authority and respectability. In much the same way that management consultants' reports can serve to legitimize decisions that might otherwise seem unequivocally partial and even vindictive, the pursuit of 'scientific' research into management supports, or at least leaves unquestioned, the legitimacy of managerial privilege and prerogative. Such research also serves to endorse the technocratic idea that, in principle, all problems are amenable to technical solutions (Alvesson, 1987). In effect, it would seem that the spell of 'science' is routinely invoked, as an ideology, to subvert resistance to the exercise of managerial power (Baritz, 1960; Wood and Kelly, 1978).

## *Techniques, Spheres of Competence and Beyond*

We have argued that the development and operation of management techniques cannot sensibly be separated from the politics of determining priorities. This understanding does not deny that management theory and practice comprise a gamut of skills and techniques institutionalized within their diverse specialisms, such as accounting, operational research and marketing (Alvesson and Willmott, 1992; see also Chapters 5 and 6). For example, within the personnel specialism, or Human Resource Management (HRM) as it is revealingly called, techniques of recruitment, selection and motivation have been developed and refined that are supposed to identify, harness and retain the energies of employees.[9]

Management techniques are complemented by a more general type of knowledge that is more directly relevant for structuring complex problems or facilitating 'strategic' levels of decision making, etc. To continue with our example of HRM, its specialists aspire to provide an integrated package of measures that are tailored to fit and fulfil 'business needs'. It is in this area of strategic management that the broad direction and operation of corporate activity is determined. It is also where conflict over spheres of influence and expertise becomes most intense, with each of the major management specialisms claiming to provide the most relevant ingredients for securing competitive advantage (Armstrong, 1986; see also Chapter 5). To elaborate further the case of HRM, Burgoyne (1993: 10) has suggested that HRM specialists' embracement of the idea of 'competences' enables them to 'justify, legitimize and explain the (HRM) function in the managerial terms which production, finance and marketing directors use . . . the concept of "competence" is crucial in presenting people as manageable commodities rather than unpredictable and self-willed agents'. In other words, the appeal and use of the competences concept is more compellingly explained in terms of its political value as rhetoric. Along with other buzz words, such as 'quality', 'empowerment' and 'reengineering', use of the competences concept can be seen as part of an ongoing effort by managers to reassert their control as they seek to 'coax, inspire, demand or otherwise produce action in their organizations' (Eccles and Nohria, 1992: 30).

Precisely because employees are wilful and unpredictable, getting to grips with the messy practicalities of managerial work always requires more than the assimilation and application of skills and techniques. At the very heart of managerial work, there is a continuous moral-political struggle to establish, build and sustain the 'credibility' and 'authority' that underpins the 'prerogative' to manage (Bendix, 1956; Storey, 1983) within particular institutional contexts (Whitley, 1989). Acquiring abstract techniques and skills is comparatively easy; establishing and maintaining the power and authority that supports their effective application in specific contexts presents challenges of a completely different order.

Managers may try to make employees, suppliers or customers act predictably, like well-oiled machines. But people are wilful. Indeed, the origins of the term 'management' can be traced to the Italian word *maneggiare*, which means 'to handle a horse'. Though seemingly obscure, this semantic root is instructive in its portrayal of the social divisiveness of management as a contradictory process: a process in which a person simultaneously takes responsibility for and seeks to control, a valuable, yet wilful and potentially resistant, resource. Given the importance of securing cooperation from wilful, potentially resistant 'human resources', it might be assumed that managers would wish to gain total control of employees. However, total pacification is unlikely to be secured in the absence of the kinds of regime envisaged by Huxley in *Brave New World* (and even there, it was not fully effective). In any event, it is doubtful whether total subjugation would be unequivocally advantageous.

The limits of total conformity are dramatically exposed when use is made of the stratagem of 'work to rule' – that is, doing precisely what is required without exercising any discretion (or extending any goodwill). Working to rule demonstrates the dependence of managers upon the judgement and cooperation of employees as it simultaneously mocks and subverts the exercise of management control. On the other hand, allowing employees a measure of autonomy, however carefully controlled (e.g. through the strengthening of corporate cultures), exposes managers to the risk that employees will abuse or redefine this autonomy for their own purposes. Managers want employees to develop and deploy initiative. But managers also want employee initiative and discretion to be exercised in managerially acceptable and disciplined ways. For this reason, managers seek to manage the meaning of work and employment. As Cohen and Camaroff (1976: 102, cited in Gowler and Legge, 1983: 198) have observed, 'a crucial variable in the construction of reality lies in the *management* of meaning: actors compete to contrive and propagate interpretations of social behaviour and relationships. . . . The management of meaning is an expression of power, and the meanings so managed are a crucial aspect of political relations.' Given the challenges encountered by managers in organizing people, it is not difficult to understand why the metaphor of horse handling was adopted. It articulates well the demanding task of marshalling and channelling the energies, habits and desires of potentially stubborn, unruly and headstrong suppliers of labour. The management of meaning, for example, is problematical because other individuals and groups are capable of supplying and developing their own preferred meanings. As we noted earlier, in the example of the manager at the chemicals plant, the preferred meaning ascribed to his being by some in the workforce was 'pig'.

The *maneggiare* metaphor also conveys the understanding that managers form an élite group or stratum, that is different from, and superior to, those they 'handle'. The metaphor does not endorse the idea of management as just one, technical element in a specialized division of labour. Rather, it highlights the *social division* of the 'handlers', who possess distinctive managerial expertise, from the 'horses' who supply the labour, and have the managerial skills applied to them: labour must be 'broken in' – by teachers in schools and colleges if not by managers in factories and offices – and continuously monitored and developed if its productive potential is to be maximized.

## Making Sense of Management – Sketching a Critical Perspective

In response to our criticisms of mainstream accounts of management, it could be objected that they present a comparatively easy target for critical analysis. Our defence is that reputable textbooks and journals are the basic storehouses of received wisdom about management and are, therefore, important and legitimate targets of criticism. That said, it is also necessary to acknowledge and address conceptions of management that diverge, in various ways, from the received wisdom discussed above. In this section, we concentrate upon contributions to the understanding of management that incorporate some appreciation of the role of ideology and politics.

### 'Progressive' Conceptions of Management and the Extension of Technocracy

The conventional criticism of classical conceptions of management is that they fail to recognize how, in practice, management decision making is 'bounded' by limited information and pressures to reach 'closure' before all options can be thoroughly scrutinized and evaluated (March and Simon, 1958). This criticism usefully draws attention to the practicalities of managerial work in which the process of reaching optimal decisions is impeded or 'bounded' by 'realities' that will not wait for the optimal solution to be found. Empirically, Mintzberg's (1973) study of managerial work presents a picture of executives rapidly moving from one activity to another, with little time for planning or to carefully assemble and evaluate relevant information before making decisions. In practice managers have been found to 'satisfice' in response to immediate pressures rather than 'optimize', having weighed the alternative courses of action.

The adequacy of this understanding of the limits of managerial rationality has been challenged by those who argue that, in addition to universal limitations of information gathering and processing, decision making is invariably guided and restricted by managers' particular allegiances, preoccupations and hunches (Pettigrew, 1973; Kakabadse, 1983; Yates, 1985). It is these hunches, proven recipes and 'biases', and not just their limited capacity to process information or the commercial pressures upon them to reach closure, that lead managers to deviate from the formal, rationalist logic of classical management theory.[10] Decision making, Child (1972: 16) concludes, 'is an essentially political process in which constraints and opportunities *are functions of the power exercised by decision-makers in the light of ideological values*' (emphasis added). Studies that pay attention to the politics of organizational decision making and the conditioning of managerial work by ideological values provide a valuable counterbalance to the over-rationalized textbook image of management. Under their influence, a new generation of researchers (e.g. Pfeffer, 1981b; Pettigrew, 1985a) and management gurus (e.g. Pascale, 1991) have focused upon the micropolitics of management decision making. Received wisdom is also now beginning to assimilate the understanding that managerial behaviour is mediated by organizational, sectoral, and societal cultures and contexts (Whitley, 1993).

Yet, despite this broadening of our understanding, 'progressive' research monographs, guru handbooks and academic textbooks continue to be written as if the question of 'management for what?' were either self-evident or of little practical consequence. In effect, academics who have drawn attention to the micropolitics of managerial decision making have criticized established, over-rationalized wisdom for being *imperfectly* managerial: if only other managers would learn to become more aware of the role of values in shaping their perceptions, and/or appreciate the nature and significance of organizational politics, they would then operate more effectively as many current difficulties and dysfunctions could be lessened, if not avoided (Kotter, 1982). Or, as Pettigrew (1985b: 314–6) has expressed this view,

> Changing business strategies has to involve a process of ideological and political change that eventually releases a new concept of strategy that is culturally acceptable within a newly appreciated context. . . . In the broadest sense, this means, prescriptively, that step one in a change process should be to improve and build upon any natural processes of change by tackling questions such as how existing processes can be speeded up, how the conditions that determine people's interpretations of situations can be altered, and how contexts can be mobilized toward legitimate problems and solutions along the way to move the organization additively [*sic*] in a different strategic direction.

So-called processual accounts of managerial work and organizational change, such as those produced by Pettigrew, begin to pay attention to what he terms 'ideological and political change'. However, all too often attention is focused upon the ideological and political dimensions of organizing simply as a means of *smoothing* the process of top-down change. Established priorities and values are assumed to be legitimate. The insights of social science into the context and dynamics of organizational change are not prized for their capacity to stimulate a debate upon the legitimacy of current priorities. Instead, social science is identified as a neutral technology for minimizing conflict associated with managers' decisions to take 'a different strategic direction'. In such 'progressive' accounts of management and organization, precious little consideration is given to the merits, or rationality, of the 'ends' of management.[11] Prescriptively, their more or less overt emphasis is upon *supplementing* and revising established means and recipes of management control (e.g. bureaucratic rules and procedures) with *the strategic reengineering of employee norms and values* in line with the 'new concept of strategy' and the 'legitimate problems and solutions' – as identified by top management or their consultants and legitimized by academics. In this process, a technocratic ideology of management is effectively reinforced, not challenged (Willmott, 1993a).

Any theory or practice that takes for granted the ends and legitimacy of expert rule, and thereby suppresses the claims of more democratic forms of governance is, in this sense, technocratic (see Burris, 1993). Taylor's Scientific Management is an obvious example. But the contemporary rise of more 'participative' and 'humanistic' techniques as embraced by the gurus of Excellence and Total Quality Management, though seemingly encouraging a weakening of the divisions between managers and managed, are not necessarily any less technocratic. On the contrary, ideologies associated with the strengthening of corporate culture (e.g. Theory Z, Ouchi, 1981) can portend a more totalizing means of managerial control (Willmott, 1993a) that aims to induce an internalization of norms and values selected by senior managers (Deal and Kennedy, 1982; Kilmann et al., 1985).

Culturist means of control have been studied in depth by Kunda (1992) in his research on Tech, a company celebrated by mainstream commentators for its creativity and progressive, people-oriented style of management. The following excerpt is illustrative of how employees at Tech are surrounded by, and continuously subjected to, Tech Culture:

> Tom O'Brien has been around the company for a while; like many others, he has definite ideas about 'Tech Culture'. . . . But, as he is constantly reminded, so does the company. When he arrives at work, he encounters evidence of the company point of view at every turn. . . . Inside the building where he works, just beyond the security desk, a large television monitor is playing a videotape of a recent speech by Sam Miller (the founder and president). As Tom walks by, he hears the familiar voice discuss 'our goals, our values, and the way we do things'. . . . As he sits down in his office space, Tom switches on his terminal. . . . On his technet mail he notices among the many communications another announcement of the afternoon events; a memo titled, 'How Others See Our Values', reviewing excerpts on Tech Culture from recent managerial bestsellers. . . . In his mail, he finds *Techknowledge*, one of the company's newsletters. On the cover is a big picture of Sam Miller against the background of a giant slogan – 'We Are One'. He also finds an order form for company publications, including Ellen Cohen's 'Culture Operating Manual'. . . . The day has hardly begun, yet Tom is already surrounded by 'the culture', the ever-present signs of the company's explicit concern with its employees' state of mind (and heart). (ibid.: 50–2)

This passage conveys the idea of Tech as an institution in which employees are continuously bombarded with positive images of the company and the reinforcement of corporate messages about what is expected from them. However, as our earlier discussion of the wilfulness of human beings suggested, employees are not necessarily submissive participants in processes of corporate brainwashing. Unlike the automatons portrayed in Orwell's *Nineteen Eighty-four* or Huxley's *Brave New World*, Tech employees bring alternative values and priorities to their work. Through processes of distancing and irony, Tech employees were able to expose and deflate the use of high sounding corporate rhetoric. On the other hand, Kunda's study also discloses a darker side of Tech's corporate culture: it could readily accommodate and exploit a degree of employee wilfulness and resistance – in the form of the parodying of values and expectations (see also Filby and Willmott, 1988) – by encouraging employees to interpret the tolerated ridiculing of Tech ideology as a confirmation of the company's ostensibly liberal ethos. The most pervasive and insidious effect of Tech culture was its repressive tolerance (Marcuse, 1964). This, Kunda suggests, was more effective in stifling and neutralizing organized forms of resistance than the imposition of a more coercive, heavy-handed approach:

'in the name of humanism, enlightenment and progress, the engineers of Tech culture elicit the intense efforts of employees not by stirring their experiential life, but, if anything, by degrading and perhaps destroying it' (Kunda, 1992: 224–5). Kunda usefully points out how modern ideologies – humanism, enlightenment and progress – are routinely mobilized at Tech, and often in subliminal ways, to legitimize the demands of the company upon its employees. Yet, despite the potency of Tech culture, the frustration and psychological degradation experienced by Tech employees prompted many of them to develop and amplify countervailing images of this seemingly benevolent organization.

We can further illuminate what we mean by taking a look at how management and organization are represented in a progressive textbook authored by John Child, whose ideas on management thought and strategic choice have been highly influential in challenging received wisdoms about management and organization. *In Organization: A Guide to Problems and Practice* (Child, 1984), Child reiterates his challenge to classical formulations of rational organizational design (see above). The redesign of organizational structures, he argues, 'cannot be expected to resolve political problems' (ibid.: 15). Why not? Because the effectiveness of any structure is understood to be conditional upon its objectives being 'regarded as legitimate by its employees or members' (ibid.). So far, so good. However, in the remainder of Child's text, the question of why securing 'legitimacy' is problematical, or how it might be more permanently secured, is not revisited. Passing reference is made to 'the coercion of formalized authority . . . reinforced by economic conflicts of interest' (ibid.). But the relevance of this insight for understanding the problems of organization or for guiding the future practice of management is unexplored. When commenting upon the legitimacy of managerial prerogative, Child suggests that problems arise when organizational structure 'becomes a victim of politics [because] it does not reflect political forces within the organization' (ibid.: 15–6). The implication is that 'politics' are present and problematical *only* when organizational structures are incontrovertibly disrupted – that is, when managerial prerogative is directly undermined or denied. Though probably unintended, one possible reading of this view is that any design of organizational control systems, however oppressive or coercive, is legitimate so long as dissent is not expressed or is effectively silenced. This interpretation is reinforced by the suggestion that manifest tensions within organizations are frequently a consequence of a hierarchy *per se* rather than, say, the institutionalization of the power and status of a managerial stratum within a hierarchy.[12]

In common with mainstream texts on management – or should one say texts *for* the preservation of the social position of the modern manager? – studies that take some account of the processual and political nature of managerial work generally soft-pedal on any sustained critical scrutiny of the conditions and consequences of management theory and practice. There is little consideration of the historical forces that promote market conceptions of freedom (as a means of raising the productivity and pliability of human labour) and which frustrate democratic control over the organizational means of their realization. Instead, the reader's attention is directed towards the opportunities and scope for refining the 'means' of management control – for example, by redesigning jobs or organizations, often by mobilizing ostensibly humanistic values (e.g. empowerment) that aspire to ease tensions while preserving the prevailing structures of domination. The image and ideal of the manager as the technocrat survives largely unscathed. Indeed, if anything, it is buttressed by the claim that formally rational solutions to problems will be successfully implemented only when the culture and micropolitics of management are effectively 'managed' and strengthened.

What Child's text fails to appreciate is that managerial work is politically charged because, in capitalist economies at least, managers are socially distanced from, and minimally accountable to, those whom they manage. Management control is rarely based upon seeking the active consent, as contrasted with conditional compliance, of the managed. As a consequence, managers are obliged to develop forms of inducement and punishment through which they strive to minimize forms of resistance and dissent.

Wherever inequalities are not founded upon unforced consent, it is necessary to develop *ideologies* that aspire to legitimize the exclusion of 'the managed' from participating in making the decisions (and meanings) that affect their lives – such as the doctrine that it is management's right to manage or the view that managers possess the requisite expertise to 'humanize' the workplace. In a word, technocracy: a system of (corporate) governance 'in which technically trained experts rule by virtue of their specialized knowledge and position in dominant political and economic institutions' (Fischer, 1990: 17).

The paradox of 'progressive' management texts is that they simultaneously go some way towards debunking the rationalist pretensions of conventional management thinking *and* facilitate the application of more sophisticated technologies of control that, in principle, enable the jurisdiction of management to be more successfully extended into the domain of culture. In effect, 'progressive' texts serve to advance and legitimize an expansion of systems of management control that aspire to infiltrate the hearts and minds of employees. Both established and 'progressive' ways of making sense of management exclude sustained consideration of how, historically, the objectives and functions of management are defined, refined and pursued through processes of moral and political struggle.

### Managers as Agents and Targets of Instrumental Reason

The moral and political dimensions of managerial work are well illustrated by Jackall's *Moral Mazes* (1988), an in-depth study of managerial work which focuses upon the dissonance between the personal values of the individual manager and the demands of the corporation (see also Dalton,

1959). The dissonance is routinely attenuated, Jackall argues, by a wide-spread compliance with 'what the guy above you wants from you' (ibid.: 6). What such 'guys' invariably want, he shows, is not just compliance with 'organizational rules or values' but a particular form of compliance that safeguards their own power and status, yet which is simultaneously capable of being represented as congruent with the rules (accepted techniques and procedures) of the corporate game: 'technique and procedure tend to become ascendant over substantive reflection about organizational goals. . . . *Even at higher levels of management, one sees ample evidence of an over-riding emphasis on technique rather than on critical reasoning*' (Jackall, 1988: 76, emphasis added). The overriding emphasis upon seemingly impartial technique and procedure attracts support from shareholders (and, in the public sector, from politicians) because it seems to define the limits of managerial discretion. According to such logic, managers are deemed to act irrationally, subjectively and unprofessionally when they deviate from refining the means of achieving organizational goals. This technicist conception of management also secures the social position of management within organizations. It reinforces the image of the impartial (apolitical) expert whose skill is deemed to be of critical importance for the maintenance of modern, complex societies. As Gowler and Legge put it, 'by conflating a hierarchy of power relationships with a hierarchy of expertise, this link between control and efficiency reinforces "the right to manage", i.e. helps to legitimate managerial prerogatives' (1983: 210).

However, endorsement of a technocratic ideology places managers in a potentially vulnerable position. The logic of neutrality 'demands' that managerial work be subjected to the same rationalizing processes that it has visited upon less powerful groups (Fletcher, 1974; Smith, 1990). Even without the development of powerful information technologies that threaten to automate the work of many supervisors and managers, employee involvement and corporate culture programmes promote the internalization of supervisory responsibilities among multiskilled, self-disciplined operatives, and thus reduce the ranks of supervisory staff and middle management. Middle and junior management are increasingly the targets of delayering in 'lean', 'reengineered' organizations. When they endorse technocratic ideology, they are not well prepared to make sense of, let alone resist, the contradictory operation of valued 'logics' that pose a threat to their very existence. As employees, managers, too, are expendable. As Anthony has observed,

> They are more likely to be the unwitting victims of reorganization (more and more frequently); transferred, retrained or dismissed at the behest of organizational plans drawn up by distant consultants; regarded as human resources, shuffled and distributed by specialists in management development and planning. (1977: 310)

Managers routinely *espouse* the goal of making their organizations more efficient and effective, as if the practical meaning of such objectives were value-free, self-evident and beyond doubt. By representing their work in this way, the meaning of management, the social position of managers and their domination of decision making are all, in principle, legitimized. The myth of order and rationality also provides an alluring sense of authority and security in conditions that are uncertain and threatening, existentially as well as 'professionally'. In the face of uncertainty and insecurity, it is confidently proclaimed that managerial expertise resides in techniques for identifying and implementing the most efficient and effective means of achieving given ends – such as growth, productivity, quality and/or productivity.

However, this image of managerial work is repeatedly shown to be incapable of addressing its complex and contradictory character (Nichols and Beynon, 1977; Willmott, 1987; Hyman, 1987). In the context of capitalist relations of production, belief in the objectivity and impartiality of avowedly neutral expertise is precarious and transitory. Keeping the faith is dependent as much, and more, upon the capacity of market conditions (e.g. strong product demand, high unemployment) to temper conflicts of interest as it is upon the capacity of managers to convince employees of the rationality of decisions that frustrate employee expectations and aspirations. When market conditions change, shareholder pressures are experienced by employees, including managers, as work intensification and increased job insecurity.

Management practice is bedeviled by tensions.[13] These tensions, it is worth stressing, are not persuasively explained or minimized as universal features of social interaction or symptoms of incompetent management. Rather, they plague *managers' contradictory social positioning within relations of production which repeatedly stimulate conflicts and struggles between employers and their employees over the organization of work and the distribution of resources.* Precisely because managers are also employees, their priorities are not necessarily congruent with those of owners. As a consequence, managers are likely to interpret and enact owner priorities in ways that promote their own career or departmental interests, perhaps at the expense of other employees to whom managers are unaccountable.

To satisfy shareholders, to facilitate control of employees and to justify their prerogatives and privileges, managers adopt the rhetoric of technical reason and profit orientation – as exemplified in the textbook definitions of management cited earlier – to rationalize their actions. We have noted how preserving the myth that they are pursuing a rational course of action can have devastating consequences for employment and career prospects. The espousal of technocratic ideology by managers can thus have perverse, counter-productive consequences for them as suppliers of labour, as well as for their subordinates. Increasingly, managers are the victims and not just the agents of a rationality that inhibits critical reflection upon, and transformation of, a structure of social relations that systematically impedes and distorts efforts to develop more ethically rational, morally defensible forms of management theory and practice.

## Conclusion

Supplying an answer to the question 'what is management?' is by no means as straightforward as mainstream, or even the more progressive, texts on management are inclined to suggest. Received management wisdom takes it for granted that the social divisions between managers and managed are either natural (e.g. based upon superior intelligence or education) and/or functionally necessary. Received wisdom then proceeds to concentrate upon refining the technocratic means of raising employee commitment and productivity. This philosophy, in our view, is symptomatic of a way of making sense of management that *reduces the political to the technical*, and represents the politics of management practice in terms of the development and application of formal procedures and impartial, 'professional' skills and competences. As Knights and Murray (1994: 31) observe in their study of the management of information technology, 'a great deal of managerial practice constructs a reality of its own activity that denies the *political* quality of that practice'.

As the political quality of management practice is denied or trivialized, consideration of the personal, social and ecological costs of the managerial methods of enhancing growth, productivity, quality and profit is largely ignored. Scant attention is paid to the increase in stress, the loss of autonomy in work and leisure or the degradation of the environment – all of which are associated with the drive for 'efficient management'. Indeed, there is a well-rehearsed response to anyone who raises such issues. It runs along the following lines: industry is responsible for the production of wealth; personal, social and ecological problems are the preserve of individuals and state governments; and government has the task of developing viable, effective (and preferably minimal) forms of action and regulation. Or, when some wider responsibility of corporations is acknowledged, it is claimed that many problems have come to light only recently; and that experts will, in due course, ensure their correction.

Received wisdom invites us to understand management to be a set of neutral techniques and functional processes employed to maximize the productive utilization of human and natural resources for our mutual benefit. It celebrates the contribution of management to corporate and national wealth; its satisfaction of people's needs for employment, job satisfaction, goods and so forth. It urges us to regard managerial work as a positive and central feature of modern, pluralistic societies. Rarely is the darker side of management theory and practice acknowledged or considered, and then most often it is presented as an aberrant and avoidable deviation from the normal state of affairs.

Of course, it is likely that the opposite complaint – namely, that we have little to say about the brighter side of management theory – could be levelled against this text. We acknowledge the difficulty of achieving a balanced view of management but would connect this with the contradictions of management theory and practice discussed earlier. Mainstream management texts present a *thesis* that is self-serving. It does not fundamentally problematize the position of management in modern society. This sets up the possibility of developing an *antithesis* that fundamentally challenges this position. Some ideas intended as a contribution to a *synthesis* are sketched in Chapters 7 and 8. For the moment, it may be helpful to summarize a number of the central understandings, themes and concerns of this text.

- *Management is a social practice.* Its content, both theoretical and practical, is derived from the historical and cultural relations of power (e.g. capitalism, patriarchy) that enable/impede its emergence and development.
- *Mainstream management theory* represents its practices as objective/ impartial/ scientific. Such claims act to mystify, more or less consciously, the power relations that shape the formation and organization of management.
- *Tensions exist* between the lived reality of management as a politically-charged process and its 'official' representation as a set of impartial, scientific techniques for directing and coordinating human and material resources.
- *Critical studies of management* recognize and examine the tensions. Instead of seeking to control these tensions through the refinement of techniques, they anticipate the possibility of resolving them through a transformation of power relations (e.g. changing the mind-sets and institutions that countenance patriarchal practices or ecological damage).
- *Critical studies are themselves a product of prevailing relations of power.* Their very existence is dependent upon tensions (e.g. suffering) in these relations which stimulate reflection upon conventional theory and practice. But the embeddedness of Critical Theory in these power relations renders its own claims partial and provisional.
- *Critical studies seek to illuminate and transform power relations* despite their embeddedness in these relations. They provide *alternative frameworks* for interpreting the practices of management. In this book, we seek to *complement and fortify* studies of management that have drawn more heavily upon labour process analysis (e.g. Braverman, 1974) or upon Foucault's work (e.g. Rose, 1989) with ideas drawn from Critical Theory.
- Critical Theory (CT) is guided by an *emancipatory* intent. In contrast to labour process analysis, it does not equate processes of liberation with working class struggle. CT is critical of the perversion of the Enlightenment tradition by positivist science but also draws inspiration from this tradition.
- CT understands *modern forms of domination* to be sustained by the power of ideas (e.g. fascism, monetarism, science). Critical analysis is therefore much concerned with the *critique of ideology* as a means of

challenging conventional wisdom and, thereby, enabling people to be liberated from ideas that are judged not to withstand critical scrutiny.

- Received wisdom (e.g. about management) may be simply *reconstructed* by critical analysis, in which case it provides an alternative body of knowledge without being accompanied by a change either in the person who adopts this analysis or in their practical actions (e.g. as a manager). Reconstruction becomes critique only when it inspires and guides a process of *personal and social transformation*.
- Emancipatory transformation occurs as people *seek to change*, personally or collectively, habits and institutions that impede the development of autonomy and responsibility. *Responsibility* depends upon the practical realization of the interdependence of human beings and our interdependence with nature. Relatedly, *autonomy* depends upon the development of institutions in which egoism is effectively problematized and minimized, thereby allowing the practical realization of undistorted interdependence.

In the place of self-serving images of managers – as impartial experts, technocrats, 'go-getters' and 'do-gooders' – it is illuminating to substitute an appreciation of the pressures that lead managerial work to become so deeply implicated in the unremitting exploitation of nature and human beings, national and international extremes of wealth and poverty, the creation of global pollution, the promotion of 'needs' for consumer products, etc. Caught in the maelstrom of capitalist organization, managers are pressured to emulate and reward all kinds of manipulative and destructive behaviours. For instance, Sculley (1987: 6) has described his experience with Pepsi-Cola, before becoming CEO at Apple, and reports that its executives were – and likely still are – 'ruthless and driven':

> Pepsi executives are pitted against each other to grab more market share, to work harder, and to wring more profits out of their business. Winning is the key value. Consistent runners-up find their jobs disappear. You must win merely to stay in place. You must devastate the competition to get ahead.[14]

Such 'driven' behaviour, we have argued, is best interpreted as an often reluctant, ambivalent or resigned response to pressures and contradictions that ferment within the prevailing structure of political and economic relations. Individual managers, like Sculley (ibid.), may privately harbour doubts about the moral value and integrity of their actions. But, in order to hold down their jobs or progress up the hierarchy, they find ways of justifying their actions as they dilute or suspend personal values and their associated doubts (Schwartz, 1987).

In principle, the theory and practice of management could be dedicated to the development of practices, commodities and services that, in addition to providing a basic level of primary goods for the world's population, would be ecologically sound and would facilitate processes of collective self-determination. All too often, however, such concerns are disregarded or deemed irrelevant as the social and ecological destructiveness of contemporary management practice is couched in terms of the rhetoric of 'progress', 'efficiency' and 'effectiveness'. As Shrivastava (1994a: 238) has noted, in mainstream management thinking, 'It is widely believed that corporations are generally beneficial, neutral, technological 'systems of production' that equally serve the interests of many stakeholders . . . This assumption ignores the destructive aspects of corporate activities.'

The capacity of human beings to reflect and think critically makes it possible to question and challenge mainstream management theory and practice. Fortunately, critical consciousness is repeatedly fuelled by the pathological consequences of 'progress': the gross exploitation of natural and unrenewable resources and associated pollution; extreme and obscene inequalities of wealth and opportunity, both nationally and internationally; institutionalized discrimination on the basis of gender, ethnicity, age, etc. The contradictory consequences of established management theory and practice stimulate alternative visions of a rational social and economic order. Even in the face of the pacification and degeneration of democratic values, 'the outcome of a struggle between critical publicity and one that is merely staged for manipulative purposes remains open' (Habermas, 1989a: 235). Precisely because capitalism is so productive in generating wealth, yet systemically incapable of distributing its bounty to those who are most disadvantaged by its operation, diverse forms of 'critical publicity' continue to be thrown up – most recently by the strength of ecological movements.

Integral to the emancipatory intent of Critical Theory is a vision of a qualitatively different form of management: one that is more democratically accountable to those whose lives are affected in so many ways by management decisions. From this critical perspective, management and organizations become more rational only when their activities are determined through processes of decision making that take more direct account of the will and priorities[15] of a majority of employees, consumers and citizens – rather than being dependent upon the inclinations of an élite of self-styled experts whose principle allegiance is either to themselves or to their masters. It would be contradictory to anticipate the precise form of such management in advance of its development by democratic processes. What can be said with some confidence, however, is that those responsible for developing and implementing its functions, of necessity, would be attentive and accountable to the concerns of a much wider constituency than is presently the case.

## Notes

1 The two major strands in the development of critical management theory have been Labour Process Analysis (LPA) and Critical Theory (see Alvesson, 1987). In LPA, management is analysed as a medium of control which secures the exploitation of labour by capital (Braverman, 1974; Knights and Willmott, 1990). In Critical Theory, management is studied more in relation to the domination of technocratic thinking and practices, and the associated emasculation of critical thinking, autonomy and democratic decision making, and

not in terms of the logic of the capital–labour relation that makes the organized working class its agent of revolutionary transformation. See Chapter 3 for a fuller discussion.

2 Watson relates how, following individual interviews with their new boss, Paul Syston, a number of the managers reported that he had said very little and had given them scant indication of his plans. His silence was experienced as intimidating, and was perhaps meant to be so.

3 Hierarchical organization can be of value in coordinating complex, technical divisions of labour. What is problematical is not hierarchical organization *per se* (see du Gay, 1994) but its use to bolster and institutionalize structures of class, gender and ethnic domination.

4 The position is made bleaker by the lack of competitive alternatives to capitalism and, especially, by the dismal record of the former Soviet Union on virtually every count, with the possible exception of its massive, propagandistic support of sport and the arts. Rarely acknowledged, though, is the pressure upon the architects and apologists of the Soviet Union to compete with the rate of growth and hostile posture presented by the capitalist West. To a limited extent, the social democratic welfare societies (e.g. the Scandinavian countries) have developed an alternative. But these are more highly regulated and socially integrated versions of advanced capitalist nations. And, indeed, differences that exist are currently coming under increasing pressure as welfare measures are identified as 'burdens' that reduce the capacity of these economies to attract investment and to induce greater productive effort from employees.

5 There is as yet comparatively little recognition of the connection between the logic of capitalist development, the destructive use of technology, the reckless plundering of natural resources and the institutionalized dependence of the 'underdeveloped' world.

6 Daft (1988: 4) ascribes this definition to Mary Parker Follett. The struggle between 'arts' and 'science' dominated definitions of management in the UK context is explored by Thomas (1980). For a comparative analysis of the role of higher education in promoting a 'science-centred' conception of management, see Engwall, 1990. See also Locke, 1989.

7 Even where the term 'science' is not explicitly used, or where management is presented as a 'practice' mediated by diverse cultural values and political systems, the basic message is maintained. As Drucker (1977: 25), a leading management guru, expresses this understanding, 'The management function, the work of management, its tasks and its dimensions are universal and do not vary from country to country.'

8 An association that represents American management academics.

9 The intent of such measures is strategically to integrate 'the needs of individuals' with 'the needs of organizations' (see McGregor, 1960; Argyris, 1964; Ouchi, 1981). In this formulation, a central purpose of HRM is to apply a set of measures that actively select and train individuals to identify and develop competences and values that are congruent with the fulfilment of organizational priorities.

10 In part, this development has been stimulated and supported by the internationalizing of management. This has fostered a growing awareness of how management practices are coloured by national cultures. An emergent knowledge of management practices in other countries, notably Japan, has made it increasingly difficult to believe that practices which appear 'irrational' from a Western standpoint pose any significant obstacle to achieving the conventional goal of profitable growth (see Pascale and Athos, 1982).

11 For example, in business schools, the inclusion of electives in 'business ethics' or the espousal of (pseudo) 'democratic styles' of managing tends to exemplify rather than challenge the acquisition and application of abstract techniques and idealized prescriptions.

12 Connecting conflict to the presence of formal, hierarchical relationships in organizations, Child (1984: 16) asserts that 'therein probably lies an *inevitable* source of conflict between managers and others' (emphasis added). The use of the word 'appear' (ibid.) to characterize employees' experience of the coercive impacts of management control is also instructive: it implies that such appearances are either deceptive and inescapable; or perhaps that they can be transformed through the use of more progressive forms of management control (e.g. the strengthening of corporate culture) that will relieve employees of their misapprehensions.

13 For example, the strengthening of corporate culture, which encourages employees to identify more closely with the mission of their organization, may succeed insofar as a stronger

sense of collective purpose assuages individual employees' experience of vulnerability and insecurity. However, there remain underlying tensions between the collectivist ideas disseminated by the gurus of corporate culture and deeply embedded Enlightenment beliefs in 'individual freedom' and, more specifically, the operation of 'free' labour markets and individual competitiveness. In the West, the use of labour markets to achieve work discipline creates and promotes the moral vacuum and individualistic behaviour that corporate culture seeks to correct without changing the conditions that operate to undermine the effectiveness of this stratagem as a medium of management control. The limits of individualistic Western management thinking and practice are well illustrated by the limited but significant departure of Japanese companies from a number of Western management's supposedly 'rational' principles. Locke (1989: 50–1) relates the paradoxical success of this deviation to the absence in Japanese history of an equivalent to Western Enlightenment. As a consequence, Locke argues, 'the Japanese worker does not think of himself as engaged in an economic function (being an electrical engineer, a production engineer, lathe operator, accountant, etc.) which is divorced from the firm, an occupational function that can be done anywhere. He is a Hitachi man, a Honda man, and so on, a member of a community' (ibid.). The Western worker, in contrast, lacks a deeply engrained ethic that binds each individual, morally as well as economically, to his or her employing organization.

14 Following his departure from Apple, Sculley discovered that the other side of winning is losing. His reputation was severely damaged when, four months after joining Spectrum Information Technologies as its Chairman and Chief Executive, he resigned and filed a $10m lawsuit against the Spectrum President for 'fraudulent misrepresentations and omissions' with regard to shareholder lawsuits against the company as well as a Secretaries and Exchange Committee (SEC) investigation into questionable accounting practices (*Financial Times*, 9 February, 1994).

15 As we argue and elaborate in subsequent chapters of this book, it is also important not to take expressions of this will and its priorities at face value, but to probe them more deeply by encouraging critical reflection upon, and communication about, human needs and interests.

# 2

# The Power of Science and
# the Science of Power

The development of modern Western societies has been dominated by two principal powers, capitalism and science, both of which have been supported and promoted by patriarchal values and priorities. A critical basis for analysing the former was established by Marx whose reflections upon the historical potency of scientific thinking were restricted to an appreciation of its role in industrializing the labour process, and thereby securing the subsumption of labour under pressures for accumulation. Comparatively overlooked by Marx was the revolutionary but *equivocal* role of scientific thinking in debunking conventional wisdoms and identifying as normative all political and ethical claims that could not be empirically proven. The equivocality of science was addressed more directly by Weber and has been a central focus for Critical Theory. This chapter explores the relationship between knowledge, values and power. At its centre are the questions of what counts as science and what are the limits of its authority. Why are we concerned with such questions? Not only because, in modern societies, science is the dominant source of legitimate knowledge but also because science tends to encourage the view that objective, value-free knowledge is attainable. As we argued in Chapter 1, the latter view is questionable and potentially dangerous.

The idea of value-free knowledge is questionable because it deflects attention from how, in practice, what counts as 'scientific knowledge' is the product of value judgements (e.g. about ontology and epistemology) that are conditioned by the specific, historical and cultural contexts of their production. Whatever grand claims science may make, its knowledge remains a contingent product of the particular values that give it meaning and direction. For this reason, it makes little sense to counterpose 'science' to 'ideology', as if it were possible to generate impartial, non-ideologist knowledge about an independently given world. Instead, the term ideology is more appropriately applied to whatever knowledge is revealed to be partial when inflated claims to be neutral, acontextual, 'scientific', etc. are debunked. As we noted in Chapter 1, social science has often given a spurious credibility to managerial expertise, and thereby provides a seemingly authoritative justification for the exercise of particular kinds of management control. It is this that makes the idea of value-free scientific knowledge potentially dangerous, especially when the aura of science is used, more or less consciously, to inhibit or suppress debate about the desirability of ends as well as the rationality of means. We develop this argument in the remainder of this chapter.

We begin by considering the view that social science is, or should be, value-free. We do this for two principal reasons. First, because the idea of value-freedom continues to exert an appeal that is as seductive as it is perilous – and not least among management academics who, since the appearance of Frederick Taylor's *Principles of Scientific Management* (1911), have sought to revise his ideas rather than contest their scientific aspirations. Second, we contend that an appreciation of the principled advocacy of value-free science, though ultimately mistaken, is helpful in illuminating key issues and problems that bedevil claims to be able to produce objective knowledge.

We then draw upon the influential paradigm framework developed by Burrell and Morgan (1979) to illustrate the claim that different value-commitments, analysed in terms of contrasting combinations of assumptions about science and society, are productive of different forms of knowledge. We commend the heuristic value of Burrell and Morgan's framework for mapping and clarifying differences of approach to the study of social and organizational phenomena. However, while we accept the heuristic value of their framework, we reject Burrell and Morgan's claim that paradigms are mutually exclusive (Willmott, 1990, 1993b). In preference, we commend Habermas' theory of cognitive interests on the grounds that the production of different kinds of knowledge is formulated in relation to 'human interests' rather than their allegiance to particular sets of ideas about science and society, and support his related plea for their mutual advancement.

## The Limits of Science and the Challenge to Technocracy

The belief that science, including management science, can produce objective knowledge assumes that it is possible, ultimately, to remove all 'subjective bias'. When armed with what are believed to be the objective facts, there is then the prospect of organizing and managing people in accordance with scientific, rather than arbitrary or partisan, principles. Taylor's (1911) advocacy of Scientific Management is perhaps the most celebrated example of such thinking. That Taylor dubbed his philosophy 'scientific' was no accident; he fervently believed that he had identified universally-valid principles for eliminating the irrationality of custom and practice from established methods of management.[1] Technocratic disciples of Taylor, the most recent of whom are the advocates of Business Process Reengineering (see Hammer and Champy, 1993), have sought to amend and refine his project – often by incorporating more sophisticated theories of human motivation and group dynamics – without doubting the wisdom or coherence of the technocratic impulse to perfect the scientific control of human productivity.

It is precisely the use – and/or abuse – of scientific thinking to promote and legitimize all kinds of divisive and destructive social technologies that Weber (1948, 1949) sought to confront and resist. Even so, Weber's attitude towards science is deeply ambivalent. On the one hand, he identifies science as a powerful, positive force for dispelling myths and prejudices: it strips away preconceptions to reveal unvarnished facts.[2] By drawing upon scientific findings, Weber argues, modern individuals can become less deluded about themselves and their world. They can also better identify how their commitment to particular values might be more effectively fulfilled. In these respects, science is understood to make a potent contribution to the development of individual clarity and responsibility. On the other hand, Weber is deeply disquieted by the disenchanting effects of science upon established traditions and moral values. Where the limits of scientific authority are not adequately appreciated, he cautions, its debunking power can be destructive of institutions and practices that, despite being scientifically indefensible, are nonetheless highly fulfilling and meaningful for those who participate in them.

In short, Weber sees both the enlightening and the destructive aspects of scientific knowledge and is therefore concerned that its limits be fully appreciated and respected. This concern is addressed in his insistence upon sharply distinguishing between (a) the production of facts by science and (b) the making of value-judgements about the merits of social institutions. Science, Weber contends, simply presents the facts; it cannot require the individual to accept these facts or to comply with their demands if these contradict the ultimate values to which the individual is committed. Questions of how to arbitrate between several different conflicting ends, for example, are deemed to be 'entirely matters of choice and compromise. There is no (rational or empirical) scientific procedure of any kind whatsoever which can provide us with a decision here' (Weber, 1949: 67). In short, fundamental to Weber's position is the claim that there is no scientific way of adjudicating between competing norms of behaviour. Views about life 'can never be the products of increasing empirical knowledge' (ibid.: 576; see also Weber, 1948: 143).

Weber's conception of science aspires to accommodate and strengthen the process of self-formation whereby individuals wrestle with the claims of competing values (see Willmott, 1993b). He does not want science to weaken or terminate the self-formation process by suggesting that there are authoritative, scientific answers to the fundamental human dilemmas of value-commitment. For Weber, it is *value-rational* to acknowledge the *scientific* indefensibility of a particular belief or practice but, nonetheless, to be *personally* fully committed to it. For Weber, the danger is that scientific knowledge is (mis)understood and applied in ways that impede or mystify the process of self-formation – for example, by suggesting that only one way of organizing work is 'scientific' and, by implication, that alternatives must be rejected. Though seductive, this kind of reasoning is unacceptable because, from a Weberian standpoint, human action that is worthy of the name (i.e. is not simply reactive, impulsive or driven by immediate material self-interest without reference to ultimate values that provide life with meaning) involves an exercise of judgement that cannot legitimately be replaced by scientific authority. While science can inform us about the likely implications of making a particular choice, it cannot remove from individuals the responsibility for choosing between competing ultimate values.

Weber's conception of the nature and limits of value-free science is of critical importance because it directly challenges the use and/or abuse of science to support or legitimate particular values or projects and, in principle, undercuts modern technocratic decision making in which allusions and appeals are routinely made to the scientific authority of experts. For example, it directly challenges the coherence of the claim made by the champions of Business Process Reengineering (BPR) that BPR is value-free insofar as it 'begins with no assumptions and no givens' (Hammer and Champy, 1993: 33). Commenting upon the common misconception that an accumulation of facts can resolve choices between values, Weber observes that

> If the notion that (value-) standpoints can be derived from the 'facts themselves' continually recurs, it is due to the naïve self-deception of the specialist who is unaware that it is due to the evaluative ideas with which he unconsciously approaches his (sic) subject matter, that he has selected from an absolute infinity a tiny portion with the study of which he *concerns* himself. (Weber, 1949: 82)

We might, for example, think of the manager who, looking at a set of accounts, declares that 'the facts speak for themselves' when seeking to justify the need for additional investment or when making a case for compulsory redundancies. Or we might think of the politician or management consultant who declares that leaders intent upon making changes that lack widespread support 'often have no choice in how they deal with those attempting to impede their efforts' (Hammer, 1994: 47). From a Weberian standpoint such claims are bogus because, no matter how many facts are accumulated about a particular subject (e.g. management), they will be insufficient in themselves to adjudicate between different value-standpoints – for example the standpoint of those who are resistant to its appeals. The denial of choice is an exercise of power, not of rationality. Or, to put this in a way that anticipates the critique of Weber's arguments from the perspective of Critical Theory (see below), the facts only speak for themselves – as 'truth' – when relations of power ensure that their basis in a value-standpoint is unacknowledged and/or undetected.

### An Evaluation of the Weberian Vision

Anxious that the idea of science would be enlisted by all kinds of cranks and demagogues to justify and champion their personal convictions (both Hitler and Hammer come to mind . . . See Bauman, 1989), Weber sought to make a sharp division between values and facts, arguing that facts could *inform* the process of making value-judgements but could not legitimately *prove* or *justify* value-judgements since this would necessarily involve a leap of faith (Weber, 1949: 55). For Weber, Scientific Method (in the singular) can determine the facts; but any amount of facts cannot, in themselves, disprove a value-judgement.

The idea that management can be made scientific – extolled in the notion of 'management science' and most famously promoted in Taylor's (1911) *Principles of Scientific Management* – clearly illustrates Weber's anxieties that the jargon of science could be used, in a specious way, to 'prove' the objective superiority of particular evaluative ideas. The separation of facts and values, Weber believed, or at least hoped, would allow science to progress unhindered by value-judgements. And, at the same time, it would procure a space for individuals to develop their own political and ethical views without being tyrannized by the seemingly compelling authority of scientific facts. What sense are we to make of Weber's ideas about the possibility of value-free knowledge? Can they withstand critical scrutiny?

Weber accepts that the choice and constitution of the topic of scientific investigation is 'coloured by our value-conditioned interest' (Weber, 1949: 76). But *he does not admit* that the commitment of science to objectivity is necessarily refracted through diverse sets of value-commitments – a social and political process that produces *different forms* of scientific knowledge. Where his argument founders is in its failure to recognize and accept that *different value standpoints promote their own distinctive conception of science*. Weber does accept that the production of facts about specific topics always depends upon a pre-existing dominant value-standpoint, but he does not reflect critically upon this insight (cf. Habermas, 1988: 16). Weber notes how the evaluative ideas with which the scientist approaches the subject matter enables him or her to select 'from an absolute infinity a tiny portion with the study of which he (sic) *concerns* himself' (Weber, 1948: 82, emphasis added), *but* he spares science from this thesis. In other words, the particular value-standpoint of science cannot be problematized within the scientific realm. In effect, this means that the scientist *qua* scientist is in no position to challenge the relevance or desirability of the agenda set by the dominant value-standpoint. The scientist simply takes up for investigation whatever 'portion of existing concrete reality (that) is coloured by our value-conditioned interest' (Weber, op. cit.).

Positively, Weber's advocacy of the value-free principle is to be welcomed insofar as it helps counter the irrational, modernist tendency to justify and realize particular value-commitments by exploiting the (seemingly incontrovertible) authority of science. By informing each individual's pursuit of valued ends, science (as contrasted with dogma and ideology) is understood to make an important, and perhaps the most important, contribution to the development of a more rational society. However, in Weber's formulation, the contribution of science is necessarily limited as it is excluded from the sphere in which choices are made between ultimate values. In this sphere, Weber contends, moral philosophy may be of assistance in identifying and debating the rights and wrongs of different ultimate values. But, reason and science can play no direct part in determining the choice of values. Why not? Because choices between competing values involve a leap of faith, a leap that is fundamentally non-rational.

This disturbing conclusion has been questioned by critical thinkers who have argued that the claimed separation between 'science' and 'morality' or between 'is' and 'ought' is itself unconvincing, except as a rhetorical gambit, because it fails to acknowledge that the scientist engages the reader or audience in a process of persuasion, and not mere demonstration. As Giddens (1989: 291–2) has observed, 'I do not see how it would be possible to maintain the division between "is" and "ought" presumed by Weber . . . Whenever we look at any actual debates concerning social issues and related observations, we find *networks of factual and evaluative judgements, organised through argumentation*' (emphasis added). Critical thinking questions the Weberian claim that the realms of science (facts) and values (judgements) are, in reality, ever separate or separable; and argues that to make this assumption is to be seduced and duped by an illusion of 'pure theory' which assumes the possibility of generating knowledge that is untainted by the practical embeddedness of theory in worldly ways of thinking about knowledge.[3]

Critical Theory (CT) shares Weber's concerns insofar as it seeks to mobilize the debunking capacity of science while avoiding the use/abuse of science to justify political and ethical claims. But, in contrast to Weber, CT situates the impulse of science firmly in the Enlightenment tradition. That is to say, it retains a belief in the possibility of applying reason to *dissolve*, and not just to expose, forms of irrationality – ignorance, superstition, dogmatism, etc. Whereas the Weberian response to potential abuses of science is to insist upon the strict separation of facts and values, Critical Theory argues that facts are invariably embedded in particular value-standpoints; and that, ultimately, the adequacy of scientific claims should be judged in terms of their contribution to the (dynamic) project of Enlightenment, and not in terms of their (static) reflection of social realities.

What, then, is the position on science developed within the tradition of Critical Theory? It is difficult to generalize (see Chapter 3). Nonetheless, we can say that instead of regarding reason as something that is found in pure form in the work of science, CT argues that the practical realization of this ideal, to which science aspires, is conditional upon transforming the social relations in which it is produced. From the standpoint of Critical Theory, a fundamental, emancipatory impulse of critical reflection is not to create or refine scientific knowledge of the world but, rather, to challenge and transform relationships that are productive of socially unnecessary suffering. CT directly contests the equation of reason with bourgeois science, as endorsed and defended by Weber.

In sum, Weber's understanding of science assumes the possibility of the value-free scientist standing outside of, or above, the society in which he/she works. For Weber, a key question is how the value and limitations of scientific knowledge can best be appreciated and recognized by those individuals (necessarily an élite) who have the opportunity to reflect upon its findings in order to frame and inform their choices. In contrast, CT focuses upon the political conditions of knowledge generation and dissemination. Its focus is not the deliberations of the individual decision maker but the structures of communication that impede or promote the very opportunity and facility to engage in such deliberations.

## The Social Production of Sciences

We have noted that any appreciation of how power relations operate to define the methods of science, and not just its agendas, is marginalized in Weber's understanding of science. His doctrine of value-freedom also excludes any rational basis for mounting a challenge to the determination of topics (and scientific procedures) by dominant values. Indeed, a perverse consequence of the Weberian doctrine of value-freedom – dubbed by Gouldner (1973b: 63) a 'salvational myth' – has been its succouring of an ideology of scientism that represents particular knowledge-claims produced by Scientific Method as indisputably authoritative. Instead of leaving a space for critical reflection, as Weber intended, scientism ineluctably acts to devalue and frustrate processes of clarification and the development of responsibility. As science is equated with value-free knowledge, all other forms of knowledge are obliged either to defer to scientistic discourse by striving to comply with its terms, or to become marginalized as unscientific. As Habermas wryly observes, when 'science attains a monopoly in the guidance of rational action, then all competing claims to a scientific orientation for action must be rejected' (Habermas, 1974: 264).

In contrast, Critical Theory starts from the understanding that whatever is deemed to be objective knowledge, whether by scientists or lay persons, is conditioned by power relations in which competing ideas, methods and findings are developed and sanctioned as authoritative forms of knowledge. CT urges that human reason be mobilized to interrogate and challenge the rationality of this knowledge, and not merely to investigate or to perfect its generation. In other words, *contra* Weber, CT directly presupposes and champions the possibility of a critical science that addresses and strives to promote the *rationality of ends* as well as the rationality of means. The Weberian conception of science is preoccupied with the refinement of 'methodology' for discovering the 'truth' about some portion of 'reality'. CT, in contrast, is concerned to show how representations of Reality and Truth are conditioned and coloured by the social relations through which truth claims are articulated and accepted. Only by transforming these relations, CT argues, is it possible to develop less partial or dogmatic representations of their reality – a shift in understanding that can itself create important conditions for social change.

As we noted above, the Weberian doctrine of value-free knowledge is an example of what Habermas (1972) terms 'the illusion of pure theory' – the belief that perfect, historical, disembodied knowledge can be produced by imperfect, historical, embodied (human) beings. When caught within this illusion, it is assumed that (scientific) knowledge can be separated from the politics that impel its production. For CT, in contrast, a belief in the idea that 'facts' can be separated from values and interests is symptomatic of a forgetfulness of the connection between the production of knowledge and the practical, human problems – of self-consciousness and self-determination – that arise out of the 'cultural break with nature' (ibid.: 312) and which cannot be suspended even when involved in science. We now elaborate this understanding.

*Three Types of Science*

The production of scientific knowledge, Habermas (1972) argues, is rooted in the distinctive relationship of human beings to nature. In an effort to come to terms with the openness of this relationship – that is, the cultural break with nature – three basic knowledges are stimulated, each of which is susceptible to more rigorous, scientific development. First, the relationship to nature provokes a cognitive interest in gaining greater *prediction and control* over unruly natural and social forces. Guided by this cognitive interest, diverse kinds of technologies have been developed in attempts to calculate and master the behaviour of humans as well as the elements of the natural world. This type of science, which Habermas characterizes as 'empirical-analytic', is not confined to the natural sciences but penetrates the social sciences, including the field of management and organization studies. It is manifest, for example, in the studies that have sought to identify the contingencies that are deemed to render employee productivity and consumer behaviour more predictable and controllable.

The second type of knowledge arises from the efforts of human beings to *understand and communicate with each other*. The purpose of such communication, Habermas contends, is not simply to improve our capacity to predict and control the natural and social worlds. Developing a fuller understanding of the lifeworlds of other people, he maintains, can be a meaningful and fulfilling project in itself. The cognitive interest that prompts the development of this kind of knowledge is not prediction or manipulation, but a concern to enhance mutual understanding. In the guise of the *historical-hermeneutic sciences*, this knowledge-constitutive interest seeks, for example, to enrich our appreciation of what organizational work means to people, thereby improving our ability to comprehend their world and enabling us to communicate more easily with them. In the field of management, the mobilization of this interest goes beyond the identification of variables that condition human behaviour (e.g. employee productivity); its concern is to appreciate what people think and feel about how they are treated as producers or customers, irrespective of what instrumental uses such knowledge may have.

The appreciation and understanding of others' social worlds can be illuminating and even enlightening. But it can also leave unexamined and unchallenged the historical and political forces that condition these worlds, and the content and process of understanding their reality. An attentiveness to the relationship between the exercise of power and the construction and representation of reality is the province of *critically reflective* knowledge, the production of which, Habermas argues, is motivated by an *emancipatory interest*. The distinguishing feature of this interest resides in a concern to expose forms of domination and exploitation – such as, for example, the connection between experiences of frustration and suffering and the existence of patriarchal practices and institutions – that can, in principle, be transformed. In the form of *critical science*, knowledge is generated that discloses such connections by *reconstructing* the processes whereby 'relations of dependence' become 'ideologically frozen' (Habermas, 1972: 310). While having an affinity with historical-hermeneutic science, the focus of critical science is upon the role of power in institutionalizing and sustaining needless forms of oppression, confusion and suffering. When this concern to expose forms of domination goes beyond a purely abstract, academic orientation, it takes the form of *critique* (see Chapter 1).

The pros and cons of the historical-hermeneutic and critical sciences has been debated by Habermas and Gadamer and, in the field of organization and management studies by Van Maanen and Deetz (Putnam et al., 1993: 221–35). Taking the side of critical science against that of the ethnographers' concern to provide a persuasive account of the field of study, Deetz has observed:

> The quality of research from a critical theory standpoint is not based on the ability to tell a good tale but on the ability to participate in a human struggle – a struggle that is not always vicious or visible but a struggle that is always present. Research should be part of a larger human struggle rooted in the right to participate in the construction of meanings that affect our lives. (ibid.: 227)

Critical science is concerned to understand how the practices and institutions of management are developed and legitimized within relations of power and domination (e.g. capitalism, patriarchy) that, potentially, are capable of transformation. Conventional approaches to the generation of knowledge about management assume that established relations of power and authority are prefiguratively rational, though as yet imperfectly so. Their mission is to produce more accurate knowledge of the reality of management so that a more efficient and effective allocation of resources can be achieved. Critical analysis subjects the rationality of such understandings and objectives to close scrutiny, arguing that the espoused rationality of conventional management theory and practice takes for granted the prevailing structure of power relations and is preoccupied with preserving the status quo, to the detriment of advancing a more rational society in which socially unnecessary forms of domination are addressed and progressively eliminated. This book can be read as a modest contribution to this project. To the extent that critical analysis provides insights that provoke or facilitate emancipatory personal and social change, it also contributes to critique.

### The Unfolding of Critical Thinking about Management and Organization

In recent years, there has been a growing scepticism about the relevance and value of empirical-analytical forms of science (see above) for addressing and solving the problems of modern society. This weakening of confidence is evident in the more progressive texts and commentaries on management and organization (see Chapter 1). Less is heard about 'management/organization science'; more is heard about 'management/ organization studies'. Less is heard about the authority of hard facts; more is heard about the persuasive power of symbols and metaphors. In this process, established analyses and prescriptions have not been displaced. But they have been complemented and somewhat unsettled by alternative perspectives. Agendas of theory and practice developed by practitioners and advocates of functionalist theory (see below) have been challenged by agendas drawn from the broader terrains of social and political theory, including the intellectual traditions of phenomenology and Marxism[4] – a development that has clearly alarmed those who would prefer to establish (*trans.*: impose) a greater degree of consensus about how to make sense of management and organization (e.g. Pfeffer, 1993).

Burrell and Morgan's pathfinding *Sociological Paradigms and Organisational Analysis* (1979) (hereafter *Paradigms*), has been particularly influential in articulating and fuelling emergent doubts about the exhaustiveness of established approaches. In addition to its impact in the broad area of organization studies, this book has inspired a series of calls for a broadening of agendas in the specialisms of marketing (Arndt, 1985), accounting (Hopper and Powell, 1985), operational research (Jackson, 1982), etc. At the heart of *Paradigms* is the idea (introduced earlier), that differing value-commitments, demarcated in terms of their assumptions about society and social science, result in different forms of (organizational) analysis. We now briefly outline Burrell and Morgan's four paradigms of social scientific analysis before using their framework to locate the distinctive contours and contribution of CT in relation to a number of other, closely related approaches. To do this, we suspend our doubts about Burrell and Morgan's rigid division of social and organizational knowledge into four mutually exclusive paradigms (Willmott, 1990, 1993b) as we commend its heuristic value. The coherence of the framework is an issue to which we return when we compare and contrast Burrell and Morgan's (1979) conceptualization with Habermas' (1982) theory of cognitive interests, as briefly outlined above.

*Competing Assumptions about Science and Society*

Burrell and Morgan (1979) draw upon diverse traditions of social and organizational analysis to identify four fundamentally different lenses, or paradigms, through which social and organizational realities can be interpreted. The four paradigms are differentiated by assumptions that are made about social science and society (see Figure 2.1). Of most direct relevance for the present discussion, Burrell and Morgan contend that each paradigm has a legitimate claim to be accepted as science. Contesting the view that only one (value-free) approach can be 'truly' scientific, they argue that both 'subjectivist' and 'objectivist' philosophies of science are coherent in their own terms. Similarly, 'consensus' and 'conflict' theories of society are understood to be as valid as each other. By perming philosophies of science with theories of society, the four distinctive paradigms of analysis are drawn up.

*Subjectivist v. Objectivist Philosophies of Science*     Objectivist philosophies assume the existence of a reality 'out there' that can be faithfully captured or mirrored by the application of scientific methods. The reality of the social world is assumed to be similar to, if not precisely the same as, the natural world. It is believed that social phenomena can be observed and measured using equivalent methods. Typically, the favoured methodology involves the careful construction of 'objective' instruments (e.g. questionnaires) that are designed to provide comparative information about the variables that are believed to make up the social world – such as the attitudes of employees or the type and variety of roles or functions performed by managers.

Subjectivist philosophies of science, in contrast, assume that social phenomena are fundamentally different from natural phenomena and therefore cannot be mirrored or captured by so-called objective instruments. Unlike the constituent elements of nature, whose properties remain constant for all practical purposes, the social world is understood, from a subjectivist standpoint, to be continuously constructed, reproduced and transformed through intersubjective processes of communication. Only by being attentive to the meanings through which reality is rendered 'objectively' real to its members, this philosophy of science contends, can an adequate appreciation of the social world be developed. Typically, the methodology favoured by 'subjectivist' researchers requires a close involvement with those who are being researched in order to discover how the meaning of concepts – such as 'centralization' or 'prerogative' – are actually formulated and interpreted by different members of an organization, and how this meaning is negotiated and changed over time.

*Regulation v. Radical Change Theories of Society*     The vertical dimension of the Burrell and Morgan matrix divides theories of regulation from theories of radical change. Theories of regulation assume that modern societies and their organizations are characterized more by order than by

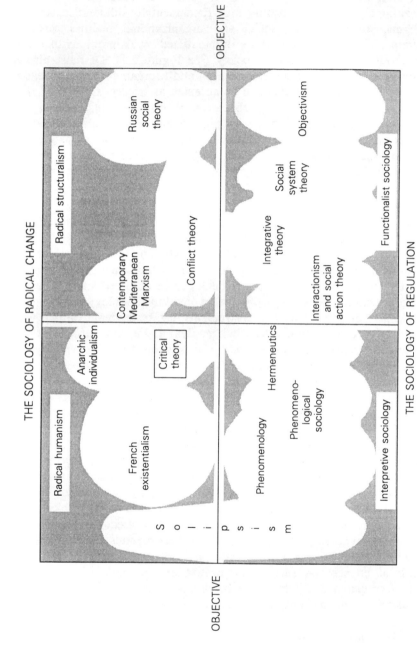

THE SOCIOLOGY OF RADICAL CHANGE

Radical humanism

Radical structuralism

French existentialism

Anarchic individualism

Contemporary Mediterranean Marxism

Russian social theory

Critical theory

Conflict theory

S o l i p s i s m

Phenomenology

Hermeneutics

Integrative theory

Social system theory

Objectivism

Phenomeno-logical sociology

Interactionism and social action theory

Interpretive sociology

Functionalist sociology

THE SOCIOLOGY OF REGULATION

OBJECTIVE

OBJECTIVE

Figure 2.1  *The four sociological paradigms (Burrell and Morgan, 1979: 29)*

conflict. Evidence of order in organizations and society is interpreted as reflective of a fundamental equilibrium and consensus among their members. Conversely, disorder is interpreted as a temporary and necessary means of re-establishing equilibrium. Consensus is assumed or taken at face value, and attention is concentrated upon the issue of how cohesiveness and functional adaptation is accomplished and sustained. Since social order is deemed to be the outcome of an unconstrained accord between the constituent elements of organizations and society, attention is focused upon how existing mechanisms for preserving social order can be strengthened – for example, by developing mechanisms that enable dynamic equilibrium in organizations and society to be sustained.

Theories of radical change, in contrast, assume that social relations are conditioned more by contradictory pressures for transformation than by forces of continuity and integration. Evidence of consensus is associated with forms of social domination that impose or instill order and consensus through direct repression or through a repressive form of tolerance in which dissenting voices are at once accommodated and marginalized (see discussion of Tech in Chapter 1, pp. 32–3). The appearance of order and stability is then connected with, for example, processes of mass subordination to the individualizing disciplines of market relations (e.g. economic dependence) and/or insidious kinds of socialization (e.g. technocratic indoctrination through education and the mass media). Needless to say, the 'same' phenomenon, such as corporate culture, can be a topic within each tradition, but their representation of its value and effects is very different (see Alvesson, 1991).

From this radical change perspective on people and organizations, to which CT makes a key contribution (see below), the reproduction (and transformation) of prevailing institutions and routines is understood to depend upon, and be potentially blown apart by, the contradictory effects of deep-seated, institutionalized inequalities and injustices. What may traditionally appear to be natural or inevitable forms of authority (e.g. patriarchy) and sources of meaning (e.g. chauvinism) can become problematical and untenable; and the effort to restore their authority is as likely to accelerate their decline and demise as to dampen the politico-economic pressures that support them. When diverse sources of tension combine, and prove resistant to suppression or accommodation, major expressions of revolt and radical change can occur – such as the widespread revolt amongst students and workers in Western Europe in 1968 and the 'liberation' of Central Europe during the latter half of 1989.[5]

## Four Paradigms for Analysing Management

So far we have identified two contrasting conceptions of social science and two divergent ways of making sense of society. By combining subjective/objective philosophies of science and regulation/radical change theories of society, four paradigms of analysis are identified. We briefly outline the two 'regulation' paradigms – functionalism and interpretivism – before paying more detailed attention to the radical structuralist and radical humanist paradigms.

### The Functionalist and Interpretivist Paradigms

The *functionalist paradigm* combines an objectivist philosophy of science with a regulation theory of society. Burrell and Morgan identify this as the dominant paradigm in social science and comment that it tends to be 'highly pragmatic in orientation . . . problem-oriented in approach . . . [and] . . . firmly committed to a philosophy of social engineering as a basis of social change' (1979: 26). In Chapter 1, we echoed this view when we noted how knowledge based upon assumptions of this kind has dominated management textbooks and is deeply engrained in the teaching of management in business schools. It is probably fair to say that much of the knowledge production and dissemination undertaken within this paradigm pays little attention to Weber's concerns about the use/abuse of science: much of its authority is derived from an unacknowledged reliance upon established common-sense values and understandings about what counts as respectable and responsible scientific activity. Below we will note its affinities with Habermas' conception of empirical-analytic sciences that are guided by a technical interest in production and control.

The *interpretive paradigm* is concerned to understand how people use symbols (e.g. words, gestures) to render their world 'objectively real'. Conceiving of organizational realities as 'little more than a network of assumptions and intersubjectively shared meanings' (ibid.: 29–31), this paradigm departs markedly from the functionalist treatment of social realities as comprising hard, measurable elements or contingencies. In the 1970s, the interpretive paradigm was viewed as highly esoteric, being sparsely populated by 'weirdo' phenomenologists and ethnomethodologists. Their concerns resonate most deeply with the interest in mutual understanding articulated by historical-hermeneutic science. Following a disillusionment with the capacity of 'hard', functionalist analysis to get to grips with the complexity and slipperiness of allegedly postbureaucratic and postmodern forms of organizational work, new watered-down and managerialized versions of interpretivism have been steadily seeping into management textbooks and the writings of management gurus.

The continuity of functionalist and interpretivist analysis lies in their shared reliance upon a regulation theory of society. This is most clearly evident in the interpretivist inclination to abstract its examination of processes of intersubjective meaning construction from any consideration of the relations of power and domination through which meanings are socially generated and legitimized (see quotation from Deetz, p. 51). To acknowledge and analyse these relations, it is necessary to flip from the paradigms of regulation to the paradigms of radical change.

## The Radical Structuralist Paradigm

The *radical structuralist paradigm* is distinguished by its combination of an objectivist philosophy of social science with a radical change theory of society. Organizational behaviour is understood to be conditioned, if not determined, by structures of domination – such as the institutionalized exploitation of labour within the capitalist mode of production. Fundamental to the radical structuralist paradigm is the understanding that what individuals think and do is conditioned more by the operation of structural forces than by their own consciousness or intentionality. As Burrell and Morgan (1979: 378) put it, 'the system as a whole retains an undiminished elementality – that is, men [*sic*] may seek to understand it but, like the wind or tides, it remains beyond their control'. In this regard, radical structuralism shares with functionalism an objectivist philosophy of science. Where it departs from functionalism is in its assumption that, latent within established structures, there are fundamental contradictions which render the reproduction of domination highly unstable. These contradictions are understood to account for the existence of more or less overtly coercive or insidious institutions (e.g. secret police, compulsory state education, mass media) that ensure continuity of social order. The structural contradictions, it is claimed, also explain the presence of recurrent conflicts and tensions in organizations and society – contradictions which contain within them a potential for radical change that is released whenever the structures are no longer able to regulate this instability.

When considering the development and prospects of capitalism, radical structuralists identify a basic contradiction between the organization of work within factories and offices (socialized production of goods and services) and the appropriation by capitalists of the surpluses produced by employees' labour (private accumulation of wealth) – a contradiction that, when not effectively massaged by the welfare state or checked by monetarist policies that bring high unemployment, erupts as industrial conflict and public disorder. Efforts to contain such contradictions in one area (e.g. increase unemployment to reduce wage demands) are understood to generate increased tensions in related spheres (e.g. fiscal crisis resulting from the fall in taxation revenues and added expenditure on benefits). To secure the appearance of order, reactionary and repressive measures (e.g. reduction in civil liberties, greater powers given to judiciary and police, etc.) are applied. Their effect is to re-establish order in the short term but at the risk of further undermining the legitimacy of the capitalist state. From a radical structuralist standpoint, then, the roots of social and environmental problems and disorder – as manifested in ecological crisis, widespread psychological distress, degraded work conditions, poor housing, juvenile delinquency, drug abuse, etc. – lie in the structures of capitalism. These problems may be moderated through reform. But they can be fully resolved only through a radical and revolutionary transformation of the capitalist system – a transformation which is propelled principally by systemic contradictions rather than by the efforts of people, either individually or collectively, to hasten its (inevitable) arrival.

Within the field of management and organization studies, Braverman's (1974) *Labor and Monopoly Capital* has been a major source of inspiration for the development of radical structuralist analyses of management and organization. Reviving and updating Marxian labour process analysis, Braverman directly challenges the claims of conventional accounts of work organization and employee consciousness, arguing that findings of studies concerned with job satisfaction, for example, take no account of how worker expectations are conditioned by wider structural factors. The finding that most workers report that they are 'satisfied' with their jobs, radical structuralists contend, tells us more about how employee expectations have been shaped to cope with (deskilled) work than about their degraded experience of employment (see Salaman, 1981; Sievers, 1986).

Subsequent radical structuralist analysis has challenged Braverman's tendency to equate the exercise of management control with the degradation and deskilling of work. *Contra* Braverman, it has been argued that managers will seek to deploy whatever strategies of control they find effective in improving profitability – including strategies that involve upskilling and expanding the sphere of employee autonomy, albeit within narrow limits (Friedman, 1977; Knights and Willmott, 1990). From a radical structuralist perspective, such moves are interpreted not as a process of 'humanizing work' or even of lowering the barriers between managers and managed, although this may conceivably be their, largely unintended, effect. Rather, they are interpreted either as a means of securing and/or extending management control – for example, by 'involving' workers more directly in their productive activity – or as a pragmatic, expedient move intended to reduce the costs of direct surveillance through the development of more sophisticated systems of self-discipline.

### The Radical Humanist Paradigm

Finally, in the *radical humanist paradigm*, a subjectivist philosophy of science is combined with a radical change theory of society. In common with radical structuralism, the radical humanist paradigm understands social order to be a product of coercion, rather than consent. But its focus is upon contradictions within consciousness rather than contradictions with the structures of (capitalist) society:

> One of the most basic notions underlying the whole of this paradigm is that the consciousness of man (sic) is dominated by the ideological superstructures with which he interacts, and that these drive a cognitive wedge between himself and his true consciousness. . . . The major concern for theorists approaching the human predicament in these terms is with release from the constraints which existing social arrangements place upon human development. (Burrell and Morgan, 1979: 32, emphasis omitted)

Critical Theory has probably been the most influential of the several approaches located by Burrell and Morgan in the radical humanist paradigm. Bracketed together with the work of other neo-Marxist traditions, such as those associated with Lukacs (1971) and Gramsci (1971), Critical Theory is positioned 'in the least subjectivist region of the radical humanist paradigm' (Burrell and Morgan, 1979: 283),[6] and is therefore adjacent to the radical structuralist paradigm. But, in contrast to the unmediated materialism of the radical structuralist paradigm, Critical Theory takes greater account of *the role of ideas* in the formation and reproduction of consciousness and society. For the radical humanist, the potential for radical change resides in the contradictions between, on the one side, the demands upon consciousness made by dominant (e.g. patriarchal) structures and, on the other side, the capacity of human beings to be creative and self-determining in ways that are fundamentally antagonistic to the reproduction of the status quo.

As the young Marx (1976) argued, the otherwise progressive, modernizing forces of capitalism are understood, from a radical humanist perspective, to exert the contradictory effect of alienating people from each other, from nature and from themselves. Communities are torn apart; industrial work is socially divisive; market relations transform people into commodities; people have limited opportunities for creative and spiritual growth. Through critiques of this kind, radical humanism makes its appeal to *every person* who is *oppressed within, and alienated from, modern institutions*, and not just those who are identified as members of the proletariat. The mission of radical humanist analysis is, first, to raise awareness of how 'normality' is oppressive; and, then, to facilitate the creative and self-determining liberation of individuals from the 'psychic prison' in which they/we are deemed to be incarcerated. Virtually everyone, radical humanists believe, is a victim of systemic oppression – oppression that is so taken for granted that it is routinely viewed as 'life'. But they also believe that, when subjected to critical reflection, such experience can spur and inspire critical reflection upon, and opposition to, forces of domination.

Within the paradigm of radical humanism, CT is best viewed as a key, constructive resource for advancing ideas and practices that share a commitment to the construction of a more rational society. Instead of focusing mainly, if not exclusively, upon the struggle between capital and labour over the control of the labour process and the distribution of surpluses, CT has consistently stressed the more Weberian view that the keys to understanding human interaction, including management and organization, are the meanings and ideologies through which institutions are organized and changed. For example, censuring Braverman (1974) for failing to appreciate the ideological importance of Taylorism as a mode of technocratic thinking (i.e. thinking that presents managers as impartial experts whose rule is legitimized by the possession of knowledge that would increase efficiency – see Stark, 1980 and Chapter 1), Burawoy, himself a leading exponent of labour process analysis, has drawn upon CT, noting that: 'Habermas and Marcuse [leading Critical Theorists] argue that under advanced capitalism political problems are no longer masked by the "natural" working of the market but are projected as problems of science and technology. . . . The pursuit of "efficiency" became the basis of a new ideology, a new form of domination' (1985: 42).

While CT certainly shares Weber's attentiveness to the role of ideas in society and their potentially mesmerizing effects upon populations, it is also important, as we stressed earlier, to appreciate its distance from the Weberian standpoint on the role of social science in relation to the understanding and critique of dominant ideas and values. Weber was more influenced by the ascetic and élitist tendencies of Nietzsche than by the worldly and democratic impulses of Marx. He was resigned to a process of rationalization from which only those with exceptional moral fibre would be spared. Critical Theorists, in contrast, have kept alive the Enlightenment idea that critical reason can be mobilized to transform society, and not just to enhance the clarity and responsibility or bolster the authority of an élite. For example, if technology is to enrich rather than impoverish human experience (cf. Marcuse, 1964), it is argued that its development and use must be placed under more democratic forms of control. To this end, the values of alternative and intermediate technologies are to be commended because, quite apart from their ecological benefits, they are seen to present decentralized means of empowering local communities to develop their own solutions and shape their own fate. Whereas a Weberian standpoint favours technocratic control by a knowledgeable élite, CT stresses the value of self-determination in which material and social technologies are developed and deployed in ways that are reflective and supportive of democratic decision making. But, equally, CT distances itself from a conception of Marxism in which scientific analysis is equated with the identification and analysis of contradictions within structures that, eventually, will produce a largely predestined process of revolutionary transformation. CT is less sanguine about the inevitability of radical emancipatory change. A socially progressive outcome of the breakdown of prevailing structures is by no means assumed. Any substantial and sustained reduction in socially unnecessary suffering is understood to be conditional upon the development and dissemination of critical science (practical rationality). By advancing and applying critical science, CT seeks to realize ends that are more *practically rational*, in the sense that they are more congruent with the expansion of autonomy and responsibility. From this perspective, the attainment of practical rationality, in contrast with the refinement of technical or instrumental rationality, is at once a condition and a consequence of the open, democratic determination of ends.

## Incommensurable Paradigms and Complementary Types of Science

Burrell and Morgan's (1979) identification of four paradigms of scientific analysis has been influential in opening up the field of organization and management studies to diverse traditions of social theory. By paying attention to the diversity of ideas about science and society, it has provided a basis for questioning the dominance of functionalist thinking in defining what counts (and what does not count) as 'scientific knowledge' of management and organizations. However, from a CT standpoint, there are also significant difficulties with Burrell and Morgan's contention that the four paradigms are incommensurable as this effectively protects each of them, including the functionalist paradigm, from external critique. In Burrell and Morgan's framework, a tendency within social science towards dualistic forms of analysis (e.g. individual v. society; action v. structure, etc.) is cast into a metaphysical principle. As a consequence, the possibility and coherence of studies that seek to synthesize 'subjective' and 'objective' approaches is denied (Willmott, 1990, 1993b; Deetz, 1994).

Consider the case of CT. Earlier we noted that Burrell and Morgan place CT in the subjectivist realm of the philosophy of social science. However, if we examine Habermas' *Legitimation Crisis* (1975a), for example, we find that this study is no less concerned with the so-called objective structures of society than are key texts of radical structuralism, even though, as its title indicates, *Legitimation Crisis* is also attentive to issues of ideology and individual motivation that are credited to the radical humanist paradigm. In fact, and revealingly, Burrell and Morgan (1979: 294) acknowledge, in passing, that their framework struggles to accommodate the interparadigmatic quality of CT. Later, they are once again compelled to acknowledge that despite Habermas' attentiveness to the role of language (which marks him as a 'subjectivist' in Burrell and Morgan's eyes), he is 'at pains to stress that the theory of communicative competence must be linked to the fundamental assumptions of historical materialism if it is to be adequate and effective'; and that 'the materialist and idealist strands within Habermas's work are always yoked in a relationship of great tension, and his theoretical orientation aims at their reconciliation' (ibid.: 296). Having saddled themselves with a dualistic framework, Burrell and Morgan are forced to pigeon-hole CT somewhere. They slot it into the radical humanist paradigm, presumably on the grounds that CT is less deterministic and economistic than structuralist Marxism and, perhaps, on the more expedient grounds that, without it, the radical humanist box would be embarrassingly bereft of content.

At this point it is appropriate to return briefly to the theory of knowledge constitutive interests developed by Habermas for identifying and differentiating between types of scientific knowledge. As we noted earlier, this theory understands the production of different kinds of knowledge to be sparked by the problems and opportunities that accompany humankind's cultural break from nature – a break that signifies the release of human beings from the compulsion of instinctual drives. In contrast to Burrell and Morgan, who connect generation of knowledge with mutually incompatible sets of *ideas* about science and society, Habermas connects the production of knowledge to the materially grounded arousal of cognitive *interests*.[7] The

degree of access. In other versions, what counts as 'feminine' or 'feminine values' has no essence but, instead, is understood to be historically and culturally contingent (Flax, 1990b). The latter position opens a space for addressing issues of gender relations in a way that subverts the, perhaps perverse, tendency to regard (and marginalize) 'feminism' as an exclusively women's issue (Flax, 1990a). Arguably, this stance, which challenges the dualism of masculine/feminine issues, is also more consonant with the Habermasian understanding that different types of knowledge are potentially complementary rather than irremediably incommensurable.

Within the field of management and organization, the feminist voice has been slow in being heard, probably because management theory and practice has been so long dominated by men and by discourses that privilege the trappings of masculinity (Hearn et al., 1989; Calas and Smircich, 1991). An early feminist contribution to critical organizational analysis was made by Ferguson (1984) who argues, *contra* Weber, that processes of rationalization can be resisted, and that the rise of feminism presents a potent challenge to bureaucratic values and practices. Others (e.g. Pringle, 1988; Collinson et al., 1990) have built upon and revised this foundation by showing how patterns of dominance and subordination are reproduced within work organizations. However, reference to radical feminist work has been conspicuously absent from critical textbooks and readers on organizations (e.g. Thompson and McHugh, 1995; Clegg, 1990; Alvesson and Willmott, 1992). To our knowledge, a broad and thorough feminist analysis and critique of the gendering of management theory and practice, including its inhibition or manipulation of emotionality (Mumby and Putnam, 1992; Jaggar and Bordo, 1989), has yet to be undertaken and, indeed, is well overdue.

## Summary and Conclusion

In this chapter we have considered the central role played by knowledge in society: it informs and justifies how we act. Whenever knowledge is, for all practical purposes, accepted as truth – when, for example, it is taken for granted that managers make decisions or that married women go to work for pin money – some forms of action are facilitated as others are impeded. In this sense, knowledge is powerful especially when it is represented and understood as neutral and authoritative (i.e. scientific). Because knowledge is a potent medium of domination, it is necessarily a focal topic of critical analysis.

In the first part of the chapter, we deployed Weber's discussion of the role of science to challenge the claims of technocracy. Here the logic of Weber's advocacy of the value of reason in guiding human affairs was not denied. But, it was argued, the idea of one, authoritative value-free science effectively devalues and suppresses alternative knowledges and conceptions of science. Burrell and Morgan's paradigms framework was introduced to illustrate the diversity of scientific analysis. It was shown to have heuristic value in highlighting the existence of different value-based approaches to the production of scientific knowledge about organizations and management. This framework also enabled us to locate CT in the wider terrain of social scientific enquiry and provided a heuristic device for comparing and contrasting other varieties of 'radical' analysis – notably labour process theory and feminist theory. However, it was also criticized *inter alia* for encouraging the dualistic idea (of 'pure theory') that scientists can stand outside of their object of study – whether this object is the world of management and organizations or the texts that present accounts of this world. Burrell and Morgan's book usefully exposes the powerful grip of 'functionalist science' upon management and organization studies and, by relativizing its claims in relation to the other paradigms, opens a space for more radical types of inquiry. However, it simultaneously disregards the central issue of how choices are made between different kinds (or paradigms) of analysis and, relatedly, the ways in which such choices are rooted in what Habermas terms knowledge-constitutive human interests.

So, while Burrell and Morgan's framework has been helpful in opening up management and organizational studies to 'radical' analysis, it demands either a full commitment to functionalist analysis or the total rejection of it. In contrast, Habermas' formulation of three cognitive interests permits, and indeed actively encourages, the development of the empirical-analytic sciences, including functionalist analysis, *within* a broader critical vision of science as a potentially emancipatory force. In short, CT complements an appreciation of the power of science with a reflexive understanding of the science of power.

From the standpoint of Critical Theory, the central problem in making sense of social reality, including the theory and practice of management, is *not* how to rid *the* scientific method of normative bias. Such an 'objectivist' ambition cannot be fulfilled, CT argues, because facts cannot be separated from values. Nor does CT advocate, in 'subjectivist' fashion, the abandonment of epistemological questions. Instead, as Habermas has argued, different types of science are understood to be embedded in different kinds of human interests. For CT, the central issue is *what kinds* of normative bias should inform the production of knowledge. CT contends that the identification and pursuit of means and ends can be more or less rational, depending upon the openness and symmetry of the power relations through which decisions about ends are reached. Accordingly, the development of less distorted forms of knowledge is conditional upon the removal of institutional and psychological obstacles, such as patriarchy and egoism, that currently impede greater openness and symmetry.

## Notes

1 Whereas established management practice relied upon the vagaries of custom and practice, Taylor's scientific principles claimed to articulate the rational specification of managerial and worker behaviour. Taylor took it for granted that everyone has a broadly equal stake in

productive activity – managers and workers as well as shareholders – and would therefore each accept the rationality of his principles of organization. Quite apart from the resistance of shopfloor workers who resented the loss of control over the pace and variety of their work, Taylor failed to grasp that managers – the experts – would not be unequivocally unenthusiastic about the additional burden of responsibility that his system placed upon them. Although the realization of this technocratic vision was found to be flawed by its unrealistic assumptions, Taylor's ideas did much to cement the ideal of managerial prerogative and control. Subsequent revisions of management theory have rejected his principles without abandoning his technocratic vision.

2 Underpinning Weber's understanding of the role of science in modern society is his existential view that the social world is essentially meaningless and devoid of ethical content. Since the world is ethically irrational, whatever meanings (or ethics) are ascribed to the world are endowed entirely by the, more or less intentional, commitment of human beings to particular values and projects. This understanding emphasizes the responsibility of human beings for the interpretations and choices that are made – a responsibility that cannot be shuffled off onto an allegedly absolute authority, whether this takes the form of, for example, the Bible or of science.

3 Critical Theory contends that science becomes ideological when its roots in the suffering of being and the preconditions of communication are forgotten. Pure theory, Habermas (1972: 314–5) argues, 'wanting to derive everything from itself, succumbs to unacknowledged external conditions and becomes ideological. Only when philosophy discovers in the dialectical course of history the traces of violence that deform repeated attempts at dialogue and recurrently close off the path to unconstrained communication does it further the process whose suspension it otherwise legitimated: mankind's evolution toward *Mundigkeit. Mundigkeit* can be loosely translated as autonomy and responsibility in the conduct of life.'

4 Clearly, there have always been criticisms from outside the sphere of management – for example, from trade unionists and from radicals of both the Left and the Right. Those on the Left have viewed management as agents of capital whose oppressive function is to keep workers in their place. From the Right, management is criticized for building self-serving bureaucratic empires that harbour inefficiency, impede competitiveness and dampen individual initiative.

5 The example of Eastern Europe serves to illustrate how the contradictions of state socialism can be contained through military oppression, routine surveillance and corruption as well as less transparent processes of indoctrination and mystification. The crushing of urban oppositional elements in China in 1989 and in Russia during 1995 and 1996 has illustrated how the use of violence by the state can be sustained and brutally exercised in the face of resistance. The coercive use of the army as well as the police during the Miners' Strike in the UK revealed the iron fist beneath the velvet glove of a modern 'democratic' state. The example of Eastern Europe also indicates how, as the coercive grip of totalitarianism is loosened, other forces can emerge to fill the vacuum. In the absence of a well-organized working class, the breakdown of order presents an opportunity for various reactionary ideologies and criminal practices to assert themselves, often with former communist *apparatchiks* remaining in key positions.

6 In this respect, Critical Theory is distanced from other elements of the radical humanist paradigm – such as the traditions of anarchism (e.g. Stirner, 1907) and existentialism (Cooper, 1990) which disregard the historical and material conditions of action. While these philosophies are directly concerned with issues of human freedom, their marginalization of the importance of the historical embeddedness of human existence leads them to become fixated upon what one Critical Theorist has characterized as the self-absorbed jargon of authenticity (Adorno, 1973).

7 As we discuss in Chapter 3, this initial formulation, which focuses upon the *consciousness* of individuals, was subsequently revised but not abandoned by Habermas when he located the emancipatory impulse in *language*.

8 Subsequently, this has been partially corrected by the contribution of Gibson Burrell to the study of gender and especially sexuality in organizations (e.g. Burrell, 1984; Hearn et al., 1989).

9 The women's movement merits only a single paragraph in *The Theory of Communicative Action*, vol. 2, p. 393 (Habermas, 1987b).

# 3

# Critical Theory: Development and Central Themes

This chapter provides an overview of the major themes of Critical Theory (CT). However, at the outset, it is worth stressing that this focus upon Critical Theory does not signal our unequivocal allegiance to this tradition of critical analysis. As we have indicated in the previous chapters and will demonstrate again in this chapter, we do not consider that Critical Theory possesses a monopoly on truth. Nothing is to be gained by denying the important insights and contributions made by labour process theory (Knights and Willmott, 1990) or Foucauldian analysis (e.g. Townley, 1993; 1994) to the study of management and organization. But, equally, we believe that Critical Theory also provides a valuable resource for making sense of management theory and practice. It is because this resource has been neglected – in comparison to labour process analysis, at least – that we have devoted this chapter to its exegesis, and not because we believe that it is the sole, or even the most enlightening, source of wisdom.

Building upon our discussion in the previous chapter, we begin by positioning CT historically in relation to the critical tradition of social philosophy, as exemplified, for example, in the ideas of 'the young Hegelians' and, most importantly, the radical thinking of Marx. Having sketched this cultural and intellectual history, we review a number of recurrent and contemporary themes in Critical Theory that are pertinent to the study of management and organizations: the dialectics of enlightenment, one-dimensionality and consumerism, technocracy and communicative action. Finally, focusing more directly upon the work of Habermas, we review a variety of criticisms – hostile as well as sympathetic – that have been directed at Critical Theory.

As in the previous chapters, the term Critical Theory is used to refer to scholars and commentators who are closely related, or strongly sympathetic, to the work of the Frankfurt School. Central figures of the School include Max Horkheimer, Theodor Adorno, Herbert Marcuse, Erich Fromm and, of greatest contemporary significance, Jürgen Habermas. At the core of Critical Theory is a concern to develop a more rational, enlightened society through a process of critical reflection upon the organization and efficacy of existing institutions and ideologies. The considerable diversity of the School is integrated around a common desire to mobilize the potentials of critical reasoning to question and transform oppressive features of the modern world by means of 'a non-authoritarian and non-bureaucratic politics' (Held, 1980: 16). Without claiming to escape the conditioning of prevailing relations of power, members of the Frankfurt School assume the possibility of subjecting established dogmas to critical scrutiny, and thereby to open up a space for emancipatory change.[1]

## A Brief History of the Frankfurt School

### The Early Years

The research institute which supported the founding members of the Frankfurt School was conceived in the 1920s by Felix Weil, the son of a successful businessman. As a student at Frankfurt University, Weil had been inspired by Leftist thinking. He approached his father who agreed to provide an initial endowment sufficient to establish an independent research centre that would employ researchers from a variety of disciplines – philosophy, sociology, economics, psychology. Crucially, this endowment made it possible for the Institute of Social Research to be more intellectually and politically independent than comparable centres directly funded by the German State. So began a pioneering and exceptionally fruitful interdisciplinary collaboration that was to have far-reaching impacts, especially in Western Europe and North America.

After somewhat uncertain and shaky beginnings, the Institute received clearer direction with the appointment of Max Horkheimer under whose leadership, during the late 1920s and early 1930s, the Frankfurt School, as it was to become known, aimed to combine social science and philosophy into a politically and practically committed social philosophy. This mission involved a fundamental questioning of the claim that social science can and should produce objective, value-free knowledge of social reality (see Chapter 2). Instead of feeling obliged to discover universal, invariant regularities and law-like patterns in social behaviour (or at least to dress up empirical findings in these terms), members of the Frankfurt School sought to show how seemingly 'given' patterns of activity (e.g. consumerism, authoritarianism) take shape within specific historical and societal contexts, and that the methods of representing these patterns are themselves inextricably embedded within these contexts. Such patterns and methods, it was contended, should be perceived as a moment in the historical movement of mankind – and not as the final form of society or of science. Underpinning this claim was a dialectically inspired concern (to be discussed below) to engender reflection upon, and emancipation from, the contradictions and restrictions inherent in advanced capitalist societies.

There is, as we indicate later, a strong thread of continuity that links the guiding ideas of the Frankfurt School and the views of left-Hegelians whose most influential member was Marx (see Jay, 1973). However, members of the Frankfurt School were not directly associated with any Leftist political party, programme or movement. In the eyes of Horkheimer and his colleagues, the proletariat was not likely to emerge as the revolutionary agent of social change. The industrial proletariat, they believed, had long since become divided and weakened – if, indeed, it had ever had the power and vision necessary to overthrow capitalism and establish a genuinely socialist society. Declining to align themselves with interests ascribed to the proletariat by orthodox Marxists, members of the School nonetheless identified themselves with the critical, emancipatory *intent* of the Marxian tradition. But, as we noted in the previous chapter, instead of focusing upon the revolutionary potential ascribed to the proletariat, attention was directed to any and all individuals who – feeling frustrated, oppressed and confused by the contradictory claims, perverse priorities and divisive effects of modern capitalist societies – were potentially receptive to the revitalization of Enlightenment ideas about autonomy and the development of responsible citizenship.

## Critiques of Totalitarianism

In the Germany of the 1930s, members of the Frankfurt School did not have to look far to find institutions and ideologies that systematically suppressed and impeded the realization of autonomy and responsible citizenship. Focusing upon the rise of Nazism and fascism in Western Europe and the increasingly authoritarian cast of the Soviet state, they asked: how could reason be so seriously eclipsed by such irrational beliefs and ideologies? Horkheimer, Fromm and the others took a large number of factors into account in their explanations: from nationalist struggles that developed out of the crisis-ridden capitalist economy to oppressive social relations and forms of socialization that fostered the mass formation of authoritarian personalities (Fromm, 1941; Adorno et al., 1950). Institutionalized nationalism, expressed as gross prejudice, was seen to be a condition and consequence of the development of authoritarian personalities. People with these personalities, members of the School argued, compulsively construct rigid and reified status hierarchies from which they derive a strong sense of identity and security. Obedient and loyal upwards, they are inclined to be intolerant and punitive downwards.

As the grip of the Nazis upon the German State and its intelligentsia tightened, many members of the Frankfurt School eventually went into exile in the USA. There they were directly exposed to, and deeply impressed if not traumatized by, the hyper-materialistic culture of the most advanced of the capitalist democracies. This experience stimulated fresh processes of critical reflection upon the seductive power of consumerist freedoms. Members of the School, notably Marcuse and Fromm, took an increasingly close interest in the (totalizing) impact of mass culture, especially in the industrialized production and distribution of news and entertainment. In particular, the media were seen by them to exert a numbing and homogenizing effect upon the consciousness of the mass of the population that inhibited reflection and normalized conformism.

the writings of Erich Fromm, who, following an acrimonious exchange with Marcuse, distanced himself from the Frankfurt School (see note 2).

During the past two decades, the tradition of Critical Theory has been carried forward by Jürgen Habermas. In the 1950s, Habermas worked as an assistant to Adorno upon the latter's return to Germany (see McCarthy, 1978). In these early years, he struggled hard to gain the respect and support of Horkheimer who was resistant to Habermas' efforts to engage more directly with the practical politics of 1950s Germany. In Germany, Habermas has consistently sought to reach a wider audience by giving interviews (see, for example, Habermas, 1986) and by publishing newspaper articles – for example on the debates in Germany in the mid-1980s concerning the reality and significance of National Socialism and the Holocaust,[3] the process of (re)unifying Germany and the significance of the Gulf War.[4]

Outside his native Germany, Habermas' influence has been largely confined to academia where he has been highly influential, as the deluge of secondary literature on his work bears witness (see note 1, Gortzen, 1982; and Nordquist, 1986), and to which this book makes a specialist contribution. In particular, Habermas has taken very seriously the complaint that the work of earlier Critical Theorists lacks any rational basis for its normative standards, and thus may be said to amount to little more than a pretentious kind of moralizing (and, some would add, by privileged intellectuals who are nostalgic for a past age in which humanistic ideas enjoyed some currency, and when academics exerted some influence). In response to this criticism, Habermas has embarked upon an ambitious and continuing programme that is intended to establish the rational foundations of CT critique. In his most recent writings this has been based upon the conjecture that the structure of human communication at once anticipates and provokes an emancipatory impulse towards the development of a more rational society in which communication is no longer distorted by relations of power and domination. In turn, this conjecture has, in principle, enabled Habermas to provide a rational basis for supporting Marcuse's rather more optimistic assessment of possibilities for counteracting the negative features of the modern technological-capitalist society, as contrasted with the more pessimistic assessments made by Adorno and by Horkheimer in his later work.

Regarded as one of the most original and influential of living Western social philosophers, Habermas has made the chief target of his criticisms the rationalization/technocratization of modern society – the domination of science, technology, administration and groups of experts over the lifeworld of its citizens (see Chapter 1). Habermas' emphasis upon the role of communication and the importance of unconstrained dialogue, together with the abstract, very wide-ranging and complex character of his major writings, makes it unlikely that his work itself will ever reach as wide an audience as that achieved by Marcuse (and Fromm) who engaged directly with popular experiential issues such as consumption, freedom, sexuality, etc. Nonetheless, his work may be of lasting value in providing a much-needed source of inspiration and guidance for diverse emancipatory movements. We return later in the chapter to explore Habermas' ideas more fully. Before doing so, we first consider the historical precedents of Critical Theory and the distinctiveness of its commitment to emancipatory change.

## The Critical Tradition

As we noted in Chapter 1, Critical Theory has its origins in the Enlightenment when knowledge based upon empirical investigation began to challenge established dogmas that had been preserved and sanctified by tradition and religion (McCarthy, 1978; Schroyer, 1973). Stimulated by the Reformation, in which papal authority and Catholic dogma were successfully challenged, key thinkers of the Enlightenment (e.g. Newton, Descartes) sought to set knowledge of the *natural* world upon a more rational, scientific basis. The understanding of scientific knowledge and 'rationality' advanced by these thinkers was positivistic or *non-dialectical*. That is to say, reality was conceptualized as an ahistorical object-world that exists externally to, and independently of, scientists' methods of representing this reality. In natural science, this dualist understanding was eventually challenged by Einstein and Heisenberg. Earlier, in philosophy, Hegelian dialectics had provided the first, systematic Western problematization of Cartesian dualism. Hegel's critique of Cartesianism was, however, confined to the realm of ideas. It was not until the young Hegelians – notably Feuerbach and, later, Marx – challenged Hegel's idealism that a materially and historically grounded conception of the *dialectical* production, or reproduction, of social reality was articulated in which subjects and objects are intertwined and mutually constitutive of each other. It is this that provides the foundations of CT (see Horkheimer, 1972).

When building upon the material dialectics of the Left Hegelians, Critical Theorists have incorporated reflections upon the major historical developments and intellectual innovations of the intervening century, including the worldwide expansion of capitalism, the rise of fascism, the degeneration of Marxism into Stalinism and Maoism, and even Right critiques of mass society (Friedman, 1981). Intellectually, phenomenology and psychoanalysis have facilitated critical reflection upon Left Hegelian residues of materialism, determinism and rationalism (e.g. Marcuse, 1955; Fromm, 1970). CT's openness to a range of intellectual traditions was initially prompted by an appreciation of the difficulties encountered by orthodox Marxism in making coherent sense of the development of welfare capitalism and the expansion of consumerism. Marx's focus upon the material exploitation of labour, in particular, has been found wanting on the grounds that it takes insufficient account of the formative role of images and ideas – and of communication and consumption, more generally – as media of socio-economic domination (Marcuse, 1964; Habermas, 1979; see also Chapter 2). Orthodox Marxism is criticized by

CT for failing to appreciate how forms of culture and communication – in the guise of ideology and the institutionalization of conflict – can serve either to diffuse the potential of negation or, indeed, can be mobilized, as in the case of Soviet Union, China and Cuba, to create a revolution in advance of the maturation of what Marx regarded as the requisite material conditions (e.g. the formation of a large and well organized industrial proletariat) for socialist transformation.

In short, CT has been concerned to expose and remedy the comparative neglect of culture and ideology in Marxian analysis, without simply making a switch or reversion from Marxian materialism to Hegelian idealism. As Habermas has observed, or claimed, with regard to his own shift of focus from production to communication:

> The paradigm-shift . . . to communicative action does not mean that I am willing or bound to abandon the material production of the lifeworld as the privileged point of reference for analysis. I continue to explain the selective model of capitalist modernization, and the corresponding pathologies of a one-sided rationalized lifeworld, in terms of a capitalist accumulation process which is largely disconnected from orientations towards use-value. (1985: 96)

Here Habermas asserts the fundamental importance of 'the material production' of the social world. The demands of the capitalist accumulation process, he suggests, are largely responsible for creating the modern world in which productive activity is directed at the generation of commodities that have utility principally as a means of exchange, and thus of capital accumulation, rather than being directed at activities that are of direct benefit, or 'use-value', for human happiness and development. This implies that an adequate understanding of processes of modernization requires a critical analysis of the organizational practices that sustain and legitimize the 'pathologies of a one-sided rationalized lifeworld'. And, in turn, this suggests that Habermas' reformulation of Critical Theory provides a relevant resource for the development of critical studies of management and organization without necessarily adopting it as the sole or even the most fruitful source of critical thinking (Alvesson and Willmott, 1992).

### Some Themes in Critical Theory

We now consider in a little more detail some of the overlapping themes and issues that have been central to the Frankfurt tradition and which are directly relevant for the study of management and organization. These are (a) the dialectics of Enlightenment, (b) the one-dimensionality and consumerism of advanced capitalist societies, (c) the critique of technocracy and (d) communicative action. There is some inevitable overlapping of these themes, but it is convenient for expository purposes to examine them separately.

*The Dialectics of Enlightenment*    At the heart of the Enlightenment project is the critique and replacement of earlier belief systems grounded in tradition, common sense, superstition, religion, etc., with ostensibly more rational forms of thought and practice. However, as we noted in Chapters 1 and 2, this project can itself encompass new and emergent forms of dogma, dependence and deprivation – notably, when appeals to science are made to establish and legitimize forms of domination. The paradox of the Enlightenment project – that it produces destruction and oppression as well as liberation and progress – is associated in Critical Theory with the expansion and domination of a scientistic and technocratic consciousness: consciousness that seeks development of instrumentally rational means for achieving ends that are deemed (by value-free science) to be beyond rational evaluation (see Chapter 2).

The rosy, positivist view of science, pictured as the benevolent agent of enlightenment, was forcefully challenged by Horkheimer and Adorno (1947a) in *Dialectic of Enlightenment*. Modern civilization, they argue, has become progressively mesmerized by the power of a one-sided, instrumental conception of reason. Beguiled by successes in conquering and harnessing nature, people in modern societies are seen to be trapped in a scientistic nexus. This nexus, Horkheimer and Adorno contend, is no less constraining, and is in many ways much more destructive, than the myopia of pre-modern traditions which the enlightening advance of science has aspired to replace: 'In the most general sense of progressive thought, the Enlightenment has always aimed at liberating men from fear and establishing their sovereignty. Yet the fully enlightened earth radiates disaster triumphant' (ibid.: 3). Perhaps the most obvious symptom of this disaster is the relentless effort to dominate nature, associated with the ruthless exploitation of scarce natural resources and widespread environmental destruction and pollution. Although Horkheimer and Adorno do not refer directly to ecological crisis as a force of negation, their analysis certainly points in this direction. For them, civilization is doomed by the inescapable instrumentalism of our relationship to nature.[5]

Whenever scientific knowledge fails to appreciate its historical embeddedness within the contexts of its production, CT argues, it stands in danger of *naturalizing* phenomena in ways which *mystify* their emergence out of a dynamic process of struggle between competing and contradictory forces in society. As Habermas has argued in relation to the double-edged capacity of science to become ideological in its effects when it is undialectically conceived and applied:

> Science as a productive force can work in a salutary way when it is infused by science as an emancipatory force. . . . The enlightenment which does not break the (mythic) spell dialectically, but instead winds the veil of a halfway rationalization only more tightly around us, makes the world divested of deities itself into a myth! (1974: 281)

Where the connection of scientific knowledge to an interest in emancipation is lost or forgotten, science becomes an ideology: an instrument of political and economic domination. In the form of technocracy, scientific expertise effectively freezes social reality and legitimizes subordination to what currently exists (see Chapter 2).

When naturalized, social phenomena are represented as existing 'beyond' human powers, rather than as social and political artifacts. CT argues that theory and practice of management, for example, cannot be adequately understood without appreciating the way beliefs, ideas and values define and legitimize the social category of managers and managerial processes (see Chapter 1). The production of (management) knowledge, CT contends, is conditioned by relations of power and domination that at once enable and constrain our capacity to reflect critically upon established 'truths' – such as our knowledge of people and organizations as these are represented in the texts and disciplines of management, and are absorbed and applied by its students and practitioners. For CT, much scientific and management knowledge is a *one-sided* expression of a dialectical process (see above) in which an appreciation of its historically-embedded production is obscured. In contrast, the dialectical imagination of CT strives to expose and critique contradictions in managerialist claims that its (ideological) theories are objective and that its (oppressive and destructive) practices are efficient and effective. In so doing, CT discloses the limits of established wisdoms and practices, and thereby opens up the possibility of more rational, less contradictory, pathways of social and economic development.

*One-dimensionality and Consumerism* The term 'one-dimensional man' was coined by Marcuse (1964) to highlight how the organization of advanced capitalist societies effectively frustrates or deflects the emancipatory impulses of oppositional movements. At the heart of Marcuse's analysis is a critique of consumerism. In affluent Western societies, Marcuse argues, people are enjoined to become passive and unreflective consumers who are incapable of imagining forms of life that differ from the present. The USA, in particular, is identified as a society that possesses enormous productive capacities. Yet, instead of being applied to facilitate qualitative improvement in the lives of its citizens, societal development is driven by the logic – or illogic – of capitalism that routinely spreads waste, destruction, superficial satisfaction and needless misery.[6]

Proponents of CT directly challenge the conventional wisdom that mass consumption actually satisfies human needs (see Chapter 5). Instead of regarding needs as objectively given by human nature, CT understands ideas about 'needs' as being shaped by powerful forces (e.g. advertising) – shaped in ways that tie people emotionally, as consumers, to the possession of more and more goods, and thereby increase their material and psychological dependence upon the goods society. The depth of this dependence, Marcuse (1969) suggests, is productive of a sense of self that is preoccupied, if not obsessed, with consuming as an end in itself, and which is therefore 'opposed to every change that might interrupt, perhaps even abolish, this dependence' (ibid.: 19). For Marcuse, forms of enjoyment provided by mass consumerism are essentially dehumanizing and 'repressive'. Their principal effect is the numbing of human sensibilities, not their refinement or fulfilment.

In a similar vein, Fromm (1955, 1976) has argued that (discriminating) processes of consumption could, and should, form an integral part of a happier and more satisfying life. Yet, perversely, an ever-inflating 'need' for more goods undermines this happiness *and* continuously spurs us on to feed the consumerist habit. The individual 'consumes' sport, films, newspapers, magazines, books, lectures, natural sceneries, social situations and even other people in the same remote and alienated way that other, everyday merchandise is consumed. The alienated consumer does not participate actively or appreciatively in these activities, but wants to 'swallow' everything there is. By celebrating the freedom of consumption, the conditioning powers of industry fill and control free time that might otherwise be devoted to reflection and communication. Still, as we noted earlier, the mass media are not considered to be irredeemably reactionary or oppressive. If placed under democratic control rather than being driven by commercial forces that celebrate the values and practices of the status quo, the mass media could be vehicles of education and emancipation.

*The Critique of Technocracy*    A distinguishing feature of technocracy is its denial of the relevance of ethics – or moral-practical consciousness (Habermas, 1979: 148) – in processes of individual and societal development. The ends of human and organizational existence are taken for granted, or they are alleged to be self-evident or, finally, they are deemed to lie beyond rational debate (see Chapter 2). In the selection of means, ethical considerations are also excluded or marginalized as the identification of the most appropriate means is deemed to be a purely technical matter. Decision making is regarded as the province of experts who, because they are deemed to know best about the field under consideration, can identify the most efficient and/or effective way of achieving (seemingly) given or self-evident ends.[7]

In the previous chapter, we noted how a concern about the use and/or abuse of science to override, rather than inform, the making of choices between competing value-commitments motivated Weber's insistence upon the separation of the realms of facts (science) and values. Weber was most anxious that science should not invade (or colonize, to use a Habermasian term) the province of values or ethics. However, as we also noted, a paradoxical consequence of lending support to the idea that authentic social science is, or can be made, unitary and value-free, rather than multifaceted and political, is its restriction to the 'positive' task of generating more accurate knowledge so as to identify the most efficient and/or effective method of achieving existing ends. To deem these ends to be given or to be beyond debate is simply to accept and reproduce the values and priorities of those groups who have been successful, through processes of political struggle, in getting their ends established as *the* ends. Technocratic consciousness fails to acknowledge the way that, far from being apolitical or neutral, it is itself *constitutive* of a particular kind of social order in which, far from being 'above' ethics, it places its own 'post-ethical' imprint on processes of individual and social development (see Macintyre, 1981).

Weber sought to ward off the technocratic abuse of science by contriving to *divide* the realm of science (facts) from the realm of values (see Chapter 2). In contrast, Habermas differentiates purposive-rational action (oriented towards efficient and effective realization of given ends) from communicative action (oriented towards understanding), *and* argues that the former is always *embedded* in, and *depends upon*, the *normative framework* provided by the latter. This is perhaps the most fundamental of the assumptions underpinning Habermas's reconstruction of Critical Theory. As well as providing a basis for his criticisms of Marx's preoccupation with production to the comparative neglect of communication (see above and Habermas, 1974), this assumption guides his interest in seemingly bourgeois ideas (e.g. those developed by Mead) concerned with interaction and the phenomenology of everyday life (Habermas, 1984). It also informs his extended efforts to ground his repeated critiques of technocratic consciousness and, most notably, technocratic systems theory (Habermas, 1989). As we noted earlier, Habermas' emphasis upon the central and relatively autonomous role of normative frameworks in processes of social interaction and development is the key element in his constructive critique of historical materialism:

> I would like to propose the following: the species learns not only in the dimension of technically useful knowledge decisive for the development of productive forces but also in the dimension of moral-practical consciousness decisive for structures of interaction. The rules of communicative action do not develop in reaction to changes in the domain of instrumental and strategic action; but in doing so they follow *their own logic*. (Habermas, 1979: 148)

In this respect, excessively materialist analysis harbours technocratic tendencies which find their expression in, for example, Soviet-style socialism. Technocracy, Habermas contends, depends and thrives upon a denial, or *forgetting*, of the embeddedness of instrumental reason in the normative framework of society (to be discussed further in the following subsection). The more that technocratic consciousness contributes to, and dominates, processes of individual and social development, the more obscured and displaced is the moral-practical quality of *all* human interaction, including the production and application of scientific knowledge. Characterizing this as an ideology, precisely because it masquerades as being above ethics when it is not, Habermas (1971: 105–6) notes how its power resides in its capacity to 'detach society's self-understanding from the frame of reference of communicative action and from the concepts of symbolic interaction and replace it with a scientific model. Accordingly, the culturally defined self-understanding of a social lifeworld is replaced by the self-reification of purposive-rational action and adaptive behaviour.' Here Habermas draws attention to the contemporary tendency in the West for the normative framework of society to be supplanted, if not absorbed, by a technocratic preoccupation with refining the subsystems of purposive-rational action. 'Old-style' politics, which sought its justification by drawing from an established (classical) pool of ethical ideas about the 'good life', are contrasted with modern politics which are much more absorbed by narrow, instrumental questions about how to maintain or regenerate elements of the (capitalist) system. A technocratic focus upon means displaces a democratic debate about ends. The traditional approach, Habermas argues, was oriented to 'practical goals . . . defined by inter-action patterns'. In contrast, the contemporary (technocratic) approach to politics 'is aimed exclusively at the functioning of a manipulated system' (Habermas, 1971: 103). Formally democratic institutions exist but, in effect, these exist to permit 'administrative decisions to be made largely independently of specific motives of citizens' (Habermas, 1973: 36). These institutions provide legitimacy for decisions. But there is minimal participation by citizens in the key decision-making processes.

The remoteness of processes of administrative decision making from the particular motives of citizens is not without its (self-defeating) consequences in terms of its corrosive effect upon public confidence and support. Policies developed to revitalize the capitalist system (e.g. tighter regulation of labour or of the restriction of civil liberties) can clash directly with cherished bourgeois freedoms and equalities (e.g. of assembly or of opportunity). And the meanings and norms developed within the institutional framework (e.g. self-discipline and trust) can become so weakened by system demands (e.g. reduced public expenditure and high levels of unemployment) that it is unable to support the weight of political and economic burdens placed upon it. But Habermas also cautions that 'we have no metaphysical guarantee' (Habermas, 1979: 188) that this erosion will not continue or that its outcome will be in the direction of democracy rather than technocracy.

To counter the degeneration of (bourgeois) democracy and its drift into technocracy, Habermas stresses the importance of distinguishing between instrumental and communicative rationality, and argues that as much – and more – attention must be devoted to the rationalization of the institutional framework by *'removing restrictions on communication'* (Habermas, 1971: 118, emphasis in original) as has been given to the rationalization of systems of purposive-rational action. Otherwise, the prospect is for ethics and democracy to be progressively weakened and eventually to 'disappear behind the interest in the expansion of our power of technical control' (ibid.: 113). Ideally, the distorting and destructive effects of technocratic consciousness are to be challenged and reversed by promoting and supporting actions that open up communications within all spheres – familial, organizational and public – and thereby facilitate the development of a *democratically rational society*. Or, as Habermas, puts it:

> Public, unrestricted discussion, free from domination, of the suitability and desirability of action-orienting principles and norms in the light of socio-cultural repercussions of developing subsystems of purposive-rational action – such

communication at all levels of political and repoliticized decision-making processes is the only medium in which anything like 'rationalization' is possible.
(ibid.: 119)

To sum up, when decisions are dominated by a technical interest in refining
means, fundamental questions about politics and ethics are marginalized as
ends are taken as given and the refinement of means becomes an end in
itself. By making more visible the primacy of communicative action,
Habermas' work problematizes the domination of technocracy as it highlights the practical rationality of the institutional framework as a resource
for contesting processes of (technocratic) rationalization that are restricted
to the realm of instrumental action.

*Communicative Action*  As we noted in the previous subsection, the
concept of communicative action challenges the conventional understanding that instrumental or strategic rationality is the only, or purest,
expression of human reasoning. Habermas (1984, 1987b) contends that all
communication depends upon a structure of understandings – such as the
understanding that utterances are truthful – which can nonetheless be
doubted in the course of interaction; and that this universal structure makes
possible the process of dialogue and argumentation through which a
*rational consensus* can be reached. Embedded in the very structure of
communication, he contends, is a 'universal pragmatics'; and this pragmatics at once anticipates an 'ideal speech situation' in which an *unforced*,
rational consensus about ends is emergent and appropriate forms of action
are pursued. Insofar as this ideal remains unrealized in practice, distortions
of communication are a potent source of frustration and suffering that
repeatedly motivates emancipatory change (to be elaborated below).

Habermas is under no illusions that, in everyday life, communications
are routinely distorted and break down whenever constraints – in the form
of sanctions and repressions – impede the practical realization of the ideal
of unforced consensus. Nor does he claim to have escaped from these
constraints. It is therefore possible, and indeed likely, that his theory of
communicative action is itself coloured or distorted, in as yet unrecognized
ways, by the contexts of its formulation. The purpose of Habermasian
critique is not to entertain the illusion of pure theory (see Chapter 2).
Rather, its critical intent is to challenge and displace unreflective, ideological discourse 'in a pragmatic and affirmative manner [that has] no
pretension to possess the *truth*' (Kortian, 1980: 134, emphasis in original).
It is intended as an invitation to a debate, and not as an authoritative move
to secure discursive closure.

The thesis that the frustrations and contradictions arising from distortions of communicative action animate the dynamics of emancipatory
action is illustrated by reference to the contemporary emergence of social
movements and forms of experimentation – the ecological movement, the
peace movement, the animal rights movement, etc. – where processes of
questioning and argumentation have been strongly encouraged and

facilitated.[8] From a neo-conservative or reactionary standpoint, activists in such movements are dismissed as moral degenerates or naïve idealists who exemplify and accelerate a continuing decline in high bourgeois standards that will be reversed only by the application of firm (e.g. authoritarian or neo-fascist) leadership. For Habermas, in contrast, the questioning of standardized patterns of action, and rejection of traditional bourgeois norms, is evidence of a vibrant lifeworld of face-to-face interaction in which, despite the pacifying effects of the mass media and pressures to accept received wisdoms, individuals articulate and advance a capacity for critical reflection and self-determination.[9] Problematizing received wisdom and values (e.g. about the natural environment as a bottomless pit for the disposal of toxic waste) is regarded as a necessary precondition for forging a consensus founded upon communicative ethics. These ethics cannot rely upon established dogmas and formulae but, instead, must be forged from a process of dialogue: 'the need for achieving understanding is met less by a reservoir of traditionally certified interpretations immune from criticism; at the level of a completely decentred understanding of the world, the need for consensus must be met more and more frequently by risky, because rationally motivated, agreement' (Habermas, 1984: 340).

Earlier we noted that Habermas' optimism regarding emancipatory currents within the dynamics of modernity is tempered by a concern that the everyday, face-to-face lifeworld is being progressively colonized by technocratic rationality. To elaborate this concern, Habermas (1987b: 151 *et seq.*) distinguishes between 'social' and 'systems' forms of integration. *Social integration* is accomplished through immediate, communicative interactions between those whose lives it directly coordinates. It involves the active and, in principle, unconstrained engagement of participants in determining the normative order of their lifeworld. In contrast, *systems integration* induces coordination by requiring participants to comply with a normative order that is imposed upon them at a distance by diverse experts and by impersonal media (money, bureaucratic rules, law, etc.). Systems integration is achieved through the use of inducements and sanctions rather than through the active, face-to-face consent of participants. Whereas interaction in the lifeworld is attentive to 'cultural tradition, legitimate orders and socialized individuals' (ibid.: 182), the operation of systems media, notably money and power, foster a:

> purposive-rational attitude toward calculable amounts of value and make it possible to exert generalized, strategic influence on the decisions of other participants while *bypassing* processes of consensus-oriented communication. Inasmuch as they do not merely simplify linguistic communication, but *replace* it with a symbolic generalization of rewards and punishments, the lifeworld contexts in which processes of reaching understanding are always embedded are devalued in favor of media-steered interactions; the lifeworld is no longer needed for the coordination of action. (ibid.: 183, emphasis in original)

The effect of coordination by means of systems integration, Habermas argues, is to devalue and weaken the moral order of the face-to-face lifeworld. Possibilities for improving the rationality of the lifeworld, opened up by modernist disenchantment with the authority of tradition, are impeded and remain unfulfilled as, in an effort to preserve the system, functional rationality feeds off, and colonizes, the meanings and understandings that are developed and valued within everyday life. For example, lifeworld values are weakened and colonized through the commercialization of leisure activities, by designing strong corporate cultures or even by extending (consumer) rights to citizens (e.g. the so-called Citizen's Charter in the UK). Even extension of such citizen's rights can have a perversely disabling impact upon the lifeworld when, instead of strengthening existing norms, it (further) reinforces the idea of citizens as passive consumers of political as well as commercial goods. In the case of the Citizen's Charter initiatives, a set of standards determined by experts is imposed upon citizens/customers who are encouraged to substitute these standards for those that they develop within the lifeworld. Individuals become increasingly constituted in passive roles – as employee/consumer/client/citizen/etc. – that are shaped principally by the technical, instrumental rationality of systems rather than by the practical, communicative rationality of the lifeworld.

As the lifeworld is colonized, Habermas contends, there is a process of cultural impoverishment as diverse experts set standards and package opinions – an impoverishment that Habermas (ibid.: 330) attributes, above all, to *'an elitist splitting-off of expert cultures from contexts of communicative action in everyday life'* (emphasis added). However, this process of colonization continuously encounters problems of legitimation. Why? Because, as Habermas (1984: 363) puts it, 'money and power can neither buy nor compel solidarity and meaning'. Systems rationality can, at best, induce dramaturgical compliance with the administrative norms of the new technocracy in which corporate cultures, for example, are managed by human resource professionals (see Chapter 1). It does not foster the trust and mutual respect that is necessary for systems rationality to be translated into effective forms of cooperation. From this it follows that a major task for critical thinkers is to expose the precarious foundations as well as the oppressive effects of technical or functional rationality. By doing this, it may be possible to open a space in which the lifeworld is further rationalized – not by experts but, rather, by groups or movements that challenge technocracy and champion democracy in ways that at once demand and support the values of autonomy and responsibility.

## Critiques of Critical Theory

To conclude this chapter without some reference to criticisms of Critical Theory would be inconsistent with CT's critical intent and self-critical claims. Many criticisms could be listed but, for present purposes, we are highly selective – though we return to make additional criticisms in

Chapter 7. Here we divide our brief review of critiques into those that are 'external' to CT, and therefore challenge its basic assumptions, and those that are basically sympathetic to CT, but identify difficulties with its project.

## External Criticisms

To those who regard social phenomena as neutral objects of investigation, equivalent to the objects of the natural sciences, the claims of CT are, of course, hopelessly value-laden and political. CT is swiftly dismissed as Leftist propaganda, peddled by deranged or disaffected intellectuals, who lack the sense and/or scientific commitment to recognize the unbridgeable difference between facts and values. In response, Critical Theorists have urged reflection upon such dogmatic dismissals. Yet, despite an ever-expanding volume of literature that argues against the neutrality and objectivity of social science (see Bernstein, 1976), many people remain indifferent to, or unpersuaded by, powerful arguments that dispute the claim of science to be value-neutral.

Some of those who share CT's scepticism about conventional images of science and society have nonetheless been unmoved by its arguments about human autonomy and processes of historical development, arguing that such preoccupations are symptomatic of a failure to grasp how the engine of history operates either largely independently of human consciousness (e.g. Braverman, 1974) or acts to reduce critical consciousness to a cynicism that 'holds anything positive to be fraud' (Sloterdijk, 1980: 546). A variant of the latter claim is that CT appeals to notions of autonomy and democracy that have little meaning or purchase in the context of modern societies, where the sense of these nineteenth-century ideas has been largely obliterated (see also Crook et al., 1992). Luhmann (1982), for example, has suggested that the basis of Habermas' distinction between technical and practical rationality is historical, and that its moment has passed – a view which, ironically, could not more fully endorse Habermas' own cautionary observation, cited earlier, that 'we have no metaphysical guarantee' (Habermas, 1979: 188) that the contemporary erosion of the lifeworld will not continue and even become total.

Alternatively, the outpourings of CT have been interpreted as the work of a disgruntled group of intellectuals whose privileged class background has impeded their identification with the interests of working people. Suspicion of the historical and élitist basis of the assumptions that underpin CT has been expressed, for example, by Bottomore who contends that:

> Reading the Frankfurt School texts on the loss of individual autonomy (and especially the writings of Adorno and Horkheimer) it is difficult to escape the impression that they express above all . . . is the sense of decline in a particular stratum of society, that of the educated upper middle class, or more specifically the 'mandarins', and the nostalgia for a traditional German *Kultur*. (1984: 42–3)

This objection is related to the criticism that Habermas' reconstitution of CT has been excessively preoccupied with questions of culture and ideology, to the neglect of the material basis of society (see Roderick, 1986). Habermas is censured for a focus upon communication that tends to deflect attention from its conditioning by the dynamics of capitalist reproduction. As we noted earlier, he has responded to such criticism by arguing that relations of production are shaped and mediated by processes of communication and identity formation that are inadequately appreciated by materialistic analysis (see Habermas, 1987b: 332 *et seq.*). But this defence cuts little ice with those who identify contradictions within, and struggles over, the productive process as the principal engine of radical social changes.

Fundamental criticisms of CT have also been articulated by post-structuralists who question whether knowledge can ever be separated from power, and therefore reject as incoherent and dangerous CT's claim to provide a rational grounding of its normative standards (e.g. Foucault, 1980; Lyotard, 1984). Such a claim is *incoherent*, the critics contend, because all forms of knowledge – including the idea of the ideal speech situation and communicative action – are articulations of power and, inescapably, exert a subjugating effect upon those who identify them as truth. The objection here is that CT is insufficiently self-reflective and self-critical about its own preconceptions – notably, its assumption that its ideas about 'autonomy' and 'responsibility' are unequivocally propitious for humankind. Such a view is *dangerous*, the poststructuralist critics declare, because it suggests that what is done in the name of humanism and emancipation is somehow exempt from (its own kinds of) oppressive effects. The risk is one of 'reason' being invoked to deny or mystify forms of subjection that ostensibly it claims to expose and remove. Habermas' response to this criticism has been to concede that CT cannot escape this risk. But he then seeks to turn the tables on the poststructuralists (see Poster, 1989) by inviting them to reflect upon what, for him, are the far more serious consequences of abandoning any basis for differentiating the true from the false, and the rational from the irrational. In which case, Habermas (1992: 209) argues, '*All* validity claims become immanent to particular discourses. They are simultaneously absorbed into the totality of some one [*sic*] of the blindly occurring discourses and left at the mercy of the 'hazardous play' amongst these discourses as each overpowers the other.' Habermas seems to be responding constructively to the post-structuralist thesis that attention must be paid to the consequences of adopting particular kinds of discourse, and not just to the way their claims are grounded. In doing so, CT is defended on the basis that efforts to differentiate the true from the false are less damaging in their, apparently conservative, effects than either a refusal to do so and/or a commitment to showing how such distinctions are solely 'immanent to particular discourses' rather than in any way being a condition of all forms of discourse (Freundlieb, 1989; see also Power, 1990).

*Internal Criticisms*

We now consider two kinds of criticisms that have been voiced by those who are broadly sympathetic to Critical Theory. First, feminists have been critical of CT's neglect of patriarchy as a pervasive source of oppression. Second, there are those who have been critical of CT, and Habermas in particular, for failing to grasp the embodied quality of human existence and the associated impediments to emancipatory change.

Radical feminism usefully draws attention to what is arguably the greatest blind spot in Critical Theory (Fraser, 1987; Meisenhelder, 1989). It highlights the vital importance of understanding patriarchy as a fundamental source of domination; and it identifies the women's movement as an important, yet neglected, source of opposition to oppressive, male-centred values and practices. Moreover, postfeminist ideas are potentially of relevance for CT, and especially Habermas' emphasis upon communication, because they open up awareness of, and communication about, gender-related forms of subjugation that have been marginalized (see Chapter 2). Rather than simply dismissing CT as 'gender blind', it is significant that some postfeminists have drawn upon, and have critically reconstructed, the insights of CT in ways that recognize their mutual concerns and seek to enrich their respective understandings (e.g. Benhabib, 1992).

Fraser (1987), for example, reviews and re-works the Habermasian distinction between, on the one hand, 'the lifeworld' – which is closely associated with the domestic and private sphere, and which escapes direct regulation by technical rationality – and, on the other hand, 'the system' where technical rationality is dominant and which is identified more closely with the world of work and the public sphere (as discussed earlier). At one level, the distinction between 'lifeworld' and 'system' is found to have *'prima facie* purchase on empirical social reality' (ibid.: 37). At the very least, it acknowledges the common experience of a division existing between the personal sphere (e.g. the family) and the more impersonal realm of economic relations (e.g. paid employment). But, Fraser argues, it is no less important to appreciate how this distinction can obscure the *continuities* between these realms – for example, by masking or marginalizing the extent to which the home is 'a site of labour, albeit unremunerated and often unrecognized' that is largely undertaken by women (ibid.). If this is accepted, then it is necessary to revise Habermas' analysis in a way that recognizes how the (patriarchal) positioning of men, as heads of family households, is underpinned by their privileged access to money and power that are the principal media of the operation of 'the system'. In fact, Habermas acknowledges the presence and oppressive influence of such media within the sphere of close, interpersonal relations. But, tellingly, these are regarded as a 'colonizing force', not as directly implicated in the constitution of the modern 'lifeworld'. In contrast, radical feminists stress the degree of mutual interdependence, interpenetration and male domination of both 'lifeworld' and 'system': 'the struggles and wishes of contemporary women are not adequately clarified by a theory that draws a basic battle line between system and lifeworld institutions. From a feminist perspective, there is a more basic battle line between the forms of male dominance linking "system" to "lifeworld" *and us*' (ibid.: 55).

Nonetheless, if CT acknowledges its relative gender-blindness, and radical feminism is prepared to learn from CT, there are possibilities for integrating their respective insights and concerns (Benhabib and Cornell, 1987; Luke and Gore, 1992). Indeed, it has been suggested that this coming together of CT and feminism is necessary if radical feminism is not to become bogged down in the mire of postmodernism (Nicholson, 1990), and CT is to become more fully engaged with contemporary struggles.[10] Within Habermas' communication theory of society, there would seem to be every reason for including patriarchy as a principal medium of distorted communication – not only between but also within gender relations as men and women struggle to recognize and emancipate themselves from the oppressive (e.g. 'aggressive'/'submissive') demands of received (and, it might be added, even radical) wisdoms about masculinity/femininity.

Another target of criticism, which is also shared by some radical feminists (e.g. Gilligan, 1982), is CT's attentiveness to cognitive processes to the neglect of human embodiment. Cognitive processes, it is argued, play a comparatively minor role in the practical process of releasing human beings from oppressive conditions (Fay, 1987; see also Keat, 1981 and Lukes, 1982). This criticism resembles the objections of those who argue that CT exaggerates the importance of consciousness in processes of radical social change (see Chapter 2). However, its intent is not so much to question the central role ascribed to consciousness as to embed it in corporal and unconscious processes (McIntosh, 1994). Forces of repression, Fay (1987) argues, exist in the body as well as the mind. Or, as he puts it, 'Changing people's self-conceptions may not be enough to change those perceptions, feelings, and dispositions which are deeply incarnated into their muscles, organs, and skeletons. . . . Humans are not only *active* beings, they are also embodied, traditional, historical, and embedded' (ibid.: 207, 209).

This objection underscores the criticism that CT (thought) and emancipatory praxis (action) are rather loosely coupled. An individual may be well versed in the (rationally reconstructive) refinements of CT, but this knowledge may exert little practical effect upon his or her conduct. In our view, this criticism is well targeted (see Chapter 8); and, indeed, as we noted in Chapters 1 and 2, it is one to which Habermas has responded by acknowledging a difference between two kinds of critical reflection. On the one hand, there is reflection that operates in the realm of ideas (e.g. about the universal presuppositions of speech and action) and has no *necessary* effect upon broader processes of self-(trans)formation. On the other hand, there is reflection that incorporates, but also goes beyond, processes of 'rational reconstruction' to dissolve destructive habits of mind and other compulsions that unnecessarily 'restrict patterns of perception and behaviour' and thereby enable 'the subject (to) emancipate himself from himself' (Habermas, 1975: 183). What Habermas has not yet successfully articulated is how reconstruction is practically translated into critique. This problem relates to a further internal criticism that concerns the lack of a substitute in CT for the proletariat as the agency of emancipatory social change.

Seeking to learn something from the lessons of modern history, leading advocates of CT have been highly sceptical about the prospects of proletarian revolution without, in most cases, becoming resigned to the prospect of total domination by instrumental reason or wholly sceptical of discourses that retain a belief in the possibility of emancipation. In contrast to other more accessible, but also cruder, forms of critical thinking, Habermas has developed a more abstract but, as yet, hazy idea of gradualist change. As Burrell (1994: 5) has observed of Habermas, he 'stands against all varieties of totalizing critique which lead to despair. For him, the philosopher as "guardian of reason" is also the sentinel of, and for, human hope'. For Habermas, change is understood to arise from a gathering, though uneven, disillusionment with the effects of modern capitalist society that are experienced as personally, socially and ecologically destructive. This disillusionment, Habermas suggests, is potentially productive of resistance and transformation for which CT aspires to provide the relevant analytical key and antidote.

However, to date, leading proponents of CT have devoted much more attention to the process of rational reconstruction than they have to the issue of how critical thinking has relevance for, and purchase upon, practical processes of collective self-(trans)formation. Despite the importance of management and organizations in modern societies, the absence of discussion of these institutions within CT is symptomatic of this tendency. Nonetheless, any lingering doubts about the practical, emancipatory relevance and potency of CT should not eclipse an appreciation of its role in raising important issues and providing inspiration for critical reflection. Of course, critical reflection upon established routines and habits of mind can simply fuel paralysing doubts, worries and anxieties, especially in the absence of a supportive culture for addressing and dissolving such concerns. But, hopefully, CT can also facilitate greater clarity about, and resistance to, forces that place socially unnecessary constraints upon open communication and personal fulfilment. It is also important not to expect or demand too much of CT – CT cannot, itself, do the practical work of emancipation.

## Conclusion

Central to CT is the understanding that, in the form of critical reflection, reason can be a stimulus and medium of human emancipation. Central figures in Critical Theory – Horkheimer, Adorno, Marcuse and Habermas – have differed in their analysis of modern irrationalities and their assessment of the prospects for their removal. But they have shared a common vision of the possibility of mobilizing the transformative power of reason to promote and guide emancipatory change. In seeking to illuminate the focus and scope of CT, we have explored briefly a number of over-lapping themes and issues that throw light upon processes of social reproduction and transformation, suggesting that CT's orientation and concerns have direct relevance for examining the development of management and organizations within advanced capitalist societies. The focus upon consumerism and the influence of mass media, for example, are relevant for analysing marketing (see Chapter 5); and the critique of technocracy and instrumental reason has broad applicability to all management disciplines where knowledge is refined and applied for purposes of buttressing or revitalizing the status quo (see Chapters 4–6).

In conclusion, it is worth noting that, with few exceptions, most other traditions of social analysis are highly resistant, if not antagonistic, to criticism. They contrive either to ignore or repel it. CT, and Habermas (1982, 1984, 1987a, 1991) in particular, has in contrast actively engaged with, and sought to learn from and even collaborate with, critics – even the most trenchant, such as Niklas Luhmann. However, there has been a weaker propensity, even and perhaps especially by Habermas, to address the question of how the tradition of Critical Theory may be extended and applied to the analysis of particular institutions or widespread practices in contemporary society (see Forester, 1982, 1993). Given that money and power figure so centrally as key media of colonization and cultural impoverishment, especially in Habermas' (1984, 1987b) theory of communi-cation, this reluctance is disappointing. For it would seem highly appropriate for the leading proponents of CT to complement a concern with grounding and refining theory with a more direct focus upon the (technocratic) domain of management and organization where, arguably, the media of money and power are most intensively enacted. One purpose of the remaining chapters of this book is to draw attention to analyses that are responsive to this concern.

## Notes

1 For overviews, many of which focus upon the work of Jürgen Habermas, see *inter alia* Jay, 1973; Tar, 1977; McCarthy, 1978; Held, 1980; Friedman, 1981; Honneth, 1991; Guess, 1981; Roderick, 1986; Keat, 1981; Benhabib, 1986; Fay, 1987; Ingram, 1987; White, 1988; Rockmore, 1989; Kellner, 1989; Rasmussen, 1990. There are also a number of collections that contain illuminating articles on particular aspects of Critical Theory. See, for example, Thompson and Held, 1982; Sabia and Wallukis, 1983; Bernstein, 1985; Wexler, 1991.

2 Marcuse's reading of Freud was by no means universally shared within the Frankfurt School. In particular Fromm, who was the first to combine the insights of Freud and Marx, not only challenged the Freudian emphasis upon sexuality and the death instinct, but also criticized Freud's crude materialism and patriarchal thinking. Fromm increasingly emphasized

the importance and precariousness of the existential basis of human freedom (Fromm, 1961). Fromm's drift away from materialism to existentialism eventually led to his break with the School and, subsequently, to an acrimonious exchange with Marcuse. Following his conflict with Marcuse (and Horkheimer), Fromm continued to share similar interests and to write, quite intentionally, books that were accessible to a wide audience (Willmott and Knights, 1982; see also Wiggerhaus, 1994). For those who were sceptical about Marcuse's belief in the power of libido and/or Fromm's humanistic appeals, only aesthetics (e.g. the work of writers like Kafka and Brecht) remained as a possible medium through which the sensibility and emancipatory praxis of the audience might be aroused (e.g. Adorno, 1967; Benjamin, 1973).

3 For an English language overview of the historian's debate on the Holocaust, see Holub, 1991, Chapter 7.

4 For his reflections on German unification and the Gulf War. See Habermas, 1994.

5 This instrumentalism is closely related by CT to the exchange principle which assumes that everything is translatable into money, an abstract equivalent of everything else. The measurement and quantification of all phenomena, associated with the demands of capitalism for exchange, forces qualitatively different, non-identical phenomena, into the mould of quantitative identity. Through the use of standardized, quantifiable instruments, the distinctive orientations and values of individuals are processed and measured according to an apparently objective set of categories or truths.

6 Marcuse's analysis parallels 'the end of ideology' thesis developed by Daniel Bell (1974), who heralds the era of the 'post-industrial society' in which class antagonisms and systematic crises are extinguished. However, whereas post-industrial theorists, like Bell, simply report and effectively endorse this trend, CT is consistently hostile to this development. The 'problem', from the point of view of CT, is that modern, affluent societies are too successful in 'delivering the goods', at least for the majority of their members. Their very success impedes the development of a critical distance from ruling ideologies of consumerism. If not wholly inconceivable, protest or rejection of dominant values becomes, for most people, irrational.

7 In the popular imagination, this is precisely what science is supposed to do, which explains why science, or the popular idea of it, is so readily associated with successive generations of innovative methods of organization and management that (claim to be) more productive.

8 This aspect of Habermas' work is particularly well discussed and critically examined in White, 1988. See especially Chapters 5 and 6.

9 It might be tempting to suggest that Habermas has an excessively romanticized view of such groups, and fails to fully recognize the constraints upon communication that arise from their own identity-securing concerns in which social pressures to comply with various forms of 'political correctness' and to respect tabooed topics impedes open debate. While this is always a danger, a reading of his highly sceptical writings on the student protest movement in the late 1960s offers considerable reassurance (Habermas, 1971, Chapter 2).

10 This task has been facilitated by Habermas' movement away from a philosophy of consciousness towards a philosophy of language (see below). Instead of locating the impulse for emancipation in the alienation of an essential – whether asexual, male or female – human *nature*, the philosophy of language focuses upon how *interactions*, including those that are constitutive of gender relations, are routinely forged within asymmetrical relations of power.

# PART II

# MANAGEMENT SPECIALISMS IN A CRITICAL PERSPECTIVE

## 4

## Critical Conceptualizations of Management

In this and the following two chapters we draw upon the ideas developed in Part I to articulate a perspective on management and its specialisms. We introduce this chapter with a discussion of the extensive range of metaphors that have been deployed to represent, or imagine, the world of management and organization. This leads us to present and discuss a number of alternative metaphors of management that are inspired by our reading of Critical Theory (CT): management as distorted communication; management as mystification; management as cultural doping; and management as colonizing power. In each case, we explore the general relevance of these metaphors for making sense of management before indicating their pertinence to the understanding of particular management specialisms. In Chapters 5 and 6, we focus more directly upon several specialisms of management, paying special attention to CT-influenced understandings of their nature and development.

### On Metaphors and Metaphorical Understanding

Everyday and political language, as well as social science, is redolent with metaphors and metaphorical expressions. For example, when Churchill talked about an iron curtain being drawn between West and East Europe after the Second World War, he was, of course, using a politically-charged metaphor. Similarly, in Chapter 1, we noted how the term *maneggiare* – meaning to handle and train horses – was first used to make sense of the emergent phenomenon of management. Metaphors are widely employed, in more or less self-conscious ways, to represent and/or (re)construct reality: 'the essence of metaphor is understanding and experiencing one thing in terms of another' (Lakoff and Johnson, 1980: 5). However, when the use of a metaphor becomes taken for granted (e.g. when reference is routinely made to organizational structure), language then appears to reflect reality rather than to offer intrinsically imperfect and playful accounts of what it represents as reality. Moreover, when a metaphor is deemed to mirror reality, the credibility of alternatives is effectively displaced and diminished.

### Language and the Mobilization of Metaphors

As the world is interpreted through the medium of language(s), our sense of reality is framed and structured in historically and culturally distinctive ways (see Chapter 2). This framing invariably involves the mobilization of metaphors. Indeed, 'framing' and 'mobilization' are themselves metaphors that serve to articulate our understanding of the metaphorical quality of much communication. By addressing metaphors as a topic *of* analysis (instead of using them as an unacknowledged resource *for* analysis), it is possible to highlight how meaning is managed – for example, by portraying organizations as 'communities' or 'battlegrounds'. Directing attention to the presence and influence of metaphors in everyday communication can, in principle, *open up* an appreciation and discussion of how different metaphors shape, enhance or shift our awareness and actions in much the same way as the appreciation of paradigms can open up the terrain of research (see Chapter 2).

In the field of management and organization studies, a number of metaphors have been widely, but unself-consciously, applied – such as those that represent organizations as 'machines', 'organisms' and 'cultures' (for a discussion of these and other metaphors, see Morgan, 1986). These three metaphors, in particular, have been promoted and reinforced by practitioners and consultants and legitimized by academics (e.g. Burns and Stalker, 1961). For reasons discussed in Chapter 1, those who deploy such metaphors have been attracted to the idea that the human world should mirror, if not mimic, the seemingly consensual, smooth-running operations of nature or engineering over which they, as the expert analysts or managers of these '*systems*', are qualified to preside.

Each management specialism (and its subsystems) has been drawn to the language of systems thinking as a rhetoric for justifying the key importance and (systemic) contribution of its procedures and requirements. So, for example, the authors of the text *Human Resource Management* formulate the Training and Development element of the Personnel/Human Resource specialism using the following terms:

> Training and development (T&D) is a *subsystem* of the HR management system. The primary objective of the T&D *subsystem* is to change the behaviour of people in the company so that performance of the company as a whole is improved. . . . *The inputs processed are the employees of the company.* . . . You

are interested in system effectiveness, that is, the degree to which the T&D system is achieving *system* objectives. You are also interested in the relationship between the benefits and the cost of the system. (Klatt et al., 1985: 337, 370–71, emphases added)

In using mechanical and organic metaphors to study organizations, there is a danger and likelihood of using managerial language and ideas as a resource for study when, arguably, they should be its topic (see Bittner, 1965). Individual metaphors might be judged as being more or less sophisticated or more or less novel. But crucially, they are rooted in particular ideas and assumptions about the world; and their popularity we submit, is associated with their role in legitimizing and sustaining particular (power-invested) world-views. Moreover, their use influences not only the way *we understand the world* but also *how we act to reproduce or transform what we do as well as how we think*. In the absence of critical reflection upon the development and (popular) use of metaphors, researchers, students and practitioners are, by default, conditioned in their thoughts and action by a few dominant metaphors and associated value-orientations for conceptualizing management and organizations.

## Pitfalls of Metaphorical Understanding

During the past fifteen years or so, a number of lively debates have drawn attention to the use of metaphors to represent and understand social and organizational phenomena (e.g. Brown, 1976; Morgan, 1980; Alvesson, 1993c). A major problem associated with the use of the metaphor concept concerns its tendency to focus upon the features of various metaphors – machine, organism, culture, etc. – without giving much attention to the way that they are selectively adopted and mobilized in the politics of management theory and practice. Many metaphors are possible, though comparatively few are widely favoured. When a particular metaphor is deemed to 'capture' some aspect of reality, the attribution of objectivity to a metaphor indicates more about the value-orientation and social position of the person or group that makes this attribution than it demonstrates any correspondence between the metaphor and what it aspires to capture. Linkages between the use of metaphors and bigger issues – concerned with power, knowledge and responsibility in modern societies – are weakly made, if not actually ignored. This danger is particularly acute when the metaphor concept is packaged in a neat, easy-to-assimilate manner.

Morgan's (1986) influential bestseller, *Images of Organizations*, is a mixed blessing in this regard. Positively, it provides an accessible overview of many different, metaphorical, orientations – including some which normally escape attention. Unfortunately, it also invites, and tacitly facilitates, an uncritical 'off-the-shelf' attitude: readers are encouraged to sample and combine competing frames of reference to achieve a more 'total' understanding of organizational phenomena. To mix our metaphors, Morgan's supermarket approach treats metaphors as elements of a common jigsaw. The suggestion is that the more metaphors one knows about, or masters, the more informed or empowered one becomes. Instead of striving to appreciate the political and historical significance of the use and popularity of particular metaphors (Alvesson, 1993a; Jackson and Willmott, 1986; Tinker, 1986), a supermarket attitude to analysis suggests that a fuller, more comprehensive understanding can be achieved simply by piling the intellectual trolley with additional perspectives (see Reed, 1990).

This supermarket attitude takes no account of how metaphors often stand in a conflicting, or at least inconsistent, relationship to each other (Heydebrand, 1980). For example, the 'root metaphor' view of culture as a reflexively accomplished process (Smircich, 1983b) is not readily reconciled with the image of bureaucracies as machines that operate independently of the will of individual members of staff. What may appear to be a 'reconciliation' is often, on closer examination, a process of colonization (see Chapter 3). Machine-like ideas continue to dominate discourses and practices on corporate culture where values and meanings are treated as building blocks in organizational design, to be engineered and controlled by corporate leaders. Thus, Peters and Waterman (1982: 11) have claimed, with regard to the development of their 7-S Framework, that what it 'has really done is to remind the world of professional managers that "soft is hard". It has enabled us to say, in effect, "All that stuff you have been dismissing for so long as the intractable, irrational, intuitive, informal organization *can* be managed".' In short, the 'soft' elements of the 7-S framework are identified as variables that the insights of post-classical organization theory render accessible to prediction and control (see Chapter 2).

This is not to deny that the use of conventional metaphors can serve valuable purposes. Understanding a company responsible for the provision of public transport as a machine, for example, may highlight and facilitate the careful integration of a very large number of tightly coupled sets of operations that are necessitated in order to carry passengers and their luggage safely and predictably around the world. As passengers, we probably want to be assured that the wheels are securely attached, and that the engine has been properly maintained. But, as staff and as passengers, we probably also prefer not to be treated as mere numbers or commodities that are processed by the system in ways that are contrived to be 'customer-friendly' only insofar as such friendliness is deemed to be consistent with profitability and/or growth. Although perhaps an extreme example, the following endorsement of Business Process Reengineering (BPR) – *the* management of change technique for the 1990s – captures well the mechanistic spirit of this manipulative thinking: 'Reengineering is, essentially, saying: this mighty machine (i.e. modern organization) – rebuild it, transform it into something better. And people too, complex instruments, transform them, rewire their emotional and psychological workings, free up new, better connections' (Leigh, 1994: 51).

The problem, from the perspective of Critical Theory, is that metaphors informed by functionalist thinking (see Chapter 2) have been dominant to the point of producing, refining and legitimizing *machine-like relationships* both within and between organizations.

## The Dominance of Functionalist Metaphors

Engineering and organic metaphors are strongly associated with the portrayal of organizations as robust, stable, unitary, apolitical and fundamentally conflict-free phenomena. Such functionalist metaphors effectively suppress awareness and appreciation of the role of organizations as media of social power and of the involvement, albeit alienated, of all organizational members in their maintenance and transformation. As Silverman has observed, 'By moving away from the actors' (i.e. organizational members') definition of the situation and of the choices available to them, we run the risk of reifying the systems that we construct' (1970: 50). Or, as Habermas has elaborated this argument:

> With systems theory, the phenomena . . . are described in a manner independent of the language and self-understanding of the actors. The objectivating change in stance triggers off an alienating effect, repeated with each individual systems-theoretic description of a phenomenon previously grasped from the participant's perspective. (1991: 254)

A widespread preference for (functionalist) metaphors that reify the operation of systems and privilege their 'survival' may not be accidental.[1] As noted earlier, whether by design or by default, metaphors that assume consensus displace and discredit the use of more challenging alternatives. From a Critical Theory perspective, other metaphors – like *totalitarianism*, *mystification* and *colonization* are more penetrating and practically relevant in their analysis of modern organizations than ideas about 'reengineered culture' or the 'turbo-charged machine'. The theory and practice of management is currently dominated by a narrow range of metaphors that deny or disregard its darker features. In marketing, for example, the dominant conceptualization is that of marketing as a 'need satisfier', as if marketing plays no role in the constitution of the needs that it professes to satisfy. To appreciate this unacknowledged role, it is relevant to mobilize other metaphors, such as marketing as *manipulation*. Conceptualizing organizations as instruments of domination (Hochschild, 1983) or as sites for ecological destruction (Shrivastava, 1993) dispels the complacency of conventional wisdom, as presumed links between the 'survival' of these corporations and their contribution to human value are challenged.

To recap, highlighting the existence of diverse metaphors for making sense of management and organization can potentially be instructive. At the very least, it can be helpful for unsettling the apparent naturalness and taken-for-granted domination of the most frequently used metaphors. However, to appreciate the significance and limitations of any metaphor, it is necessary to recognize its underlying value-orientations and associated commitments (see Chapter 2). In the absence of critical reflection upon the connections between power structures and the development and use of particular metaphors, the presentation of a supermarket of metaphors (e.g. Morgan, 1986) invites the uncritical selection of familiar 'brands' that broadly confirm, rather than challenge, the consumer's preconceptions and prejudices. The alternative is to develop metaphors that chime with experience but, in doing so, offer a fresh and more challenging interpretation of the realities of management and organization.

## Critical Theoretic Conceptualizations of Management

Having noted the pervasive presence of metaphors and identified some problems in their use, we now present some counterpoints to dominant metaphors of management. To this end, we identify a number of metaphors that are broadly informed by a CT perspective on social and organizational reality, as outlined in earlier chapters.

### Management as Distorted Communication – Communication and the Instrumentalization of Reason

As we argued in Part I, the theory and practice of management routinely privileges instrumental rationality in which communication is focused upon, and is largely restricted to, the refinement of means – including the 'strengthening' of corporate culture – such that this attentiveness to means threatens to become an end in itself. The displacement of debate about goals in favour of the perfection of means, we argued, occurs when ends are taken for granted and/or when ends are deemed to lie beyond rational debate. We also noted how the perfection of means is inevitably coloured, mediated and not infrequently displaced by other considerations, such as the sectional (e.g. career) values and priorities of managers. Nonetheless, *official* corporate language is frequently one of monolithic deference to seemingly apolitical, instrumental rationality. Companies, and to an increasing extent other organizations (hospitals, schools, etc.), are enjoined to function as carriers and supporters of a rhetoric of instrumental rationality that is most evident in corporate mission statements, press releases and annual reports.

To be clear, there is nothing intrinsically evil or inherently undesirable about instrumental rationality or the metaphors that it favours. On the contrary, as we suggested in Chapter 2, instrumental reason is fundamental to human well-being: it enables us to organize resources – both natural and human – in ways that can reduce needless divisiveness, suffering and waste. When applied with the unequivocal and uncoerced consent of organizational members, instrumental reason can be productive of human welfare. But, in the absence of practical reason – that is, political-ethically informed judgement – instrumental reason pays little attention to its unintended effects, effects that include 'externalised costs', such as the destruction of human communities and the natural environment (Shrivastava, 1993). When unchecked by critical reason, instrumental rationality is liable to produce a means–ends dystopia where, over time, even the relevance and value of ends becomes assessed in terms of what is achievable with the available means. Beliefs and practices that are deemed not to comply with this logic, nor to make a functional contribution to the efficiency and/or effectiveness of means, are then regarded as *passé*.

In contemporary society, the dominance of an ideology of instrumental rationality – which is routinely assumed to be superior or more rational when compared to other values, goals and discourses (e.g. democratic, ecological, etc.) – places a major constraint upon the development of communicative, as contrasted with instrumental, rationality. Indeed, Deetz and Mumby (1990) have suggested that, 'the legitimation of managerial rationality through the dominance of the technical interest necessarily produces systematically distorted communication insofar as all forms of discourse are made sense of (i.e. judged as valid) via the interpretative template of technical-rational knowledge'. In Chapter 3, we noted how Habermas (1984, 1987b) has recast and elaborated the critique of instrumental rationality within his communication theory of society. According to this theory, there are four conditions of communicative action: truthfulness, legitimacy, sincerity and clarity. If, for example, the truth and/or sincerity of communication is radically and continuously doubted, then it is impossible for communication to proceed. In this sense, the four conditions are a necessary, though generally taken-for-granted condition of any form of communication. Without an anticipation of, and respect for, these conditions, communication would soon break down. Communication can thus be assessed and evaluated in terms of its approximation to, or distortion of, these criteria. The issue of whether communication in organizations approximates to dogma (closed communication) or dialogue (open communication) can also be addressed. The value of the distorted communication metaphor is that it directly highlights the restriction of free dialogue. As Forester has argued:

> When organizations or polities are structured so that their members have no protected recourse to checking the truth, legitimacy, sincerity, or clarity claims made on them by established structures of authority and production, we may find conditions of dogmatism rather than of social learning, tyranny rather than authority, manipulation rather than cooperation, and distraction rather than sensitivity. In this way critical theory points to the importance of understanding practically and normatively how access to, and participation in, discourses, both theoretical and practical, is systematically structured. (1983: 239–40)

This view emphasizes that organizations do not only produce goods and services. They are also, and more fundamentally, producers and reproducers of media of communication, in which employees are often induced to pay attention to a very limited range of organizational activities and outcomes (see Chapter 1). Indeed, modern corporations can be perceived as proto-totalitarian institutions insofar as they assess the value and relevance of all contributions predominantly in terms of the monolithic 'template of technical-rational knowledge' (Deetz and Mumby, 1990). Instead of actively

enabling communicative interaction, thereby encouraging more differentiated world-views and dissolving traditional hierarchical forms of
authority, the reproduction of the modern corporation tends to require
and preserve communications that are systematically distorted (Deetz,
1992a and b).

*The Case of Business Process Reengineering*   Common to all recent major
ideologies and techniques for improving corporate performance (e.g.
Excellence, TQM, BPR) has been the contradictory championing of
empowered employees and strong leadership. This circle is squared by the
claim that the discipline of firm leadership is productive of greater autonomy. Or, as Peters and Waterman (1982: 322) articulate this argument, 'a
set of shared values and rules about discipline, details and execution can
provide the framework in which practical autonomy takes place routinely'.
In other words, the individual employee is free to do what he or she wishes
as long as this is what the boss wants the employee to wish (Willmott,
1993a).

Consider the latest of recent managerial techniques: Business Process
Reengineering (BPR). Business Process Reengineering is distinguished by its
identification and promotion of new information and communication
technologies as a means of radically transforming work. For example, reengineered work may enable customers to deal with a single representative/
VDU operator who responds to their requirements simply by activating the
relevant databases and networks and then monitoring progress. Instead of
designing organizations as a production line with production and service
work being completed by a series of employees undertaking a sequence of
tasks, BPR aspires to turbo-charge the productivity of labour by moving to
parallel processing. In principle, all activities are then dramatically speeded
up and unproductive duplication is eliminated (Willmott, 1994b; Grint,
1994).

Despite the lip service paid to concepts like 'empowerment' and 'teamwork', there can be little doubt that the intent of BPR is to *impose* and
sustain a *totalizing* solution. Hammer and Champy (1993), the leading
advocates of BPR contend that:

> It is axiomatic that reengineering never, ever happens from the bottom up. . . .
> The first reason that the push for reengineering must come from the top of an
> organization is that people near the front lines lack the broad perspective that
> reengineering demands. . . . Second, any business process inevitably crosses
> organizational boundaries . . . some of the affected middle managers will
> correctly fear that dramatic changes to existing processes might diminish their
> own power, influence and authority. . . . *If radical change threatens to bubble up
> from below, they may resist it and throttle it. Only strong leadership from above
> will induce these people to accept the transformations that reengineering brings.*
> (ibid.: 207–8, emphasis added)

Most recent recipes for improved corporate performance, such as Excellence and TQM, have been couched in the velvet language of humanism

and employee involvement that favours incremental change and continuous, sustained improvement. In contrast, BPR is couched in engineering language and charges senior management with the task of imposing the BPR recipe for revolutionary change upon employees, who are to be 'induced' into accepting its requirements. Senior managers may carry those wounded by reengineering for a little while but they must '"shoot the dissenters!"' (Hammer in Kalgaard, 1993: 71). Hammer and Champy brazenly identify the need for 'Czars' (not champions) who will ruthlessly push through reengineering programmes without regard for the personal, social or even the economic costs involved in such a coercive approach to organizational change (Grey and Mitev, 1995a).

From a CT perspective, such developments are interpreted as nascent technocratic totalitarianism. Whatever is deemed by experts to be effective in terms of gaining a competitive advantage or maximizing output, however insidious or demeaning, is regarded as legitimate because, it is argued, leaders committed to change 'have no choice in how they deal with those attempting to impede their efforts' (Hammer, 1994: 47). When *instrumental* rationality is elevated to *rationality per se*, it becomes an *ideology*, as the value-based ends and the value-laden means for attaining these ends are shielded from reflection and critical evaluation.

*Technocratic Totalitarianism in Human Resource Management* Human Resource Management (HRM) elaborates a battery of 'objective' techniques for managing the selection, motivation and promotion of employees (Hollway, 1984; Steffy and Grimes, 1992; Townley, 1993) which, in principle, are yoked to the strategic objectives of the organization (Legge, 1989, 1995). HRM specialists do not go to the root of the problem by advocating the removal of constraints that impede employees discovering for themselves what is meaningful for them. Instead, they contrive to design and reward work in ways that are intended to increase employee motivation, flexibility and productivity. Within HRM discourse, employees are understood to be 'motivated' so long as they are productive – regardless of whether their work is experienced as personally meaningful. In this sense, as Sievers (1986) has argued, the idea of motivation is a 'surrogate for meaning' in a world where experts dominate decisions about how organizations and jobs should be designed, and work frequently lacks any deeply valued meaning.

In HRM, the idea of making work more motivating serves to legitimize piecemeal social engineering (e.g. Human Relations). As a surrogate for meaning, the literature on motivation allows non-meaningful work to be interpreted through a technocratic lens so that 'the human resource' becomes a manipulable object of management control (Rose, 1990). Through the systematic design of programmes of selection, induction and training, the province of management is being expanded by Human Resource specialists to include teaching employees how to think and feel about their work, as well as how to do it more productively. The aim of these HR programmes, often guided by consultants, is to place under systemic control the potentially disruptive and subversive extra-organizational values which employees bring with them into employment (see Chapter 1 and below). Likewise, marketing specialists are currently promoting the idea of 'internal marketing' and 'relational marketing' – developments that aspire to provide a technology for forging and sustaining social ties (see also Chapter 5); while accountants represent their specialism as 'the language of business' and themselves as its impartial 'score-keepers' or 'map-makers' (see also Chapter 6).

Money and power provide the media for designing and redesigning the norms that regulate interaction between employees and their internal and external customers (Wilkinson and Willmott, 1995a). As reason is instrumentalized, albeit in the name of empowerment and even love, important questions concerning ends, values and ethics are excluded from the corporate agenda (see Alvesson, 1987; Carter and Jackson, 1987; Reed and Anthony, 1992). Managers remain *personally* preoccupied with career goals and organizational politics. But management is *publicly* represented as a matter of impartial professionalism, not of politics. An ideology is developed in which management is viewed as responding expertly and dispassionately to 'objective' factors. Communications are routinely distorted as issues are defined and pursued through the application of expertise – competences, skills and techniques which are assumed to be dedicated to the realization of a common social good (see Chapter 1).

### Management as Mystification – the Selective Constructing and Confusing of Needs and Understandings

The mystification metaphor can be used to draw attention to the ways in which managers strive to construct a favourable image of themselves and/or their organization through the careful arrangement of symbols and ceremonies (Rosen, 1985; Alvesson, 1996). The mystification metaphor, it is worth stressing, does not necessarily imply that researchers or other analysts occupy a position that permits them privileged access to an 'objective' reality behind the mystique (though some may fall victim to this delusion). Rather, it can be used to draw attention to how management contrives to shape the way people – employees, consumers and citizens – make sense of the social world and participate in it. It understands management as an institution whose agents mould and influence people's beliefs, meanings, values and self-understandings.

*Mystifying Liberation and Creativity*  Currently fashionable ideas promise to 'liberate' managers and employees from the drudgery of traditional patterns of work (e.g. Peters, 1992). But, in effect, these ideas impose a new set of disciplines upon employees who are encouraged to equate processes of liberation and creativity with unequivocal dedication to corporate values and objectives, as they induce employees to regard their fellow workers as customers (Oakland, 1989). 'Soft' versions of Total Quality Management, in particular, incorporate Human Resource thinking as they proclaim that: 'Total quality management is part of a holistic approach to progress . . . there is a tremendous unlocking of energy in management and the workforce . . . *liberating people at work to become more truly themselves and more creative*' (Bank, 1992: 195 emphasis added). The basic problem with such claims is that they assume emancipation and creativity to be gifts that can be bestowed upon employees by managers whereas, arguably, they are necessarily the outcome of individual and collective struggles to overcome forms of dependency. In the absence of such struggles, it is others – e.g. managers – who decide how and when people are 'truly themselves' and what counts as being 'more creative' (Willmott, 1993a).

HRM, Keenoy and Anthony (1992: 243) have suggested, aspires to operate as a cultural filter that 'embraces the uncertainties of employee existence, imposes order and meaning on them and provides the employee with a predictable, secure and carefully projected and rewarded understanding of organizational life'. However, as they also observe, organizational life is not (yet) the only source of symbolic or cultural meaning. Not only are occupational and professional subcultures likely to be resistant to the demands of HRM, but employees bring to the workplace (moral) notions of fairness, justice and so forth that are not necessarily compatible with either the content of HRM policies or with the procedures used to implement them. Effective management, Keenoy and Anthony (ibid.: 249) contend, is dependent upon the maintenance of community bonds of a more substantial and more coherently moral nature than can be constructed by HRM consultants and practitioners. In other words, to translate this criticism of HRM into Habermasian language, the systems logic of impartial professionalism is likely to collide with 'lifeworld' understandings of equity and legitimacy.

*Mystifying the Hierarchy*   In contemporary management theory and practice, there is much talk about the flattening of hierarchies and the reduction – if not the deletion – of middle management. Consider, then, the following example (taken from Alvesson, 1995). In a Swedish computer consultancy company, top management expended considerable time, energy and financial resources in encouraging its staff to adopt the norms and values of the company. Employees were repeatedly told that the hierarchy was extremely flat, with only two grades – subsidiary managers and consultants – and no intermediate levels. In general, social relations within the firm were represented to staff as non-hierarchical, close, friendly and family-like.

One consultant in this company was asked to compare it with his former workplace. In doing so, he repeated many of the themes contained in the corporate ideology, notably the relative lack of hierarchy. At his previous place of employment, this consultant had had a group manager as his immediate superior, while at his present workplace there was a flat structure. 'My only boss is Alf (Subsidiary Manager)', he said. Later in the interview, he was asked about possibilities for exerting some influence in the allocation of assignments. It turned out that his last assignment had been given to him by Sten, without his being asked whether he was particularly interested in it. The researcher then asked if Sten, a consultant, had managerial responsibilities and received the answer: 'Yes, he works directly under Alf'. In practice, then, it seemed that Sten functioned as a middle manager with semi-formal status as second-in-command. As far as the interviewee was concerned – a graduate engineer with several years of working experience – there was no doubt that Sten was his superior.

This example suggests that this employee had not fully reflected upon the plausibility of the official representation of the organization as 'flat'; or, at the very least, that he was willing to disregard the anomaly by regurgitating, without qualification, the official view that Alf was his only boss. Certainly, the direct reference to Sten's managerial responsibilities seems to contradict directly his earlier description of the company. Yet he revealed no awareness of the discrepancy.[2] While any interpretation of such examples is (fortunately) contestable, we suggest that it illustrates how continuous exposure to a dominant set of ideas can produce an unreflexive regurgitation of their content and, indeed, can operate to dull sensitivity to experiences that could potentially disrupt and debunk their authority.[3]

*Mystifying the Customer*   Perhaps the most obvious area of management for the use of the mystification metaphor is marketing, and especially its role in selectively constructing how, as consumers, our 'needs' are identified and satisfied. Marketing represents itself as a technically-rational apparatus for closing the gap between producers and consumers by identifying, and satisfying, 'customer needs'. 'Marketing is all about mutually satisfying exchange relationships for which the catalyst is the producer's attempt to define and satisfy the customer's need better' (Baker, 1987: 8). And yet, arguably, the nature and extent of human need is something that is socially ascribed and negotiated rather than objectively given (Knights and Willmott, 1974/5; Willmott, 1995c). Marketing is thus implicated in the constitution and mystification of what human need is rather than simply reporting upon, and responding to, given needs.

Consider advertising images. Very often, these function as ambiguous symbols, capable of containing various sorts of meanings and stimulating various kinds of impulses and desires (Leiss, 1983; Sahlins, 1976). Commercials for cars or cigarettes are displayed against a picture of unspoiled wilderness, or a liqueur bottle is set in a farmhouse room full of hand-crafted furniture. The fluidity of the symbolism that surrounds these products acts to encourage individuals to associate the purchase of these goods with a satisfactory level of 'need satisfaction' – for status, identity confirmation, self-esteem, etc. Marketing in particular, but also management in general, is engaged in processes of myth-making as it exploits ambiguity and insecurity to procure and expand its influence.

Techniques of mass persuasion developed to shape and control processes of consumption are now being applied to the task of 'internal marketing' within organizations. Criticisms of consumer manipulation are therefore of relevance when addressing how, within the sphere of production, Total Quality Management programmes seek to induce employees to identify themselves as customers within a supply chain (Wilkinson and Willmott, 1995a). Such programmes are at the centre of a contemporary offensive by corporations to increase productivity, quality and flexibility by securing control of the 'soul' of each employee (Rose, 1990; see below) – for example, by directly intervening in the design of work cultures through which a sense of work identity is acquired. Their intent is that employees should derive a sense of self-esteem from the service given to the next person in the chain rather than from the intrinsic meaning or pleasure associated with the work they do. Here, customer satisfaction is the preferred surrogate for meaning. In such programmes, metaphors such as 'team' and 'customer' are mobilized in ways that mask and mystify, more or less intentionally, their embeddedness in and contribution towards relations of domination and control (Kerfoot and Knights, 1994).

In sum, the metaphor of mystification highlights the ongoing processes of influencing how people make sense of ambiguous phenomena (arrangements, changes, acts, product qualities, etc.), showing how critical evaluations are denied, normalized or counteracted, and how 'positive' perceptions and attitudes are developed. To explore further this aspect of mystification, it is appropriate to use the metaphor of cultural doping, as this suggests a process that penetrates deeply into the formation of self-identity. Doping is a matter of ensuring that people have the 'right' orientations.

## *Management as Cultural Doping – the Corporation as a Socialization Agency*

The cultural doping metaphor represents management as a socialization agency. Socialization is the process through which humans acquire, and identify with, the values, customs and aspirations of the social groups in which they live and grow up. Socialization can also be defined as cultural learning. Cultural doping is firmly on the agendas of Human Resource Management and (Total) Quality Management initiatives, for example, and is increasingly identified as the key to the success of such initiatives (Wilkinson, 1993). In induction and development programmes, employees are told – more or less explicitly – how they must perceive and relate to the established organizational reality, and how they should participate in organizational rites where the 'correct' values, virtues and ideals are communicated. Often the influence is exercised on a sub-conscious level, making it difficult for employees to recognize it and subject it to critical scrutiny (for critical discussions, see Kunda, 1992 and Willmott, 1993a).

The dominant, technicist orientation inculcated into management education is an example of such doping (see also Chapter 1). Much education and training of managers is as much and more about acquiring the 'right' (i.e. self-assured and 'positive') orientations towards managerial work. Personnel specialists, for example, are increasingly encouraged to adopt the jargon and orientation of Human Resource Management – a label that suggests and legitimizes an equivalence of human beings with other factors of production, as it further erodes the traditional welfare-oriented role of the personnel specialist (Watson, 1977; Keenoy and Anthony, 1992). In the marketing field, the cultural doping metaphor highlights how people are brought up to be, above everything, 'sovereign' consumers, to such an extent that a great deal of a person's subjectivity – values, feelings and thinking – is associated with, and evaluated in terms of, the level and content of consumption.

To own and consume becomes a core element in affluent societies. With the segmentation of markets, and the increased emphasis upon the acquisition of lifestyles, marketing has tended to increase its appeal and to institutionalize its influence, especially when it appears to pay for public goods – through the sponsorship of sport and through its contribution to entertainment or good causes, such as education and ecology. In the commercialized process of educating people about how to make sense of life, corporations and marketers have strengthened their position while parents and cultural traditions have lost ground (Lasch, 1979).

The effect of the expansion of marketing and consumption has been illustrated by historical studies of the changes in 'people production' during the last century (see especially Rose, 1990). Fromm (1941) and Riesman (1950) identified the market-oriented, 'other-directed' person as an increasingly common character type in the USA (see also Chapter 3). The attributes of such a person include flexibility, dependence on other people's opinions and a willingness to adapt to fashions and social changes. More recently, Lasch (1979; 1984) has characterized the personality type of Western capitalist societies, pre-eminently the USA, as narcissistic – being distinguished by a combination of an unstable level of self-esteem and recurrent self-doubt – a volatile mix that is concealed from self as much as from others beneath an outward appearance of gregariousness, self-confidence and conviction (see also Goffman, 1959). The narcissist believes (or desperately wants to believe) in the appearance that he or she presents to others. However, the schism between self-confidence and self-doubt, which lies at the centre of narcissism, is keenly felt as an experience of alternation between (publicly expressed) feelings of satisfaction and grandiosity, on the one hand, and (privately repressed) feelings of emptiness and vulnerability, on the other. Advertising and images of consumption are understood to normalize narcissism as they stimulate grandiose fantasies which simultaneously arouse and compensate for feelings of unhappiness and inadequacy. The outcome, Lasch argues, is resentment and self-contempt:

> *Modern advertising seeks to promote not so much self-indulgence as self-doubt. It seeks to create needs, not to fulfil them*; to generate new anxieties instead of allaying old ones. By surrounding the consumer with images of the good life, and

by associating them with the glamour of celebrity and success, mass culture encourages the ordinary man to cultivate extraordinary tastes, to identify himself with the privileged minority against the rest, and to join them, in his fantasies, in a life of exquisite comfort and sensual refinement. Yet the propaganda of commodities simultaneously makes him acutely unhappy with his lot. By fostering grandiose aspirations, it also fosters self-denigration and self-contempt. (1979: 180–1, emphasis added)

The metaphor of marketing-as-cultural-doping (socialization) draws attention to how, when marketers influence the demand for products, they are affecting not only tastes, wants, understandings and needs; they are also involved in producing and governing people, as their sense of personal identity becomes more closely associated with, and dependent upon, *what they own and consume*. Current marketing talk about tailoring products and services to the profile or specifications of individual customers proclaims that niche marketing and the customization of goods will enable modern consumers to express and secure their individual identities without discrediting the framework of mass consumption (e.g. McKenna, 1991; Pine, 1993). However, as Lasch (1979) emphasizes, programmes and techniques that seek to exploit or colonize the lifeworld are inherently problematical and unstable. Instead of developing a less precarious basis for processes of self-formation and reproduction, they can compound the precarious and fluid nature of (modern) identities and stimulate the development of resistance (e.g. social movements and protest groups) that challenge their legitimacy.

*Management as Colonizing Power – the Erosion of the Lifeworld*

Colonization describes the way that one set of practices and understandings, which are strongly associated with the instrumental reason that is dominant in the organization and management of complex systems, comes to dominate and exclude other practices and discourses that are present within the everyday cultural media of 'the lifeworld' where human beings develop their basic sense of being purposive, wilful subjects with distinctive social identities (as discussed in Chapter 3). Instead of understanding social phenomena from the cultural perspective of the participants, instrumental reasoning represents these phenomena as impersonal, interchangeable elements of the system. 'The system' refers to the presence and operation of more abstract and formal structures of relations, governed in the modern era by money and (formally based) power. Within the rationality of the system, individuals are treated as numbers or categories (e.g. grades of employees determined by qualifications or types of clients by market segment) and, more generally, are viewed as objects or instruments whose value lies in reproducing 'the system'. Most work organizations, Habermas (1987b: 309) contends, 'not only disconnect themselves from cultural commitments and from attitudes and orientations specific to given personalities; they also make themselves independent from lifeworld contexts by neutralizing the normative background of informal, customary, morally regulated contexts of action'. 'The system', Habermas argues, poses a potential challenge to the sense of self-identity and value that develops within the lifeworld. This is a tendency to which each of the three metaphors discussed in the previous sections of this chapter draw attention in different ways. The colonization metaphor can be seen to pull together their insights into a broader framework for interpreting contemporary developments.

When pointing to the colonization of the lifeworld by systems thinking and values, Habermas is concerned that, in advanced capitalist societies, the lifeworld is too often regarded as an irrational impediment to the perfection of systems' properties, or is viewed purely as a resource for breathing new life into tired bureaucratic structures (Willmott, 1992). Such a devaluation of lifeworld properties is not so much viewed as 'bad' as *perverse*. It is perverse because the instrumental rationality of the system depends upon the communicative rationality of the lifeworld, even though it appears to function independently of the understandings and competences that are developed within the lifeworld. At the very least, 'systems' rely upon human beings who are capable of communicating effectively; and who are not manipulated and demoralized to the point of being incapable of cooperation and productivity. It is when the connection between 'system' and 'lifeworld' is denied or distorted that the normative and ethical sensibilities developed within the lifeworld are weakened and eroded. Current talk of 'business ethics' and the strengthening of corporate culture to facilitate empowerment, trust and teamwork can be seen as a – largely synthetic – 'system' response to its own corrosive effects upon lifeworld values and practices.

Perhaps the most obvious case of colonization occurs in the sphere of consumption where individuals are increasingly encouraged to identify with 'system' images and packages of 'the good life'. Obliged to consume in order to exist, the consumer is exhorted by assorted advertisers and experts to realize how his or her lifeworld should be ordered, including leisure and even sexual identity. The space for face-to-face formation and control of the lifeworld, spared from 'system' pressures, is progressively reduced. Processes of defining the meaning and identity of the self are colonized by techniques developed by 'expert' promoters and packagers of goods and services, including education and training programmes that encourage recruits to substitute 'systems' values (or, at least, learn how to manage the appearance of doing so) for those of the lifeworld (see Chapters 1 and 8). Engineered, top-down meanings are intended to replace the bottom-up meanings which employees and consumers bring from the lifeworld.

Each of the management specialisms currently competes to demonstrate their relevance and effectiveness to processes of colonization. In the UK and USA, at least, accounting has historically established itself as *the* specialism of management control by providing impersonal, quantitative measures of individual and organizational performance, and it is now busily promoting its relevance for bringing 'value-for-money' to public sector organizations, such as hospitals and schools (Ezzamel and Willmott, 1993). Similarly, Information Systems (IS) has been promoted as something that must be introduced with the utmost urgency into all spheres of production and consumption so that computers are now poised to mediate and control many aspects of our day-to-day transactions and communications.[4] Databases organized and managed using computers are often deemed to be 'better' or 'more authoritative' as well as quicker, just as television news is widely deemed to be more neutral as well as immediate than the equivalent newspaper coverage. However, the use of new technology is not unremittingly colonizing. Satellite communications (e.g. faxes) and especially the Internet are as yet largely unregulated (and, indeed, are very difficult to regulate or censor effectively), and are therefore actual and potential carriers of all kinds of subversive material and person-to-person communications.

The complete subjugation of employees and consumers to 'system objectives' may be an unstated, though perverse, aspiration of managerial theory and practice. But it is doubtful whether this (totalitarian) vision can ever be realized. This view is clearly illustrated by the following quotation from an employee in one of the biggest UK supermarket chains. Having expanded by taking business from individual shops and small chains, an oligopoly currently exists in this sector. An appealing alternative to price-based competition – which, of course, is the least attractive option for the chains that have established the biggest margins and/or the highest operating costs – is differentiation through improvements to customer service. In the following quotation, an employee who has been trained to smile at customers – posters at all entrances to the shopfloor at her workplace were emblazoned with the injunction 'smile, you're on stage' – commented, 'the company has to be realistic . . . it's alright for someone to tell you to smile but you can't smile at someone who's calling you a stupid bitch' (Ogbonna and Wilkinson, 1990: 12). The company's expectation that its employees will be civil towards customers is, of course, consistent with established values of the lifeworld where impersonal, off-hand behaviour is expected to be the exception rather than the norm.[5] Lifeworld values (e.g. of quality and care) are selectively invoked to introduce and legitimize programmes of 'customer care', 'total quality' and the like, in an effort to project the idea that the customer is valued *as a person*, and is not being 'cared for' simply as a means of retaining market share and increasing profitability. However, while the notion of being civil to employees is broadly consistent with established lifeworld values, the tactic meets its limits when employees are required to sustain the smile even when customers are deemed, according to lifeworld values, to be unreasonable or even personally offensive (see also Van Maanen, 1991). A polite, diplomatic attitude towards rudeness and hostility *at all times* may be consistent with retaining custom. But it also violates lifeworld values. More generally, as Habermas has suggested, the exploitation, abuse and colonization of lifeworld values is productive of tension and resistance:

> The new conflicts arise along the seams between system and lifeworld . . . the interchange between the private and public spheres, on the one hand, and the economic and administrative action systems, on the other . . . it is institutionalized in the roles of employees and consumers, citizens and clients of the state. It is just these roles that are the target of protest. Alternative practice is directed at the profit-dependent mobilization of labor power. . . . It also takes aim at the monetarization of services, relationships, and time. (1987b: 395)

Compliance with demands by employers to be polite and diplomatic, even under the severest provocation, are likely to be grudging as well as insincere ('I smile because I'm told to') (see Hochschild, 1983). It is compliance that may wear very thin and turn to resentment when, for example, the injunction to be a smiling shop worker is placed in the contradictory context of being understaffed, overworked and undervalued by customers and employers alike. Resistance arises from the values of the lifeworld that can be antithetical to what are sensed to be obtrusive and manipulative demands. Colonization is also impeded because it depends, paradoxically, upon respecting and preserving central elements of the lifeworld. If processes of self-formation and social integration are undermined, morale is sapped, with the associated risk of crises of motivation and legitimation (Habermas, 1973; 1987b). Each new philosophy of management – from Scientific Management to Total Quality Management – can be seen to address aspects of the contradiction as managers strive to extend their sphere of governance from bodies (the design of jobs) to souls (the socialization of employees). The fact that demand for new techniques of management control remains buoyant suggests that the colonization of the lifeworld by experts who manage 'the system' is far from assured or complete.

**Conclusion**

The four metaphors (or metaphor-like conceptualizations) – management as distorted communication, management as mystification, management as cultural doping and management as colonization – discussed in this chapter illustrate how organizations and management can be conceptualized in ways broadly inspired by Critical Theory. We certainly do not claim that the metaphors explored here perfectly reflect or fully illuminate what organizations and management are about. Metaphors simply provide alternative ways of making sense of social reality. They do not mirror it; nor do they even capture particular aspects of reality that can then be aggregated to provide a total picture. Our counter-metaphors simply give attention to issues that are often unacknowledged or poorly appreciated by mainstream representations of management. We have also stressed that, while they are seductive, forms of mystification and cultural doping can offer only temporary and partial solutions to the problems and anxieties of self-formation. As Giddens has remarked, when challenging a tendency to exaggerate the extent to which people are passive, helpless victims of the power of media images that colonize their consciousness, 'In assessing the prevalence of narcissism in late modernity, we have to be careful to separate the world of commodified images . . . from the actual responses of individuals . . . powerful though commodifying influences no doubt are, they are scarcely received in an uncritical way by the populations they affect' (1991: 178–9).

Each of our metaphors offers an alternative to mainstream images of management and provides a springboard for further theoretical and empirical work. By challenging the authority of conventional wisdom, the metaphors may perhaps inspire a more critical understanding of modern work organizations, and thereby prompt and guide their emancipatory transformation. It is relevant to recall how, historically, imperialistic colonizers sooner or later have encountered local resistance to their oppressive ambitions. It is to be hoped that a comparable process of opposition and revolt will develop within modern societies, and that it will draw support from diverse social movements and protest groups whose members are also antipathetic to the erosion and distortion of communicative rationality by an overbearing systems mentality. This is a common thread that, potentially, could bring together alliances of oppositional groups around a political agenda for radical change.

## Notes

1 The very idea of *survival* is strongly associated with natural selection theory. Like many words that appear to be neutral and innocent, the concept of survival is not. For it evokes ideas about the natural world, where adaptation has nothing to do with sectional interests and is unmediated by *socially constructed* (and transformable) divisions of class, gender and ethnicity. Likewise, reference to 'organization' and even 'organization studies', rather than to (the study of) diverse organizing discourses and practices, tends to marginalize consideration of issues of action, conflict and oppression (Willmott, 1996b).

2 It is also possible that Sten was aware of the discrepancy but was only partially successful in concealing this awareness. However, if this interpretation is favoured, then there is the difficulty of reconciling a tendency or pressure to hide this awareness with the espoused corporate ideology of open communications, even with external researchers.

3 An example of dulled sensitivity that is closer to home for British academics concerns the comparatively recent rating of the research and teaching performance of all University departments. For research, all departments are rated on a scale of 1–5; and for teaching they are assessed as unsatisfactory, satisfactory or excellent. Though initially viewed with scepticism and hostility, these rating exercises have become progressively institutionalized, with the tendency for academics to evaluate departments in terms of these reified categories rather than in terms of their localized knowledge of their distinctive strengths, quirks and weaknesses. See Willmott (1995a) and Prichard and Willmott (1997) for a fuller discussion of these developments.

4 For example, it has been found that customers purchasing travel and insurance products are much more likely to be persuaded of the reliability and genuineness of 'deals' if they are flashed up on a computer screen rather than presented in glossy brochures.

5 As was demonstrated by Garfinkel's (1967) notorious breaching experiments, in which students living at home were instructed to take on the role of lodgers.

# 5

# Critically Assessing Management Specialisms I: Organization Theory, Marketing and Strategic Management

In this and the following chapter, we draw upon our earlier discussions of critical thinking, and of Critical Theory (CT) in particular, to consider a number of management specialisms. Limitations of space prohibit consideration of all the subspecialisms of management. Our review is necessarily selective in both its focus and its coverage.[1] We attend first to organization theory, before turning to the specialisms of marketing and strategic management. These three specialisms are grouped together as they share a more explicit concern with the 'softer', human side of management. They are also generally less preoccupied with quantification and with avowedly objective forms of measurement. In the next chapter, we examine the fields of accounting, information systems and operational research where quantification is more in evidence.

Of course, it is difficult to make a sharp distinction between the respective domains and orientations of the management specialisms. Service management, for example, incorporates elements of marketing and organization theory. Within the more quantitative disciplines (e.g. accounting and operational research) there has recently been some 'softening' of approach as behaviourial (organizational) elements are incorporated into their field. And, indeed, contemporary trends towards teamworking and networking are intended to encourage and facilitate closer cooperation between specialists and foster the development of 'hybrid' managers. In general, behaviourial aspects of work, generally drawn from organization theory, are exerting an increasing influence on the development of other management subspecialisms.

Finally, it is worth stressing that we are not seeking to provide a comprehensive review of critical studies of the management specialisms or even of those studies that resonate most deeply with the concerns of Critical Theory. Instead, our intent is to provide a broad discussion of each of the specialisms that can provide a point of departure, and hopefully a source of inspiration, for anyone who has been frustrated by, or disaffected with, conventional representations of these specialisms. To repeat what we said in Chapter 1, we view our commentary as a stimulus to emancipatory forms of management theory and practice, and not as anything approaching a definitive statement on how each of the specialisms has been subjected to critical scrutiny.

**Organization Theory**

Organization theory is the most fundamental and pervasive of the management specialisms. Organizing is endemic to all the specialisms and, indeed, is not infrequently identified as the very medium of management (Hales, 1993). Organization theory is also the most important for critical management theory as it has the greatest knock-on effects in the other specialisms.[2]

*Beyond Classical Organization Theory*

The basic outlines of the critique of mainstream (functionalist) organization theory and practice were sketched in Chapters 1 and 2, and we will not repeat these here.[3] Instead, we will briefly review two trends that have shifted organization theory away from its classical formulation in the writings of Taylor (1911) and Fayol (1949). *First*, there has been a re-assessment of the belief that modern management is concerned with the design of organizational structures and working practices that eliminate the disruptive, counter-productive effects of tradition and sentiment. This has been evident in the development of varieties of Human Relations (Mayo, 1949) and Socio-Technical Systems thinking (Emery and Trist, 1960), where sentiment is identified as an *untapped resource* for securing improved levels of commitment and productivity. But it is also evident in neo-Human Relations ideas (McGregor, 1960; Argyris, 1964) where the attainment of corporate objectives is understood to be secured through the realization of individual employee needs, with self-esteem and self-actualization being championed as 'key motivators'. In its most recent manifestation, the recasting of classical thinking takes the form of building strong corporate cultures in which the scope for attaining self-esteem and self-actualization is carefully managed through the development of more 'organic' organizational systems (see Chapter 4). Associated with this managerial focus upon culture and symbolism as potent, organic media of control, there has been keen academic interest in this area (Weick, 1987; Frost et al. 1985, 1991; Alvesson and Berg, 1992).

The *second* shift away from classical theory has occurred with the move from an assumption that organizational members share identical interests (e.g. in applying the principles of scientific management) to understanding that organizations comprise a plurality of stakeholders – such as employees, consumers, suppliers, government, the law, the local community and sources of finance (Cyert and March, 1963). Organizations are increasingly understood to 'satisfy the needs' of a plurality of groups; and the task ascribed to professional managers is one of ensuring that the diverse needs of these groups are recognized, that conflicting interests are regulated, and that a dynamic equilibrium is maintained. Contemporary organizational analysis has done much to highlight the presence of different forms of rationality and even 'irrationalities' (Brunsson, 1985). However, an emphasis upon diversity tends to imply that power relations between stakeholders are more or less equal, if not wholly symmetrical.[4] This overlooks the extent to which plural rationalities are the medium and outcome of institutionalized inequalities of wealth and influence, and are the product of ongoing conflicts between various groups (see Chapter 1).[5] From this latter perspective, the establishment of a strong corporate culture, for example, is interpreted less as a means of improving the balance between a plurality of stakeholders than as a stratagem for inducing conformist attitudes and values (see Chapter 4).

In order to break with pluralist understandings of organizations, it is necessary to shift to a more radical standpoint, such as those developed within the Marxist and radical feminist traditions. We begin by expanding the brief discussion of feminist thinking that we introduced in Chapters 2 and 3.

### Gendered Organization Theory

Initially, most of the interest in gender and management emerged from a liberal feminist position, as outlined in Chapter 2, and concentrated on women managers (e.g. in terms of leadership style and other problems, etc. compared to male managers). It included consideration of difficulties experienced by women in attaining managerial positions because of prejudices and resistances that were biased against women making careers (e.g. Marshall, 1984). As we noted in Chapter 2, such an approach is rather restricted: it concentrates on those organizational and psychological conditions that are of immediate relevance for women aspiring to function as managers. While it challenges male-biased practices and beliefs, it does not question the wider institutional arrangements or the overall logic of corporate organizations (Alvesson and Billing, 1992; Collinson et al., 1990; Calas and Smircich, 1992, 1993).

A broader, gendered vision of organization understands all aspects of modern organization as infused with values, rules, priorities and orientations that are deeply gender-biased. It notes, for example, how corporations and public bureaucracies have traditionally been, and remain, dominated by males (Mills and Tancred, 1992). Because women have taken primary responsibility for the reproductive sector – child care and other 'logics' that are developed within the reproductive sphere (Gilligan, 1982) – many features of organizations are sensed to be alien and frustrating to women. Moreover, when women adapt to organizational conditions and managerial demands, it has been argued that there is the risk that 'conformity and the abandonment of critical consciousness are the prices of successful performances' (Ferguson, 1984: 29).

As we noted in previous chapters, there are similarities between CT and many versions of feminist thinking, including their respective critiques of (the dominance of) instrumental reason (Alvesson and Billing, 1992; Hearn and Parkin, 1983). However, while CT contends that the dominance of instrumental reason is problematic irrespective of gender, feminists are

inclined to contend that 'the feminist case against bureaucracy goes beyond
. . . (the "traditional" critique of CT and Marxism) because it constructs its
alternative out of concrete and shared experiences of women, rather than
out of a romantic vision of pre-capitalist life or an abstract ideal of "human
nature"' (Ferguson, 1984: 27). To this, the CT response is that many men
share with many women similar experiences of frustration in relation to
bureaucracy, and that while men generally are probably more at ease in the
impersonal culture of bureaucratic organizations, this is a mixed blessing,
and it is a relatively small élite of men who are the major material
beneficiaries of contemporary forms of work organization. One could also
challenge the idea of the uniform experiences and values of women.
Females vary substantially, not only in political opinions and career
interests, but also in experiences of dissatisfaction in organizations (Billing
and Alvesson, 1994). Drawing attention to what is most acute for female
workers may obscure what is common among many employees irrespective
of gender. In this respect, at least, there is scope for a closer alignment
between feminism and Critical Theory.

Indeed, in recent years there has been a growing challenge to the idea of
the dichotomy between males and females as robust categories (Flax, 1987).
It has been questioned whether this dichotomy mirrors, rather than
constitutes, two distinct groups corresponding to biological sexes or even
reflects the existence of stable and distinct socialization patterns which fix
the meaning of, and ideas about, men and women. There has been an
increasing interest in how masculinity and femininity are socially
constructed and transformed. Instead of being fixed by nature or history,
gender identities and relations are seen as precarious and unstable. Associated with this deconstruction of gender is an interest not only in women but
in men and masculinity (Collinson and Hearn, 1994), and also in the social
and organizational processes through which forms of femininity and
masculinity are produced within corporate settings. For example, sexual
imagery and jokes (Collinson, 1992; Hearn et al., 1989), and discourses
about corporate strategy and leadership, are understood to involve strong
elements of masculinity that act to strengthen male identities and thereby
reproduce asymmetrical gender relations in organizational life (Calas and
Smircich, 1991; Hearn and Parkin, 1987).

## Critical Organization Theory

In Chapter 2, we overviewed a number of strands of critical thinking in the
study of organizations. In the following sections of this chapter, we focus
upon the contribution of Critical Theory (CT). It will be recalled that
analysis informed by CT aspires to go beyond the historical-hermeneutical
project of seeking to appreciate members' interpretations of organizational
phenomena. Additionally, it interrogates the conditions that support, and
perhaps impede, the capacity to develop and articulate particular interpretations. In so doing, CT-guided studies move away from the idea that

researchers can 'objectively' capture others' interpretations without placing their own gloss upon the meaning of such findings. Although we are uncomfortable with easy, and dangerously arrogant, references to 'false rationalities' and 'delusions', we agree with Steffy and Grimes (1986) that the CT researcher 'is not a passive observer or even a participant' but, rather, is 'a "reconstructionalist" . . . who finds within empirical structures and members' interpretations false rationalities usually reflecting organizational ideologies. . . . researchers should increase members' understanding of their conditions and, subsequently, establish conditions for organizational change' (ibid.: 333–4). What is conventionally viewed as a vicious problem of eliminating bias from research design can be reinterpreted as a positive virtue that permits the development of a dialogue in which the question of how interpretations are conditioned by forces, of which individuals, including researchers, are often only dimly aware, is brought to light and subjected to critical scrutiny. In short, CT seeks to open up radically new understandings of organizational life that have a potential to promote new modes of work that give voice to, and promote, critical reflection and autonomy (Benson, 1977; Heydebrand, 1977; Jermier, 1981).

There are two principal versions of organization theory inspired by CT. One approach focuses upon the alienation of individual consciousness and understands emancipatory action in the context of the conflict between an essential human freedom and its negation by oppressive social institutions. A second approach, which Habermas' work has inspired since the early 1970s, proceeds from the pragmatics of communication whose violation is understood to provoke emancipatory action.

*On the Alienation of Human Consciousness*   As we noted in Chapters 2 and 3, a major concern for leading Critical Theorists (e.g. Marcuse) has been the way people can become psychologically dependent upon, and 'imprisoned' within, modern institutions. Workaholism and the psychological (as contrasted with material) anxieties associated with the loss of employment or lack of promotion are symptomatic of such dependencies. As we have suggested earlier and in previous chapters, managerial interest in Human Relations and Corporate Culture can be interpreted as moves to exploit employee anxiety (e.g. about self-esteem) by contriving to provide a corporate antidote for it.

This interpretation can be contrasted with traditional psychoanalytic theory in which the irrationalities of the human psyche are viewed as intrinsic to human nature. From this perspective, reason is regarded as a precarious accomplishment, always vulnerable to the play of unconscious motives and fantasies (Freud, 1917; Fenichel, 1945) that are only marginally affected by the dampening or amplifying influence of social and cultural conditions. CT, in contrast, contends that culture plays a central role in the development of the human psyche – for example, by increasing the conflict between libidinal drives and the standards and restrictions of civilization and/or by reinforcing the power of immature fantasies (Marcuse, 1955;

Fromm, 1970). The neurotic and narcissistic character of the modern individual is, according to this view, much more a function of a particular form of civilization than it is a pure reflection of a woman or man's essentially problematical psychology (cf. Lasch, 1979; see also Chapter 4).

From a CT perspective, then, the confusion, anxiety and emotional turmoil that impedes the process of organizing personal and social life in accordance with so-called 'rational' ideals is, in large part, socially and organizationally produced (Frost, 1980). Authoritarian social relations, degraded work conditions and low discretion are all understood to be detrimental for employees' psychological well-being (Fromm, 1955). Strongly non-democratic and non-egalitarian relations between superiors and subordinates are understood to induce more or less conscious feelings of dependence, anxiety and vulnerability. It is precisely for this reason that the business of counteracting hierarchical and authoritarian relations can be deeply threatening. The (unconscious) tendency is to comply, albeit with repressed feelings of resentment, with their demands (Sennett, 1980; Knights and Willmott, 1989). Jobs that provide little discretion and little intellectual stimulation are linked to rigid attitudes to life, passivity, and broadly conservative and authoritarian opinions (Kohn, 1980). Instead of striving for clarification of the life situation, and then engaging in action to change it, there is a tendency for passive adaptation and compensatory consumption to be pursued and endorsed.

This does not mean that the development of the human psyche works solely against emancipation or that it necessarily acquiesces to the status quo, however problematic. On the contrary, the tensions associated with the denial of autonomy and responsibility are understood to provide the basis of personal and collective resistance to forms of domination. As we noted in Chapters 3 and 4, Marcuse (1955) argued that human instincts, which are mostly unconscious, stand in potential opposition to the oppressive disciplines of modern organization and society. According to Marcuse's account, contradictions arise between, on the one hand, the modern ego administration that programmes people – through education, training and mass media – to produce and consume, and, on the other hand, libidinal drives that repeatedly call for pleasure and satisfaction. Libidinal impulses recurrently present a challenge to the status quo and may, therefore, foster emancipatory change[6] – when they do not fall foul of repressive desublimation, where forms of pleasure are pressed into the service of corporations (e.g. 'hoopla' in the guise of competitions, parties, prizes and 'gongs' for performance).

Habermas, in contrast to Marcuse, is sceptical about placing too much emphasis upon instinctual impulses towards emancipation, arguing that the ascription of instinctual impulses is an historically and culturally mediated process. Or, as he puts it, the concept of instinct is 'rooted in meaning structures of the lifeworld, no matter how elementary they may be' (Habermas, 1972: 256). Instead of a focus upon the alienation of human consciousness – produced either by the loss of control of the means of

production (Marx), or the denial of instinctual impulses (the id) by the
formation of the super-ego (Freud) – Habermas turns to *language* as the
medium of all human understanding *and* the source of human autonomy
and responsibility:

> the human interest in autonomy and responsibility is not mere fancy, for it can be
> apprehended *a priori*. What raises out of nature is the only thing that we can
> know: *language*. Through its structure, autonomy and responsibility are posited
> for us. Our first sentence expresses unequivocally the intention of universal and
> unconstrained consensus. (ibid.: 314)

In his later work, Habermas endeavours to make good this claim by
seeking to show that communication could not proceed without making the
(unarticulated) assumption that human beings are autonomous and
responsible, and that an unconstrained consensus is anticipated (see also
Chapter 3). We now turn to analysis of management and organization that
has been influenced by 'the linguistic turn' in Critical Theory.

*Organizations as Structures of Communicative Interaction*   The analysis of
organizations as structures of communicative action, rather than sites
of psycho-social imprisonment, is symptomatic of a (Habermasian) shift in
CT from a focus upon the alienation of *individual* consciousness to a
consideration of distortions in *intersubjective* communication (see Chapter
3). Instead of assuming that humans possess an essential autonomy that is
frustrated and deformed by the demands of oppressive organizational
structures, the focus upon communication sidesteps the question of what is
essential to human nature in favour of an understanding of the fundamental conditions of human communication. The critical issue then
becomes whether particular structures of communication allow these
fundamental conditions to be fully realized; or whether relations of power –
in the form of capitalism, technocracy, consumerism, sexism, racism, etc. –
systematically impede this possibility by, for example, representing such
impediments as natural or functional rather than social and enslaving.

    Drawing upon Habermas' ideas on communicative interaction and
rationality, Forester (1983, 1989, 1993) has identified four kinds of mis-
information or communicative distortion that are of particular relevance
for understanding organizational work. His analysis is attentive to two
dimensions. The first concerns the inevitable/unnecessary character of the
distortion. The second concerns the question of whether the distortion is *ad
hoc* (where it is more connected to individual action than a reflection of
social structure) or structural/systematic (where it is inherent in a particular
social order). Combining the two dimensions leads to the model shown in
Figure 5.1. Even though all sources of communicative distortion must be
considered, a focus on communicative interaction suggests that square 1
(cognitive limits) is of least interest and that square 4 (structural legitimation) is of greatest significance for analysing the theory and practice of
management and organization.

| Contingency of distortion | Autonomy of source of distortion | |
| --- | --- | --- |
| | Socially *ad hoc* (personbound) | Socially systematic/ structural |
| Inevitable distortion | Cognitive limits: complexity, random noise, idiosyncratic personal traits disrupting communication  (1) | Division of labour: information inequalities due to legitimate division of labour, problems in the transmission of meaning  (2) |
| Socially unnecessary distortions | Interpersonal manipulation: deception, bargaining, wilful unresponsiveness  (3) | Structural legitimation: monopolistic distortion of exchange, ideological creation of needs  (4) |

Figure 5.1    *Types of communicative distortion (adapted from Forester, 1982)*

While drawing attention to forms of communicative distortion that, in principle, can be counteracted, the model acknowledges the significance of universal problems for the emancipatory project. For example, the emotional and cognitive state of human beings places limits upon communicative rationality (square 1), as do the unpredictable dynamics and ambiguities of social life (square 2). The proposed means of uncovering the link between power and distortion, and thereby facilitating emancipatory change is, first, to evaluate empirical phenomena by considering their immediate character in terms of their necessary or unnecessary bounds; and, secondly, to examine their structural or non-structural character in a given social context. When phenomena are discovered to be socially unnecessary and structurally based, the consistent response is to question and reach some grounded agreement upon how things are, and how they should be; and then, to act in order to facilitate the emancipatory change of the existing structures. As Forester (1988: 9) puts it, the idea is to challenge 'any perceived "necessity" or "natural" or reified character of such constraints. Here we have the link between a tradition of ideology critique and political action and a previously altogether depoliticized understanding of administrative and planning rationality.'

Habermas' communication theory encourages a readiness to say 'no' to statements with problematic validity claims, and a preparedness to engage in communicative processes of challenging such statements when deemed necessary. The criteria for rationality and legitimacy is the degree to which statements indicating standpoints about values, goals and means can be probed in a process of dialogue to warrant their 'truth' (are statements well grounded in what we recognize as facts?), their 'legitimacy' (do they express acceptable values and norms?), their 'sincerity' (are they referred to in a sincere or manipulative way?) and their 'clarity' (are they diffuse, could they be clarified?) (Forester, 1993; see also Chapter 4). It is possible to conceive of a strong and a weak version of critical organization analysis guided by Habermas' theory of communication. The strong version suggests that the truth, legitimacy, sincerity and clarity of statements can be decisively tested through a process of critical scrutiny. The risk associated with such a programme is that it may pay insufficient attention to the contingent conditions of the judgements that are made and thereby slide into authoritarianism. Equally, as poststructuralists (see Chapter 3) have warned, the strong version of Habermas' communication theory does not encourage reflection upon the disciplinary effects of its own presuppositions.

It is therefore important to explore how Habermas' ideas may be used in a weaker, critically pragmatic way, where the working principle is not to try to get rid of all communicative distortions or indeed to accomplish an ideal speech situation, but to open up a space for increased communicative action with regard to beliefs, consent, and trust, thereby challenging and reversing the tendency of work organizations to devalue, corrode or appropriate the values of the lifeworld (e.g. family, neighbourhood, voluntary associations). A developed capacity to question and discuss the rationality of significant statements can consequentially alter the way that these discourses act to maintain the position of a ruling, managerial élite. This capacity can also provide a basis for the critique and transformation of organizational practice (Alvesson, 1996; Forester, 1989, 1993). Support for this endeavour can be derived from studies which show that, despite an official rhetoric of purposive-rationality, 'interactions are still connected via the mechanism of mutual understanding' (Habermas, 1987b: 310). Not only is there considerable scope for so-called 'informal behaviour', but the effective operation of organizations is heavily dependent upon it. Or, as Habermas makes this point: 'If all processes of genuinely reaching understanding were banished from the interior of organizations, formally regulated social relations could not be sustained, nor could organizational goals be realized' (ibid.).

The tendency, nonetheless, is for organizations to disempower the validity of family and community ethics as each employee is legally required to subjugate his or her values to the authority of systems in which 'there is no *necessity* for achieving consensus by communicative means' (ibid.: 311, emphasis in original). Yet, by the same token, there is a managerial risk of growing separation between, on the one hand, what is subjectively meaningful and, on the other, what is deemed to be necessary according to 'the objective meaning of a functionally stabilised nexus of action' (ibid.). It is the tensions and identity crises associated with this separation that, *inter alia*, are understood by Habermas to generate processes of critical reflection that can challenge and reverse the tendency for systems' logic to devalue and displace lifeworld values fostered by family and community.

*Summary*

Organization theory guided by CT has shared the concern of post-classical organization theory to highlight the perverse effects of suppressing the contribution of lifeworld values (e.g. sentiment and tradition). But it has also analysed how relations of power in organizations operate to impede open communication, as more or less subtle forms or coercion are applied. From a CT perspective, the purpose of studying organizations and organizing practices is not simply to 'map' their contours, to appreciate the diverse meanings attributed by actors to their organizational conduct or to identify means of raising productivity by reducing forms of dissatisfaction and poor morale. Rather, its purpose is to stimulate and contribute to a dialogical process of challenging and removing discourses and practices that are incompatible with the development of greater autonomy and responsibility.

**Marketing**

Marketing is perhaps the most visible and controversial of the management specialisms. Its academic status is also rather precarious. Brown (1993: 28), for example, talks about 'marketing's perennial search for academic respectability' and of 'the discipline's lowly standing in the scholarly caste system'. More salient are the widely expressed doubts about its contribution to the social good of society. However, debates about the credibility and social contribution of marketing have tended to take place outside, or at least at the margins of, the marketing specialism. Indeed, it is probably fair to say that, of the management specialisms, marketing has been one of the least self-reflective and, seemingly, the most self-satisfied. As a discipline, marketing is generally at a low level of theory development (Arndt, 1980, 1985) in which the question of whether it has scientific status has been periodically raised – but then only, it would seem, to argue for a positive answer, and thereby legitimize the claims of the discipline (Hunt, 1976). Nevertheless, there are signs of a growing interest in critical and reflective work among a small but growing minority of marketing academics.[7]

Mainstream marketing gurus claim that marketing is concerned with satisfying the needs of customers (see also Chapter 4). Kotler (1976), for example, defines marketing as 'human activity directed at satisfying needs and wants through exchange processes' (ibid.: 5). This is a very broad and imprecise definition that accommodates and encourages the (colonizing) extension of marketing into diverse spheres of social and economic life (Morgan, 1992). Our consideration of the marketing specialism begins with a review of doubts that have been expressed about its key claims. We then focus upon the key role of consumer marketing in societies where massive resources are committed to the management of demand for products and services for which there would otherwise probably be little call.

*Marketing as the Science of Exchange Behaviour*

Marketing theory and research remains staunchly positivistic in its disregard of the historical and political construction of its research 'objects'.
According to Brown (1993: 28), the low and rather disreputable status of
marketing, which is strongly associated with doubts about its claims to
serve (rather than hoodwink) consumers, has meant that marketing has
long felt obliged to prove itself 'more scientific than science' by applying
'rigorous methods'. This move has led to the critique that much marketing
is conservative, passive, sterile and conceptually colonized by empiricism
and micro-economic theory (Arndt, 1985). Certainly, marketing research
and the leading marketing journals are heavily committed to the application and legitimation of such approaches. Their overriding concern has
been the scientistic refinement and testing of instruments that are intended
to measure the ever-increasing number of variables that supposedly
enhance the capacity to predict consumer behaviour. This view has been
defended in terms of 'scientific realism' (e.g. Hunt, 1990), which pays little
regard to the relationship between knowledge and wider issues, including
history, culture and power (Willmott, 1996a).[8]

When seeking to rectify marketing's attachment to positivism, Arndt
(1985) has suggested that ideas drawn from the non-functionalist paradigms
identified by Burrell and Morgan (1979; see Chapter 2) can enable
marketers to explore various neglected dimensions of marketing theory and
practice, including subjective experiences, conflicts and liberating forces. In
recent years, there has been a slowly growing interest in such approaches –
notably, in interpretive marketing and consumer research (e.g. Belk et al.,
1989; Hirschman, 1990). These less objectivistic (e.g. ethnographic)
methods generate forms of knowledge that directly challenge the conventional wisdom by taking more direct account of the practical reasoning of
consumers as they decide which products and services they will buy. Yet,
despite some signs of disillusionment with, and departures from, the
established positivist paradigm of marketing knowledge, alternative
methodologies have not yet seriously begun to reshape marketing theory
and research.

In presenting itself as 'the discipline of exchange behaviour' (Bagozzi,
1975: 78), marketing excludes consideration of how 'exchanges' are
mediated by asymmetrical relations of power. As Baker (1987: 8) has
proclaimed, in defence of marketing, 'it is all about mutually satisfying
exchange relationships for which the catalyst is the producer's attempt to
define and satisfy the customer's need better'. Identifying exchange as its
central concept, marketing provides a deceptively simple, easy-to-under-
stand formulation of the complexities of human interaction and neglects to
discuss how structures of domination and exploitation shape and mediate
relationships.

Of course, all relationships, including those that are most personal and
intimate, *can* be represented in the language of exchange. And, insofar as

these relationships are increasingly targeted and influenced by marketing practices – which take it for granted that 'exchange forms the core phenomenon for study in marketing' (Bagozzi, 1975: 32) – they may indeed come to conform more closely to the 'truths' that such knowledge is sensed to convey (Foucault, 1977). A practical outcome of conceptualizing social interaction as exchange is to depersonalize and commodify relationships. In such relationships, individuals are routinely encouraged to represent, and relate to, each other as commodities in a marketplace – a development that exchange theory and associated discourses actively promotes (see Chapter 3).

The concept of exchange is beguiling because it suggests that each individual is a sovereign consumer who is free to pick and choose in the marketplace. The discourse of exchange appeals to a common-sense humanism and voluntarism that inflates the individual's sense of autonomy and provides a central plank in marketing's professional ideology. Its promise is to recognize and expand, through the medium of market relations, the individual's sense of freedom. What this obscures, or at least fails to address, are the *social* relations of inequality that privilege or exclude participation in *marketized* transactions. Or, as Giddens (1979: 272) articulates this argument, the basic deficiency of exchange theory is that it 'does not incorporate power . . . and tends to remain tied to a framework of utilitarian individualism'. Through the (ideological) concept of exchange, social interactions are portrayed and naturalized as processes of reciprocal manipulation between (egoistic) parties who individually derive benefit from such transactions.

Far from securing consumer sovereignty and satisfaction, it has been argued that many of the marketing methods celebrated in the academic literature frustrate or even undermine the realization of this ideal (Jonsson, 1979). For example, it has been noted how students of marketing are presented with theories and methods that claim to weaken or circumvent the will of consumers by inducing them to act in a habitual way (e.g. by encouraging brand loyalty), or in an impulsive way (e.g. by legitimizing a compulsion to consume), etc. More specifically, Jonsson's (1979) examination of the contents of marketing textbooks reveals their advocacy of the following:

- The use of cosmetic product differences in order to make it difficult for the consumer to identify more substantive differences between products.
- The use of background music in order to distract the consumer, and make it more difficult for him or her to suggest counter arguments to what the seller proposes.
- The appeal to the consumer's guilt feelings through a small gift, which makes the consumer feel inclined to buy as a response.

Jonsson (1979) contends that the satisfaction of consumers' given needs and wants is frustrated and counteracted by particular forms of marketing practice. His goal is the development of less manipulated, more autonomous patterns of consumption. However, by focusing only upon the tendency of marketing methods to undermine customer sovereignty, which is itself unproblematized, a limited critique of the process of marketing and consumption is presented. From a CT perspective, the problems that attend processes of consumption are not restricted to specific forms of marketing management, but include a broader social dynamic that is impelled by, and serves to fuel, consumer capitalism. A more penetrating critique must address the question of how consumers become aware of their preferences and how their decisions are shaped by social processes, including the process of marketing products and services.

In countering the fetish of consumerism, it is relevant to recall the existence of groups (e.g. environmentalists) that more or less explicitly question the rationality of continuously increasing consumption. Garrett's (1987) study of the effectiveness of marketing policy boycotts against companies deemed to be operating unethically (e.g. polluting the environment, etc.) is indicative of one way forward for the academic field of marketing. Knowledge gained from such studies is of relevance not only for boycott organizers, but also for other potential targets of boycotts (companies) which may be encouraged to reform their practices in order to avoid such unwanted attentions. However, from a CT position, Garrett's study has a narrow focus on the effectiveness of boycotts. It does not, for example, address questions of how an interest in changing company policy is formed; and no distinction is made between normatively and communicatively anchored standpoints for identifying unethical policies or organizing boycotts. Nonetheless, this study is suggestive of ways in which a critical knowledge of marketing and consumerism can be forged, thereby enabling marketers to free themselves from narrow, technicist research and anodyne textbook accounts of their specialism.

## Marketing, Needs and Consumerism

As we have noted, most marketers – academics as well as practitioners – routinely assume that marketing theory and practice broadly serves the interests of customers, and thereby contributes to the well-being of individuals and society. Intuitively, one might indeed expect that an increase in consumption would lead to an increase in satisfaction. However, given a comfortable material standard of living, it is certainly debatable whether increases in consumption do bring about any lasting happiness or increased satisfaction. Many investigations in wealthy countries suggest that this is not the case (Scitovsky, 1976; Wachtel, 1983; etc.). Such studies indicate that levels of satisfaction do not increase, and can even decline, when material living standards improve substantially.

One explanation of this paradox is that many so-called 'needs' that consumers strive to satisfy are unreflectively acquired. Needs for products and services may be induced by others who are in the business of suggesting to us that our life, or sense of self-identity, is incomplete or impoverished unless we fulfil the ascribed need, which may be material or symbolic. In this regard, Pendergrast (1993) notes that Coca-Cola's midfield signs at the playoffs of the 1990 Football World Cup reached a worldwide audience of 25 billion viewers, and that Coca-Cola invested $80 million on its 1988 Olympic promotions. 'Regardless of the sport – field hockey, basketball, volleyball, gymnastics, sumo wrestling, motorcycle races – Coca-Cola sponsored it in almost every country in the world' (ibid.: 389). Such campaigns serve to reinforce the idea that the consumption of such goods is not only desirable and fashionable, but also entirely normal. The message is not that their consumption satisfies a material need, for which there are many, less expensive substitutes, but that it does so in an exceptionally gratifying (identity-enhancing) way.

Leiss (1978) has argued that mass consumption society – promoted by its greatest advocates, the marketers – induces the following psychological problems: a fragmentation and destabilization of 'needs'; difficulty in matching 'needs' with the characteristics of goods; and a growing indifference to more basic needs or wants. When, for example, Coca-Cola or Levis associate their products with youth – or, at least, with people's 'need' to appear young – an imaginary relationship between needs (for warm clothing) and goods (jeans) is produced and reinforced. The 'need' for clothing or drink becomes associated more closely with the image (and value) of glamour and youthfulness than it is with the use as protection against the elements or the relief of thirst. In such ways, commercial forces feed off the largely repressed fear of old age and death as they amplify the ideal of immortality (Willmott, 1995c).

The unfortunate effects of advertising, according to its critics, include the reinforcement of social (e.g. gender) stereotypes, the trivialization of language; the promotion of conformity, social competitiveness, envy, anxieties and insecurities; and disrespect for tradition by appealing to newness and youth (Pollay, 1986; see also debate between Holbrook, 1987 and Pollay, 1987 on this issue). A focus upon consumption as a good in itself is productive of a moral vacuum, it is argued, which advertising simultaneously stakes a claim to fill. As desires are unremittingly aroused and exploited, people become more cynical (e.g. they become used to incomplete information, half-truths or deceptions), irrational (e.g. they become compulsive about consuming), greedy and narcissistic (see Chapter 4).[9] Other strivings and desires (e.g. individuality, solidarity) that are either in conflict with, or resistant to, the fuelling of possessive individualism and capital accumulation processes, are deemed to be peripheral, naïve, or are in other ways marginalized. The propaganda of consumption, Lasch contends:

addresses itself to the spiritual desolation of modern life and proposes consumption as the cure. It not only promises to palliate all the old unhappiness to which flesh is heir; it creates or exacerbates new forms of unhappiness – personal insecurity, status anxiety, anxiety in parents about their ability to satisfy the needs of the young. Do you look dowdy next to your neighbours? Do you own a car inferior to theirs? . . . Advertising institutionalizes envy and its attendant anxieties. (1979: 73)

Advertising through the mass media (and, more recently, through more selective targeting, such as personalized mail shots), plays a central role in the process of stimulating and legitimizing consumption (see Harms and Kellner (1991) for a discussion of Critical Theory and advertising). Through the use of sophisticated advertising and marketing techniques, the mass(ive) consumption of goods and services is routinely presented as *the* answer – perhaps the only answer – to widespread feelings of insecurity, frustration, disorientation and meaninglessness. Consumption is identified as the 'fix' that alleviates, albeit temporarily, the existential pain to which it needlessly contributes by inhibiting the development of more value-rational consumption (see below). It is clearly possible to critique the effectiveness of this fix in terms of the transient nature of the satisfaction produced and, more fundamentally, in terms of its reinforcement of the very feelings that it contrives to mitigate. But, of course, from a conventional marketing perspective, both effects are prized because they keep the wheels of consumptionism and accumulation spinning.

As marketing becomes respectable and institutionalized, it becomes applied to larger and larger terrains of human existence. All social relations are potential targets of its discipline as market mechanisms become the preferred means of monitoring and evaluating social relations. As Morgan has observed, this involves:

> a monetization and commodification of social relations. In this world, marketing can tell us the 'price of everything, but the value of nothing'! Anything can be marketed. It does not have to be the more obvious goods and services; it can be 'good causes', 'political parties', 'ideas'. The whole world is a market and we are consumers in a gigantic candy-store. Just sit back and enjoy it! (1992: 142–3)

The most important impact of marketing discourses and practices is not to make individuals buy a *specific* product or service. Rather, its more important and insidious effect resides in establishing the *generalized understanding* that consumption, which is increasingly customized and individualized, is entirely normal and unequivocally desirable. As Featherstone has observed:

> Within contemporary consumer culture (lifestyle) connotes individuality, self-expression, and stylistic self-consciousness. One's body, clothes, speech, leisure pastimes, eating and drinking preferences, home care, choice of holidays, etc. are to be regarded as indicators of the individuality of taste and sense of style of the owner/consumer. (1991: 83)

In this light, marketing is identified as a powerful and seductive agency of social control. Its pervasive effect is to place mass consumption at the centre of our awareness and sense of self-identity so that we become dependent, like addicts, upon the consumption of commodities for maintaining our lifestyle/lifeworld: 'I shop therefore I am' or 'Shop Til You Drop' as 1980s T-shirts ironically declared, in deadly humorous fashion.

*Consumption, Status and Value Rationality*

Far from highlighting the adverse consequences of consumption, the subliminal message of much advertising and packaging is that consuming is pleasurable – aesthetically as well as materially (Haug, 1986) – and that it will enhance the individual's social status and/or self-esteem. Goods and services are transformed from 'being primarily satisfiers of wants to being primarily communicators of meanings' (Leiss et al., 1986: 238). As marketing seeks to fix our attention upon its 'solutions' to our 'problems', it distracts and deflects attention from values and goods that are less readily satisfied through the marketplace – such as quality of work, more fulfilling personal relationships and ecological concerns such as air quality and water purity (Haug, 1986). All kinds of personal services become commodified, or mediated by the market – from 'chat lines' to computer dating agencies. And yet, however sophisticated the means of satisfying the needs ascribed to consumers becomes, the connection between consumption and satisfaction remains weak – satisfaction is, at best, fleeting.

One explanation of the weak connection between consumption and satisfaction focuses upon the relative or positional character of consumer goods (Hirsch, 1976). Goods, it is argued, are not in themselves necessarily sources of positive satisfaction. Instead, what is important is what one owns, or what one consumes, in relation to other people. A person is likely to be more satisfied to own a bicycle in a village where everyone else has to walk than a person who owns a small car in a town where every other car is bigger. People very soon become accustomed to their possession of new goods, which they then take for granted. They then start to crave something else – for example, ownership of a small car to replace the bicycle. Something similar is indicated by the concept of mimetic rivalry (Asplund, 1991). This phenomenon concerns people's inclination to value and want what other people want. It has also been suggested that much consumption by the middle and upper classes derives its value from being differentiated from the products and services consumed by other people (Hirschman, 1990). Satisfaction is thus largely a matter of distinguishing oneself from, and elevating oneself over, others – in terms of taste, prestige and, consequently, power (Veblen, 1953; Bourdieu, 1984). This status competition serves to fuel economic growth, but the number of people who can score higher than the average is constant, so levels of satisfaction remain relatively unchanged while, arguably, levels of expectation and frustration tend to increase.

From a CT perspective, the major problem with consumerism, and the social and ideological processes that support this ideal, is that it narrows and distorts processes of communication and self-formation. By inducing an emotional commitment to maintaining the flow of goods, and being dependent on its mass producing and distributing capacities, consumerism ties people to the present social order.

Drawing upon Weber's (1978) ideal-typical distinction between four forms of action, we can say that marketing routinely promotes and legitimizes a preoccupation with either the *affective* pursuit (e.g. shopping to get a psychological boost), or the *rational calculation* of material self-interest, with the intent of identifying and satisfying immediate subjective wants. Where affect dominates, consumers simply indulge whatever desire happens to flood their consciousness. Consumption is driven by forces (e.g. advertising) about which the individual consumer has little conscious knowledge, and over which he or she is able to exert little rational control (i.e. in the extreme, what has been termed 'compulsive shopping disorder'). Where instrumentally rational action is dominant, the consumer is able to calculate which of many possible forms of consumption is likely to yield the greatest satisfaction. Unconstrained by ultimate values or predetermined commitments, the individual is 'free' to consume in all directions (see Chapter 2). Only the rules of marginal utility impede the desire to consume. As du Gay and Salaman (1992) have characterized the cult(ure) of the (instrumentally rational) customer, it is a world in which customers are constituted as seemingly sovereign, self-actualizing actors who are 'seeking to maximize the worth or their existence to themselves through personalized acts of choice in a world of goods and service' (ibid.: 623).

To these possibilities of affective and instrumental rationality, Weber (1978) counterposes *value-rational* action. Value-rational behaviour, Weber argues, involves the individual in orienting his or her choices to ultimate values. In contrast to the affective and instrumentally-rational customer, the 'value rational' actor is guided/constrained by particular value commitments that necessarily focus and limit the pattern of consumption. Needless to say, such constraints are not likely to be good for business! They are nevertheless often significant where, for example, religious and ethical considerations play a role in economic behaviour (Etzioni, 1988).

Marketing techniques rarely promote or serve the development of value-rational consumption. In general, their objective is to encourage individuals to maximize and sustain consumption, not to focus and constrain it within the confines of a specific value-orientation. Their intent is to enable potential customers to overcome moral and rational resistances and reservations about buying particular products or services. Presenting themselves as championing the 'needs' of the consumer, marketers cast consumption within a quasi-therapeutic ethos that promises fulfilment through consumption (Fox and Lears, 1983). All constraints upon consumption (e.g. resistance to credit) are regarded as irrational; appeals are made to erode the established norm of saving money by encouraging customers to spend it; suggestions are repeatedly made to the effect that a particular life (-style) is incomplete without the purchase of a product.

Of those most directly influenced by CT, Fromm has been consistently critical of marketing and advertising. Identifying marketing as a contemporary character trait, he talks about 'the marketing personality' (Fromm, 1976) who is preoccupied with presenting a self in a form that is desirable to others. Fromm examines how marketing values shape and 'possess' individuals who are 'without goals, except moving, doing things with the greatest efficiency; if asked *why* they must move so fast, why things have to be done with the greatest efficiency, they have no genuine answer, but offer rationalizations, such as "in order to create more jobs"' (Fromm, ibid.: 147). Such people always keep 'moving', they never stop to reflect upon how their frenetic activity undermines the very purpose (e.g. need fulfilment) that it professes to serve. They rarely manage to penetrate beyond the rationalizations of their action to reveal the sense of emptiness that is driving them on to make themselves desirable, and to maintain the sense of accomplishing something.

More generally, Fromm (1976) describes the development in the Western world as a massive social experiment concerning whether materialism might be the answer to the problems of human existence and concludes that the answer is clearly negative. All the evidence suggests that many problems remain (see above), and that some social problems (e.g. pollution and crime) can get much worse, as affluence increases and social divisions in society become more visible and acute. Though highly relevant for the theory and practice of marketing, issues and debates of this kind are conspicuously absent from marketing texts and journals. Only a small number of commentators has directly challenged the connection between consumption and lasting satisfaction.

The cultural doping and mystification metaphors, described in Chapter 4, are relevant here. An image of individuality is sold through the purchase of goods that signal the possession and pursuit of particular – seemingly distinctive, yet fundamentally conformist – lifestyles. For example, a junk mail brochure from a major UK electrical chain used the following banner headline: 'Improve your Lifestyle with a Mobile Phone'. This was accompanied, seemingly without humorous intent, by a large photograph of a man engaged in the supposedly tranquil sport of fishing with a phone tucked in his breast pocket, threatening to disturb his peace at any moment!

Critical marketing studies can usefully debunk the seductive images promoted by companies that supposedly cater for consumers. Consider McDonalds. This company has successfully promoted an image of being a highly desirable place to eat, especially for families. Yet, upon critical reflection, it is apparent that McDonalds requires customers to wait upon themselves (by giving orders, fetching the food and disposing of the mountains of cardboard and plastic containers) and to eat with their fingers. As Letiche and van Hattem have observed:

> The choices for employees and customers are very limited. Every aspect of the food and its presentation has been calculated. The hamburgers look large because they stick out, just a bit, from the buns; the portions of french fries look large because the stripes on the little carton boxes are drawn to create an illusion of length, etc., etc. Every dietary facet, dimension of presentation, aspect of preparation, has been measured and is controlled. Hereby McDonalds maximizes predictability – eating at one McDonalds is the same as eating at any other; time

of the day or year plays no role. Every aspect of the experience is as uniform as is possible. To achieve this goal a very high level of control is exerted. The cooks cannot influence the taste of hamburgers; the drink dispenser, not the employee, measures how much Coke you get. The work is entirely de-skilled; there's no real cooking just the 'heating up' of pre-prepared products. Customers are controlled via the uncomfortable seats which limit visits to twenty minutes, and the 'saccharine music' which drives 'punks' away. Is McDonalds really rational? If the criteria is the quality/cost ratio of food the answer is 'No'. McDonalds food is expensive and unhealthy; it overuses fats, salt, sugar to achieve the taste impression that one is 'getting a lot'. McDonalds makes eating 'fun'; at the cost of downloading the 'kids' into the 'playground', and still further reducing parent-child contact. (1994: 12–13)

Arguably, McDonalds is successful not because of what happens to their customers but because they have successfully associated notions of speed, precision, uniformity and predictability with images of what is desirable (Ritzer, 1993). Its success is a product of inviting the customer to focus upon what McDonalds can offer (consistency, etc.) by disregarding and devaluing what it cannot.

*Summary*

Marketing is perhaps the subdiscipline of management to which CT (and related intellectual traditions) can contribute most, and yet it is also in this specialism that the influence of critical analysis is weakest. Whereas marketers assume the existence of needs and point to consumer demand as a way of justifying this assumption, proponents of CT have been concerned with the ideological, symbolic and psychoanalytical significance of consumption, arguing *inter alia* that the appeal of advertising and other forms of demand management feeds upon, and reinforces, infantile impulses and fantasies (1979) and is associated with various problems, such as:

- a widespread belief that consumption is the route to happiness, meaning, and the solution to most personal problems (Fromm, 1955, 1976; Marcuse, 1964);
- a displacement of feeling from the valuing of people to the valuing of objects;
- the creation and reinforcement of consumer identities leading to a precarious and vulnerable sense of self (Lasch, 1979);
- distorted political priorities, giving extra emphasis to private goods and neglecting public goods; the over-stressing of economic goals and down-playing of other ends such as peace and justice (Galbraith, 1958);
- ecological wastefulness and damage (Leiss, 1976).

The potential for CT-inspired thought to foster an alternative to traditional marketing is strong. As we have indicated, a CT approach to marketing can bring fresh insights and provide a more penetrating appreciation of its wider ethical and social significance.

## Strategic Management

Strategic management is both one of the oldest and one of the newest of the management disciplines. It is old in the sense that owners and managers have always made key decisions – for example, about which business to be in, or about how human and material resources are to be deployed. But strategic management is also new because only comparatively recently has this responsibility been labelled, studied and prized as 'strategic management' (Knights and Morgan, 1991). The recent preoccupation with strategic management has led one American management guru to remark about North Americans that 'We get off on strategy like the French get off on good food and romance' (Pascale, 1982, quoted in Wensley, 1987: 29). Strategic management focuses upon the competitive positioning of organizations in relation to the perceived opportunities and constraints posed by the (changing) contexts of their operation. From a managerial perspective, successful strategic management is conceived in terms of mobilizing resources in ways that strengthen the focal organization's command of its environment and/or weakens the position of competitors. Strategic management is generally associated with the work of senior managers (and their advisors) and is currently closely identified with the work of particular specialists, such as industrial economists and marketers. However, strategic management also encompasses the development of strategically-conscious 'human resources' who are knowledgeable about, and committed to, the successful implementation of strategic plans.

### Orthodox Contributions to Strategic Management

Conventional approaches to strategic management are preoccupied with the rational identification of competitive advantage and the design of corporate structures, policies and business units. These approaches involve, *inter alia*, the identification and refinement of plans that are shaped through an analysis of the market structure of the firm, the resources at its disposal, and an appraisal of its actual and potential competitive advantages in comparison with its rivals (e.g. Porter, 1985). Plans may include the formation of strategic alliances and networks with other organizations or the pursuit of growth through acquisitions. Orthodox understandings of strategy and strategic management foster a mentality where the financial criteria are central and the development of a deeper understanding of businesses is down-played (Mintzberg, 1990). This is most salient in the USA, where the use of case studies in education may lead students, erroneously, to believe that, based on a twenty-page report, they can develop a strategy that will revive the fortunes of an ailing corporation. (For an interesting cross-cultural comparison with regard to strategy, see Whittington 1993.)

Such thinking about strategic management tends to ascribe to the managers of corporations immense powers to identify sources of competitive advantage, and then to direct their businesses to secure the strategic objectives. This thinking also assumes that 'environments' are predictable, and that long-term plans can be sensibly made and progressively implemented. Against this view, it has been argued that the scope for exercising strategic choice is severely constrained (or enabled) by the capabilities, or 'core competences', present within any given organization (Hamel and Prahalad, 1989). Strategy, it is argued, should be driven by the 'leveraging' of these competences, not by the identification of a niche that might be beyond an organization's capabilities.

It has also been objected that, in mainstream thinking on strategic management, little account is taken of the unpredictability of events and the volatility of market forces. It is argued that many successful 'strategies' are more likely to 'happen' as a consequence of accident and good fortune, rather than as an outcome of rational planning. This view implies the strategic relevance of being alert and prepared to exploit new openings, and being willing to experiment with a range of options rather than carefully formulating a strategy and then systematically implementing it. But, against this view, it has been suggested that the scope for opportunism is severely constrained because firms are frequently grouped in similar populations lodged in shared market niches; and that, in practice, established routines and modes of response constrain the capacity to move into new niches (Hannan and Freeman, 1977; Aldrich, 1979). To this objection can be added the view that many markets are dominated by a few key players who alone command the resources sufficient to exclude new entrants; and that firms are deeply embedded in social systems and networks that at once impede and promote particular kinds of (strategic) thinking and action (Granovetter, 1985; Whittington, 1993).

## Strategic Management as Process

Orthodox efforts to elaborate and refine highly idealized, *prescriptive models* of strategic management or to identify those variables that are deemed to inhibit or constrain the pursuit of 'ideal' courses of action, have been challenged by strategic management researchers who have sought to understand how strategies are *practically organized* and realized. The resulting pattern of activity, Mintzberg et al. (1976) argue, may in practice deviate – for organizationally sound reasons – from the intentions of those who originally formulated the strategic plans. In a similar vein, Quinn (1980) has challenged the idea of strategy as a rationally ordered cycle of stages from formulation to implementation. Instead, strategic management is represented as a highly recursive and incremental activity.

Strategic management is then more readily understood to be 'crafted' rather than planned (Mintzberg, 1987).[10] The craft metaphor suggests a comparatively 'open' approach to strategy-making that is appreciative of the existence of recursive processes through which strategic *learning* is accomplished, and continuous adjustments are made. It suggests that the practicalities of strategic management involve fuzzy and intuitive processes of understanding in which managers 'learn about their organizations and industries through personal touch' rather than by reading 'MIS reports and industry analyses' (Mintzberg, 1987: 73). As Johnson has commented, such research suggests that:

> In the process of strategic decision-making there is a much greater reliance on management judgement and past experience than the evaluative techniques of the management scientist would suggest. . . . What becomes clear is that the selection of strategy is primarily by means of management judgement and is likely to be bound up in a process of bargaining within the organization. *Solutions are not so much likely to be adopted because they are shown to be better on the basis of some sort of objective yardstick, but because they are acceptable to those who influence the decision or have to implement it.* (1987: 29, emphasis added)

From this perspective, the practicalities of strategic management involve processes of bargaining between parties in which decisions are reached that are 'subjectively' acceptable rather than 'objectively' rational. When attention is paid to the practical accomplishment of strategic management, the relevance of 'ask(ing) questions about *the processes of knowing* – those processes that produce the rules by which an "organization" is managed and judged' – becomes apparent (Smircich and Stubbart, 1985: 727, emphasis in original).[11] And when these processes are located in a wider institutional context, it becomes possible to appreciate and address how strategic management is an expression of (senior) managers' efforts to organize, secure or advance their sectional interests in relation to such factors as continued employment, promotion prospects, divisional or departmental empire building, etc. (see Chapter 1). Entrenched ideologies and practices may preclude the consideration of alternative strategies (Whittington, 1989; see also Huff, 1982). The very opportunity to identify, and choose between, alternative strategies is enabled/constrained by the patterns of thought or 'ideology' that make these choices imaginable (Pettigrew, 1985a; Wilson, 1982). This perspective accepts and illustrates the understanding that established assumptions or beliefs held by decision makers routinely shape processes of strategic management. But instead of regarding their recipes and repertoires as forces that are given by the culture of the industry, or forces that can be honed to enhance performance (Grinyer and Spender, 1979; Peters, 1984), attention shifts to consider how strategic recipes are socially constructed and reproduced through *relations of power*; and how, by implication, the transformation of strategic decision making is conditional upon changing these relations (see, for example, Child and Smith, 1987).

'Systemic theorists' of strategy, as Whittington (1993: 28) has described them, contend that strategic management is guided by norms derived from 'the cultural rules of the local society. . . . The internal contests of organizations involve not just the micro-politics of individuals and departments but the social groups, interests and resources of the surrounding context'. In other words, it is argued that in order to understand the

exercise of managerial judgement, it is necessary to appreciate how processes of strategic decision making are enabled and constrained by the play
of wider social forces – forces that are a condition as well as a consequence
of organizational decision makers' judgemental work.

However, to date, processual and institutional studies of strategic management have tended to abstract the politics of strategic decision making
from the wider historical and social contexts of managerial action (see
Wood, 1980). Reference is made to the organizational and sectoral contexts
of decision making but this is largely taken as a given in the analysis of the
empirical material (e.g. Pettigrew, 1985a). The outcome is a recognition and
trivialization of the politics of strategic management (see Alvesson and
Willmott, 1995). Insufficient account is taken of how managers are
positioned by historical forces to assume and maintain a monopoly of
strategic decision-making responsibility (see Chapter 1). And there is
minimal concern to explore how managers' practical reasoning about
corporate strategy is conditioned by politico-economic structures that extend
well beyond the boundaries of any particular organizational sector. There is
little consideration of how managerial values are laden with ideological
assumptions about the 'facts' of strategic management. Corporate strategies
are rarely assessed in terms of their wider impact on society. To address such
issues necessitates a shift from the study of strategic management as a
process of organizational politics to a perspective that locates this process
within the wider context of contemporary capitalist society.

### Strategic Management as Domination

The common limitation of orthodox and processual approaches, from a
critical perspective, is their failure to analyse strategic management as a
condition and consequence of wider, institutionalized forms of domination.
This is most transparent in orthodox accounts of strategic management
where managers are urged to perfect the (technocratic) rationality of their
decision making. When surveying the orthodox literature, one is struck by
the continuity between Frederick Taylor's mission to rationalize the design
of shopfloor work and the efforts of strategic management theorists – such
as Porter (1985), Hamel and Prahalad (1989) and even Pettigrew (1988) –
to generate technocratic methods for building and sustaining a position of
competitive advantage. As Fischer has noted:

> for technocrats, the solution is to replace the 'irrational' decision processes of
> democratic politics (group competition, bargaining, and compromise, in
> particular) with 'rational' empirical/analytical methodologies of scientific
> decision-making ... Nothing is more irrational to technocratic theorists than
> the disjointed, incremental forms of decision-making (typically described as
> 'muddling through') *that result from a political commitment to democratic
> bargaining and compromise.* (1990: 22, emphasis added)

It is, of course, precisely the 'disjointed, incremental' quality of decisions
that advocates of the processual perspective valuably recall and illuminate.

However, as we have stressed, when focusing upon the organizational politics of interaction and negotiation between different individuals and groups of managers, processual analysts of strategic management largely take for granted the structure of domination through which such interactions are socially accomplished. This structure includes the dominant discourses of strategy – processual as well as orthodox – that organizational members are induced to use in order to define and realize their purposes. We now discuss three aspects of domination in the theory and practice of strategic management: the colonizing effects of talk about strategies; practices associated with mergers and/or acquisitions, that weaken or avoid competition; and the issue of power and accountability in strategic decision making.

*Strategy Talk* Debates about what strategy 'is', and how should it properly be understood, take place against the taken-for-granted assumption of the importance of the subject matter. The strategy industry includes a large number of writings – on everything from strategic human resource management to strategic information management – that contributes to the colonization of management thinking and practice by talk of 'strategic' relevance. It could, of course, be argued that the relationship between strategy talk and managerial practice is very loose, but this does not prevent strategy from having a far reaching impact in the ideational world. The colonizing tendency of strategy is productive of some peculiar effects – such as people saying 'strategically important' when by 'strategically' they simply mean important. In an academic seminar, one participant who was conducting research on strategic management confessed that by 'strategic', he just meant 'big' decisions. The term 'strategic' is bandied about to add rhetorical weight, misleadingly one might say, to managerial activity and academic research projects. One could argue that such name calling is innocent and trivial, but the expansion of strategy talk from the military to all sectors of organizational and everyday life has political effects (Knights and Morgan, 1991). Like other discourses that have a colonizing impact, by weakening alternative ways of framing issues and assessing values, its effect is to close rather than open debate. Strategy talk frames issues in a way that privileges instrumental reason; it tends to give the initiative with those who successfully claim to be 'strategists'; it also has clear masculine connotations that reproduce and reinforce gender biases.

When Mintzberg, for example, conceptualizes strategy as 'pattern in a stream of decisions' (1976) it could be said that such processes have little to do with strategy as more conventionally defined (i.e. a plan followed by implementation) or, indeed, that such formulations actively disrupt such conventional wisdom. Nonetheless, such literature uncritically contributes to the construction of strategy as a highly significant phenomenon. Once the idea of strategy becomes established and widely accepted as a primary concern of competent organizational members, it can quickly become an important benchmark for guiding and legitimizing plans and actions.

Among middle and senior managers at least, demonstrable knowledge of the existence, and significance, of 'internal' resources and 'external' constraints becomes a way of displaying competence and suitability for promotion. In effect, the adoption of strategy talk has self-disciplining effects as employees contrive to gain credibility and influence by demonstrating and promoting the relevance of their work for attaining objectives that are deemed to be 'strategic'. As Knights et al. have noted, 'an effect of strategic discourse is to constitute the organization and the individual subject as self-consciously aware of the competitive struggle for power and to render them "open" to techniques of rational control and evaluation in its pursuit' (1991: 9–10).

To the extent that the discourse of strategy is successfully introduced and disseminated by a powerful, managerial élite, it serves to construct (or reinforce) the perceived common-sense understanding that organizations are strategy-driven and that employees outside the strategic core should realize their limited overview and understanding, and subordinate themselves to the implications of the strategy. In turn, this understanding helps to encourage, as well as to justify, the introduction and development of new forms of management control (e.g. Total Quality Management) without careful scrutiny and discussions involving all those concerned. The hegemonic effect of disseminating knowledge and awareness of strategic management among employees may be to weaken employee resistance to techniques of control, and forms of work intensification, that are legitimized on the grounds that they are strategically necessary. Against 'non-traditional' authors (e.g. Mintzberg) who seek to understand strategy in more processual, cultural – even sociological – terms, one could argue that not only different talk about strategy is needed, but also less talk.

*Domination Through Concentration*   The espoused intent of strategic management is to weaken competitive pressures by finding niches, acquiring competitors or expanding vertically. Growth and forms of 'strategic collaboration' are each means of securing economic power. Corporations deploy their resources to stifle innovations which pose a threat to established patterns and interests (Frost and Egri, 1991) as well as to influence government policies and to shape public opinion. An example of how corporate strategies have sought to exploit and control the use of mass media for purposes of marketing products and services is given by Rose, who notes how, in the USA:

> Hill and Knowlton, in 1986 the largest public relations firm, bought the lobbying company owned by Robert K. Gray. Five years later, not to be outdone forever, the public relations firm of Burson-Marsteller bought Black, Manafort, Stone and Kelly, also a lobbying firm. Prior to the purchase of lobbying companies designed to affect the outcome of the passage of laws in legislatures and the U.S. Congress, P.R. companies had endeavoured to affect opinion in mass market audiences through the stories they placed on television and in the print media. Various media conveyed their messages. After the acquisition of (the) lobbying firms, new thinking and new strategies for influencing the public sector were

formulated. I should mention that both Hill and Knowlton and Burson-Marsteller were owned by even more massive advertising agencies and when they acquired lobbying firms, a fuller institutional and utilitarian conceptual order was made possible. *This is called 'integrated marketing'. Now advertising messages can be coupled to public relations campaigns and with lobbying efforts all directed out of the same firm with enormous resources.* (1993: 21–2, our emphasis)

Strategic management, encompassing mergers and acquisitions as well as product and organizational development, can be evaluated in terms of its consequences for establishing centralized economic power as well as suppressing public debate over key politico-economic issues. In general, strategy often aims at reducing competition and increasing corporate control over suppliers as well as markets (Whittington, 1993). There are, therefore, strong reasons to evaluate corporate strategies less one-sidedly in terms of their contributions to corporate profits, and more in terms of a debate about the social good and, most fundamentally, the ecological consequences of the exploitation and depletion of natural resources.

A particularly glaring weakness in most strategic business thinking is its exploitation and/or predatory neglect of the natural environment. In managerial thinking, analysis of 'the environment' is framed in terms of a combination of technological, economic and social factors, with little attention being paid to nature. In effect, nature is assumed to be a free good. This devaluation of the natural environment is somewhat perverse, given that so much organization theory draws more or less explicitly upon biological metaphors, such as organism and population ecology (see especially Chapter 4). However, a few studies in strategic management are now beginning to pay attention to ecological issues (e.g. Shrivastava, 1993; Stead and Stead, 1992) in a way that urges a radical re-thinking of how decision makers in companies relate their activities to ecological concerns – such as the effort to minimize the use of non-renewable supplies of energy and to support policies of sustainable growth. For example, Shrivastava talks about *ecocentric strategic management,* in which the corporation is seen as a part of a living natural environment. Instead of regarding the natural environment as separate from companies and using it as a free receptacle for externalized costs (e.g. waste), an ecological orientation to strategic management demands that full account be taken of how corporate goals, production systems and products interact with ecological systems.

*Power and Accountability in Strategic Management*   The most entrenched obstacles to wider participation in strategic decision making – for consumers and citizens as well as immediate employees – are political, not natural or even technological factors. Orthodox representations of strategic management take for granted institutionalized structures of power – of patriarchy and ethnicity as well as ownership. Processual studies tend to focus upon the local (i.e. organizational and sectoral) dimensions of their reproduction, to the neglect of their societal embeddedness. From a critical perspective, the study of strategic management must make central an investigation of how processes of strategy-making involve an exercise of power over how people interpret reality and develop opinions.

Most writers on strategic management take it for granted that processes of strategic decision making are necessarily and legitimately the monopoly of top management. Yet, there are examples of companies that incorporate groups of employees, or even involve the entire organization, in discussions and decisions on core issues in ways that depart quite radically from established, top-down conceptions of strategic management (e.g. Raspa, 1986; Weisbord, 1987). A minority of writers on strategic management has argued that a bottom-up orientation to strategic management should complement, and be fused with, the top-down direction of strategic management (Bourgeois and Brodwin, 1984; Westley, 1990). So long as those at the top remain largely unaccountable to those at the bottom, this may do little to change the structure of domination within organizations. Nonetheless, calls for a bottom-up orientation can help to highlight the contradiction of excluding those affected by the provision of goods and services from participating directly, and effectively, in processes of strategic decision making.

From a critical perspective, a basic problem with established strategic management theory and practice is the assumption, noted earlier, that senior managers have a legitimate monopoly over processes of strategic decision making; and that their decisions will ensure the best means of generating and allocating technological and human resources. Inadequate account is taken of the diversity of groups – citizens, consumers and employees among others – who may be positively or adversely affected by these decisions. Within orthodox and processual accounts of strategic management, these groups have relevance only when the implementation of strategic plans is understood to depend upon their support or compliance (e.g. the receptivity of consumers to promotions that encourage them to purchase new products). The issue then becomes one of calculating how employee or customer support can be cost-effectively engineered, rather than how their concerns can best be appreciated or addressed.

Strategic management that lacks participation by those who have direct and up-to-date knowledge of the volatility of 'environments' is unable to recognize the on-the-ground knowledge of employees or to secure their full commitment (Nord, 1983). It is, of course, tempting to be dismissive of approaches that encourage employee participation in strategic management on the grounds that they seek to appropriate employee knowledge. Certainly, it is relevant to question whether participative, bottom-up approaches to strategic management are motivated by a commitment to develop industrial democracy rather than a concern to manage the contradictions of capitalist control without changing existing structures of domination (see Chapter 4). Nonetheless, moves to encourage greater participation by employees and other groups in processes of strategic management can be welcomed, especially when they openly recognize that orthodox, top-down, technocratic methods of managing strategy fail to address the social organization of productive activity. However, from a CT point of view, participation is necessary but insufficient. The crucial issue is whether discussion and identification of goals, priorities, values, directions and means for accomplishing objectives is based upon a sufficiently broad set of social as well as economic criteria, and whether these criteria are themselves open to question and reconsideration. Of central interest is the quality of the communicative processes through which such questions are addressed and resolved. We return to these issues in Chapters 7 and 8.

## Summary and Conclusion

Our discussion has challenged the narrow basis of both rational and processual approaches to strategic management. It has been suggested that critical thinking can make a valuable contribution in moving us beyond the 'soft technocratic' framework of processual approaches where wider social and ethical questions are – conveniently – omitted from the agenda of management, and the legitimacy of placing decision making in the hands of an élite of self-appointed experts is unquestioned. Our discussion of organization theory, marketing and strategic management has suggested a number of ways in which critical analysis of established theories can foster the development of new understandings of these specialisms. In particular, CT-inspired analysis of the management specialisms is committed to developing ways of organizing that are more socially responsible in their identification and implementation of strategic objectives. Attention is then focused upon contradictions that harbour a potential for reconsidering goals, questioning means–goals assumptions and enabling new forms of practice.

## Notes

1 For example, we do not provide further coverage of the domain of human resource management from which illustrations were drawn when discussing metaphors in previous chapters.

2 The most obvious example is the impact of Burrell and Morgan's *Sociological Paradigms and Organizational Analysis* (1979) upon the conceptualization of the other specialisms.

3 *Inter alia*, there have been studies that highlight the central role of power and politics (Frost, 1980; Clegg, 1989), class relations and control of the labour process (Braverman, 1974; Knights and Willmott, 1990), ambiguity, confusion and lack of rationality in organizations (Brunsson, 1985), the subjective and interpretative nature of social life and organizations (Silverman, 1970; Czarniawska-Joerges, 1992), culture and symbolism (Alvesson and Berg, 1992; Martin, 1992), and gender issues (Mills and Tancred, 1992). The interested reader is encouraged to consult Reed (1985, 1992), Clegg (1989) and especially Thompson and McHugh (1995) for overviews.

4 Fox (1974), for example, has interpreted the shift from 'unitarism' to 'pluralism' as a sophisticated ideology for 'maintaining the status quo of highly unequal power, wealth and privilege' (ibid.: 282). Widespread acceptance of the status quo, he contends, is more a

reflection of the power of the few to shape the views and priorities of the many than it is an expression of unforced consensus (see Chapter 1). This is not just because employees are forced to earn a living by selling their labour. It is also because the powerful few have control of 'the many agencies of socialization through which conformist attitudes and values are shaped' (ibid.: 284; see also Chapter 4).

5 Pluralist analyses have been plundered by managerialists who argue that conflicts are functional, that they can be managed and, indeed, that they are of critical importance for engineering more effective decisions (Pascale, 1992; Robbins, 1983). Limited forms of conflicts in organizations are then represented as a healthy sign of 'pluralism' – a pluralism that legitimizes managerial authority and is actually or potentially functional for the affirmation of instumental rationality (see Chapter 1).

6 For a discussion of diverse perspectives on ideas on eroticism, sexuality and pleasure in organizations, see Burrell (1984, 1992).

7 See, for example, Alvesson (1994), Anderson (1983, 1986), Belk et al. (1989), Brown (1993), Firat et al. (1987), Muncy and Fisk (1987), Peter (1992) and Peter and Olson (1983).

8 It would seem that, in common with economists, politicians, business and union leaders, marketing academics are caught in a logic of action in which ends most readily associated with quantifiable measures are given priority (Offe and Wiesenthal, 1980), despite the risks attached to this myopia – especially in terms of ecological catastrophes (Shrivastava, 1993; Stead and Stead, 1992).

9 For example, a survey of 1,000 readers of *Company* magazine, reported in the *Observer* (16 October 1994), found that 'given the choice between having £2,000 to spend on clothes, a job promotion, going on holiday, falling in love and losing a stone in weight, more would choose to go shopping than any other option'.

10 Mintzberg identifies diverse patterns of strategy-making that range from the totally deliberate, where deviation is minimal (this parallels the orthodox approach to strategy-making), to the totally emergent, where no plans were made or where planning was impossible given the uncertainty about environmental conditions (Mintzberg and Waters, 1985).

11 Placing 'organization' in scare quotes indicates that the differentiation of the organization from its environment is a product of strategists' social knowledge rather than a reflection of empirical reality (for an elaboration of this argument in relation to discourse on strategy, see Knights, 1992).

# 6

# Critically Assessing Management Specialisms II: Accounting, Information Systems and Operational Research

In this chapter, three of the more quantitative fields of management are examined. In common with the previous chapter, our purpose is to show how critical thinking can provide us with fresh understandings of the specialisms of management. When addressing each of the specialisms – accounting, operational research and information systems – we note how a reliance upon quantification has been complemented and attenuated by a growing appreciation of the 'behaviourial' conditions and consequences of using quantitative techniques. We also consider how, in each field, CT, in particular, has been deployed to challenge orthodox methodologies and to advance a critical alternative to the received wisdom.

## Accounting

Accounting is conventionally viewed as a rather dry, unexciting field of management that is concerned with the technicalities of measuring and reporting economic values, as exemplified by the practices of bookkeeping and external reporting. It is understood to comprise the principles and methods used to record transactions and prepare statements about assets, liabilities, costs, profits, etc.

Within accounting, a basic division can be made between its internal provision of management information and external reporting. The former is concerned with methods favoured within particular enterprises to monitor and control costs associated with the accumulation or transfer of economic values. It is termed 'management accounting' because its principal function is deemed to be the support of management decision making (Arnold and Hope, 1983). Calculating and recording the cost of materials or machinery, or the unit-cost of producing goods, are examples of the focal concerns of management accounting. Financial accounting, in contrast, is concerned with the preparation of information to relevant people outside the organization – notably creditors, shareholders and tax authorities – although these figures may also be relevant to other parties, such as employees seeking to improve the terms and conditions of the sale of their labour. As conventionally defined, the purpose of financial accounting is to supply a quantified report or picture – principally in the balance sheet and profit and loss account – of the financial standing of an organization. Despite an established division between management and financial accounts, they are related as the former frequently provides the raw information from which financial accounts are derived; and those who audit financial accounts can make recommendations about the internal production of management accounting information.

## The Behaviourial Dimension of Accounting

On the face of it, accounting can appear to be a straightforward, mechanical activity, comparable to basic mathematics. Indeed, it is quite often gently ridiculed, not least by accountants themselves, as 'score-keeping' or 'bean counting'. This metaphor suggests that accountants, as independent and impartial observers, simply monitor and record the scores in a game played by other players. However, the mundane unproblematical appearance of accounting is deceptive. Despite an image of objectivity, accounting is founded upon contestable conventions; and the construction, meaning and implications of its figures are always subject to contest and interpretation.

To elaborate briefly upon the 'game' metaphor, it is relevant to note that players in business do not necessary accept the current methods of keeping score (for a broader discussion of the use of metaphors, see Chapter 4). The players may seek to influence how the scoring is conducted and what is recorded. Not infrequently, the very playing of the game is influenced by how accountants keep score as the players identify the easiest way to make an impact upon the relevant, most visible performance measures. For example, the way that a budgeting system is designed and operated can have non-trivial consequences upon the allocation of resources between specialisms of management or upon how the performance of managers (in keeping to budget) is assessed. Once it is recognized that accounting principles and methods are 'mere conventions' that construct economic reality in particular ways, rather than as mirrors that faithfully reflect reality (Hines, 1988), it becomes possible to appreciate better how accounting standards that, in principle, reduce the scope for 'subjectivity' are produced through a process of debate and contestation in which there is always one (or more) rival way of proceeding from currently accepted methods; and that effective lobbying can have very considerable implications for the levels of performance or profit that are recorded.[1]

When the social and organizational contexts of accounting are recognized, it becomes possible to appreciate how techniques – such as budgeting or costing – are developed and applied through *the medium of organizational relationships* in which different groups are engaged in a *political* process of supporting or resisting different ways of constructing and interpreting accounts. With regard to internal management accounting, this concern has been explored through the development of what has been labelled a 'behaviourial' perspective. Borrowing heavily from organization theory (see

Chapter 4), this perspective has explored the relationship between accounting techniques and the psychological and organizational variables that are deemed to condition their development and use. For example, behaviourial accounting research has studied how local conditions or 'cultures' selectively adapt and apply accounting techniques such as budgeting (e.g. Argyris, 1952; Wildavsky, 1968; Hopwood, 1972; Rosenberg et al., 1982).

Within behaviourial accounting, considerable attention has been focused upon the question of how different configurations of accounting practice are associated with variables (or contingencies) that are deemed to determine their effectiveness in improving organizational performance (see Otley, 1980 for an early review). An alternative, more sociologically informed, approach has endeavoured to appreciate how accounting techniques – such as budgeting – are actually interpreted and negotiated in organizations (Colville, 1981). This approach, which has strong affinities with the interpretive paradigm (see Chapter 2), has addressed the ways that accounting practices are shaped and operated through the medium of organizational members' diverse values and priorities (see Chua, 1988 for a review).

A broadly similar pattern is discernable in financial accounting. Here too, the socially constructed character of accounts has become an increasingly influential focus of attention. Fuelled by the lack of effective accounting regulation, coupled to the development and complexity of international business, there has been considerable scope for an expansion of 'creative accounting' (Smith, 1992). Associated with such developments, there has been a growth in studies that examine how principles and methods of external reporting are determined and enforced.[2]

From these brief remarks, it can be seen that accounting is not inherently the dry discipline that it is often assumed to be. Without suggesting the existence of a conspiracy, it is interesting to note that accountants have little incentive to debunk or discourage this understanding. This is not just because their training urges them to believe in it (Power, 1991), but because the conventional image of accounting as a technical, score-keeping activity inhibits critical scrutiny. So long as accounting appears to be purely technical, concerned only with varieties 'scorekeeping', there seems to be very little of interest to catch the critical eye. It is therefore somewhat surprising to discover that, of all the fields of management, accounting has been subjected to the most vigorous and extended critical examination (Morgan and Willmott, 1993).[3]

*Towards a Critical Perspective on Accounting*

We have already noted how, even among fairly 'mainstream' accounting academics, there has been a growing interest in understanding how accounting techniques and procedures are developed and used within the context of organizations and society. In a seminal paper that highlights the value of situating accounting in its social and organizational contexts,

Burchell et al. (1980) begin by noting how accounting has come to occupy a dominant position in the functioning of modern societies. Among its many roles, accounting is seen to act as a definer, regulator and monitor of economic performance within private and public sectors. It is also an adjudicator in the distribution of resources, and a key contributor to national and corporate planning. Finally, it is a principal medium in the construction of organizational realities, including the attribution of a specific, quantifiable identity and self-understanding to employees (Miller and O'Leary, 1987).

Burchell et al. (1980) directly challenge the idea that accounting is a passive reflector (or scorekeeper) of economic reality, arguing that it should be recognized as both a product and a producer of socio-political processes. This view, which echoes our earlier emphasis upon the motivation of the players in relation to the activity of the so-called scorekeepers, is dramatically expressed in their thesis that the appropriate metaphor for accounting is *not* that of an 'answering machine' that simply records what is fed into it. Rather, the more relevant metaphor is that of the 'ammunition machine' that is developed and refined in struggles between different groups in the belief that accounting can best advance their most cherished beliefs or privileges (ibid.: 15).

Burchell et al. (1980) associate accounting procedures with mechanisms of social and organizational control developed to deal with 'the conflictive nature of organizational life'. But they are decidedly vague on the question of how the politics of accounting should be analysed. Reference is made to the work of pluralists (e.g. Cyert and March, 1963; Pettigrew, 1973; Pfeffer, 1978, see Chapter 1) who argue that more effective managerial control, and improved performance, can be achieved by acknowledging, and managing, the existence of competing interests within organizations. However, in pluralistic analysis, there is a vagueness about how to theorize power relations within organizations (see Chapters 1 and 4). Burchell et al. (1980) tend to abstract the study of the politics of organizations from the wider, historical context of the political economy in which accounting practices are developed and legitimized (Tinker, 1980, 1985). Despite connecting accounting practices to Weber's (1968) discussion of the growing dominance of formal rationality, based upon quantitative measures of efficiency, the development of this rationality is disconnected from an appreciation of the political struggles through which accounting's contemporary influence has been promoted and resisted. Burchell et al. make only passing references to Braverman (1974) and to Foucault (1977), and make no mention at all of the potential relevance of Critical Theory for illuminating the social significance of accounting, as a medium and outcome of instrumental reason masquerading (or interpreted) as a value-free 'answering machine'.

Since the early 1980s, the theoretical vacuum in critical accounting scholarship has been filled by a diversity of theories and perspectives that have presented equally diverse challenges to narrow, technicist treatments of accounting theory and practice.[4] In addition to Critical Theory, critical accounting academics have drawn upon structuralist Marxism (e.g. Tinker et al., 1982; Tinker, 1980, 1985), labour process analysis (e.g. Hopper et al., 1987; Armstrong, 1987) and Foucauldianism (e.g. Hopwood, 1987; Miller and O'Leary, 1987), as well as studies that are more synthetic or eclectic in orientation (e.g. Lehman, 1992; for overviews of their respective contributions, see Chua, 1986; Roslender, 1990, 1992; Puxty, 1993 and Morgan and Willmott, 1993a).

## Critical Theory and Accounting

Structuralist Marxism, labour process analysis and Foucauldianism all have some affinities with Critical Theory (see Chapter 2). They broadly share a 'radical change' conception of society: power and domination, rather than consensus and community, are at the centre of social and economic relationships – including the theory and practice of accounting.[5] Structuralist Marxism and orthodox labour process analysis anticipate a process of radical transformation, a change that is provoked by the exploitative and unstable structure of capitalist society and struggled for by the organized working class. Both Critical Theory and Foucauldianism, in contrast, have serious doubts about the revolutionary credentials of the working class. Foucault urges us to recognize the indivisibility of knowledge and power, and to remain sceptical, if not pessimistic, about the prospects of a domination-free society (see Chapter 7). Critical Theory, in its Habermasian formulation at least, pins its hopes upon a more diffuse and sustained process of emancipatory change, guided by critical reason and non-distorted communication, that is propelled by the agency of diverse social movements (see Chapter 3).

Although comparatively small in number, at least when compared to studies of accounting informed by structural Marxism and Foucauldianism, there now exists a growing body of accounting research that draws upon Critical Theory.[6] In the main, the influence of CT upon this work has been confined to the work of Habermas, with little sustained interest being shown in the writings of Horkheimer, Adorno or Marcuse to enrich the radical critique of accounting (although see Laughlin, 1987: 484).

Arrington and Puxty (1991) take up a recurrent theme of Habermas' analyses – that 'technical' work is inescapably grounded in the 'practical' or 'moral' realm of social relations (see Chapters 2 and 3) – to suggest that Critical Theory provides the most relevant and penetrating critical resource for remembering accounting as 'a form of moral action' (ibid.: 48). Accounting, they argue, represents the social action of economic life through the '"delinguistified" media of money' (ibid.). As such, it is a very fertile ground for empirical inquiry into distortions in communicative rationality. The hidden moral quality of accounting, they propose, can be revealed by undertaking studies that appreciate how, in practice, accounting information is routinely produced, mobilized and contested in the pursuit of particular values and interests. To this end, Arrington and Puxty commend the use of Habermas' discussion of formal pragmatics as a conceptual framework for reinterpreting existing research and guiding future studies of the empirical realm of accounting practice (see also Puxty, 1991). Their suggestion is that Habermas' ideas could be used to explore *'how* interests are in fact adjudicated in accounting and *how* particular accounting acts do and must transpire with both empowering and pathological consequences' (ibid.: 51). In this way, accounting theory and practice is identified as an important empirical site for understanding and challenging how communications are shaped within, and distorted by, asymmetrical relations of power (see also Power and Laughlin, 1992).[7]

The fullest case for using Critical Theory in accounting research has been made by Laughlin (e.g. 1987, 1991; Laughlin and Broadbent, 1993). It is argued that CT provides a powerful vehicle 'through which understanding about reality can be achieved and transformation of concrete institutions [can] occur' (Laughlin, 1987: 482). The particular merit of Critical Theory, Laughlin contends, is that it is directly geared to the practical concern to change the world without recourse to the simplifications and historicism of structuralist Marxism. Moving beyond earlier applications of Habermas' ideas that simply critique the limitations of alternative methodologies (e.g. Willmott, 1983), Laughlin advocates the development of a research programme that takes full advantage of the insights generated by Habermas' (1984, 1987b) more recent writings on universal pragmatics and juridification.[8]

Laughlin (1991) applies a Habermasian framework to explore the use and potency of accounting in the operation of steering mechanisms that facilitate and legitimize the colonization of lifeworld values and practices. Specifically, Laughlin commends the relevance of Habermas' distinction between the self-formative 'lifeworld', where norms and values concerning 'ends' (e.g. personal creeds) are dominant and, in contrast, formalized 'systems' where purposive-rational calculations about the effectiveness of 'means' (e.g. the design of jobs) are central, and where 'steering media' (e.g. the law) direct the development of the 'systems' – including their colonization of processes through which the norms and values of the lifeworld are developed and sustained (see Chapter 4).

For example, Laughlin shows how, in the case of European Railways (Dent, 1986b), traditional engineering values – which identified the soundness and quality of engineering practice as the essential activity and skill of running railways – were challenged and marginalized by the increasing application of financial criteria in decision making about how the railway should be run. New forms of accountability introduced during the 1980s, Laughlin argues, acted to undermine the established (lifeworld) engineering craft values of railway workers, in which 'financial considerations were secondary', as a much stronger emphasis was placed upon the design and operation of effective and profitable systems of management control (Dent, 1986a: 27, quoted in Laughlin, 1991). In this example, the increasing deployment of accounting techniques in management decision making in

European Railways is seen to have problematized and undermined the rationality of established values. Traditional operational and engineering concerns were translated into 'the profit calculus' and railway matters 'came to be reinterpreted through the accounting thereof' (1991: 228; cf. Broadbent et al., 1991 where a similar analysis is applied to the UK's National Health Service). The lifeworld of the railway(wo)men was disrupted and severely damaged, Laughlin argues, as systemic rules were imposed – in the form of abstract accounting measures and controls. Laughlin's key argument is that established accounting disciplines did not act neutrally to facilitate the reproduction or survival of the existing lifeworld by enabling its practices to become more efficient or effective. Rather, their introduction tended to be corrosive of established lifeworld values.

The European Railways example is helpfully contrasted by Laughlin (1991) with the case of the Church of England where, despite a continuing resource crisis, accounting was found to play a secondary role. In contrast to the railways, Laughlin argues, the lifeworld values of the Church have been largely preserved because, he suggests, in this context the corrosive potential of an accounting mentality has, to date, been successfully resisted. Other examples fall between these extremes, but nonetheless illustrate the tensions between norms and values concerning 'ends' and purposive-rational calculations about the effectiveness of 'means' – such as the recent struggles by public sector workers in the UK, notably medics and teachers, to frustrate or circumvent the accounting logic of unit-costs in an effort to protect and preserve welfare and educational values. (For a more developed analysis that focuses upon recent reforms in health and education institutions in the UK, where accounting is identified as an 'active partner' in the possible disintegration of established 'organizational lifeworlds', see Laughlin and Broadbent, 1993.)

More recently, Laughlin and Broadbent have turned their attention to building more prescriptive models which are drawn from Critical Theory. Rather than simply showing how particular expressions of accounting are inappropriate and are being resisted, as in their public sector work, they have tried to speculate on what enlightened and enabling accounting would look like. They have also used Habermasian work to build a critical evaluatory process for the public sector reforms that they have been analysing over the last few years (see Laughlin and Broadbent, 1994). While this work is still only in its early stages, it promises to provide an important dimension of the Critical Theory research programme in accounting.

## Information Systems

There is a considerable and increasing degree of overlap between the fields of accounting and (management) information systems, particularly as management accountants seek to extend the boundaries of their expertise

(Earl, 1983). Management accounting systems provide information and, consequently, there can be something of a struggle for control over the design and operation of management information systems. What is distinctive about Information Systems (IS) is its *computer-based* provision of information and its aspirations to provide information support for *all* management functions – from accounting to personnel.

Using computer power, it is theoretically possible to gain instant access to diverse sources of information – not only to changes in 'the environment' (see Chapter 5), such as sales information on different products, but also information on every operation within the organization, including the performance of each department and even each employee. There is also enormous potential for the development of shared networks between organizations, although their realization and implementation is often impeded as well as promoted by competitive pressures (Knights et al., 1993). Although the focus of IS to date has been principally upon the hardware and software of computer science, it has become increasingly concerned with the 'behaviourial context' and organizational media of IS applications. In this respect, it parallels developments within other areas of management practice.

*The Behavioural Dimension of Information Systems*

In principle, the IS specialism aspires to take responsibility for the computer-based processes through which information in organizations is collected, stored, manipulated and accessed. Its objective is to apply computer and behavioural science to make this process more systematic and, in recent years, more 'user-friendly'. However, most effort in IS has been directed towards the abstracted modelling of information systems which are then imposed, as it were, upon organizations. In this process, the users of the systems have, until quite recently, been largely excluded from processes of design and development on the grounds that they lack relevant IS expertise, and are therefore unable to make any relevant contribution (Murray and Willmott, 1993). This situation is gradually changing in response to the substantive irrationalities – that is, failures – of formally rational systems. Because the designers of the systems have often concentrated on the perfection of the technology, to the neglect of the 'needs' of the users, the outcome has frequently been the development of cumbersome, user-hostile systems that fall well short of the effective and efficient systems that were promised. The shift from mainframe operations to the client-server networking of PCs has further hastened this development.

Problems encountered in making systems work have enhanced the credibility of behaviourally-oriented IS research. Much of this work has been preoccupied with the effective integration of social and technical systems (e.g. Bostrom and Heinen, 1977; Mumford, 1983). As in the case of other management specialisms, this has shifted attention away from the technical and towards the behavioural dimensions of systems design

(Walsham, 1993). *Inter alia*, the examination of the organizational politics of designing and implementing information systems has been stimulated (e.g. Robey and Farrow, 1982); and an awareness of the struggles between different specialist managers over the control and use of these systems has increased (Knights and Murray, 1994). However, in common with behavioural studies that have developed in other areas of management, interpretive treatments of issues of power have been criticized for failing to penetrate the institutional and ideological barriers to improved forms of communication and organization (see Elkjaer et al., 1992; Murray and Willmott, 1993).

### Towards a Critical Perspective on Information Systems

An interest in the political and processual aspects of IS has grown as their non-benign use and effects have become better recognized and understood (for an overview of work in the field, see Orlikowski and Baroudi, 1989). Instead of seeing IS simply as a means of providing more detailed, speedier and more reliable information, systems are increasingly viewed as changing and often tightening the ways in which activity within organizations is monitored and controlled (e.g. Sewell and Wilkinson, 1992). To take a comparatively trivial example, the computerization of supermarket checkouts can supply immediate and reliable information about the sale of goods which assist the process of re-stocking. But this innovation also presents an opportunity for management to monitor the speed, accuracy and honesty of checkout operators. As the potential of IS as surveillance systems is recognized and exploited, a 'darker' side of their development and implementation becomes more evident.

Partly because IS is a new field and partly because it has been dominated by computer engineers and systems analysts, who are interested in developing the power and elegance of their machines and methods, critical reflection upon the social and political significance of IS has been rather limited. An early but influential exception is Weizenbaum's *Computer Power and Human Reason* (1976). A computer expert, Weizenbaum highlights the potential of IS to deny reason and extend the abuse of power. Familiar with, and informed by, the insights of Critical Theory (see especially pp. 249 *et seq.*), Weisenbaum highlights a number of possible social dysfunctions of our increasing dependence upon computer-produced information. Commenting upon the use of computers in the Vietnam War (let alone the Gulf War, where their use enabled TV spectators to attend to the conflict less as war involving massive loss of life and perhaps more as something comparable to a game of virtual reality space invaders), Weizenbaum observes that:

> When the American President decided to bomb Cambodia and to keep that decision secret from the American Congress, the computers in the Pentagon were 'fixed' to transform the genuine strike reports coming in from the field into the false reports to which government leaders were given access. George Orwell's Ministry of Truth had become mechanised. . . .

Weizenbaum continues:

> Not only have decision-makers abdicated their decision-making responsibility to a technology they do not understand – though all the while maintaining the illusion that they, the policy makers, are formulating policy questions and answering them – but responsibility has altogether evaporated. . . . The enormous computer systems in the Pentagon and their counterparts elsewhere in our culture have, in a very real sense, no authors. Thus, they do not admit of any questions of right or wrong, of justice, or of any theory with which one can agree or disagree. They provide no basis on which 'what the machine says' can be challenged. (Weizenbaum, 1976: 238–40)

To be clear, Weizenbaum is not suggesting that computers should be programmed to make judgements. Nor is he denying that the 'fixing' of computers is done by human beings, not computers. Rather, he is arguing that computer power can and does exert an insidious influence upon how people – particularly powerful people – are able to think, make decisions and act. Though not inevitable, the effect of this power, he argues, tends to reinforce a myth of technological rationality and inevitability in which moral choices between alternative ends become reduced to a decisionistic process that is exclusively concerned with the computer-assisted calculation of means (see Chapter 1). A major difficulty with IS, Weizenbaum argues, is the widespread technocratic understanding that a continuous expansion and refinement of computer systems is an inescapable part of human progress, progress that is driven ever onward by what appears to be the impersonal march of science.

> Technological inevitability can be seen to be a mere element of a much larger syndrome. Science promised man power. But, as often happens when people are seduced by promises of power, the price exacted in advance and all along the path, and the price actually paid, is servitude and impotence. Power is nothing if it is not the power to choose. Instrumental reason can make decisions, but there is all the difference in the world between deciding and choosing. (ibid.: 259)

Weizenbaum's central point is that the development and use of computers has tended to reflect and reinforce an instrumental conception of reason in which making choices between competing ends (e.g. using computers or not using them; using them selectively in ways that preserve the status quo or using them in ways that question the status quo, etc.) is subordinated to making decisions about how their power, speed, reliability, etc. could be increased – often 'for the morally bankrupt reason that "If we don't do it, someone else will"' (ibid.: 252–3).

Although highly critical of the ways that computing technology is used, it is relevant to note that Weizenbaum does not reject the use of computers or even the efforts being made to increase their power and speed. Rather, he calls for the development of *critical* reason (as contrasted with instrumental reason) so that it becomes both possible and desirable to exercise human, democratic judgement about how computer power may be most effectively used for human purposes. Or, as Weizenbaum puts it: 'The alternative to the kind of rationality that sees the solution to world problems in psychotechnology is not mindlessness. It is reason restored to human dignity, to authenticity, to self-esteem, and to individual autonomy' (ibid.).

Of course, the meaning of 'dignity' or 'authenticity' is not uncontested. Just as it is problematical to reify the meaning of 'science' (see Chapter 2), the meaning of 'autonomy' is properly a subject for critical interrogation that reveals the embeddedness within a peculiarly modern conception of the individual (Winograd and Flores, 1986; see also Chapter 7). However, if we are to follow the tradition of Critical Theory, it is to be stressed that this Enlightenment conception of the nature and rights of the individual is worth valuing and defending – a defence that must also allow, rather than deny, a full recognition of its historical relativity.

## Critical Information Systems

From the perspective of Critical Theory, the challenge of developing a more rational society is not principally a technical one, involving the design and implementation of more powerful systems of control (e.g. the development of management information systems). Rather, the challenge is fundamentally social and political. It involves the transformation of institutions so that computer power acts to facilitate emancipation rather than preserve the status quo. This challenge has been taken up by a small but growing number of IS specialists who have drawn upon CT, especially the work of Habermas, to develop a critical alternative to mainstream, instrumental forms of IS theory and practice (e.g. Klein, 1986; Klein and Hirschheim, 1985; for an overview, see Lyytinen, 1992).

The application of CT in IS is comparatively recent and is still at an early stage. It has yet to progress much beyond a critique of existing approaches to systems development. This has been done either by drawing upon Habermas' theory of knowledge-constitutive interests, as outlined in Chapter 2 (e.g. Klein and Lyytinen, 1985; Lyytinen and Klein, 1985), or by commending Habermas' more recent work on communication (see Chapter 3) as a promising, but as yet untested, approach to the study of IS (Lyytinen and Hirschheim, 1988). The critique of conventional IS has challenged its epistemological and ontological assumptions, along similar lines to the objections raised by Weizenbaum (see above). For example, when attacking the mainstream conception of information systems as scientistic, Klein and Lyytinen (1985: 143) argue that 'the separation of information systems goals from human purpose and the identification of data with measurable facts conceals the real nature of information systems as social communication systems'; and that, 'under scientism, science, rather than being a critical conscience and teacher of practice, becomes its myopic servant' (ibid.: 151).

To counter the dominance of instrumental, scientistic reason within IS, Klein and Lyytinen (1985) commend two changes in the orientation of the IS community. First, they argue for a broadening of the education and training of IS specialists so as to increase awareness of the relativity and poverty of 'the scientistic paradigm' (cf. Hirschheim and Klein, 1989). Teachers of IS are asked to recognize and honour a responsibility for grasping and disseminating a plurality of approaches to IS development, including those informed by Critical Theory. This education and training, Klein and Lyytinen contend, should incorporate a consideration of 'the ethical-moral position which legitimizes preferred tools and methods as "good" and which is to guide their application' (ibid.: 152).[9] Second, when turning to consider the practice of IS, Klein and Lyytinen (1985) invoke the Jeffersonian dictum that the powers of society are best put in the hands of the people. From this position, they urge that systems designers should engage in a dialogue with the users of IT, the users being not just those who operate IT within organizations but everyone who is an end-user. They note that the prevailing philosophy and practice of IS does not permit users to exercise discretion over the development and use of IT, and comment: 'if industry leaders cannot explain how their approach to system design differs from that practised in totalitarian societies (e.g. by being able to demonstrate how they design systems with the people for the people by the people), then the Western world is in trouble' (ibid.: 154). Relatedly, it is suggested that movement in a Jeffersonian direction can be facilitated by industry leaders becoming more open to studies that provide insights into the practical, processual operation of IS.

A good indication of CT's potential for studying and transforming IS is to be found in the work of Hirschheim and Klein (1989), where they draw upon the Burrell and Morgan paradigmatic framework (see Chapter 2) to identify the distinctive contribution of CT to IS development in comparison to diverse other approaches.[10] Following Habermas, Hirschheim and Klein's (1989) basic argument is that the legitimacy of system objectives and design is dependent upon a process of free and open communication, guided by an appreciation of the presence and value of each of the three knowledge-constitutive interests identified by Habermas (1972) – in production and control, mutual understanding and emancipation (see Chapter 2). In this formulation, the goal of IS design and development would be to enable:

> [the] institutionalization of an ideal speech situation which in turn validates a consensus about system objectives and modes of design and implementation. The ideal speech situation would legitimate a moving balance between the fundamental three objectives of information systems development, namely improved technical control, better mutual understanding and continued emancipation from unwarranted social constraints and psychological compulsions. (Hirschheim and Klein, 1989: 1209)

Hirschheim and Klein (ibid.) recognize that Habermas' conception of the ideal speech situation (see Chapter 3) is indeed an ideal that may never be fully implemented; and that, in practice, people may be unwilling or unable to engage in open debate or change their behaviour. Nonetheless, they suggest that it can be used as a benchmark for assessing the quality of IS design and legitimizing its implementation. A number of ways of mitigating socially unnecessary impediments to, and distortions of, rational discourse are suggested. These include the reorganization of systems development processes so as to encourage 'rational motivations to participate, share and elicit missing information'; the introduction of conferencing systems that 'motivate people to contribute their expertise'; and the design of information systems that would 'motivate people to communicate criticisms and radical change proposals by shielding them from the threats of the powerful' (ibid.: 1209; see also Hirschheim and Klein, 1994).

This 'wish list' has yet to be translated into a series of empirical studies or methodologies of change. As Lyytinen (1992: 175) has observed, 'more detailed and explicit critical studies of ID development' are required if CT is to penetrate the IS community as a viable research approach. Perhaps the most receptive audience in the field of IS for Habermas' ideas on communication is likely to be in Computer-Supported Cooperative Work (CSCW) where there has been a greater openness to social theory (see, for example, Bannon et al., 1991 and especially Dietz and Widdershoven, 1991). In commending the relevance of Critical Theory to IS specialists, Lyytinen suggests that they could usefully pay greater attention to developments in other management disciplines where such work is rather more advanced (e.g. Forester, 1992; see Chapter 4), and where CT-influenced studies have borrowed from traditions and theorists whose work provides more assistance in researching concrete practices. Specifically, Lyytinen (1992: 175) identifies work developed within the specialism of operational research (e.g. Ulrich, 1983, 1988) as relevant 'for elaborating a critical methodology of IS development'.[11] It is to this specialist field that our attention now turns.

## Operational Research

The origins of operational research (OR, which in North America is more commonly known as operations research) lie in military operations where mathematical models were developed in an effort to identify the most efficient method of deploying available weaponry, supplies and manpower (see Checkland, 1983 and Rosenhead, 1989 for summaries). It is also the case that a number of the key figures in the early history of OR regarded its development as a scientific means of creating a planned, socialist society based upon the efficient husbandry and use of scarce resources (Mingers, 1992a). However, this early idealism has subsequently been marginalized within the discipline of OR, though it has recently experienced a modest revival in the form of 'community OR' (Parry and Mingers, forthcoming; *Dragon*, 1987). Commenting upon this history, Tinker and Lowe (1984) have observed how the discipline 'has lost much of the vitality and vision it had a decade ago. It languishes in a morass of technical specialization; it lacks overall coherence, and direction' (see also Tinker and Lowe, 1982).[12]

OR techniques have been most widely adopted by industry and government – often applying computer power – to develop more effective
systems, such as those designed to improve logistics, stock control and
manpower planning. In the process, Mingers (1992a: 93) comments, 'Messy
and complex problems were reduced to that which the technique could
handle, and people were just another component of the system like
machines and money. OR's "solutions" gained their legitimacy through
their supposed scientificity as embodied in the idea of optimality.' However,
disillusionment subsequently set in as the mathematical models developed
by OR specialists were perceived to be remote from, and frequently
irrelevant to, managing an increasingly complex and changeable world. A
concentration upon the perfection of mathematical technique had the
unintended effect of reducing the influence and contribution of OR to
managerial decision making. Accountants and, more recently, information
systems specialists have been viewed as possessing more relevant (e.g.
'behavioural') knowledge and skills, and a more pragmatic orientation, for
undertaking tasks that had previously been undertaken by OR specialists
(Bain, 1992).

### 'Soft' OR

The response of OR specialists has been divided. Some have been content
to concentrate their efforts in limited fields where their models continue to
have some purchase – such as in queuing theory or in stock control. Others
have sought to broaden OR methodology to encompass 'soft' factors that
had been excluded from the 'hard', quantified models. A variety of approaches and techniques has been developed (e.g. Ackoff, 1979; Checkland,
1981; Eden, 1989; reviewed in Mingers, 1992a), all of which share the
concern to appreciate the interactive, messy nature of most real-world
activities and problems. Of these, Checkland's (1981) 'soft systems methodology' (SSM) is perhaps the most theoretically sophisticated and influential.

SSM departs from 'hard' methodologies by arguing that systems models
do not, and cannot, capture or map the world that they study. At best, they
can provide one possible language for communicating about this world.
The purpose of SSM is to appreciate and model how different actors
working within a particular situation (e.g. a company or a department)
interpret and communicate their sense of reality. Whereas 'hard' systems
thinking studies the world as something that is given, and is accessible
through the use of scientific methods, SSM studies this world as the continuously negotiated outcome of interactions between people who mobilize
diverse interpretive frameworks. The 'messiness' of much problem-solving
is understood in terms of shifting negotiations, where there is frequently no
common and shared definition of what the problem is or of the
appropriateness of alternative solutions. The value of SSM, it is claimed,
resides in its capacity to model the diversity and complexity of these
interpretative frameworks and thereby to facilitate a process of dialogue by

enabling different groups to appreciate how others see the world, with the anticipation that, by engendering greater mutual understanding, consensus will be reached on the nature of the problem and how it is to be effectively solved.

Paralleling critiques developed within other specialisms of management, 'soft' thinking has been attacked for its failure to deal adequately with issues of power and conflicts of interest. Lacking in SSM, its critics argue, is an understanding of how different interpretive frameworks are historically embedded in, and sustained by, relations of domination and exploitation (for a review, see Willmott, 1989). When this shortcoming is acknowledged, it is evident that attaining consensus between different groups is likely to require a radical transformation of these relations. Otherwise, whatever agreements may emerge are likely to be conditioned by the position of comparative dependence or autonomy of some groups in relation to others. Views will not be freely formed, developed or expressed: since their meaning is embedded in the power relations from which they derive their plausibility and force, few 'communication problems' are likely to be fully resolved by modelling meanings in the way that SSM proposes.

## Critical OR

Initially, critiques of the neglect of the material conditions of OR theory and practice came from the tradition of structuralist Marxism and labour process analysis (e.g. Hales, 1974; Rosenhead and Thunhurst, 1982). More recently, these have been joined, and perhaps overshadowed, by OR specialists who have commended CT as a resource for advancing critical OR theory and practice.[13] There has been considerable debate about how critical OR might best be formulated and advanced.[14] As with the specialisms of accounting and IS, the banner of Critical Theory has been carried in OR by a fairly small group of active researchers.[15] These critics have often taken some version of 'soft' thinking as a point of departure for advancing what they deem to be a more adequate approach that takes appropriate account of power and domination in processes of decision making. Particularly influential is the work of Jackson who argues that 'the kind of unconstrained debate envisaged (by Checkland's SSM) cannot possibly take place. The actors bring to the discussion unequal intellectual resources and are more or less powerful. . . . The result of the inequalities of power is that the existing social order, from which power is drawn, is reproduced' (1982: 25).

From a critical perspective, the consensus identified or encouraged through the use of 'soft' methodologies is viewed with suspicion. Little confidence is placed in the agreements reached since these are understood often to take shape within asymmetrical relations of power that inhibit the open formation and expression of views. However, with the possible exception of Flood and Jackson's (1992) approach, which draws heavily upon Ulrich's Critical Systems Heuristics (CSH, see below), critical OR, in common with the IS specialism, has yet to move far beyond reflection upon the epistemological foundations of OR.

One of the most developed attempts to apply Habermas' ideas has been made by Ulrich (1983, 1988). Briefly, Ulrich's thesis is that all statements – such as those made by managers or public planners – are necessarily founded upon unjustified judgements about the world. The intent of his Critical Systems Heuristics (CSH) is to press those in positions of authority to make transparent, and thereby make available for further interrogation, the normative basis of their policies and statements. By employing reason 'polemically' to recall how all statements rest upon undeclared 'break-offs' of justification, it is intended that authorities become provoked into articulating the values and assumptions upon which their claims are based – the objective of CSH being to facilitate debate about the adequacy and legitimacy of these claims. In this way, Ulrich (1988) contends, the understandings of Critical Theory, concerning the relationship between knowledge and power, are transformed from 'a mere research program into a practical tool of critical social inquiry and design (ibid.: 155).

CSH itself makes no claim to enjoy a privileged access to the truth. Its critical intent is not to reveal the falseness of others' claims by contrasting them with the truth of CSH. Rather, its objective is to develop the conditions in which a plurality of parties can be reminded that their diverse positions have in common a basis in some undeclared 'break-off' which can be clarified only by challenging their authority. In principle, Ulrich (1983: 74) argues, 'the polemical employment of reason secures to both sides an equal position for reasonable dialogue' (see Flood and Jackson, 1991b for an application and evaluation of CSH; and for a dismissive treatment of CSH and the claims of CT more generally, see Tsoukas, 1992 – of which more below). However, Ulrich's thesis is somewhat disingenuous since the *effect* of CSH, if not its intent, is to deconstruct the position of those whose authority is most widely accepted or deeply entrenched (see Willmott, 1989, 1995b). It is likely that these authorities will also feel, rightly or wrongly, that they have much to lose from a dialogue that tenaciously questions their claims. If, as Ulrich argues, statements are founded upon unjustified judgements, it is to be expected that authorities will strenuously resist efforts to make these more transparent. Emperors do not willingly admit their nakedness! Even if authorities are privately persuaded by the arguments of CSH, they are unlikely to give strong support to its public application (see Payne, 1992). An adequate critical study of management must squarely face up to the likelihood of this response (see Chapter 8 for a fuller discussion of CSH).

To overcome resistance to change, a methodology of emancipation informed by the insights of CT must openly acknowledge, and work with, the tensions and contradictions within power relations, as experienced by those who are privileged and those underprivileged by these relations. For example, while recognizing that there will be resistance from those in positions of authority, it is necessary to appreciate how each 'side' is a victim and a perpetrator of unnecessarily oppressive social arrangements and cultural traditions. Mingers (1992a) reaches broadly similar conclusions when he suggests that Habermas' highly abstract formulation of the organization of power must be complemented by approaches that are more directly concerned with the study of concrete practices and processes, a view that is also expressed by Lyytinen (1992) in relation to IS.

### Addressing the Backlash

Finally, before concluding this chapter, it is relevant to take note of the sweeping critique of Critical Systems Thinking, and of Critical Theory more generally, advanced by Tsoukas (1992, 1993). Although Tsoukas directs his fire at the use of CT in OR, a similar tirade could be launched against its application in other realms of management studies reviewed in this and the previous chapter. We do not have the space here to summarize and challenge this critique at any length. And, indeed, we accept a number of the criticisms that Tsoukas makes of the Critical Systems Perspective developed principally by Jackson and Flood (e.g. Flood and Jackson, 1992) – for example, their tendency to regard society as a coherent subject and the inclination to favour an essentialist conception of human beings (see also Chapter 7). We also agree that 'Total Systems Intervention' (Flood and Jackson, 1991a) falls well short of a commitment to emancipation required by CT. As Mingers (1992b) cuttingly observes, Flood and Jackson's *Creative Problem Solving* reads 'more like a management consultant's handbook than an emancipatory tool' (ibid.: 734).

The basic difficulty with Tsoukas' critique stems from his feverish desire for certainties and a related unwillingness to accept the problematical status of all knowledge, including science (see below). His many complaints about the philosophical weakness of Critical Systems Thinking arise from a naïve faith in the separation of knowledge/facts and opinion/values. This leads Tsoukas, unsurprisingly, to challenge the claims and coherence of analyses that borrow heavily from Critical Theory (see Chapter 2). It also leads him to make quite wild claims, such as the assertion that those sympathetic to a Critical Systems perspective believe in, and seek the abolition of the means–ends distinction, whereas, arguably, the ambition of CT is not to abolish this distinction but to scrutinize, clarify and secure the (communicative) rationality of means and ends.

CT does not claim that critical reason is, or ever could be, supreme or free-floating in the process of developing human societies but, rather, that it is of value in loosening the grip of power relations, such as patriarchy, that impede and distort open communication and rational societal development. To repeat, a number of Tsoukas' (1992) criticisms of the comparatively unsophisticated formulation of power in CT-guided research can be accepted (see also Mingers, 1992a). But he fails to demonstrate that a more satisfactory conceptualization is incompatible with CT's assumptions and ambitions. With regard to his understanding of science, we have no quarrel with the contention that self-criticism has (in principle!) been 'the corner-stone of scientific inquiry' (ibid.: 654). Yet, paradoxically, this observation fails to appreciate how CT (and, for that matter, Foucauldian analysis) has persuasively challenged assumptions about the autonomy of the scientist's self, the constitution of this self within relations of power and domination, and the limited capacity or preparedness of scientists to reflect critically upon the discourses and practices that have provided defences of positivist science, such as those advanced by Popper (see Habermas, 1976).

Refusal to reflect critically upon the assumptions (e.g. cf. the auton-omous scientist) that underpin such objections to CT leads Tsoukas to conclude that CT is no different in spirit, or in practice, from the estab-lished interpretive perspective found in assumptionist analysis (Mason and Mitroff, 1981), second-loop learning (Argyris and Schon, 1978) and soft-systems methodology (Checkland, 1981). Instead of seeking to appreciate how a critical perspective favours a dialogical and less imperious approach to assessing the plausibility of competing truth claims, Tsoukas (1992: 654) insists upon evaluating the claims of CT in terms of an unreflexive, self-congratulatory conception of 'methodological rigour'. Tsoukas (1992) is disinclined, or unable, to recognize that the relationship between positivist/ interpretivist and critical perspectives is not inherently zero-sum. While there are fundamental differences in the assumptions and values that constitute these perspectives (see Chapter 2), there is no particular difficulty for CT in engaging with the 'dominant rationalities' of management or in providing interpretations that are of interest and value to managers. To assume that managers are entirely indifferent, if not wholly antagonistic, to ideas that directly challenge received wisdom about their 'problems' is, in effect, to embrace an essentialism that takes inadequate account of the complex and contradictory positioning and constitution of managerial work (see Chapter 1 and Willmott, 1996c).

## Conclusion

In this and the previous chapter, we have sought to highlight the existence of research into the specialisms of management that draw upon critical thinking, and especially CT, to provide an alternative to orthodox ways of making sense of management. We have also sought to make apparent the continuities with, as well as the departures from, other 'behaviourial' and 'soft' portrayals of its various subfields. In reviewing each field, we have sought to show how CT contributes fresh ideas and inspiration to those who are disillusioned with, and even despairing of, the perverse and destructive social and ecological consequences of established ways of organizing and managing. In each of the fields, we identified a small but active and growing number of researchers who are engaging CT in an effort to question and to change orthodox theory and practice. It is our hope that recognition of their pioneering efforts in applying critical reason to advance the theory and practice of management will inspire others either to join them or, at least, to debate their concerns.

## Notes

1 For example, there are different methods for calculating depreciation, determining Research and Development expenditure and writing off bad debts. The means of assessing the coherence and credibility of these methods depends upon what assumptions are made, and upon the balance of advantage that is calculated to accrue from the use of different techniques.

2 In the Anglo-American context, at least, financial accountants as well as those who check their accounts (the auditors), have tended to favour very general principles. This affords them the flexibility to choose between a range of approaches so as to place the performance of the organization in the best possible light. On the other hand, the users of financial accounts (e.g. creditors and shareholders) and government regulators have favoured increased standardization in order to achieve greater ease of comparability between financial statements. This comparability argument is contested by the providers of financial information who argue that organizations operate in highly diverse conditions, and that standardization necessarily favours some sectors or organizations to the disadvantage of others. Only flexibility, and the opportunity to choose between competing methods, they contend, allows a 'true and fair' picture to be presented. However, as regulators have become better informed about the consequences of seemingly impartial accounting conventions for national as well as corporate economic performance – such as the determination of research and development expenditure or accounting for inflation – they have sought to intervene (thereby reducing the self-regulating autonomy of the profession) to limit the scope for variation in the preparation of financial statements (see Cooper et al., 1994).

3 Even the field of organization studies struggles to match accounting in the number and depth of broadly critical journals that have appeared during the last decade or so. In large measure, this has been facilitated by one journal – *Accounting, Organizations and Society* (AOS) – which has actively sought and supported the development of critical accounting studies. AOS has published work informed by Marxism, post-Marxism and especially the writings of Foucault, as well as a smaller number of articles grounded in Critical Theory. Subsequently, AOS has been joined by three other broadly 'critical' accounting journals – *Public Interest Accounting*, *Accounting, Auditing and Accountability Journal* and *Critical Perspectives on Accounting*. The series of tri-annual *Interdisciplinary Perspectives on Accounting* conferences (1985, 1988, 1991, 1994) have provided an international forum for the presentation and discussion of critical accounting studies. These have been complemented by similar conferences held in the intervening years in North America and Australasia. Many of the papers given at these conferences have subsequently appeared either in one of the journals or in Cooper and Hopper (1990). In addition, several conferences convened in association with AOS have promoted the development of critical thinking among accounting academics, often by inviting participation from scholars drawn from other fields – linguistics, history, etc. A number of textbooks that take a broadly critical approach or which review critical accounting studies have appeared recently or are in preparation (e.g. Roslender, 1992; Puxty, 1993). The influence of critical thinking is also beginning to creep into what, in terms of the list of contents, are fairly conventional textbooks. In Wilson and Chua's *Managerial Accounting; Method and Meaning*, for example, the techniques of accounting are situated within an organizational context, and attention is paid to how accounting information is 'used to legitimize decisions which have already been made on political or social grounds in order that an air of objectivity may be created' (Wilson and Chua, 1988: 9).

4 In quite marked contrast to other management specialisms, leading 'critical' accounting scholars have been very active in encouraging non-accounting academics to bring their insights to accounting – a development that has been assisted by an exceptionally tight labour market

for accounting academics and, arguably, by the professional aspirations of accounting as a rigorous intellectual discipline.

5 Here it is also relevant to note the violent disagreements among Marxian and Foucauldian accounting academics about what counts as 'radical scholarship'. See, for example, Neimark's (1991) polemical critique of the radical potential and aspirations of Foucauldianism and the special issue of *Critical Perspectives on Accounting* (1994) that contains responses and a rejoinder.

6 This includes Laughlin and Puxty, 1983, 1984; Willmott, 1983, 1984a; Laughlin, 1987, 1988, 1991; Arrington and Puxty, 1991; Dillard, 1991; Broadbent et al., 1991; Dillard and Bricker, 1992).

7 To date such studies, which use the idea of the ideal speech situation as their basis, have not been undertaken within the field of accounting. An indication of what such analysis would look like can be found in Forester (1992). See also Chapter 4.

8 Juridification refers to a process or situation where the law goes beyond its established function of providing a formal framework, in which autonomy is in principle supported and enabled, to specify 'the social processes, relationships and often the outcomes . . . which are determined by a definable political agenda and purpose' (Laughlin and Broadbent, 1993: 339).

9 To facilitate this process, they call for additional channels for the dissemination of non-scientistic research papers – for example, by having special issues in existing journals. In contrast to the field of accounting, IS has lacked a journal that actively stimulates and disseminates critical research. However, the recent appearance of journals such as *Accounting, Management and Information Technology* and the recent broadening of policy of the *Journal of Information Systems* and *MIS Quarterly* suggests that this position is changing.

10 Each paradigm, they argue, is associated with a different conception of the systems analysts: as systems expert (functionalist), as facilitator (interpretive), as labour partisan (radical structuralist), and as emancipator or social therapist (radical humanist).

11 Lyytinen's interest in critical work developed within the field of operational research and is indicative of a degree of overlap between these fields (see also Jackson, 1992).

12 The engagement of these accounting academics in this debate also signals the degree of affinity between debates in accounting and OR.

13 As in the case of accounting, this has been assisted by the appearance of a journal, *Systems Practice*, which provides an important focus and outlet for critical OR.

14 See, for example, Jackson, 1990; Mingers, 1992c and the series of exchanges between Jackson and Mingers in the *Journal of the Operational Research Society*, 43, 7: 729–35; 44, 2: 205–10; 44, 7: 729–35.

15 See Jackson, 1982, 1985; Mingers, 1980, 1984, 1992; Ulrich, 1983; Oliga, 1988; Flood, 1990; Jackson and Flood, 1991a, 1991b.

# PART III

# TOWARDS AN INTEGRATION OF CRITICAL THEORY AND MANAGEMENT

---

## 7

## Recasting Emancipation in Management and Organization Studies

Following the general spirit of Critical Theory (CT), the previous chapters have presented critiques and counterpoints of conventional wisdom in the fields of management and organization studies. In this and the concluding chapter, we reflect upon the claims of CT and explore its continuity with more progressive forms of management theory and practice as we investigate the possibilities for forging links between the insights and ideals of CT and humanistic forms of management. In this chapter, we are principally interested in the theoretical aspects of such a synthesis. More specifically, we seek to re-evaluate Critical Theory's concept of emancipation – that is, the understanding that, through a process of critical self-reflection and struggle, people can become freed from diverse forms of domination. In Chapter 8, management practice receives more explicit attention.

As we noted in Chapter 3, major critiques of CT have come from orthodox Marxism and, more recently, from poststructuralist theory (PS).[1] Orthodox Marxism regards CT as excessively cerebral. Criticized for failing to appreciate how transformations of consciousness emerge from the blood-and-guts process of class conflict and struggle, CT is attacked for lacking any well-defined agency of emancipatory change. As Cleaver (1979) expresses his frustration with CT, 'the basic character of the analysis remains its commitment to ideological critique and its impotence in dealing with the growth and development of working-class power'. In contrast, PS doubts whether the 'truths' assumed by CT's critique of ideology can be separated from relations of power; and, relatedly, whether the autonomous subject who overcomes the oppressive, consciousness-distorting effects of power is an attainable ideal. Taking the arguments of PS seriously suggests a more cautious vision of emancipatory transformation, since different forms of knowledge – including CT – are understood to have the potential to become new sources of domination. From quite different directions, then, doubts have been cast upon the relevance and claims of CT.

This chapter is written in the form of a dialogue between management and organization studies (MOS), Critical Theory (CT) and poststructuralism (PS). By engaging in a kind of conversation between these three orientations, we explore what space there may be for advancing the emancipatory project. Our discussion circles around various topics that have been touched upon in the earlier chapters – power, knowledge, improvement, autonomy, ends, etc. We first present a brief account of the idea of emancipation in management. We then consider kinds of critique that CT, particularly in the context of management and organization studies, must take seriously. Following this, we sketch a framework for a modified understanding of emancipation as a response to such critique. Finally, we have some more specific suggestions for emancipatory research concerning ways of listening, writing and reading, where space is given to critical reflection and emancipation as well as to other, more traditional, concerns.

Exploratory and perhaps provocative, the following reflections do not presume to provide some fully worked out, definitive answer to the many questions that are raised. Nor do we claim to provide an 'integration' or 'reconciliation' of the different perspectives and positions that we examine. Recognizing the difficult territory in which we move, the chapter offers a set of brief exchanges, comments and ideas as a contribution to a debate about the idea of emancipation in management studies, with CT taking centre stage. Because the various themes explored have more or less salience for other voices – principally, poststructuralism and humanistic management theory – these can be heard at different times and to different effect. Our concern is to encourage greater dialogue between the 'mainstream' and 'critical' wings of management, but without harbouring any illusions about the philosophical and political differences that distinguish their respective positions (see Chapters 1 and 2). To this end, we have sought to make our discussion more open-ended and more self-critical, in terms of CT (see also Chapter 3).

## Management and Emancipation

In previous chapters, we have suggested and explored various ways in which CT can be mobilized to examine and critique contemporary developments in management and organization studies. As Kellner (1989) has persuasively argued, CT's analyses of the administered society, the culture industries and the consumer society can provide vital resources for analysing their crisis-ridden development in which there is 'a peculiar combination of streamlined rationality and intense irrationality, of organization and disorganization, of crisis tendencies and efforts at crisis management' (ibid.: 203). But, against this, it must be recognized that Habermas, in particular, has not addressed the significance of new forms of communication – computer, communication satellites, etc. – preferring instead to concentrate upon 'the traditional (one might say metaphysical) project of determining the ontological foundation of a free society' (Poster, 1989: 133). As Forester (1982) has observed of Habermas' contributions to CT, 'conspicuously lacking has been an account of those institutional and organizational forms which mediate between the analytic levels of social system and social action: e.g., factories, hospitals, schools, unions, churches, firms and companies, cultural and ethnic associations, and the like'. As a consequence, for a majority of practitioners and academics who work in the field of management, Critical Theory may well appear not a little remote and irrelevant. Not only does its concern with emancipation fail to provide 'fixes' for managerial problems or even engage with the substantive fields of organization and management theory, but also its analysis is highly abstract and esoteric.

Within mainstream management and organization studies, two dominant attitudes to the notion of emancipation can be found. One immediate, 'hard-nosed' response is to dismiss any suggestion that the domain of work organizations and the study of management, in particular, is – or ever conceivably could be – associated with such a fancy idea as emancipation. The role of managers, this response insists, is 'to ensure the survival/ growth/profitability of the organization'; and/or 'to satisfy the immediate demands of shareholders/customers/(and to some extent) workers'; or, more cynically, 'to keep the shareholders/customers/employees off the backs of managers'. The business of *management* – managerialists and orthodox Marxists might agree – is about safeguarding the interests of shareholders by controlling the productive capacity of workers (Storey, 1985). It has nothing to do with emancipation which, at best, is a private matter for the individual, and one that is legitimately pursued away from work: emancipation is simply not an issue for, or responsibility of, management.

An alternative response to talk of emancipation – and one that is closer to, yet still at considerable distance from, the position of CT (and of this book) – is that much modern management theory is indeed concerned with freeing employees from unnecessarily alienating forms of work organization. The current jargon term for this concern is 'empowerment'. From Human Relations through Quality of Working Life (QWL) to Corporate Culture, it could be claimed, a priority (of humanistic management theory) has been to redesign material and symbolic conditions of work in 'enriching' ways that serve higher-order needs (e.g. self-actualization), improve job satisfaction and, thereby, raise productivity. When management provides opportunities that are deemed to satisfy such needs, the 'emancipation' of employees from alienating conditions of work is said to be well advanced, if not pretty much complete.

Normally, proponents of CT consider humanistic management theory to be a fatally crippled, ideologically polluted version of 'emancipation' that merits harsh critique. Our own work has sometimes expressed such a position (Alvesson, 1987; Willmott, 1993a). Elements of the earlier chapters of this book echo this view. We basically believe that humanistic management theory merits highly critical examination. But we are also ready to concede that a more nuanced appreciation of humanistic management theory is possible, and that it may even receive a *carefully qualified* welcome. To its credit, humanistic management theory begins to understand employees as subjects, albeit ones from whom more productive effort can be gleaned and garnered. In principle, at least, (some) employees are recognized to possess 'higher-order needs'; and a moral as well as material value is explicitly placed upon managing people in a caring, responsible manner. However, it is also necessary to recognize and emphasize that the 'softness' of humanistic management theory is founded upon a narrow understanding of key prerequisites of emancipation. Humanistic management theory assumes that 'emancipation' is identical to providing employees with training and jobs that allows them to progress up 'the needs hierarchy'. And 'empowerment' is seen as an essentially passive process that is *bestowed* upon employees by progressive, enlightened managers.

In contrast, a CT-guided perspective insists that emancipation and empowerment necessarily involve an active process (or struggle) for individual and collective self-determination. CT is sceptical about – though not necessarily implacably opposed to – the emancipatory claims and effects of top-down change even, and perhaps especially, when this change is couched in the language of 'empower-and-facilitate' rather than 'command-and-control'. *For CT, emancipation is not a gift to be bestowed upon employees but, rather, is an existentially painful process of confronting and overcoming socially and psychologically unnecessary restrictions.* The latter include a broad range of phenomena extending from sexual and racial discrimination to dependency on a consumerist lifestyle for self-esteem, and the fear of failure in relationship to ideologies of careerism. In the absence of struggle, increased opportunities for employee 'initiative' and 'discretion' bestowed by humanistic varieties of management theory can easily have the paradoxical, but not always unintended, effect of weakening employees' capacity to reflect critically upon their work situation and corporate objectives. An example of where empowerment can reduce the capacity for critical self-reflection is when the cascading down of responsibility is accompanied by a (centralized) strengthening of corporate culture. Redesigning work in ways that expand opportunities for exercising discretion can make it more enjoyable and/or meaningful for those who remain in employment. However, it is also relevant to consider the extent to which redesign projects are driven by pressures to raise productivity or flexibility, to reduce managerial overheads, etc. Most crucially, it is necessary to assess whether the new design encourages or impedes opportunities for self-determination.

For CT, any substantial and lasting form of emancipatory change must involve a *continuing process* of critical *self-reflection* and associated self-transformation. Emancipation is not to be equated with, or reduced to, piecemeal social engineering directed by a more or less benevolent managerial élite. Rather, CT's conception of the emancipatory project encompasses a broad set of issues that includes the transformation of gender relations, environmental husbandry, the development of workplace democracy, etc. But, equally, it is implausible, and undialectical, to assume a zero-sum game between improvements in organizational performance and emancipatory movement. Even *within* the constraints of capital accumulation and the domination of instrumental rationality, the contradictory dynamics of modern organizations are capable of accommodating – and indeed promoting – some degree of increased employee responsibility and autonomy, at least for those (core) members who are deemed to be most pivotal for securing competitive advantage.

## Critiques of Critical Theory

Having briefly sketched a rationale for interpreting CT in a way that allows a degree of rapprochement with humanistic management theory without losing its critical edge, we now move on to identify a number of critiques of CT. We identify three types of problems with CT's ideal of social science as a facilitator of emancipation. We first consider criticisms concerned with its 'intellectualism' and 'essentialism'. We then relate the 'negativism' of CT to the marginalization of CT within management and organization studies (MOS). The types of critique differ substantially. But we believe that they are each worthy of consideration in the present context. We will then argue that each of the three criticisms can be answered in a way that is responsive to the respective objections.

### Intellectualism

At the heart of Critical Theory is an assumption that human reason is an emancipatory force, a force that is constrained and distorted by historical conditions that can be changed (see Chapters 1 and 3). These conditions (e.g. managerialism, chauvinism), it is asserted, inhibit and deflect the ability of human beings to act collectively to determine their own needs and shape their own destinies, a process of distortion that is experienced as frustration and suffering. It is this experience of frustration that, in principle, fires a process of critical reflection upon the social conditions of suffering and stimulates their emancipatory transformation. In practice, however, pain and frustration may be eased in other ways – for example, through immersion in work (workaholism) or through escapist involvement in forms of distancing and entertainment, etc. that effectively reduce the individual to an object of passified 'ego administration'. As Fay has observed, stressing the suffering aspect:

> Critical social science arises out of, and speaks to, situations of social unhappi-
> ness, a situation which it interprets as the result both of the ignorance of those
> experiencing these feelings and of their domination by others. It is this experience
> of unhappiness which is the wedge a critical theory uses to justify its entrance
> into the lives of those it seeks to enlighten and emancipate. (1987: 83)

Reflecting further upon the claims of CT, Fay (1987) has questioned
whether the sequence of problematical conditions → suffering → critical
reflection → emancipation is as unproblematical as Habermas, for example,
is alleged to suggest. Without denying that critical reason is a potent source
of emancipatory force (see Chapter 1), Fay argues that its powers are
'inherently limited' by somatic (embodied) learning in which the sense and
(socio)logic of the contemporary social order becomes deeply embedded in
the body. In other words, Fay contends that people become physically
habituated or addicted to, and highly dependent upon, the world as they
know it. The somatic impulse, unmediated by critical reason, is to cling to
and defend this world – almost regardless of how unsatisfactory or futile
such action may be – rather than engage in the demanding and threatening
process of transforming it.[2]

Insofar as human beings are 'historical, embodied, traditional and
embedded creatures' (Fay, 1987: 83), the responsiveness of subjectivity to
rational, critical argument may be quite limited. The cognitive emphasis in
CT may therefore prove less than effective in communicating its message
and promoting critical self-reflection, let alone emancipatory practice. Or,
as critics of CT have articulated this criticism, the rationalist bias of CT is
evident in its neglect of the sentient and emotional aspects of human action.
Yet, it is precisely these aspects that are necessary 'to provide sufficient
inducement or motivational inspiration to command the allegiance of its
potential addressees' (see also Whitebrook, 1984; McIntosh, 1994). Moreover, an emphasis upon reflection, evaluation and freedom in social life
may simply lead to recurrent self-questioning and suspicion of all social
arrangements. Recurrent doubts about what one is doing, and of the
optimality of the social order, are perhaps as likely to create despondency
and paralysis as to inspire a process of personal and social reconstruction.

In response to such criticism, it is first worth noting that leading
proponents of CT, such as Horkheimer and Adorno (1947b), were very
conscious of the limitations of human reason – to the point of despair,
since they saw no way of dealing with this problem. Broad-brush critiques
of the 'totally administered' or 'one-dimensional' society were, arguably, as
much statements of desperation as they were serious efforts to stimulate
emancipation. But, even so, as we noted in Chapter 3, Marcuse's *One-
Dimensional Man* (1964) had the paradoxical effect of contributing directly
to a late-60s questioning of dominant values (e.g. materialism and consumerism) and social arrangements (e.g. hierarchy), a questioning which he
considered had all but been disabled by modern, technocratic consciousness
and the widespread identification of consumption as the principal means
of happiness. Thus, our response to doubts about the transformative

contribution of CT is to retain and foster a belief in the *limited* power of reason to question conventional wisdom and current practice, while, at the same time, asserting its vital contribution to processes of emancipation. Furthermore, instead of understanding the power of reason either as something universal *or* as something that is peculiarly dominant in 'modern' society, we are inclined – in the after-shock of the Holocaust, McCarthyism and the Gulags – to regard the critical deployment of reason as an historical phenomenon that is more or less salient during different eras. In our view, the contemporary means of sustaining, and perhaps reviving, the limited and depleted potency of critical reason is to adopt and develop the insights of Critical Theory, but in ways that are less preoccupied with Grand Theorizing and more prepared to learn from, and contribute to, localized practical concerns. Criticism of the intellectualist bias of CT is paralleled in poststructuralist arguments against metanarratives and totalizing critiques, to which we now turn.

*Essentialism*

The criticism of CT for being essentialist is directed at its inclination to advance all-embracing frameworks that necessarily reduce or 'totalize' the complexity and heterogeneity of phenomena so that they 'fit' into a single, integrated vision. Poststructuralists, in particular, have complained about this tendency (Calas and Smircich, 1987; Cooper and Burrell, 1988; Lyotard, 1984). A second issue, which is also central to the challenge of poststructuralism (PS), has been the assault on the idea of an autonomous subject. Against the 'essentialist' idea of an integrated, coherent, homogeneous individual, PS accepts and indeed celebrates the inevitability of fragmentation, inconsistency, undecidability, variation and heterogeneity.

A basic assumption of humanist thinking, whether in management theory or social philosophy, is that beneath the alienated, fragmented surface of human consciousness there is an autonomous individual striving to get out.[3] Or as Weedon (1988: 21) puts it, humanism 'presupposes an essence at the heart of the individual which is unique, fixed and coherent'. In management theory, there is a widespread assumption of the existence of a fixed set of needs which, when fulfilled by the employer, maximises the individual's contribution to the organization as well as his or her job satisfaction. CT, in contrast, rejects the bourgeois humanist idea that human autonomy can be fully realized within the constraints of modern work organizations. To CT, the death of God as *the* source of authority and purpose is the beginning, not the end, of the humanist project. Although modern individuals have been freed from feudal illusions (e.g. the divine rights of kings), CT stresses that we remain ensnared by contemporary illusions – such as the idea that 'freedom' is fully realized by the opportunity to buy and sell commodities including labour, to participate passively in representative democracy and/or to apply behavioural science to rationalize existing means of organization. To justify its critique of contemporary illusions and 'social unhappiness', CT has not infrequently appealed to the radical humanist idea that, at the core of individuals, is a (potentially) unified, autonomous subject who is currently alienated and degraded by routines and priorities that unnecessarily impede the full flowering of a value-rational society.[4] In MOS, this thesis is paralleled by McGregor's (1960) opinion that the autonomous core of individuals can be liberated by shifting from a 'Theory X' to a 'Theory Y' philosophy of management or, more recently, by Peters' (1992) claim that managers can liberate themselves by making their jobs totally 'flexible' and 'networked'.

It is the assumption of an essential autonomy that is challenged by PS. Subjectivity, PS argues, taking issue with CT, is the product of diverse and contradictory discourses and practices through which individuals routinely come to be (misleadingly) identified, and to (mis)identify themselves, as autonomous subjects. For PS, 'The individual is both the site for a possible range of subjectivity and, at any particular moment of thought and speech, a subject, subjected to the regime of meaning of a particular discourse and enabled to act accordingly' (Weedon, 1988: 34). Habermas assumes that, in principle at least, 'regimes of meaning' can be cleansed of power by achieving symmetry in communicative relations; and that, in such a situation, the autonomous and responsible individual will, at last, be fully realized. PS, in contrast, contends that the true/false and alienation/ emancipation dichotomies are unsupportable. Foucault (1980), in particular, has challenged the idea, which is central to CT, that the relationship between 'knowledge' and 'power' is wholly negative; and, relatedly, that the ideological aspects of the former can be eliminated by removing the latter. Foucault contends that most, if not all, power relations incorporate elements that are 'positive' for, and valued by, those populations whose subjectivity they constitute (e.g. career ladders that are being valued and defended by managers whose sense of identity they serve to shape and reproduce). Foucault also draws attention to the way that forms of knowledge, however enlightened, exert truth effects that are contradictory in their consequences. For example, the idea that human reason has emancipatory potential can produce a form of social theory – namely, Critical Theory – that privileges abstract theorizing and critiques over the fostering of critical insights into mundane philosophies and practices; or, worse, there is the risk that Critical Theorists 'know best' and establish themselves as Authorities, thereby silencing a dialogue that they profess to promote.

Turning away from grand critiques of exploitation and domination, which treat society or organizations as a totality, Foucault has commended a focus upon what he terms the microphysics of power. By this he means the diverse and intersecting ways in which power is exercised through shifting networks of power relations and struggles. The principle value of this approach, we believe, resides in its capacity to appreciate the complex and precarious dynamics of social organization. It avoids reducing the messy and often paradoxical qualities of management and organization to a product of some single, unified power (such as capitalism, technocracy, top management, the State, unions – or even mass culture or consumptionist ideology). In turn, this approach opens up the possibility of appreciating the frailty and vulnerability of processes which, from a totalizing perspective, appear uniform, inevitable and unshakeable. What, from a more distant or abstracted position, can be readily categorized and dismissed as an expression of 'bourgeois ideology' or as a generator of 'false-consciousness' may be appreciated as a more ambiguous phenomenon that, upon closer examination, is contradictory in its formation and effects (Knights and Willmott, 1989).

*Negativism*

A third, related complaint against CT concerns its 'negativism'. Undermining the basis and plausibility of conventional beliefs and assumptions is, or is supposed to be, a principal task of academic research and scholarship. However, if criticism is not accompanied by more constructive suggestions, it becomes an easy target for the charge of 'negativism'. One-sided negativism can present a mirror image of the hype and one-dimensional technicism of much management theory. This negativism can create problems, both in terms of how the objects and subjects of CT critique are represented, and in terms of demonstrating the practical relevance of its concerns.

   It is not unusual for far-reaching critique to result in marginalization, if not ostracism or excommunication. The credibility of CT is especially stretched in the field of management studies where there is such keen devotion to (the engineering rhetoric of) instrumental action and problem-solving. However, the case for CT is not assisted when it is sensed to embrace a 'holier than thou' attitude that is fundamentally uncompassionate and, as a consequence, uncommunicative. CT is (unintentionally) uncommunicative when it is perceived to be engaged *exclusively* in 'knocking' and 'putting down' conventional wisdom rather than appreciating how, in Habermas' terms, the findings of empirical-analytic and historical-hermeneutic sciences have a potential role to play in the development of a more (value-) rational society (see Chapter 2). We are, of course, not saying that conventional wisdom should be spared critical examination. But the capacity for CT to exert an influence is conditional upon its willingness to engage with mainstream ideas and practitioners in ways that are understandable and, hopefully, appealing to others (see Chapter 8).

   Outright dismissals of 'managerial ideology' are perversely undialectical. This is because they disregard or marginalize the contradictions and countertendencies within managerial ideology (see Chapter 1). For example, in emphasizing the difference between the oppressive logic of management practices and the emancipatory ideals of CT, there can be a deep reluctance to acknowledge and explore the progressive potential in certain theories – for example, the contribution of some of the neo-human relations and corporate culture philosophies in unsettling, if not deeply problematizing, some of the more traditional, rationalist theories of management and organization. Despite their considerable weaknesses, practically as well as ethically (Willmott, 1993a), these ideas have at least challenged the excessively narrow conception of 'rationality' that has governed classical approaches to the field. A reluctance to engage dia-logically with the mainstream, pro-managerial approach contributes to CT's marginalization[5] when its proponents, ourselves included, present arguments that are excessively one-sided, negative and unconstructive.

Superficially, at least, recent developments in management theory share with CT a recognition of how a narrowly technical conception of rationality inhibits creativity and innovation as it exerts a divisive and deadening effect upon human organization. Shared, too, is the belief that people will often respond positively to opportunities that are found to enable them to expand their discretion or autonomy; and that, in doing so, they may tend to act more responsibly towards others. However, instead of emphasizing these areas of common understanding, there is a tendency for CT to focus exclusively upon the negative features of modern management theory – such as the mystification of autonomy and the domination of employees' hearts and minds, in addition to their bodies. Which is not to say that these features should be overlooked or that, for example, the contradictions associated with claims that 'strong' corporate cultures can expand employee discretion should be glossed over. On the contrary, attentiveness to issues of discretion, autonomy and empowerment within management theory present opportunities to engage in a constructive dialogue in which the potential for corporate culture to inhibit critical thought can be articulated (see, for example, Wilkinson and Willmott, 1995a).

## A Rejoinder to the Critiques of CT

Having reviewed a number of criticisms of CT, primarily from PS but also from the position of conventional management theory and practice, we note that these criticisms are, in some cases, somewhat double-edged. Essentialism certainly pervades humanistic MOS, with its timeless, ahistori-cal conception of human nature that it presses into a theory of human needs. Other significant problems with MOS include an anti-intellectualism associated with the preference for simple solutions, and its hyped presentation of its own transformative power. In contrast, the intellectual history of the Frankfurt School indicates a considerable interest in taking seriously historical variations in rationality and subjectivity, thus weakening the essentialism in its view of human nature (see Chapter 3).

A number of critical students of management have turned to PS, and especially to the writings of Foucault, for guidance and inspiration (e.g. Knights, 1992; Townley, 1993). Although some of Foucault's writings can compete with the most abstract offerings of CT, much of his work – and especially his later books – cannot be accused of excessive esotericism or intellectualism. But neither does Foucault leave his readers in an optimistic state concerning the chances for liberation. Geertz (quoted in Hoy, 1986) views Foucault as writing a story of 'the Rise of Unfreedom'. Despite highlighting the positive quality of power, its disciplinary effects are seen by many commentators to be all-pervasive. Reflecting upon the political thrust of Foucault's work, Rorty (1985: 172) has remarked that Foucault 'forbids himself the tone of the liberal sort of thinker who says to his fellow-citizens: "We know that there must be a better way to do things than this; let us look for it together"'.

Such criticisms can be challenged for seeming to reflect the élitist view that writers of Foucault's stature should produce a 'blueprint' for a better society. Foucault, it is worth noting, was highly sceptical about such ambitions. Finding no overwhelming merit in the rational discipline of consistency, Foucault was empowered to say many seemingly contradictory things. Some of these things appear to echo the critical intent of CT. For example, when commenting critically upon the value of critiques that rely upon the essentialist assumptions of 'Utopian schemes', rather than engaging more directly in analysis of the microphysics of modern institutions, Foucault observes that:

> It seems to me that the real political task in a society such as ours is to critique the working of institutions which appear to be both neutral and independent, to criticise them in such a manner that the political violence which has always exercised itself obscurely through them will be unmasked, so that one can fight them.' (Foucault in Elders, 1974: 171 cited in Rabinow, 1986: 6)

In any event, the differences between CT and Foucault's (shifting) stand-point should not be exaggerated, as Foucault (1991) himself acknowledged. Reflecting upon his intellectual development and his ignorance of the Frankfurt School until quite late in the development of his thinking, Foucault remarks:

> At that point, I realized how the Frankfurt School people had tried ahead of time to assert things that I too had been working for years to sustain. . . . When I recognise all these merits of the Frankfurt School, I do so with the bad conscience of one who should have known and studied them much earlier . . . if I had read those works earlier on, I would have saved useful time, surely: I wouldn't have needed to write some things and I would have avoided certain errors. (ibid.: 117, 119)

Indeed, some commentators group CT and PS together as counterpoints to bourgeois ideas about the autonomous individual (Firat and Venkatesh, 1992; Sampson, 1989). Nevertheless, the PS critique of essentialism raised above is worth taking seriously. The differences between CT and PS, particularly Foucault, may create fruitful tensions on these issues (Alvesson, 1996; Alvesson and Deetz, 1996; Deetz, 1992b; Willmott, 1994a).

Equally, despite his criticisms of Foucault's subjectivism, Habermas (1989a: 294) is by no means dismissive of Foucault's analysis of power/

knowledge relations, arguing that 'he did indeed provide an illuminating critique of the entanglement of the human sciences in the philosophy of the subject'. Our own inclination is to interrogate and mobilize Foucault's writing in a project that is proto-emancipatory in intent (see White, 1986), even though his ideas are not without ambiguity in this enterprise. This ambiguity is at once a strength and a weakness: a strength because his ideas inject a healthy dose of scepticism into the heady, intellectualistic realms of CT (as well as into the naïve optimism of MOS). Foucault has also shown the value of undertaking genealogical analyses of mundane processes and institutions (e.g. prisons and prison-like organizations) in a way that sheds new light upon their oppressive consequences, and thereby contributes to a critique of these practices. But, with the possible exception of an ethical stance that was emergent in his final work (*History of Sexuality, vols 2 and 3* – see Foucault, 1985, 1986), the positive features of Foucault's writings should not distract us from the fundamental difficulty in Foucault's position: the absence of any *consistent* normative bearings (Willmott, 1994a). Associated with this aporia, perhaps, is Foucault's reluctance to situate his penetrating analysis of power/knowledge relations and the constitution of subjects within a discussion of political economy, the functions of the capitalist system and its consequences for ecology as well as for the distribution of wealth and opportunity. As Dews has argued, in defence of Critical Theory and of Habermas in particular, against poststructuralist critique:

> It is true that Habermas' work does not hold up a mirror to contemporary experiences of fragmentation, loss of identity, and libidinal release, in the manner which has enabled post-structuralist writing to provide the 'natural' descriptive vocabulary. . . . But neither does it pay for its expressive adequacy and immediacy with a lack of theoretical and historical perspective. (1986: 33)

This critical assessment of PS is directly relevant for the arguments of Lyotard (1984) and many authors interested in 'deconstruction' and 'the postmodern condition'. Despite the best of intentions, an emphasis upon the open, ambiguous character of language and a preoccupation with the precarious nature of writings and texts can degenerate into an exclusive, intellectual, intra-academic enterprise. In terms of accessibility and constructive critique, much PS is hardly an improvement upon CT. A tendency toward the unqualified dismissal of contemporary society and its institutions in CT is paralleled in PS's dismissive rejection of what it terms 'grand narratives', i.e. all forms of large-scale frameworks and projects, including the idea of a progressive development, which are said to be 'totalitarian' (Lyotard, 1984). On this particular point, PS is perhaps culpable of harbouring its own 'essentialism', in which all sorts of 'grand narratives', excepts its own, are viewed as essentially the same, in an indiscriminate way (see Kellner, 1988.) On balance it may be concluded that, for all its problems, the progressive ideals associated with the emancipatory project of CT makes its blend of positive/constructive and negative/

critical elements somewhat less alien (e.g. to practitioners and MOS) than the more consistently 'uncommitted' and recurrently deconstructive inclinations of PS (Willmott, 1996b). However, if CT is to have greater relevance for actors in 'ordinary' organizational settings, its tendencies towards intellectualism, essentialism and negativism must be acknowledged and addressed. This, in our opinion, does not necessitate the jettisoning of the idea of emancipation as a guiding value of analysis. On the contrary, if social science is to avoid becoming a nihilistic enterprise in which the generation of knowledge is completely divorced from the values which inspire and guide its production, a commitment to emancipation must be retained and reconstructed.

## Reconceptualizing Emancipation

A degree of disillusionment with the development or elaboration of 'grand critiques' can be helpful in assisting the expansion of critical analysis of ordinary, everyday power relations and struggles. Geertz (1973) has argued that the (anthropological) concept of culture should be cut down in size so that it covers less and reveals more. Likewise, the concept of emancipation may be cut down in size in a way that avoids making excessively or exclusively grandiose claims. In this section, we draw upon the previous discussion to elaborate a reconceptualization of emancipation. This favours an increased emphasis on smaller-scale, open projects.

### Micro-emancipation

When focusing upon possibilities for 'micro-emancipation', the multifarious activities, recipes for action and techniques developed within organizations are viewed not only as means of control but also as objects and facilitators of resistance and, thus, as potential vehicles of emancipation. In this formulation, organizational processes are understood to be uncertain, contradictory, ambiguous and precarious. Within systems of power and control there are invariably contradictions and 'loopholes' that can be exposed and exploited for purposes of critical reflection and emancipatory transformation. As Deetz (1992a: 336) expresses it: 'with every "positive" move in disciplinary practices, there is an oppositional one'. Control is conceptualized not only as discipline and restriction of the space for action, but also as a potential source of critical thought and emancipation. All sorts of control stratagems are understood to be mediated by, or unintentionally productive of, 'signs' or 'messages' that can trigger off suspicion, resistance and critical reflections – that is, impulses that can provide the basis for emancipatory change.

The dialectic of control and resistance has been noted and more fully explored by authors working outside of the tradition of CT (e.g. Edwards, 1979; Giddens, 1979). But they have analysed this dialectic principally as a succession of conflicts between major, integrated managerial control strategies and large-scale resistance (or aggregates of similar small-scale reactions) to dominant control forms. What we seek to emphasize here is the relevance and significance of another type and expression of emancipatory action that is less grandiose in conception and focus. This might, for example, be the redefinition of a verbal symbol launched by management for a particular purpose. Instead of being a vehicle for managerial control and integration, this symbol can become a manifestation of irony and distance – such as the idea of 'empowering' employees or the 'mission statement' ascribed to an organization (see, e.g. Smircich, 1983a). Similarly, status symbols such as office space, luxury equipment, controlled access to privileged areas, etc. often reinforce formal hierarchy, feelings of superiority/inferiority and support careerism. But they may simultaneously and inadvertently draw attention to the arbitrary and political nature of corporate arrangements, thus nurturing scepticism rather than tighter discipline.

Inherent in the concept of micro-emancipation is an emphasis on partial, temporary movements that break away from diverse forms of oppression, rather than successive moves towards a predetermined state of liberation. This 'micro' view of emancipation differs markedly from the traditional conception of a one-way transformation of consciousness from 'false' to 'true' as the crucial element in the change from an oppressive social order to one that is in harmony with clarified wants and ethical principles. The emancipatory project is instead formulated as a precarious, endless enterprise, continuously fighting to increase the space for critical reflection and change as it counteracts the diverse, oppressive effects of unexamined traditions, prejudices, the ego administration of mass media, consumerist pressures, etc., that combine to place socially unnecessary limits on the ways in which the social world can be understood and enacted. It portrays the emancipatory idea not as one large, tightly integrated programme, but rather as a myriad of projects, each limited in terms of space and time (and of success).

*A Brief Illustration*   We will briefly illustrate the idea of micro-emancipation with one example drawn from an 'information meeting' about reorganization at a Swedish industrial company (Alvesson, 1996). Present during this two-hour long meeting were about a hundred junior and middle-level managers. The top manager opened the meeting with a rhetorical question: 'Why are you here?' To which he immediately replied, 'It is because you are the managers in this company.' By examining this opening gambit, we will suggest that such an unremarkable way of addressing the audience is far from innocent and is a suitable theme of micro-emancipation (see also Knights and Willmott, 1987).

Let us first say that it is not self-evident that the people present are 'managers', even though they have this title. If it were self-evident, it is doubtful that the top manager would have begun by defining the reality of the situation in this way. To identify and constitute someone as a manager is not just a question of appointing the person to a particular formal position. The identity and the ideology which characterize the appointee are also crucial (cf. Deetz, 1992a; Therborn, 1980). It cannot be taken for granted that people who are appointed to such positions regard themselves *primarily* as managers, or that they are regarded as managers by others. A given person who has the title of department manager may regard themselves, first and foremost, as a member of a family, as a female, as middle-aged, perhaps as a 'green', or even as a union member, and so on.

Corporate management competes with other groups and categories for the individual's time, self-perception, attention and loyalty. Ideally, from top management's point of view, 'managers' *should* regard themselves primarily as company people. It is therefore important to maintain and reinforce this managerial identity. Appealing to them as managers means that certain ideas and values about the job are being accentuated – such as responsibility, loyalty, work morale, result orientation, etc. In effect, members of this audience are being urged to disregard or suspend all other identities. As Galbraith (1983) has pointed out, managers are more strictly controlled in many respects than other employees; for instance, they have to be more careful about what they think and say. Thus, it is an important task for top management to continually constitute people who take 'managership' very seriously, and who give priority to values, ideas, feelings and actions – including self-discipline – associated with being a 'manager'. The basic idea of the meeting could be to remind the audience that they should perceive the reorganization through pro-managerial spectacles, and not as a family member who, for example, fears the loss of employment or as an ambitious individual who is poised to seize an opportunity for self-advancement.

Micro-emancipation, in this example, means resistance to stratagems deployed in efforts to fix people's identities and self-understandings. Rather than pointing at false consciousness – it is certainly not simply false to see oneself as manager – the constraints associated with an uncritical, institutionalized acceptance of a particular prescribed identity are the target of the researcher's interpretation. Micro-emancipation occurs when critical reflection enables the development of an open attitude to the ascription of identity in which the negative (e.g. subordination to certain norms and self-constraints) as well as the positive (e.g. status confirmation) aspects of the use of the term 'manager' are acknowledged and explored. At the core of micro-emancipation in this particular example, then, is the consideration of resistance to the power technique of defining another person in a certain way. A small-scale liberation is encouraged – as a response to a specific move of power (temporary fixation of identity) – not a more ambitious call for transformation of the situation (and the organizational context) into a full-scale democratization. The latter is not inconsistent with, but falls outside, the idea of micro-emancipation.

### The Costs and Paradoxes of Emancipation

In this light, emancipation is seen as an element in everyday life, involving recurrent struggles between the oppressive exercise of power and resistance to its exercise. This reconceptualization of emancipation also acknowledges that domination (e.g. mechanization of craft production) can facilitate an expansion of productive capacity as well as providing a possible starting point for emancipation. Correspondingly, emancipatory change might involve a loss of productive capacity. Employees seeking to expand their autonomy and control over productive forces may either choose, or be faced with, a reduction in their productivity, with consequences for their sense of self-identity as well as their employment security. Similarly, women emancipating themselves from dominant socialization patterns and gender roles may reduce their interest in, and capacity for, caring and thereby reduce their contribution to the unpaid economy. Employees freeing themselves from a Protestant work ideology may be less committed to, and less capable of, acting as 'socially responsible' citizens. Not only capitalists but also client groups (e.g. hospital patients) may suffer. A critical questioning of beliefs and values may well facilitate more rational thinking, recognition and clarification of neglected needs, ideas about fairness, etc. But, in so doing, this thinking may also estrange the individual from the tradition which has formed his or her very subjectivity. It is possible that anxiety, identity loss and other severe problems may accompany (or impede) emancipatory transformation (Fay, 1987).

It is naïve and unrealistic to ignore or gloss over the 'costs' of emancipation. The possible costs must be fully acknowledged, especially in critical studies of management and organization where received wisdom about effective and productive organizing comes into immediate conflict with emancipatory thinking. It must be recognized that the price to be paid for many forms of liberation from dominant ideologies and external constraints can be high. For example, an outcome of enhanced ecological consciousness and greater freedom and creativity at work – which are likely priorities emerging from critical reflection and emancipatory change – may be reduced wages and consumption, or even bankruptcy and unemployment. It is far too simplistic to assume that only 'irrationality', apart from the repressive power of an egoistic social élite, stands in the way of liberation. Emancipation involves a trade off between certain gains and certain losses. People might have persuasive reasons for refusing emancipatory invitations, including both fear of failure and fear of the effects of 'successful' emancipation. These fears can only be addressed if they are fully recognized, not dismissively swept away as 'irrationality'.

Just paying attention to certain aspects of management and organization inevitably means that complex phenomena are selectively represented and illuminated. This can easily create a closed and fixed appearance of an open and ambiguous phenomenon. Unless we are to assume that some people are already fully emancipated, it must be recognized that an anti-emancipatory tendency runs through all projects – even those with the best intentions and preceded by careful reflection. The dynamics and dialectics of emancipation also mean that an idea, or an intended practice, can be subverted in its practical application. Even if it begins by opening up understanding, or facilitating reflection, it can end up locking people into fixed, unreflective thinking (Willmott, 1993b). Critique and liberation from old dogma is then followed by new dogma: somewhere in the process, a theory guided by critical, emancipatory intent turns into an anti-emancipatory force (see Horkheimer and Adorno, 1947a).

So, the dark side of CT's emancipatory project must be acknowledged. Having said that, defeatism must also be exposed and challenged. For example, as we noted earlier, it can be acknowledged that Habermas' (1984) ideas on communicative action and reflective dialogue contain 'anti-emancipatory' potentials – such as an intellectualist ideology that stresses cognitive capacity and communicative skills as core values, and which offers a 'total' framework (thereby possibly excluding 'other voices') and, arguably, has a pro-male bias (Meisenhelder, 1989). Awareness of the anti-emancipatory potentials in all 'good' suggestions and recipes encourages deeper reflection upon how ideas lend themselves to ideological (ab)usage. If this is true of CT, it is doubly so for humanistic management theory. A greater sensitivity to anti-emancipatory elements might mean that some influential authors and gurus are taken less seriously – and less widely, and superficially, read. It would also almost certainly improve the chances of the outcome of their prescriptions being more in accordance with their stated intent.

*A Note on Emancipation Myopia* Having argued for the virtues of emancipatory micro-projects as well as the ambiguities of emancipation – irrespective of scope and intention – we must also sound a cautionary note about an over-reliance upon local projects of emancipation. There is a danger that an emphasis upon struggles around local practices could leave unchallenged wider sources of irrationality and oppression – such as those endemic to the organizing principles of capitalism, historically and culturally anchored gender stereotypes, the hegemonic role of the mass media, the exploitation of the environment, the technocratic domination of professional and managerial ideologies, etc. Efforts to make space for increased discretion and autonomy on the purely local level could lead to a narrow kind of liberation in which local difficulties are (temporarily) ameliorated but the deeper, structural problems largely escape attention and correction.

With these important considerations firmly in mind, we believe that it is desirable to move away from a conceptualization of organizations either as a tightly integrated chain of institutions operating according to the logic of the iron cage, as CT tends to do, or as settings in which fragmentary, uncoupled forms of micro-power and local struggles are at play, as PS does. Instead, organizations can be viewed as loosely coupled orders harbouring elements of oppression and opportunities for emancipation which are, to varying degrees, connected to, or are products of, the cultural and politico-economic contexts of their formation and reproduction. We are not prepared to trade off 'totalizing' thinking for myopia. Many of the most significant sources of oppression associated with environmental pollution, domination of multinational corporations and poverty are of a global nature. A PS turn in critical management theory risks ignoring or trivializing these problems. But, equally, global issues exist on the local level. For example, worldwide pollution is contingent upon how people think about and relate to everyday decisions – which may be more or less ecologically damaging. By focusing upon micro-power, analysis can have more direct relevance to the *lived experience* of people who are con-tinuously engaged in local struggles – for example, by raising awareness of the consequences of everyday decision making. At the same time, as we have stressed, these struggles must be appreciated as a medium and outcome of broader processes of transformation.

### Emancipation: Types and Foci

To elaborate on our reconceptualization of emancipation further, it is necessary to develop a more refined understanding of the nature and direction of emancipatory moves. To this end, a distinction can be drawn between the type of emancipatory project and the focus of its interest. As with many such distinctions, its value is heuristic: in practice the different types and foci of emancipation merge into one another. Nonetheless, this model provides a point of departure and offers a stimulus for developing a more adequate conceptualization of some key dimensions of emancipatory projects. The matrix in Figure 7.1 summarizes the types and foci of emancipation.

On the first, *horizontal axis* we distinguish everyday questioning of ideas and practices from a totalizing type of emancipatory project. *Questioning* is principally directed at challenging and critiquing dominant forms of thinking. Dominant ideas and current social arrangements are met with suspicion and are scrutinized. The aim is to combat the self-evident and the taken for granted. This type of emancipatory project is primarily concerned with investigating and problematizing. Its intent is to doubt and resist authority (and its disciplining effects) without, necessarily, proposing an alternative agenda or set of prescriptions. At the other end of the con-tinuum of emancipatory projects, a *Utopian* approach develops an overall 'vision' that frequently ignores or marginalizes the relevance of immediate, 'micro' problems. It should perhaps be stressed that the Utopian project does not necessarily present a recipe for 'the good life' or for fixing the mind in a narrowly specified direction: insofar as CT has a Utopian element, it is also overtly anti-authoritarian. It aims only to counteract ideologies and social arrangements that obstruct human freedom, not to fill the latter with particular contents. In CT, the Utopian element takes the form of a counterfactual proposition (e.g., the unalienated individual or the ideal speech situation) that aims at opening up consciousness for engage-ment with a broader repertoire of alternatives. Utopianism represents

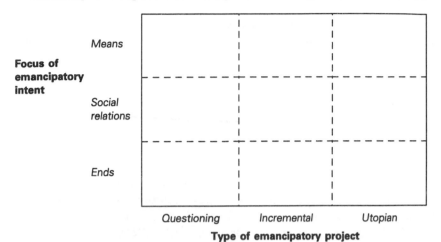

Figure 7.1   *Model summarizing types and foci of emancipation*

alternative thinking rather than the suggestion of a ready-made, 'better' alternative or the provision of recipes for action.

Between the questioning and Utopian types of emancipatory project, we identify *incremental undertakings* that favour and articulate a gradualist or reformist approach to emancipatory transformation. These often concentrate on participatory processes. Of course, questioning and incremental approaches may also involve a Utopian element. As we stressed earlier, the distinction between these approaches is heuristic; and it may be more helpful to think of them as dimensions of emancipation upon which more or less emphasis is placed in different emancipatory projects. Clearly, many forms of critique implicitly assume or anticipate a superior state or emancipatory change of direction. Even ideas about 'deconstruction' are, arguably, informed and influenced by an alternative set of ideas that claim to provide a more adequate account of how accepted understandings (e.g. about gender) are constructed (see, for example, Martin, 1990).

Turning now to consider the *vertical axis* of our matrix, by 'focus' we mean the primary object of emancipatory efforts. Here we make an analytical distinction between 'means', 'social relations' and 'ends'. Again, it is necessary to acknowledge the purely heuristic quality of this distinction. *Means* is intended to refer to discourses and practices that are valued for their supposed ability to make ends achievable. Emancipatory projects which address 'means' challenge the necessity and value of established methods of organization, including the hierarchical and fragmented division of labour, autocratic leadership styles, psychological testing, etc. – which, of course, have also been challenged, albeit in less radical ways, by humanistic management theory.

At the other end of the vertical axis, *ends* refers to the purpose of organizational or managerial activity. The emancipation of ends is concerned with the unfreezing of institutionalized priorities, thereby opening up debate about issues such as the practical value of economic growth, consumption, the quality of life, and so on. The horizontal axis indicates the range of orientations, or emphases, that may inform such a focus. For example, a questioning approach might ask why it is that certain values and objectives are given priority over others. Alternatively, a Utopian conception of communication may be deployed to challenge the way in which particular ends have been selected and are defended by suggesting radically different values. An incremental orientation would seek to point towards ways in which (limited) opportunities for emancipatory change may be identified and pursued.

Finally, the inclusion of *social relations* as a focus of emancipatory intent draws attention to the social organization of privileges and power. Of course, social relations can be divorced from neither means nor ends. But the focus on social relations is particularly attentive to the way that means and ends are embedded in structures of social relations. For example, a focus upon means, such as participatory styles of coordinating work for the attainment of ecologically sound production, does not necessarily touch upon issues like segmented labour markets, pay differences or other forms of class, gender or ethnic inequality. Actions directed against oppressive means and taken-for-granted ends do not exhaust the prospects for emancipation, since it is possible to contemplate efforts directed at the emancipation of social relations from power asymmetries that would not significantly change ends and/or means. Workplace democracy or gender equality, for example, do not necessarily exclude high productivity as a taken-for-granted goal. Nor do they necessarily challenge an extensive division of labour (as long it is not gendered) as the appropriate means.

*Illustrating the Framework*

Having discussed the elements of our heuristic framework, we now indicate how it may be used by comparing and contrasting approaches within management and organization studies (MOS) and CT. We start from the three foci and briefly explore types of emancipatory projects in relationship to each of these.

The primary focus of study in MOS is 'means'. Mainstream MOS is preoccupied with the refinement of means in a purely technical, non-emancipatory fashion. Sociotechnical and QWL movements and, more recently, Corporate Culture may express aspirations to be emancipatory. However, since an instrumental rationality pervades their recipes for change, such approaches are problematic in relationship to less compromised ideas about emancipation (Alvesson, 1987). Some weak emancipatory potential is present, nonetheless, in their concern to remove overtly degrading and fragmenting forms of work. Since the questioning and Utopian elements of these approaches are largely absent, their emancipatory elements are best viewed as incremental.

When it comes to emancipatory projects directed at changing social relations, there is greater variety in terms of the type emphasized. Some contributions to participation are, like most means-focused research, incrementally oriented, but they may also incorporate a more ambitious interest in modifying social relations (e.g. Gustavsen, 1985). Typically, the interest lies in facilitating workplace democracy, often through action research and sometimes in collaboration with unions (Sandberg, 1981). Most Marxist-inspired approaches (such as Braverman, 1974; Clegg and Dunkerley, 1980) conceptualize emancipation as a matter of radically changing social relations. Their emphasis is typically Utopian (and often questioning). They push for a classless society in which the coordination of productive activity is based on consensual social relations.

CT-inspired authors and other radical humanists also challenge the rationality of existing ends but are more interested in the realization of the somewhat abstract goals of human freedom, creativity, rational dialogue, etc. They are generally concerned with ideology critique (e.g. the critique of scientism) that has a strongly questioning orientation (Alvesson, 1987; Mumby, 1988). Sometimes there is also an interest in more incremental projects, such as Forester's (1989) suggestions for the emancipation of planning practices from institutionalized forms of domination; or in Utopian ones, like Schumacher's (1974) ideas on small-scale, ethical production, Shrivastava's (1993; 1994a; 1994b) ideas on ecologically oriented ('ecocentric') management, or Burrell's (1992) ideas on pleasure as a driving force and end that can subvert its contemporary use as a source of profits (e.g. the leisure industry).

As we argued earlier, it is extremely difficult, if not impossible, to maintain a hard and fast distinction between 'truly emancipatory' and 'falsely emancipatory' discourse and practice. We have stressed our scepticism about the possibility and value of 'purist' formulations of CT. We believe instead in fostering an approach that opens up and explores – theoretically and practically – a space between the heady abstractions of CT and the glitzy hype of humanistic MOS. But, in doing so, we are anxious to discredit attempts to equate micro-emancipation with (pseudo-) humanistic versions of MOS in which conflicts between the material requirements and/or ethical sensibilities of human populations, on the one hand, and the priorities of capitalist corporations, on the other, are obscured through the presentation of a seductive package of humanistic management techniques.

We have suggested that the emancipatory contribution of both CT and MOS can be enhanced if reflection upon the potential of its discourses and practices is not restricted to the narrow space covered by only one of the squares in Figure 7.1 above.[6] Emancipation, even in a micro-version, should encourage thinking and acting that transcends a singular type or focus, whether it is 'means', 'social relations' or 'ends'; 'questioning', 'incrementalism' or 'Utopianism'. The narrow targeting of a specific space within our matrix is to be avoided because it fragments and subverts the

idea of emancipation, which is to open up, challenge and transcend constraints. Here we might be misread as advocating a 'grand' approach to
emancipation. It would be a misreading because, in our view, combating a
narrow targeting of emancipation does not necessarily lead to 'grand
critique'. It is the connective space between a narrow, yet concrete, consideration of the micro-politics of emancipation and a broad, yet abstract,
formulation of the historical and politico-economic conditions of change
that we are seeking to open up.

## Reorienting Emancipatory Studies

We have argued that the problems exposed by critiques of CT invite a
reformulation of the idea of emancipation in social science in general, and
in MOS in particular. An important element in such a project is the
development of a new research strategy in which an overtly Utopian
version of Critical Theory – including its promises of fulfilling an emancipatory project of freeing people from 'ideologically frozen social relations'
– is de-emphasized in favour of a more eclectic framework, which includes
perspectives and voices other than CT. Abstract, totalizing attacks on the
prevalent social order (late capitalism, class society, etc.) are then complemented and qualified, if not backgrounded, by studies that explore and
critique particular, local practices without losing sight of the relevance and
potency of more 'global' insights.

In the remaining pages of this chapter, we seek a number of possible
lines of development by considering: (a) the value of ethnography for
emancipatory studies; (b) a new approach to writing and the transmission
of ideas; and (c) new modes of reading in the interpretation of ideas. Our
purpose here is not to offer completely novel approaches. Instead, our more
modest intention is to indicate and illustrate possibilities for micro-
emancipation in the sphere of management and organization.

### Listening to People

The conduct of ethnographic studies of organization presents an opportunity for employees to speak out in a way that can moderate and
challenge the adequacy of more 'totalizing' accounts of management and
organization. Ethnography is a research process in which the researcher
'closely observes, records, and engages in the daily life of another culture
. . . and then writes accounts of this culture, emphasizing descriptive detail'
(Marcus and Fischer, 1986: 18). In ethnography, the researcher is not just
interested in behaviour and structures, but also, and quite often more so, in
symbols and meanings (Rosen, 1991). *Critical* ethnography takes seriously
the complexity, ambiguity and inconsistency of people's discourse and
practice without falling into the empiricist trap of naturalizing the ideology,
power and communicative distortions (including the ambiguity of language)
that are central to the reproduction of management and organization.

While acknowledging the important contribution of interpretive ethnography, the intent of a critical approach is to appreciate how meanings may carry privileged interests (Deetz, 1992a; Putnam et al., 1993). An important challenge for the critical ethnographer is to place local actors' meanings, symbols and values within a wider political, economic and historical framework, while, at the same time, minimizing any tendency for such a framework to press the empirical material into a particular theory and language (a dominating voice). In this way, the politics of management and organization can be disclosed without unduly obscuring the ambiguities and variations of local practice and the multiple ways in which it can be interpreted.

Such a proposal is not entirely novel. There are a number of examples of ethnographic-type studies of organizational work that are informed by a broadly critical standpoint (e.g. Filby and Willmott, 1988; Knights and Collinson, 1987; Kunda, 1992). These studies illuminate and challenge the oppressive and self-defeating features of modern organizations. Critique is concretized and brought to life through analysis of deeply qualitative data. However, instead of unsettling prevailing preconceptions and dogmas, there is a danger that the debunking of conventional wisdom simply conveys a sense of self-righteousness and superiority which seems, paradoxically, to be dismissive of, or to poke fun at, the dilemmas and struggles of the people whose practices are the targets of critique. Of course, critical analysis demands a deflation of pretensions, including the (self-)deceptions of those who occupy positions of relative power and advantage. But it must also be sensitive to their accomplishments, and in particular relate their pretensions to the historical and existential conditions within which their subjectivity is constituted (Knights and Willmott, 1989). Otherwise, critique is needlessly vulnerable to being interpreted and dismissed as 'one-sided', 'axe-grinding', 'negative' and/or 'irrelevant'. It then becomes self-defeating in its mission to communicate the value of emancipatory change.

To counter this tendency, one possibility is to undertake ethnographic studies that proceed from, and include, different critical perspectives and combine 'critical' and 'non-critical' perspectives. Critical ethnographies depart from this approach when the negative, self-defeating aspects of organizational work gain attention without the acknowledging or exploring of more positive, productive features. Their thrust has been necessary and valuable as a corrective to mainstream, functionalist accounts of organizational processes in which the negative aspects are either undisclosed, naturalized or explained away by interpreting them as symptomatic of managerial incompetence. But, in focusing upon the negative, oppressive features of organizations, there is a danger of critical ethnographies alienating readers who, potentially, are open to learning from their insights. It is possible, in principle at least, to emphasise the presence of contradictions and the potential for emancipation without ignoring or devaluing positive advances in the management of concrete organizational problems (e.g. pollution control) under contemporary conditions and restrictions. Such an approach presents one possibility for reducing the gap between CT and conventional MOS.

### New Styles of Writing

The development of an empirically-grounded, more accessible form of CT-informed research can also be facilitated by new styles of writing. Current ideas about writing and experimenting can provide challenging sources of inspiration for CT (see e.g. Calas and Smircich, 1991; Clifford and Marcus, 1986; Marcus and Fischer, 1986; Jeffcutt, 1993). An alternative is to toggle between 'practitioner-friendly' and 'critical-emancipatory' textual elements.

One could imagine a supplementary (or opposite) role of CT in writings which take a traditional approach to established topics. Emancipation can reside in the wings, taking centre stage in a text only when it has something of direct importance to say. Instead of focusing strongly on emancipation and critique in the overall approach, expressions of these impulses could be more selective. Stimulation of critical reflection is perhaps more likely when, instead of concentrating upon the production of devastating critiques of conventional wisdom, there is more exploration of competing interpretations. Through a process of 'critical signalling', portions of texts can point to problems by highlighting the linkages between management theory and capitalism, male domination, manipulation, distorted communication, privileged interests, repression, etc. The idea of emancipation then enters by stealth, in the form of disruptive asides in the text.

This possibility highlights the relevance of designing texts in ways that stimulate self-reflection (Alvesson and Sköldberg, 1996). Wherever possible, reflection should be encouraged not only upon the object of critique but also on the authority of the critique. Of course, this point – like many others in this chapter – is relevant not only for CT (and not least for mainstream MOS). The dangers of simply exchanging the authority of one account (e.g. MOS) for the authority of another (e.g. CT) must be recognized and addressed. If the selection and interpretation of the teaching material illuminates problems and tensions that are widely encountered, and struggled with, then it is perhaps less likely that the text will simply be 'banked' as another nugget of knowledge rather than applied, through a process of critical self-reflection, to illuminate and perhaps transform practice (Grey et al., 1996).[7]

Sometimes a text can be reinterpreted to assume a more emancipation-oriented character. Take, for example, Pondy's (1983) discussion of myths and metaphors. He believes that these are important because 'they place explanation beyond doubt and argumentation' (ibid.: 163). He also argues that 'in myth, the ordinary rules of logic are suspended, anomaly and contradiction can be resolved within the mythical explanation' (ibid.), and that they therefore fulfil important managerial functions. Pondy's interpretation of myths and metaphors parallels the arguments of deconstructionists who seek to reveal how a sense of closure is accomplished by a text. In Pondy's case, closure is understood to be achieved through the use of metaphors and myths – devices that effectively exclude alternative, and potentially disruptive representations of organizational reality. From the standpoint of CT, the presence of myths is oppressive where they impede rather than promote reflection, and thereby inhibit emancipatory change. However, from Pondy's managerialist standpoint, myths are uncritically embraced on the grounds that 'attention to symbolic aspects is necessary for the effective management of organizations' (ibid.: 163).

Processes of emancipation value doubt, for doubt can open a space for critical self-reflection and transformation. In contrast, Pondy's observations have an anti-emancipatory thrust. His argument would have encouraged more critical thinking *if*, instead, he had suggested that: 'critical attention to symbolic aspects is necessary for the discovery of anomaly and contradiction, and – through that – the development of critical reflection among organizational participants'. This conclusion is entirely consistent with Pondy's thesis that myths and symbols obscure contradictions. But it acts to trigger ideas and thoughts in a more emancipatory direction. An alternative to this would be to present both types of interpretation or to make alternative and parallel readings and interpretations of the 'same' phenomenon. In which case, a critical-emancipatory interpretation could follow, or be followed by, alternative kinds of understandings without any compulsion to integrate them (for an illustration, see Alvesson, 1996; Martin, 1992). By creating a series of tensions and (precarious) resolutions, a text can allow the reader to take from it what he or she will. Clearly, the anxiety about this approach, from a CT perspective, is that the reading will be dominated by common-sense interpretations that either dismiss its peculiarly open-ended character or lack the intellectual resources with which to challenge the wisdom of the conventional account. The counter-argument is that where the text resonates with the reader's experience without relying upon an all-guns-blazing critique of conventional wisdom, it may well have a more penetrating and lasting impact.

### Looking for Emancipatory Elements in Texts

Our third illustration of the way that a reconstructed concept of emancipation may be applied relates to the possibility of identifying emancipatory elements in management texts. As noted earlier, Critical Theory is inclined to dismiss ideas that are intended to enhance managers' capacity to raise the productivity of labour (such as Scientific Management, Human Relations and Corporate Culture). On the rare occasions when these ideas are considered, the emphasis tends to be upon their manipulative features. Little attention is given to their – limited – progressive qualities or the contradictory consequences of their application (Alvesson, 1987; Fischer, 1984; Marcuse, 1964).

Yet, as we observed earlier in this chapter, common to humanistic management theory (e.g., McGregor, 1960; Weisbord, 1987), the Corporate Culture literature (Kanter, 1983; Peters and Waterman, 1982) and CT is a challenge to the adequacy of theories that reduce human nature to a more or less sophisticated form of economic rationality. In each case, rationalistic theories are criticized for fostering forms of organization and job design that have the unintended consequence of inhibiting creativity and exerting a generally depressive effect upon morale and productivity. By acknowledging employees' creative capacities, and by expanding opportunities for them to respond to situations in innovative and 'responsible' ways, humanistic MOS theory prescribes a move away from the mechanistic application of bureaucratic rules and procedures to diverse approaches that share a concern to mobilize the sentiments of employees – for example, by seeking to promote flexibility and innovation within the parameters set by a few core values. Those who favour the strengthening of corporate culture to improve organizational performance contend that competitiveness can be increased by encouraging employees to identify with, and internalize, a limited number of superordinate corporate values:

> Let us suppose that we were asked for one all-purpose bit of advice for management, one truth that we were able to distil. . . . We might be tempted to reply, 'Figure out your value system. Decide what your company stands for. What does your enterprise do that gives everyone the most pride?' (Peters and Waterman, 1982: 279)

Such prescriptions can be interpreted simply as manipulative and ideological (see Chapter 1). Managers are being advised to commit resources to identifying and nurturing, and if necessary creating, the values that guide, or will guide, corporate behaviour in ways that exploit the desire of employees to gain a sense of pride, and thus make them more willing to work hard and cooperatively (e.g. flexibly and creatively) for their employer. Though their example of IBM looks somewhat dated from the perspective of the mid 1990s, Deal and Kennedy provide the following illustration of corporate culture thinking:

> A strong culture enables people to feel better about what they do. . . . When a sales representative can say 'I'm with IBM', rather than 'I peddle typewriters for a living', he will probably hear in response: 'Oh, IBM is a great company isn't it?' He quickly figures out he belongs to an outstanding company with a strong identity. For most people, that means a great deal. The next time they have the choice of working an extra half hour or sloughing off, they'll probably work. (1982: 16)

It is not difficult to argue that the insecurity of employees is being exploited as a corporate image is marketed whose purpose is to convince them (as well as customers) that their self-esteem will be boosted by identifying more closely with the superordinate values of the company for which they work. Yet, such invocations also implicitly invite employees to question the existence and value of many established forms of organizational control. For example, the Corporate Culture gurus stress that people are more complex, and have greater potential, than is generally attributed to them (Peters and Waterman, 1982: Chapter 3). No longer are employees being required simply to work accurately and productively in exchange for a wage. Rather, they are being encouraged to view their working lives as a series of opportunities to apply and develop their capacities to be innovative and to exercise discretion. Within the boundaries defined by the culture – and here is the rub for Critical Theory – 'people are encouraged to stick out, to innovate' (ibid.: 106).

It is not too difficult to expose the limitations and anti-emancipatory impulses of such a philosophy (Willmott, 1993a). It can be objected, for example, that the effect of its implementation is to make corporations more illiberal, if not totalitarian, as they hire and fire individuals on the basis of whether they demonstrate a sufficient deference towards their sacred values (Soeters, 1986): 'you either buy into their values or get out' (Peters and Waterman, 1982: 77). Corporations remain shackled to the task of achieving profitable growth to which end, despite failures of strong cultures to deliver improved performance, the strengthening of corporate culture continues to be perceived as a relevant means. Yet, an attentiveness to the virtues of creativity, innovation and discretion also opens up some opportunities for questioning the gap between the promise of these words and the actual conditions of work within such companies (see Wilkinson and Willmott, 1995b). Where this promise is not fulfilled, there is a stimulus to reflect critically upon the rationality of organizations that impede the expression of creativity and innovation (Binns, 1993). Where the promise is realized, albeit in partial and distorted form, its effect is to constitute employees whose sights are, in principle, continuously raised by the expectations about 'autonomy' and 'responsibility' that the corporations aspire to instil into them.

To be clear, we are not saying that Corporate Culture qualifies as (micro-) emancipation. The anti-emancipatory elements are too salient; they concentrate solely on means, taking corporate goals and management prerogatives as given, and thereby cement the social relations through which they are reproduced (Stablein and Nord, 1985). Rather, we are saying that the limited recognition of human creativity, as well as the individual capacity to make choices and exercise discretion, etc., can provide the basis for a more sustained questioning of the ends and priorities of companies and working life, when these are identified as restricting opportunities for the expression of this human potential.

## Summary and Conclusion

In this chapter, we have sought to initiate and develop a conversation between humanistic management theory, Critical Theory and poststructuralism. More specifically, we have explored the question of how the emancipatory impulse of CT may be retained, albeit in revised form, in the

face of quite different theoretical and practical critiques from poststructuralist and practitioner positions.

We have suggested that emancipation does not have to be conceptualized
or realized only in terms of 'grand' projects. Instead, it may be partially and
imperfectly fulfilled in everyday management and organizational practice.
This view, we argued, is consistent with a critical interpretation of
humanistic management theory. It is a view that resonates too with the
scepticism expressed by poststructuralism about all-embracing theoretical
projects envisioning far-reaching, contradiction-free programmes of social
improvement. Encouraging a dialogue between CT and PS (especially the
work of Foucault) can be supportive of less abstract, understandings of
management and organization that can make more accessible the often
remote, philosophical arguments of CT. Indeed, this is a view that Habermas (1994) himself seems to endorse when he observes that 'Foucault's
microanalysis of power calls our attention to an invisible dialectic between
the egalitarian tendencies of the age and those new unfreedoms that settled
into the pores of simultaneously emancipated and systematically distorted
communicative practices' (ibid.: 119). Gains, however small, in terms of
increased discretion and improved job satisfaction should be appreciated as
such, and not be measured solely against Utopian visions of autonomy,
creativity and democracy – visions that may have little meaning for the
everyday life experiences and struggles of many organizational participants.
This positive aspect of contemporary organizational transformation should
not be disregarded or dismissed when drawing attention to its more sinister
and oppressive features.

## Notes

1 We recognize that there are significant differences and tensions within Critical Theory –
for example between Adorno and Habermas (see Chapter 3). We are also aware that the
poststructuralism label has been actively resisted by many of the theorists to which it has been
applied, including Foucault. For us, the contribution of poststructuralism is more important
than disputes over the labels. While Foucault's corpus as a whole cannot be identified with
poststructuralism, his work on the relation between power, truth and subjectivity does have
close affinities with its central concerns (Weedon, 1988).

2 This criticism resonates with the concern, most forcefully articulated by Sloterdijk (1980),
that ideology critique has become too weighty and solemn. By cutting itself off from 'the
powerful traditions of laughter within satirical knowledge, which have their philosophical roots
in ancient kynicism', they have come to assume 'a complete air of bourgeois respectability'
(Sloterdijk, 1984: 202).

3 The intellectual origins of humanism can be traced to the Enlightenment when Man,
through the agency of reason, 'postulated the human, as opposed to a divine, construction of
the ideal' (Dawe, 1979: 375).

4 Marcuse (1955), for example, identified human instincts at the core of human existence
that would disrupt and transcend the totalizing control of advanced society (see Chapter 3).
Currently, Habermas' more cerebral formulation of the core of human activity is dominant.
Autonomy and solidarity is coupled to communicative action. Central here is the anticipation
of a speech act of a free dialogue in a non-authoritarian society where the potentials in
language for questioning, checking and arguing are fully developed (see Chapter 3).

5 When combined with the intellectualism and essentialism in CT, its negativism may account for the marginal presence of CT within, and impact upon, management theory and practice. As we have indicated, this situation is partly attributable to the inaccessibility of the language employed within CT as well as to the dominance of values that are antithetical to CT. Difficulties experienced in publishing critical management research in leading journals, especially in USA, mean that its contribution has been muted, if not entirely 'silenced' (Calas and Smircich, 1987), even though there is clearly an increasing amount of critical work produced – as witnessed by this book. As a consequence, CT struggles to attain a position from which its voice can be heard.

6 The argument against restricting the project of emancipation to one focus or type does not strike solely against 'grand' versions of improvement and liberation. Certainly, it is unsatisfactory in emancipatory projects to exclude the more mundane levels of incremental change – and thereby the concerns of organizational participants. But it is equally unsatisfactory to improve means without critically considering the wider context of social relations or alternative ends. Without the latter, we can hardly talk about emancipation. Many (most?) forms of Organization Development and neo-Human Relations techniques fall victim to this criticism since they routinely abstract organizational behaviour from its context and/or alternatively, reduce the analysis of context to the interaction of a set of conditioning variables. They typically take efficiency and profit motives for granted and subordinate 'humanization' to these dominant goals (Alvesson, 1987). Similarly, as we argued in Chapters 2 and 3, ideas about women in management, for example, are inadequately understood when they are boiled down to the issue of equal access to career possibilities, without any consideration of the more profound relationship between gender relations and organizational arrangements and goals (Alvesson and Billing, 1992; Calas and Smircich, 1993; Ferguson, 1984). Emancipatory discourses and practices are partial and incomplete without full recognition of the role of macro-level forces – such as class, race and gender structures and associated ideologies of domination that pervade and legitimize the world of organization and management. Taking the idea of emancipation seriously – even when revised along the lines suggested here – does not leave the social totality unexamined, taken for granted or undisturbed, but keeps a critical eye on how it puts its imprints on the micro-level. Likewise, a focus on elements for micro-emancipation – such as the message of an advertisement appealing to the desire to feel young and beautiful – may, for example, strengthen a general questioning of how corporations and marketing create consumer-centred identities (see Chapters 3 and 5).

7 The banking concept of knowledge is drawn from Freire (1972). It is a notion which directly echoes Horkheimer's (1937: 222) critique of the Cartesian understanding of knowledge in which the 'essential unchangeableness between subject, theory, and object' is assumed.

# 8

# Critical Theory and Management Practice

In Chapter 7 we argued for an approach, broadly informed by Critical Theory (CT), that acknowledges and explores commonalities between CT and progressive elements in management and organization studies. In this chapter, we explore further the relevance and impact of CT for people working in organizations – academics and students as well as practitioners – who are potential agents of (micro-)emancipatory transformation. An important task and contribution of Critical Management Theory (CMT), we argue, is to promote a more systematic and critical consideration of the contexts of organizational work; and to strengthen resistance to pressures to comply with the reified logic of functional imperatives and the demands of corporate conventional wisdom.

Individual employees (or groups of these employees), including managers and academics, are an important audience for CMT.[1] Our image of these people, ourselves included, is not that of heroes or 'black belt' emancipatory warriors who have already achieved self-clarity and autonomy. Rather, we picture diverse individuals and groups struggling to 'get by' – to deal with everyday challenges and frustrations – in conditions that are psychologically demanding, and where personal ambitions, the threat of unemployment and other pressures often militate against progressive, emancipatory forms of practice. The ideas presented in this chapter are directed at practitioners and students who are open to incorporating elements of critical reflection in their work and careers. We also address the situation of management teachers and the socio-political conditions that provide obstacles, but to some extent also openings, for more radical research and teaching agendas. Because we explore some of the implications of CT for the working lives of different groups (e.g. management practitioners but also academics), the chapter is inevitably somewhat fragmented.

We begin by setting CT within a discussion of alternative means of promoting social change. We then review alternative CT-inspired models of reflective practice before contemplating the possible consequences of critical thinking upon corporate employees. There we return to the argument, sketched in earlier chapters, that decisions are often complex, ambiguous and involve trade-offs between competing objectives and rationalities. As a consequence, there is frequently some space for exercising judgement and discretion in ways that can reduce dependence and apathy, and expand autonomy and responsibility. However, such opportunities are not always seized; and we therefore address and discuss the resistance to research and teaching that is critical of received wisdom and corporate ideologies. Finally, we reaffirm our view that there remain opportunities to debunk and transform dominant forms of discourse and practice.

## Means of Promoting Progressive Social Change

Before dealing with the question of how Critical Management Theory may inspire more reflective forms of organizational practice, we consider alternative means of putting into practice the ideals of contemporary critical thought. In principle, and without focusing particularly on CT, the following four means of promoting progressive reform can be identified:

1 *'Better', more enlightened, forms of social engineering, including management and public administration.* Here it is assumed that modern, progressive forms of management may accomplish greater individual autonomy, community and/or self-fulfilment in organizations. Although intended principally to improve productivity, quality and flexibility, a number of contemporary management techniques and programmes (e.g. quality circles, Total Quality Management) can encourage limited, local forms of teamworking and involvement, as we acknowledged in Chapter 7. There is some shading of this model of social improvement into point 4 below.

2 *Political reforms, often championed by leftist parties and movements, enshrined in legislation on consumer policy, worker safety, environmental protection etc.* Through regulations mediated by the legal system, constraints on corporations are applied, and examples of 'best practice' and 'good citizenship' are promoted, often in 'partnership' with industry.

3 *Political struggles pursued mainly outside the formal political system* (e.g. by environmental protection groups or by members of the women's movement). These struggles often aim to influence politico-legal systems, but they also routinely achieve other, more far-reaching effects that act to change understandings and attitudes in a progressive way. For example, more ecologically-informed customers may make choices that induce manufacturers to produce 'cleaner' or more sustainable products; female (and male) employees may be strengthened by the women's movement in their resolve to resist traditional, gendered employment practices and divisions of labour.

4 *Forms of collective action and participation in the community or the workplace.* In some organizations (e.g. universities, cooperatives and knowledge-intensive firms) forms of participation, or at least 'networking', are to some degree institutionalized, as a consequence of their collegial development.[2] In comparison to the programmes identified in point 1, forms of local participation are less orchestrated from above and can be productive of less hierarchical forms of organization. More far-reaching forms of involvement are usually conditional upon a change in the legal base favouring co-determination, sometimes backed up by co-ownership.

These four means of progressive reform are all relevant ingredients for challenging and counteracting ideologies and practices that impede and/or suppress the development of greater autonomy and responsibility. Critical Management Theory (CMT) can in various ways support these kinds of reform. It may, for example, contribute to the critical evaluation of participative modes of management by (a) highlighting the limitations of manipulative methods and techniques (e.g. their use in Total Quality Management, Wilkinson and Willmott, 1995a), (b) researching how organizations are involved in implementing progressive legislation and policies (e.g. Flood and Jackson, 1991a), (c) studying progressive social movements and new organizational forms to assess their effects and suggest paths for future development (e.g. Grimes and Cornwall, 1987), and (d) conducting research that is of direct relevance from the subordinates' or union's point of view (e.g. Brown and Tandon, 1983). In many cases, such evaluations can be facilitated by non-managerialist methodologies as well as by other radical schools of analysis (see Chapter 2).

Critical Management Theory is a relevant source of inspiration and guidance for such studies and projects. But CMT's major contribution to reform differs from the four means of promoting change summarized above, and from associated theories and methodologies. As we indicated in our discussion of micro-emancipation in Chapter 7, the most distinctive and far-reaching contribution of CMT resides in its capacity to stimulate and nurture the development of critical consciousness and less distorted communication. Its strength – like that of CT in general – lies in reflection that encourages emancipatory thinking, communication and change rather than specific problem-solving or answering distinctly empirical questions. It is in the (re)formation of consciousness that CT can make a difference by presenting challenges to what is taken for granted, and by inspiring and supporting new forms of thinking and action. Reality 'out there' (ecology, material structures, economic forces) is, of course, of utmost significance for the quality of life. Polluted air and water, for example, immediately affects life's quality in dramatic ways. But, from a CT perspective, how people think about, monitor, and enact this reality is no less important because, arguably, *we can only communicate, critically evaluate and transform the 'quality' of this 'external reality' through our knowledge of it and our capacity to reflect critically upon it*. This is why communication, and the encouragement of critical reflection upon the (ideologically distorted) media and contents of communication, is a cornerstone in CT's project; and it is equally relevant for CMT.

By assisting in a process of engendering and extending local forms of critical consciousness within organizations, CMT can make a contribution to a broader movement of emancipatory transformation. When complemented and enriched by Foucauldian analysis (see Chapter 7), attention can be directed towards 'the endless everydayness of small, insignificant claims and counterclaims (which) provides the full measure of the functioning of power in corporations' (Deetz, 1992a: 302). Promoting changes in the orientations of individual employees is vital, not just for the improvement of local situations but for wider processes of emancipatory change. As we emphasized in Chapter 7, micro-settings do not exist in a social vacuum. It is therefore necessary to challenge and dissolve a tendency to divorce private troubles from public issues by appreciating how local tensions and frustrations form an integral part of the larger context.

## Ideas for More Reflective Work Methods

CMT assumes that organizations must be managed by critically minded and reflective human beings if we are to weaken the grip of instrumental rationality and its deleterious consequences in terms of ego administration, pacification, conformism, wastefulness, pollution, etc. (see Chapter 1). Committed to the development of dialogically based micro-decisions and actions in everyday working life, the intent of CMT is to encourage critical reflection along a broad scale which, though focusing upon local forms of domination (e.g. distortions in communication found in micro-settings), interprets these in relation to wider historical forces (e.g. patriarchy). To illustrate how CMT addresses emancipatory change within organizations, we consider the contributions of Forester and Ulrich on planning and the work of Payne on corporate ethics. In each case, Habermas' work is applied to advance and facilitate pro-emancipatory principles for organizational work.

Forester (1985, 1992, 1993) has used Habermas' theory of communicative competence to argue that planning should be viewed as attention-shaping (communicative action), and not purely, or principally, as a means to a particular end (instrumental action). Close attention is paid to the subtle communicative effects that shape and mediate the planning process. Commenting upon its dynamics, Forester observes that: 'Actions as diverse as threatening, promising, and encouraging . . . may be instrumentally oriented toward some end, but each is fundamentally and practically communicative too . . . action *seeks ends and meaningfully communicates*: the most instrumental action without meaning would be simply *meaningless*, not even recognizable as an action' (1993: 24). Applying the theory of communicative competence, Forester shows how each of Habermas' types of validity claim can be used to reveal distortions of communication, and thereby expose forms of domination (see also Chapters 3, 4 and 5). This research is guided by a concern to reduce communicative distortions through practical measures so as to re-member the norms of comprehensibility, sincerity, legitimacy and truth[3] at various levels: the face-to-face level, the organizational level and the political economical (structural) level. In this process, the following vision of local planning practice emerges:

> As we broaden our understanding of the planner's action (from technical to communicative), we come to understand the practical organizational problems planners face a little differently. We come to understand that problems will be

> solved not by one expert, but by pooling expertise and non-professional contributions as well; not by formal procedure alone, but by informal consultation and involvement; not predominantly by strict reliance on data bases, but by careful use of trusted 'resources', 'contacts', 'friends'; not through formally rational management procedures, but by internal politics and the development of a working consensus; not by solving an engineering equation, but by complementing technical performance with political sophistication, support-building, liaison work, and finally, intuition and luck. (Forester, 1985: 212)

Forester's research illustrates the relevance of Habermas' theory of communicative competence for interrogating the discursive acts that are a routine feature of organizational work. More specifically, it enables us to raise and explore systematically the critical issue of whether communications are genuinely cooperative achievements or the product of strategic action in which force is overtly or covertly substituted for open discussion. Forester (1983) suggests that where conditions for questioning communications are impoverished or absent, such that organizational members have little or no possibility for challenging and debating demands that are made upon them, there are strong grounds for suspecting that the framework of social norms is founded upon 'tyranny rather than authority, manipulation rather than cooperation, and distraction rather than sensitivity' (ibid.: 240). By providing us with a framework for exposing and analysing the way domination is institutionalized in mundane organizational work, CMT can stimulate the process of challenging and transforming its rationality.

In Chapter 6 we noted how, within the field of Operations Research (OR), a similar set of concerns has animated Ulrich's (1983, 1986) Critical Systems Heuristics (CSH). Ulrich, like Forester, is concerned to engage with the lived experience of organizing and planning, as contrasted with theoretical models of an ideal discourse. He seeks a form of *practical discourse* that provides the necessary (dialectical) mediation between reason as an intellectual ideal and practice as an experiential reality. In this discourse, the emphasis is upon facilitating a movement towards forms of practice that approximate more closely to the abstract principle of generalizability of interests enshrined in Habermas' conception of the ideal speech situation and his theory of communicative competence. The intent of Ulrich's CSH is to subject experts' claims to unrelenting scrutiny by seeking to expose and debate their normative basis.

> Critical Systems Heuristics . . . is intended to serve a critical purpose against the objectivist illusion in prevailing concepts of rational planning. . . . If it succeeds in its purpose, it will provide planners and concerned citizens alike with an effective tool of reflection and criticism – reflection on the inevitable normative content of all planning. Planning is rational, from the perspective of this study, if the involved planners and the affected citizens make transparent to themselves and to each other this normative content. (Ulrich, 1986: 20)

Ulrich's concern is to develop a methodology that reveals the normative content of the boundary judgements associated with what he calls 'justification break-offs' – which occur when, sooner or later, people cease to provide any rationale or defence of their claims. To this end, Ulrich has constructed a checklist of twelve questions which are intended to enable the people involved to interrogate 'a design's normative content and challenge the "objective necessities" by which the other side may seek to justify or dispute the underlying boundary judgements' (ibid.: 6). Overall, the purpose of the checklist is to stimulate reflection and debate concerning issues of: who the beneficiaries of a given system are; who controls the system; upon what authority sources of expertise draw; how the design of the system is legitimated, etc. In each case, those involved in, and those affected by, the design of systems are invited to compare their understanding of what *is* actually the case with their conception of what *ought* to be case. Recommending this approach, Ulrich (ibid.: 9) argues: 'Contrasting "is" and "ought" boundary judgements provides a systematic way to evaluate the normative content of planning while at the same time rendering transparent the normative basis of the evaluation itself.'

The boundary judgements applied in these definitions are then subjected to critical examination. This can be done, Ulrich argues, by recognizing and applying 'polemic'. The term is used in a somewhat ironical way to recall that all definitions and statements necessarily rely upon 'justification break-offs' and, in this sense, share a common limitation. Ulrich argues that an awareness of this shared characteristic can empower lay persons to challenge the definitions favoured by the expert without any special obligation to justify the rationality of such a challenge. So long as these lay persons do not privilege the validity of their own definition of the situation, it is possible – in principle – to impose the burden of proof or justification upon those who do (implicitly) make positive validity claims about their own definitions and plans.

Payne's (1991) interest in corporate ethical reform is quite similar to Ulrich's CSH. Briefly, Payne seeks to create a setting in organizations in which diverse stakeholders are relatively free to discuss ethical issues. Without denying the restrictions and practical difficulties of achieving an ideal speech condition, he commends a middle course 'between awareness of the impossibility of ever realizing the ideals of true participant autonomy and responsibility versus the dangers of readily accepting conventional organizational communication and meanings' (ibid.: 75). Payne's proposal is that an 'ethical dialogue group' be created and developed within organizations that would serve an interpretive *and* critical role in raising issues and critical consciousness, rather than acting directly as a change agent. His justification for this separation between discourse and transformative action is that the latter activity calls for other skills and priorities, and that a focus upon the practicalities of managing change would tend to constrain and prejudice processes of critical reflection. The modest role of the ethical dialogue group is to identify and explore stakeholder views and moral claims, and to propose a critical standard by which to improve theory and practice (see also Guba and Lincoln, 1989 which is critically assessed by Laughlin and Broadbent, 1994).

As with practical problems associated with Ulrich's CSH (discussed above and in Chapter 6), the obvious limitation of Payne's proposals concerns the probable resistance by some stakeholders (e.g. investors and owners) to an institution – the ethical dialogue group – that threatens to legitimize the claims of, and perhaps give equal or greater recognition to, other stakeholders (e.g. employees, citizens) whose values and priorities may directly challenge the status quo. On the other hand, the separation of consciousness-raising from practical intervention may at least allow a critical questioning of existing priorities to be voiced, and, perhaps, a gradual incremental shift in understanding, policy and practice to be fostered (see Chapter 7). Even if it fails to attract support or, if implemented, becomes no more than a talking shop that immediately changes nothing, an ethical dialogue group may nonetheless be of value in revealing how some stakeholders are more dominant, and unaccountable, in shaping processes of communication and decision making in organizations.

Besides the work of Forester, Ulrich and Payne, there are a number of other researchers who have attempted to apply the ideas of CT to facilitate change. Gustavsen (1985), for example, has addressed the issue of creating preconditions for a dialogue in labour/management interaction in relation to the implementation of workplace reform. Others (e.g. Herda and Messerschmitt, 1991) have suggested that Habermas' ideas of undistorted communication could inform programmes of organizational development. While we are broadly supportive of such initiatives, and accept that they may involve some compromising of 'purist' CT (see Chapter 7), translating the insights of CT into practical situations does risk the trivialization and dilution of its critical, emancipatory intent. Adaptation to pragmatic concerns carries with it the danger of deflecting attention from more fundamental issues (e.g. those concerned with the preconditions and quality of communication). Nonetheless, we believe that efforts to apply CT in ways that may facilitate micro-emancipation should be actively supported and developed. It is only by struggling to apply CT-type thinking that its relevance for understanding and transforming everyday, organization work can be appreciated and assessed. In turn, it is hoped that these efforts can be refined and developed to advance CMT in directions that are theoretically rigorous *and* practically relevant.

## CMT as a Source of Inspiration for Working Life

Using CT as a source of inspiration for distinct methodologies is, of course, not the only way in which it may influence organizational practice. CMT also can equip students, managers and other practitioners with concepts, ideas and understandings that act as a counterweight to the ideological indoctrinations and functional imperatives encountered in corporate settings. As students and managers become acquainted with, and (hopefully) persuaded by, the relevance and value of CMT, they may be drawn to develop practices that actively encourage critical reflection, self-clarification and collective and individual autonomy. Among the possible consequences of this developmental process are more reflective career choices and managerial decision making that incorporates a broader spectrum of criteria. Of course, the practical effects of critical consciousness do not end here, but we identify these two areas as pertinent examples.

## CMT and Career Choices

Given wider exposure to CMT, it can be expected that more people will become rather more discriminating in their choice of employers and careers. The choice of employment is already shaped by values, irrespective of encounters with CMT. Vegetarians are not inclined to work in slaughterhouses. Many people would not actively seek work in the defence/war industry, etc. But, as critical reflection upon the ethical nature and implications of corporate activity develops, it can be anticipated that employees will become increasingly sensitized to, and discriminating about, the obvious and not-so-obvious dimensions of employment – ranging from gender policies and work environments to the social value and ethical acceptability of the products and services that they produce and distribute. Potential recruits may ask themselves, for example, whether particular products and services, and the jobs attaching to them, are vital or marginal for human well-being.

Instead of treating the labour market predominantly in an economically rational way, and instead of assuming that legal corporate activities are also morally just (or simply beyond ethical reach), the development of a more sceptical and questioning attitude is anticipated. People – or at least those with options in the labour market – may be more inclined to work for companies and organizations that, upon reflection, are considered to fulfil socially productive purposes or, at least, engage in activities that have comparatively limited harmful effects. Conversely, organizations whose contributions are perceived to be more dubious, in terms of social and ecological impacts as well as employment practice, would become less attractive places of employment.

Of course, it is also likely that the attractiveness of an employer or a job will be greatly contingent upon concrete benefits such as job security, work climate, pay and career opportunities. It is to be expected that the risk of unemployment will continue to compromise and limit employee sensitivity to the ethical-political virtues of different employers. It is unrealistic to expect a sacrifice of family responsibilities to some higher, collective ideal (although historically such sacrifices are not unknown). But, at the same time, it is relevant to recognize that neither egoism nor altruism are social constants. They are each contingent upon socio-cultural conditions (see Perrow, 1986, for a discussion of how different types of organizational conditions influence such orientations). Pressures of the market economy and consumerist ideology in respect of, for example, undergraduate (business) education in the UK and elsewhere tend to promote a self-centred, instrumental 'consumption' of education. But against this pressure is a countertendency, especially among the younger generation, towards an appreciation of the interdependent, synergistic nature of human activity, and an emergent awareness that self-interested actions are frequently counterproductive for personal as well as social development. This is perhaps most evident in growing ecological awareness.

Without denying that unconditional altruism is unlikely to become, in the foreseeable future, a stable or reliable basis for occupational and career choice, the influence of CMT can make a valuable contribution to shifting perceptions and priorities – for example, by focusing attention upon otherwise neglected or 'hidden' dimensions of corporations with regard to such matters as employee involvement, recruitment and promotion policies, environmental policies, etc. At the very least, exposure to CMT is likely to challenge conventional views on the importance of pay and consumption 'needs' in relation to other concerns – such as the ecological soundness or the social contribution of one's job. As we indicated in Chapter 5, CT shows that consumptionism is an unreliable source of happiness. Critical insights into consumption may encourage new priorities in life.

Having said this, it is necessary to acknowledge that CMT provides no ready-made answers or blueprints for action. Its contribution is to encourage broader reflection upon what is rational and valuable, and, relatedly, to counteract ideologies and discourses that pre-structure choice in accordance with narrow sets of ascribed needs and values. Consequently, it is not possible to predict outcomes following exposure to CMT. Any such specification would be inconsistent with the understanding that action is mediated by processes of interpretation whose patterning and effects cannot be reliably predicted. The contribution of CMT is to unsettle the rationality of what is taken for granted, not to provide an alternative source of authority that can be blindly or mindlessly accepted.

### CMT and Decision Making

As we have argued in earlier chapters, corporate life produces and reproduces a number of social and environmental irrationalities. These include unsustainable growth, pollution and class, gender and ethnic forms of domination and exploitation, in addition to the construction of compulsive (consumer) 'needs' and identities. CMT can prompt managers and other corporate participants to (a) consider the implications of their work for these wider concerns and (b) take these effects into account in decision making, so as to limit unnecessary suffering and increase opportunities for emancipatory action.

One example of socially irrational decision making that can also have devastating human and ecological consequences is the design and operation of systems that are unsafe and result in major industrial accidents. In many cases, such accidents could have been avoided if only a more reflexive and less cavalier approach to the management of risk had been adopted. However, it is all too easy to attribute blame for such accidents to careless individuals or rogue organizations when, arguably, the absence of reflection and care is symptomatic of a politico-economic system in which short-term advantage is sought without regard for the longer-term consequences – human and ecological. As Gephart and Pitter (1993) have argued, accidents are 'often seen to be caused by the failure of individuals to acquire, possess, or implement (relevant) skills or traits' (ibid.: 248) when they are more plausibly interpreted as a manifestation of a web of social and economic relationships in which a blind eye is turned, more or less knowingly, to the risks inherent in particular activities. Analysing accidents in the oil and gas industries, Gephart and Pitter (ibid.) apply Habermas' (1976) ideas on the connection between economic, political, legitimation and motivation crises to argue that 'rational' decisions, inadvertently, produce major industrial accidents; and that risks inherent in the pressures of capitalism[4] (e.g. to reduce costs and increase returns) are transferred from corporations, via the State, to individual citizens who either suffer directly the consequences of these pressures or, as taxpayers, pick up the tab for remedying their effects. The Challenger disaster provided an exceptionally traumatic and shocking example of the effects of such pressures.

We are not (quite!) naïve or idealistic enough to believe that increased awareness among decision makers of the negative consequences of their decisions will make them more willing to sacrifice profits and, by implication, their jobs or career prospects. But, to a considerable extent, irrationality and socially unnecessary suffering is a consequence of narrow, technocratic thinking that simply disregards alternative priorities and forms of action that could be supported without necessarily damaging profits or jobs. Even though the market economy routinely condones wastefulness (e.g. packaging and disposability) and promotes a predatory attitude to nature, it is often possible to develop designs and processes that are humanly and ecologically less destructive *and* equally, if not more, profitable. The idea that there is only one 'best' (i.e. profitable) way of managing organizations has long since been debunked. Neither this myth, nor the reactionary Leftist resistance to all reform on the grounds that it extends the life of capitalism, should impede the reduction of needless suffering and waste.[5]

To summarize, we have briefly explored three areas in which critical thought may have an influence on managerial decision making: (a) when there is scope for letting various values and criteria make a difference, and enabling other ideals to complement, if not replace, profit maximization; (b) when there is a non-competitive relation between business goals and other ideals; and (c) when decisions are sufficiently ambiguous to permit the inclusion of alternative means of achieving conventionally 'acceptable' outcomes. People who have developed a capacity to think critically, and thereby challenge conventional wisdom, we believe, are better equipped to shift the balance away from established priorities and objectives towards other, more socially and ecologically defensible goals. CMT can inspire and guide a cognitive shift in which wider concerns put their imprints on the criteria and considerations governing decisions and actions. Despite the pressures of capitalism and its promotion of egoism, 'common decency' and 'good intentions' continue to play some part in the shaping of management practices and organizational development. CMT at once supports and appeals to such orientations. But critical thought then seeks to stiffen such well-intentioned, liberal concern.

### The Reflective and the Unreflective Practitioner: Two Illustrations

We now illustrate elements of the preceding argument by giving examples of two top executives who exhibit very different orientations in terms of reflectiveness. We highlight: (a) variations in terms of managers' ways of relating to what they are doing, (b) the possibilities for reflection, and (c) the relevance of reflection.

The first case is taken from John Sculley's book *Odyssey* (1988), to which we made passing reference in the conclusion to Chapter 1. Sculley, subsequently CEO at Apple, describes his time as a top executive at Pepsi when the company was embroiled in the so-called 'Cola Wars'. The following is an extract from an important executive meeting:

> Like the other meetings, this one was a ceremonial event. We marked it on our calenders many weeks in advance. Everyone wore the unofficial corporate uniform: a blue pin-striped suit, white shirt, and a sincere red tie. None of us would ever remove his jacket. We dressed and acted as if we were at a meeting of the board of directors. (ibid.: 2)

During the meeting, Pepsi is declared now to be Number One in the USA market. It had captured a 30.8 per cent share compared to Coca-Cola's 29.2 per cent. The executives were, to say the least, elated:

> It was one of those moments for which you worked your entire career. We always believed, since the early seventies, when Pepsi was widely viewed as the perennial also-ran, that we could do it. All of us started out with that objective, and we never took our eyes off it. (ibid.: 3)

John Sculley then goes on to disclose, with a touch of self-deprecation, his own attitude towards this enterprise:

> If I was brash or arrogant on my way to the top, it mattered little to me. I was an impatient perfectionist. I was willing to work relentlessly to get things exactly right. I was unsympathetic to those who couldn't deliver the results I demanded. (ibid.: 4)

> Winning to me, was an obsession. I was driven not only by the competition but by the force of powerful ideas. I demanded the best of myself. If I walked away from an assignment not totally consumed or absorbed to near exhaustion, I felt guilty about it. Dozens had failed at this regimen, but to me, Pepsi was a comfortable home. (ibid.: 7)

Sculley assures his readers that the rules at Pepsi were fair, even though executives who failed were quickly replaced ('either your numbers went up and continued to grow, or you began to comb the classifieds for a job elsewhere'). He and his colleagues (Pepsi appears to have been populated exclusively by male executives) 'didn't complain'. Being critical of the company was taken as a mark of personal failure to adjust and deliver. Complaining was simply inappropriate behaviour among the Pepsi managers who regarded themselves as:

> the best of the best. In a corporation populated with bright, ambitious achievers ... they had proven they were intellectually and physically fit survivors in America's corporate Marine Corps. (ibid.: 2)

Sculley and his colleagues appear to have behaved like the members of a religious cult whose prospects of salvation were measured in the sales of sweetened water. In this context, it became unreasonable to ask: What is the purpose of the Pepsi Corporation? Does it accomplish anything socially valuable? Work was self-evidently purposeful so long as more sweetened water was sold, and the ultimate prize was to outsell Coca-Cola. A person working for the Red Cross, saving people from starving to death, a member of a resistance group fighting a cruel dictator, or a researcher tracking the mystery of cancer or Aids, could not have been more committed than Sculley was to increasing Pepsi's sales. Through rigid codes (e.g. dressing), and through carefully orchestrated rituals ('public hangings' for poor performance), discipline and conformity at Pepsi were tightly maintained. According to Sculley, executives willingly subordinated their working lives to a strict logic of winning market share. Friendship, family and other interests were pushed to the margins. This corporate hegemony was so strong that no sign of complaints, doubts or questioning was tolerated. When working for Pepsi, the purpose was self-evident and unquestioned: to be Number One. To doubt, or to become deflected from this purpose was heresy.

When instrumental rationality exerts such a powerful, hegemonic influence, the purpose and the reason guiding the objectives are of no interest (see Chapter 2). For Pepsi executives, the sales figures were more significant and real to them than anything else. To raise questions about this priority, save to question how sales might be further increased, was viewed as a symptom of personal inadequacy or irrationality, if not insanity. Commenting upon the values and priorities routinely pursued by capitalist corporations, Braverman (1974) has suggested that capitalists are the contemporary equivalents of King Ahab who boasted 'my means are wise, my goals are insane'. Reading Sculley's account of the Pepsi Corporation gives the critical reader a similar feeling, except that the ascription of wisdom to the means might be deemed a tad generous.

In responding to such censoriousness, it may be objected that CT acts as a killjoy: it draws attention only to hidden psychological injuries following from the discrepancy between the manager as a rational broker of diverse stakeholder interests and the executives at Pepsi who were consumed with the mission of becoming Number One; or between the grandiose images of the product commercials and the less perfect looks and 'lifestyle' of the viewer.[6] Our response to this criticism is that the demands placed upon Pepsi executives (by peer pressure as much as by any 'external force', notably shareholders) are symptomatic of a capitalist economy in which the pursuit of profitable growth – in this case, by increasing market share – can come to take priority over all other concerns, for individual managers as well as corporate investors. It simply doesn't matter *how* profit is made – in terms of the usefulness of the product or the conditions under which employees are required to work. Profitable growth alone dictates where human effort is to be directed in the production of goods and services. Enormous amounts of human effort are therefore marshalled and expended in selling sweetened water and similar goods in preference to other activities that, by almost any criterion, would be of greater personal and social value. Executives and consumers are pawns in the game of increasing market share and maximizing profit as they are persuaded that the good things in life are obtainable only by devoting their lives to, or spending money on, commodities whose significance is constructed wholly through an association with other desirable and pleasurable forms of activity (see Chapters 4 and 5). From this perspective, the senior executives at Pepsi, no less than the consumers of their products, are victims as well as perpetrators of a mind-numbing fantasy that mystifies and distorts what, upon critical reflection, is of greater personal and social importance.

A different orientation is articulated in an interview with Mr Harald Agerley, chairman of one of Denmark's largest industrial companies (published by the Danish daily newspaper *Information*, 14 October 1991). Agerley, a businessman nearing retirement, describes how, for many years, his company invested heavily in the cleaning of waste, reducing the usage of water and energy consumption, and reducing pollution from heavy metals, etc. He stresses the possibility and importance of greener strategies in business life. But he also offers the opinion that this is *not sufficient*. For he questions whether ecologically sound business practice can be fully reconciled with profitable operation. He acknowledges that his own company has traded on a positive image (which, in common with an increasing number of PR-conscious executives – such as Richard Branson, Chairman of Virgin – he promotes without cost through newspaper interviews). But Mr Agerley argues that the commercial contribution of securing a favourable 'green' image is quite limited. The commercial pay-offs of ecologically correct business policies, he suggests, are much exaggerated (because they rarely are worth the opportunity cost in terms of delivering requisite levels of profitable growth).

In Mr Agerley's judgement, the idea that companies will reform their policies by being persuaded that ethical and ecological soundness is 'good for business' is seductive but ultimately chimerical. For substantial change to be achieved, he argues, governments must intervene to reform business practice. *Inter alia*, the following measures are identified: forcing companies to provide information about the ecological consequences of their products, taxing materials that are in short supply, increasing taxation on energy usage, and requiring companies to dispose of exhausted products. Unusually for a businessman (even one nearing retirement!), doubts are also publicly raised about the wisdom and sustainability of continuing economic growth, at least in the industrialized world. Given the standard of living enjoyed by a majority of people in the West, Mr Agerley asks whether 'we have not arrived at a point where we should end our apparently insatiable hunger for more material goods'. He suggests that the West could sensibly produce more only if this were directed to the development of other countries.

When considering the respective reflections of Mr Scully and Mr Agerley upon their business experiences, it is a little too easy to identify Sculley as 'the bad guy' and Agerley as 'the saint'. It is true that Sculley does not directly question Pepsi's mission or its business practices – including its cavalier treatment of staff. Nonetheless, his account provides a wealth of insights into the values and priorities of companies like the Pepsi Corporation. Although Sculley does not relate his observations to the logic of capitalist enterprise, his account of Pepsi is not uncritical and can indeed stimulate critical reflection upon its purpose and demands, as we seek to show in a later section of this chapter. In the case of Agerley, it is worth noting that the company's success in decreasing pollution is partly a function of its previously high levels of energy consumption and pollution, which occurred when Agerley was also its CEO. It can also be argued that the expression of such views by people like Mr Agerley (and ourselves) is a luxury that cannot be afforded by those who are less comfortably off. Nonetheless, the views expressed by Mr Agerley, in particular, suggest that there is considerable scope for the development of theory and practice through an alternative logic to that routinely followed by business (see Nord and Jermier, 1992).

## A Garbage Can Model of Critical Thought

In earlier chapters, we have argued that decision making in modern organizations tends to be represented, and idealized, as the product of an instrumentally rational process. Executives are obliged to wrap up their proposals in a rhetoric of rationality and to articulate their decisions in the language of efficiency and effectiveness (Meyer and Rowan, 1977; Gowler and Legge, 1983). In a similar vein, March and Olsen (1976) have suggested that the rhetorical gloss of rationality can belie the extent to which decision making is so often a 'non-rational' activity, and that decisions are frequently the product of more or less random, unsystematic and unpredictable processes. Prefiguring elements of later processual analyses of managerial work and strategic management (see Chapters 1 and 5), March and Olson suggest that decision makers find themselves in a more complex, less stable, and less understood world than the one described by standard theories of organization and organizational choice (see Chapter 4). Decisions, March and Olsen claim, are outcomes of four relatively independent 'streams' of activity within organizations: problems, solutions, participants and choice opportunities. A choice situation, they argue, 'is *a meeting place for issues and feelings* looking for decision situations in which they may be aired, solutions looking for issues to which they may be an answer, and participants looking for problems or pleasure' (ibid.: 25).

To simplify, we identify two intertwined issues that are looking for decision situations. First, those related to the sphere of instrumental rationality (efficiency, profits, etc.); and, secondly issues falling within the politico-ethical sphere (ecology, democracy, autonomy, equality, etc.). With these two types of issue in mind, it can be suggested that the contents of March and Olsen's four streams may be more or less consistent with the ideals of CT. The process may be more or less distorted in communicative terms; the problems addressed and the solutions chosen can be more or less subordinated to a profit maximization/satisficing logic; and the minds of the participants can be more or less technocratically oriented. However, as we have repeatedly argued, the *ambiguity* of many situations may stimulate and promote critical reflection. The iron grip of instrumental rationality is loosened to the extent that decision situations are resistant to closure by its logic (see the earlier discussion of Critical Systems Heuristics).[7] If we combine the notion of a *potentially* reflective and critical manager, as a person capable of instantiating critical discourse, with the ambiguity of decision processes, we can then posit critical reflection as a fifth stream running alongside the other four. When a capacity for critical reflection intercedes with a particular problem (people/solution/choice opportunity), it may be activated and inform a person's efforts to influence a decision (see Forester, 1981, 1993).

At least two kinds of links between critical reflection and the other four streams can be made. The first concerns interpretation. Problems are normally open to many interpretations – upon which the possible solutions depend – which may be more or less technocratic or critically reflective. Deetz (1992a) speaks of the politics of representation, arguing that the language used to perceive and describe a phenomenon is of critical importance. A critical interpretation serves to highlight how 'favoured' representations routinely operate to reproduce the prevailing pattern of domination as alternative representations are marginalized or suppressed (see Chapter 4). In Chapter 7, we used the example of a top manager explicitly identifying his audience as the managers of the company in order to illustrate this point. The same goes for solutions: there are alternative solutions available for most problems, but conventions and institutionalized thought patterns restrict the options. The contribution of critical thinking is to open up awareness of other possibilities for interpreting and acting upon streams of problems and solutions.

A second link between critical reflection and garbage-can decision processes concerns the way that 'the meeting place for issues and feelings' can trigger processes of critical reflection when found by a 'fifth' stream of activity (see Mumby and Putnam, 1992). Diverse politico-ethical dimensions of issues may then be discerned and addressed – including domination, gender inequality, exploitation of personnel, environmental pollution, waste of resources, communication of misleading (dishonest) images to the public, marketing strategies that have harmful social and psychological effects, acquisitions of companies to gain a monopoly position, etc. (see Chapters 4 to 6). Given critical thinking, there is a possibility that the decision making situation – the problem and the solution – is interpreted in a way that is attentive to wider circumstances and effects, and not just those most tightly coupled to growth or profits. Such thinking may not be continuous. Indeed, it is more likely to be sporadic – though accumulative – as it is provoked and developed by issue-specific circumstances. As Deetz has observed:

> The struggle is not against some powerful force out there that directs thought and action, but against the forgotten, hidden, misrecognized, suppressed conflict – the disciplinary power – of the momentary practice. Understanding the micro-practices of closure in the corporation, and as they extend out of the corporation, is a first step. The ideal is to engage in corporate discourse in a way that regains significant conflict and reopens experience on critical social issues. (Deetz, 1992a: 290)

Despite the restrictiveness of corporate discourse – well illustrated by Sculley's account of the meeting at the Pepsi Corporation (and see below) – it is often possible to devise skilful means of unsettling conventional wisdom and stimulating critical reflection without suffering outright rejection. Disrupting the habitual tendency towards cognitive closure is certainly not easy. Yet as many of the new management gurus are also proclaiming, it is necessary to 'undo' embedded assumptions, thought patterns and institutional practices if corporations are not to become moribund. The authority ascribed to such views may, for example, enable employees to appeal to the ideology of 'empowerment' and 'constant change' (Peters, 1988) as they raise questions about the status quo (Binns, 1993; Wilkinson and Willmott, 1995a). Of course, improving the odds for discursive openness and critical thought in corporations is not a panacea. But recognizing and contributing to the existence of critical thinking in the contents of the 'garbage cans' is nonetheless an objective worth pursuing. As we now contend, management education can provide important inputs into such projects.

## Situating CMT in the Context of Management Education and Research

For CMT to have a role in managerial practice, it is of decisive importance that managers and managers-to-be become acquainted with critical thinking during their education. What is the prospect of CMT influencing management research and education? This is less an issue of the strength of CMT in intellectual terms than the politics and practice of educational institutions and learning media. While we recognize that much management education and training occurs, formally or informally, 'in-house' within workplaces, we restrict our discussion to the content and delivery of management education within educational establishments.

Perversely, perhaps, current ideological and material conditions favour the appointment of critical scholars within colleges and university management and business schools, where academic credibility is at a premium. Despite reservations about their ideological credentials, CT-oriented or receptive staff continue to be recruited and promoted, perhaps because they are often highly committed to education, can provide some intellectual weight and are less likely to exploit their position to attract private consultancy work. For a variety of reasons, then, business schools are becoming an increasingly common location for people who are concerned with the development and application of critical reason. While it is probably unrealistic to expect this group to exert a leading or dominant influence in the field of management, the current situation presents interesting opportunities.[8] The number of students taking management courses continues to grow as increasing numbers of students in other disciplines, such as engineering and languages, elect or are required to take courses in management as an integral part of their studies.

## Education as Agenda Setting

Management departments and business schools in colleges and Universities are becoming key socializing agencies for the intelligentsia of advanced capitalist societies. By dint of their numbers alone, management teachers and academics are exerting an increasing influence – over university committees, for example, where they are set to become more directly involved in shaping the very meaning and future of education. Such openings and opportunities are particularly precious from the standpoint of CT because, as we noted in Chapter 3, in contrast to traditional Marxism, CT does not claim the support of any particular class or party (or unions), which means that all educational media become primary channels for facilitating change. Working in management departments can offer opportunities for gaining research and advisory access to decision making centres in society. In turn, this can facilitate the generation of findings and the dissemination of ideas that provide a more grounded illumination, illustration and critique of the operation of the 'purposive-rational sub-systems' in contemporary society (see, for example, Sikka and Willmott, 1995). While acknowledging the pressures upon management academics to comply with the expectations of managerial élites and the temptation to undertake lucrative consultancy projects, Rosen has observed that:

Although such forces reduce the likeliness of critical scholarship, they at the same time provide management academics with a varied tool kit – professional and technical skills, social legitimacy and esteem, access to funding, access to various forums for communication, and so on – to develop the praxis concept by engaging contradictions as a conscious force for change. (1987: 579)

Teaching and the wider dissemination of critical thinking is a key aspect of this praxis. The approach to education most consistent with CT is one of dialogue, rather than formal lecturing, in which students are enabled to see themselves and their situation in a new and meaningful light (Comstock, 1982; Grey et al., 1996). What Forester (1993) has said of public planners is no less true of management teachers and researchers. Namely, that they are not simply engaged in information processing or even problem-solving but are actively involved in shaping attention and agenda setting: 'In their everyday, ordinary questioning of possibilities, planners and policy analysts open or foreclose possibilities, alert or ignore others, call forth or disregard particular concerns, and spread or narrow the bases of design, criticism, participation, and thus decision making' (ibid.: 27). That said, many management teachers and researchers continue to adhere to the view that their mission is to present potential or existing managers with the techniques that, it is anticipated, will equip them to improve corporate and employee performance; and not, for example, to reflect upon the political and ethical significance of issues of ownership and managerial control.[9] In effect, the latter issues are marginalized as matters for the consciences of individual managers or for legislation by the State.

It is necessary to acknowledge that the world of business, management and organization is widely associated with values and practices that conflict with those of Critical Theory. These include the treatment of human beings as means rather than ends, the conformism associated with cultural-ideological control and the manufacturing of consumer identities, 'the bottom line' as the criterion of effectiveness, the reckless pursuit of wealth regardless of the social costs and ecological consequences, etc. (see Grey and Mitev, 1995b). Whereas Critical Theory is identified with the idealist pursuit of an ethics of community and collective self-realization, management is routinely absorbed in the instrumental quest for corporate expansion and careerist gratification. As Fischer has tellingly observed:

As long as the political model remains only a *theoretical* challenge to technocracy, the stakes are largely relegated to the intellectual realm. Once it is introduced as a central theory in the education and training of aspiring managers, however, it begins to take the form of a challenge to existing organizational relations. (1990: 293)

Cultural resistance to CMT is fuelled by external dependencies on the labour market, business, government and political élites – dependencies that frustrate, as well as stimulate, processes of critical reflection. But, equally, when making comparisons between the respective worlds of management and CT, there is a danger of succumbing to an undialectical view: a view that is capable only of grasping points of difference as it overlooks possible points of rapprochement and commonality (see Chapter 7). For, arguably, there is an important (albeit partial and precarious) overlapping of concerns with regard, *inter alia*, to 'the exposure of issues that politico-economic structures would otherwise bury from public view [and] the opening and raising of questions that otherwise would be kept out of public discussion' (Forester, 1993: 6). Despite institutional and ideological resistance to its claims, critical thinking is beginning to infiltrate the management sciences, as our review of the growing literature indicates (see especially Chapters 4–6).

### From Action Learning to Critical Action Learning

Thinking, planning and managing processes are guided by taken-for-granted assumptions about what makes 'good sense'; and managers are not wholly immune to changing expectations and values in society. So, despite efforts to justify and rationalize the making of judgements according to impersonal, technically-rational criteria, it is difficult to deny that the process of identifying and applying technical criteria is a product of political and ethical choice (see Chapter 2; Anthony, 1986). Only in the world of 'decisionism', as Habermas (1974) characterizes it, is it assumed that the values currently dominating corporate activity are natural or lie beyond the reach of rational debate. These criticisms are paralleled by senior practitioners who have questioned the curricula of business schools in which there is an emphasis upon the acquisition of techniques, to the neglect of interpersonal and communications skills (*Harvard Business Review*, September–October and November–December, 1992). To be sure, their criticisms are generally motivated by quite different concerns and values – notably, worries about global competition and eroding competitive advantage. Nonetheless, *each problematizes the value of a technicist orientation to the theory and practice of management* (see also Reed and Anthony, 1992). Each recognizes that knowledge of techniques is of limited value when abstracted from the practical (i.e. morally and ethically charged) realities of human relations and organizational politics (Willmott, 1994b; Fox, 1994a, 1994b). Such concerns have been addressed most directly by the advocates of Action Learning who have developed an alternative to mainstream educational practice.

Action Learning encourages participation in sharing knowledge and constructively criticizing others' diagnoses and prescriptions (McLaughlin and Thorpe (1993).[10] This process is directed to, and by, self-development rather than a concern to learn about theories or models merely as a means of passing exams. Action Learning thus depends upon, and aspires actively to contribute towards, a process of maturation in which ignorance, confusion and uncertainty are openly acknowledged and shared. Instead of concealing these seemingly negative attributes and emotions behind an often defensive front, they are positively valued as a basis for becoming better informed, gaining greater clarity and coming to terms with

Table 8.1   *Traditional and Action Learning approaches to management education (adapted from McLaughlin and Thorpe, 1993)*

|  | Traditional management education | Action Learning |
|---|---|---|
| Worldview | The world is something to learn about | The world is somewhere to act and change |
|  | Self-development is somewhat important | Self-development is very important |
|  | Some notion of correct management practice, established by research, defines the curriculum | Curriculum defined by the manager or organization |
|  | Managers should learn theories or models derived from research | Managers should be facilitated by a tutor to solve problems |
| *Modus operandi* | Experts decide on what should be learnt, when and how much | Experts are viewed with caution |
|  | Models, concepts, ideas are provided to offer tools for thinking and action | Models, concepts, ideas are developed in response to problems |

uncertainties. Some key differences between traditional management education and Action Learning are set out in Table 8.1.

An important feature of the Action Learning process is a growing appreciation of, and sensitivity towards, 'darker' aspects of organizational life that are routinely marginalized, or coded, within everyday management practice. As McLaughlin and Thorpe (1993: 25) have observed: 'At the level of their own experience, managers undertaking Action Learning programmes can come to know themselves and their organization much better. *In particular, they can become aware of the primacy of politics, both macro and micro, and the influence of power on decision making and non-decision making, not to mention the 'mobilization of bias'* (emphasis added). As this reference to 'the primacy of politics' and 'the "mobilization of bias"' implies, there is a direct link to be made between the embodied insights generated by Action Learning and the theoretical contributions of diverse traditions of critical analysis explored in the previous chapters. However, this linkage is by no means automatic. It depends upon the meaning and significance that is attributed to the embodied insights of Action Learning.

It is illuminating to compare and contrast three possible ways of responding to the insights into 'the primacy of politics' generated through processes of Action Learning. The *first* response is to regard these insights as just another 'nugget of knowledge' about people, organizations and society. In which case, they have little more significance for the life of the learner than his or her knowledge of a complex chemical formula. In effect, as this 'nugget' is 'banked', there is a 'cutting off' or compartmentalization between knowing and being (Freire, 1972). A *second* response is to integrate the insights of Action Learning into the individual's established repertoires of knowing and acting. In effect, the insights add to, or refine, the individual's range of tools and techniques for pursuing an established schedule of priorities. This response is distinguished and circumscribed by limited critical reflection on the question of *why* the new 'insight' into 'the primacy of politics' had been previously hidden. Was it no more than a simple accident or oversight? Or was it symptomatic of the interplay of power and knowledge in society? The second response either understands a prior ignorance of politics as a 'one-off' oversight or, more cynically, understands it to be symptomatic of dominant power/knowledge relations but treats *this* understanding as a 'nugget of knowledge' that is equivalent to a chemical formula. In short, the second response effectively disregards, or is blind to, tensions or discontinuities between established knowledge, which had marginalized the significance of politics, and the new knowledge that accords it 'primacy'. Perhaps the recognition and experience of such tension undermines the sense of self-identity that has been invested in the pursuit of established priorities to an extent which makes it too threatening to embrace.

Finally, a *third* response explores further the possibility that some forms of knowledge, and methods of learning, are *systematically* encouraged as other forms of knowledge and insight are routinely marginalized, devalued or suppressed. As we noted above, the second response may integrate this insight, instrumentally, into the pursuit of an established schedule of priorities (see Kotter, 1979; Pfeffer, 1981a).[11] In contrast, the *third* response mobilizes the new insight in a way that interprets the previous lack of awareness as in some way *a medium and outcome of power relations*. Instead of assuming that the insight into 'the primacy of power' is either irrelevant for, or that it can be integrated within, existing repertoires of knowing and acting, the individual is provoked into reflecting upon, and reassessing, the value of previously established priorities and their means of attainment (Coopey, 1995). Of course, this reflection may be partial and temporary: it may not be sustained. Nonetheless, it sows a seed of tension and doubt that may subsequently be regenerated.

Before proceeding, it is perhaps worth emphasizing that the distinction between the three responses is heuristic. If, instead of differentiating the types of response, our focus were upon the lived experience of individual people, we would doubtless discover a complex and dynamic mix of responses. Few individuals, if any, would consistently embody any one type of response. Instead, we would find tensions and alternations between the three types of response – not least because the practical, embodied meaning of 'the primacy of power' takes time and effort to develop, and because individuals invariably experience both personal regression as well as social resistance as they – and we – struggle to change our priorities and repertoires of thought and action.

Critical discourses on management resonate with Action Learning's challenge to traditional approaches to learning and, more specifically, with the insights into power generated by unplanned as well as organized forms

Table 8.2  *An alternative approach to management education using a framework adapted from McLaughlin and Thorpe (1993)*

| | Conventional Action Learning | Critical Action Learning |
|---|---|---|
| Worldview | The world is somewhere to act and change | The world is somewhere to act and change |
| | Self-development is very important | Self-development and social development are interdependent |
| | Curriculum defined by the manager or organization | The interdependence of beings means that no individual or group can gain monopoly control of the curricula |
| | Managers should be facilitated by a tutor to solve problems | Managers are potentially receptive to, and be facilitated by, the concerns of other groups, in addition to individual tutors, when identifying and addressing problems |
| *Modus operandi* | Experts are viewed with caution | Received wisdom, including that of experts, is subject to critical scrutiny through a fusion of reflection and insights drawn from critical social theory |
| | Models, concepts, ideas are developed in response to problems | Models, concepts and ideas are developed through an interplay of reflection upon practice and an application of ideas drawn from critical traditions |

of Action Learning. This fusion, which can be described as Critical Action Learning (CAL), understands that 'the encouragement to think' is provoked by the contradictory forces that play upon everyday life; and that the attentiveness of critical thinking to 'the primacy of power' makes it capable of providing explanations that are rationally more persuasive than those offered by traditional theory (see Table 8.2).

The role of CT and CMT, we have suggested, is to prompt and sustain critical reflection by identifying and challenging forces (e.g. patriarchy, consumerism, technocracy) that are productive of socially unnecessary suffering and/or inhibit critical reflection upon their rationality. Its intent is to nurture, legitimize and give momentum to everyday processes of reflection. These processes may be developed and sustained to the point of transforming the conditions that are productive of the tension. Or reflection may be truncated, weakened and overwhelmed by other forces. It is difficult and potentially dangerous (and, indeed, not a little contradictory!) to provide a formula or blueprint for what is a complex and varying process of critical action learning. However, because it can also be helpful to illustrate what may otherwise be viewed as a highly abstract notion, we offer the following schematic view. We then illustrate the early stages of this schema by reference to John Sculley's account of his experience at Pepsi-Cola that was sketched earlier in this chapter (for a more extended discussion of these issues, see Kjonstad and Willmott, 1995).

In broad outline, the process of Critical Action Learning involves the following moments:

1   An experience of tension (e.g. anxiety or doubt) or the identification of contradiction (e.g. success *and* unhappiness).
2   The interpretation of tension/contradiction as avoidable, i.e. as a social and political phenomena rather than as a 'given' or a natural law.
3   Analysis of the tensions/contradictions, including the conditions that are understood to produce them.
4   Recurrent efforts to resolve tensions/contradictions through struggles to change their conditions of possibility. This includes strengthening the capacity to identify and analyse tensions/contradictions.
5   An experience of new tensions and/or the identification of contradictions arising from the process of struggle. Go back to point 2.

One way of reading Sculley's account of his time at Pepsi (see above) is as a confession that usefully moves beyond the purely self-celebratory books penned by 'heroic' senior executives in recent years. While clearly keen to stress the exceptional talents and quality of Pepsi executives, and thereby trumpet his own outstanding abilities, Sculley (1988) is also somewhat reflective, and even mocking, about the managerial culture at Pepsi in which 'everyone wore the unofficial corporate uniform', including 'a sincere red tie'. He also describes himself, unflatteringly, as 'an impatient perfectionist' who was 'unsympathetic' to anyone who failed to perform to his standards. This is perhaps suggestive of an admission of personal weakness rather than a celebration of macho strength. So, however partial and self-indulgent Sculley's account of his time at Pepsi may be, we suggest that it is expressive of *some degree* of critical reflection. Consider, more specifically, the following passage where Sculley draws attention to the experience of tension, in the form of guilt, that occurred whenever he was not totally consumed with, or absorbed by, his work:

> Winning to me, was an obsession. I was driven not only by the competition but by the force of powerful ideas. I demanded the best of myself. If I walked away from an assignment not totally consumed or absorbed to near exhaustion, I felt guilty about it. Dozens had failed at this regimen, but to me, Pepsi was a comfortable home.

Reflection upon his time at Pepsi enabled Sculley to appreciate how his sense of identity and purpose had become totally invested in the Pepsi Corporation – to the extent that it had become his 'comfortable home'. With the benefit of hindsight, he recognizes how he was captivated by the force of the powerful idea that Pepsi could become Number One in the USA market, even though his commitment to the realization of this idea resulted in expelling family, friends and other interests to the margins of his life. Slavish devotion to the success of the corporation led Sculley to give Pepsi the 'best' of himself, leaving only the residue for others.

Sculley's book can be read, and possibly was intended, as a cautionary tale for executives (and academics!, like ourselves, for whom 'writing' or 'publishing' might be substituted for 'winning' in the above quotation from Sculley) who are vulnerable to the seductions of 'the powerful ideas' generated within corporations. To this extent, the experience of tension is represented as an *avoidable* product of corporate seduction. Sculley's realization that slavish devotion to the corporation was not inevitable (even though it might have meant dismissal from 'America's corporate Marine Corps') gives a critical edge to what might otherwise have been a purely celebratory account of Pepsi culture. It makes it possible for Sculley to be self-deprecating about his obsessive concern to win the 'Cola Wars' (the academic equivalent in the UK being the 'Rating Wars' between different universities and departments, see Willmott, 1995a). However, the lack of *analysis* of Pepsi culture and Sculley's participation within it, ultimately results in a comparatively entertaining read that offers only minimal stimulation and support for critical reflection – an outcome that we associate with Sculley's inclination to naturalize capitalism and egoism (and, of course, the conventions of the genre of popular management books), governed by common-sense ideas and understandings about the value of commercial success.

Sculley entertains us by poking fun at the specifics of the Pepsi culture (e.g. 'the sincere red tie') and its managers who fancied themselves as the 'corporate Marine Corps'. But he makes little connection between the pressures applied to Pepsi managers and the organization of capitalism as a politico-economic system that demands the commodification and exploitation of those who sell their labour to its corporations. The title of Sculley's book, *Odyssey*, alludes to the Homeric original discussed at length by Horkheimer and Adorno in *Dialectics of Enlightenment* (1947a), where it is deployed to illustrate the difficulties that attend the realization of critical reason. In contrast, Sculley tells his story but incorporates little direct reflection upon the significance of his experiences. In effect, the process of Critical Action Learning plateaus at stage 2. Any further reflection is impeded by the naturalizing of capitalism and, relatedly, by the idea that Pepsi executives were sovereign individuals who freely chose to devote themselves to its objectives and felt guilty when they did not. The natural and irreversible egoism and careerism of individuals is assumed to explain the behaviour of the Pepsi executives. No link is made between a confession of 'brashness' and 'arrogance', and the process of socialization that actively fostered and rewarded these 'winning' qualities, precisely because they are conjoined with an obsessive willingness 'to work relentlessly to get things exactly right'. Nor, most crucially, does Sculley connect his commitment to Pepsi values and objectives with a process of socialization and education (to a high level) that seemingly incapacitated him and other senior Pepsi executives from taking or developing a more critical and autonomous position in relation to 'the powerful ideas' internally marketed by Pepsi.

Analysis of the tensions and contradictions identified by Sculley is truncated by the lack of critical thinking about the conditions that were productive of these problems. As we argued in Chapter 1, this limitation should not be diagnosed in terms of Sculley's personal failure but, rather, in relation to his education and social positioning as a senior executive. As a consequence of this positioning, he is unlikely to be familiar with critical thinking and, even if he were, is unlikely to disclose or apply this knowledge – not just because it might disrupt the telling of an entertaining story but because it would involve a demanding process of personal transformation (from that of apologist to critic of corporate capitalism).

In his *Odyssey*, Sculley identifies and describes some of the perversities of corporate capitalism but lacks the analytical tools (and probably the inclination) to diagnose them. His limited reflections upon corporate practices are not sustained. Pepsi executives, himself included, are gently lampooned. But there is scant appreciation of how a reduction in the tensions and contradictions described by Sculley is conditional upon struggles for social development as well as self-development. These struggles, it can be speculated, would include efforts to challenge and change ideologies and practices that are productive of an obsessive commitment to what, upon reflection, are very likely to be viewed as trivial objectives, such as those described by Sculley. They would also involve an effort by Sculley, probably through a process of dialogue with others, to move beyond self-deprecation to address directly whatever frustrations, unhappiness or sense of inadequacy fuels his obsessive (macho) concern with winning – an obsession that offers a socially acceptable, yet contradictory, means of escape. Needless to say, personal struggle is an important condition for participation in processes of social transformation that is not driven by a (sado-masochistic?) urge, institutionalized in the 'comfortable home' of Pepsi culture, to dominate and dispose of those who, in Sculley's words, 'couldn't deliver the results I demanded'.

## Conclusion

We have suggested that the irrationalities and contradictions associated with the theory and practice of management make it fertile ground for the application and development of critical thinking in general and CT in particular. Tensions within organizational practices and relations can promote critical reflection as established recipes for survival and success, both individual as well as organizational, are found to fail; and this pain spurs a search for fresh ideas and perspectives. When investigating the world of management and organization, the challenge is to show and explore how the abstract reflections of CT and related critical thinking can have relevance for illuminating and transforming mundane realities of organizational work. As Luke and White have noted of the different meanings that are currently being assigned to the development of 'post-industrial', informational capitalism:

> One set of alternatives, based on corporate capital's instrumental rationality, points towards an informational transformation of labor in the production and consumption of information. Another range of ecological alternatives, based on communicative rationality, decentralized institutions, vernacular cultures, and global moral consciousness can empower producers and citizens with the competence to decide for themselves the meanings and direction of the informational revolution. (1985: 49)

A key contribution of Critical Theory (CT) and Critical Management Theory (CMT) is to highlight the *interpenetration* of the technical and practical dimensions of social life and, in doing so, to question common-sense discourses and established practices – including much of management theory and practice – that subordinates the moral practical to the technical – instrumental. As Ray (1993: 25) has observed, 'even when actors are behaving in a purely instrumental fashion, in a market or in a bureaucracy, their communication must be bound by shared norms and beliefs which can be reconstructed and critically examined'. By undertaking analyses and disseminating research findings that are 'empirical, historically situated, phenomenologically cogent, normatively insightful' (Forester, 1993: 13) and accessible to students and practitioners of management, CT can provide a timely contribution to the reconstruction of management education and practice.

If the ideals of CT are to be realized, it is necessary to stimulate and advance a process of dialogue in which its insights make a forceful contribution to the self-understanding and practice of managing and organizing. To this end, CMT must move beyond abstract theorizing to address and critique the mundane realities of management theory and practice. Otherwise, as Agger (1991: 133) has argued, CT is accessible only to a small group of academic devotees who 'ignore the contribution their own argot makes to hierarchy, empowering only those who speak in the arcane phrases of European high theory'. As we have repeatedly acknowledged, the project of applying critical reason to make sense of management is likely to encounter considerable resistance as it contests the rationality ascribed to conventional wisdom and established practices. But these sources of resistance can be enlivening and inspiring rather than threatening and disheartening. Resistance can be viewed as a carborundum for sharpening the human capacity to cut through the claims of conventional wisdom in ways that redress the imbalance of instrumental and communicative rationality.

## Notes

1 In contrast to the breadth of concerns explored within CT – such as legitimation crises within advanced capitalist states and Habermas' (1989b) identification of social and political

movements outside of the workplace as the most promising source of modernization along non-capitalist paths (see also Chapter 3) – CMT is more restricted and modest in its focus.

2 This working principle is, however, always subject to erosion by divisive pressures, such as individual incentives – as is clearly evident in the continuing reforms of higher education (Willmott, 1995a).

3 The *truth* claim concerns the veracity of the statement. When accepted, this claim has the effect of shaping the listener's beliefs. A *comprehensibility* claim concerns the clarity of the statement's expression which, when it is registered, shapes the listener's attention. A *sincerity* claim concerns the speaker's good faith. When accepted, this gains the listener's trust. Finally, there is a *rightfulness* claim. This concerns the appropriateness or legitimacy of the statement. When accepted, it facilitates the listener's cooperative involvement. See Chapter 3 for a fuller discussion.

4 Gephart and Pitter (1993) acknowledge that industrial accidents also occur in industrialized State socialist societies and, indeed, argue that the lack of separation between political and economic sectors in these economies makes industrial accidents more likely as they are more easily covered up by the State, and the citizenship has even fewer means of articulating its opposition to a system that claims to represent the interests of the people while simultaneously exposing them to high levels of risk.

5 We elaborate upon this point later in this chapter when we discuss the case of Mr Agerley.

6 In common with many other high-margin consumer products, soft-drinks are heavily marketed by appealing to idealized images of youth, popularity, freedom, lifestyle, etc. – the fantastic quality of which has been exposed by Pepsi's recent difficulties in promoting media heroes whose lifestyle is subsequently alleged to be tarnished by a real involvement in drugs and unorthodox sex in addition to (the by now safely commodified and commercialized) rock and roll. Positively, its advertising campaigns celebrate health and freedom. Partly in order to counteract adverse publicity and to gain public attention and support, corporations like Pepsi often make substantial contributions to charitable organizations. However, ideas about ageing, self-esteem and health education are not left untouched or undamaged by powerful campaigns showing (and celebrating) young, beautiful, healthy people drinking sugared water. Indeed, nothing particularly commendable would seem to flow from the enormous effort devoted by Pepsi executives to their corporation – in terms of personal development, healthier customers or other, comparable outcomes.

7 Of course, the logic of communicative rationality – undistorted dialogues grounding good decisions – may also be subverted by garbage-can processes and decisions. However, in the current situation, where instrumental rationality is dominant, ambiguity may more often favour efforts to loosen, if not counteract, its domination.

8 As we noted in Chapter 6, it is instructive to look at the membership of the editorial boards on, say, *Organization, Accounting Organizations and Society* and *MIS Quarterly*.

9 Here it might be objected that 'business ethics' is an established and expanding specialism within the field of management. We concur with this objection and see this specialism as a promising area for the development of an orientation informed by Critical Theory. In our view, CT provides a much firmer foundation for exploring the ethics of business since it incorporates an attentiveness to issues of domination and indoctrination that are largely absent from business ethics courses. For a fuller exploration of this argument, see Deetz, 1985. See also Payne (1991) and Kjonstad and Willmott (1995).

10 The following paragraphs have been extracted and revised from Willmott (1994b).

11 A notorious example of this syndrome is the conversion of Maslow's radical exploration and critique of the institutionalized neglect of the 'further reaches of human nature' into a 'needs hierarchy' that individualizes the problems of, and solutions to, psychic and economic alienation within modern work organizations (Knights and Willmott, 1974/5).

# References

*Accounting, Auditing and Accountability Journal* (1989), Special Issue on 'Contextual Studies of Accounting and Auditing'. 2, 2.

*Accounting, Organizations and Society* (1987), Special Issue on 'Critical Studies in Accounting'. 12, 5.

Ackoff, R. (1979), 'The Future of Operational Research is Past', *Journal of the Operational Research Society*, 30: 93–104.

Adorno, T. (1967), *Prisms*. London: Neville Spearman.

Adorno, T. (1973), *The Jargon of Authenticity*. London: Routledge.

Adorno, T., Frenkel-Brunswik, E., Levinson, D.L. and Nevitt Sanford, R. (1950), *The Authoritarian Personality*. New York: Norton.

Agger, B. (1991), 'Theorizing the Decline of Discourse or the Decline of Theoretical Discourse?', in P. Wexler (ed.), *Critical Theory Now*. London: Falmer Press.

Aldrich, H.E. (1979), *Organizations and Environments*. Englewood Cliffs, NJ: Prentice Hall.

Allen, V.L. (1975), *Social Analysis: A Marxist Critique and Alternative*. London: Longman.

Alvesson, M. (1987), *Organization Theory and Technocratic Consciousness: Rationality, Ideology and Quality of Work*. Berlin/New York: de Gruyter.

Alvesson, M. (1991), 'Organizational Symbolism and Ideology', *Journal of Management Studies*. 28, 3: 207–25.

Alvesson, M. (1993a), *Cultural Perspectives on Organizations*. Cambridge: Cambridge University Press.

Alvesson, M. (1993b), 'Cultural–ideological Modes of Management Control', in S. Deetz (ed.), *Communication Yearbook, Vol. 16*. Newbury Park, CA: Sage.

Alvesson, M. (1993c), 'The Play of Metaphors', in J. Hassard and M. Parker (eds), *Postmodernism and Organizations*. London: Sage.

Alvesson, M. (1994), 'Critical Theory and Consumer Marketing', *Scandinavian Journal of Management*. 10, 3: 291–313

Alvesson, M. (1995), *Management of Knowledge-Intensive Companies*. Berlin/New York: de Gruyter.

Alvesson, M. (1996), *Communication, Power and Organization*. Berlin/New York: de Gruyter.

Alvesson, M. and Berg, P.O. (1992), *Corporate Culture and Organizational Symbolism*. Berlin/New York: de Gruyter.

Alvesson, M. and Billing, Y.D. (1992), 'Gender and Organization: Toward a Differentiated Understanding', *Organization Studies*. 13, 1: 73–103.

Alvesson, M. and Deetz, S. (1996), 'Critical Theory and Postmodern Approaches in Organization Studies', in S. Clegg, C. Hardy and W. Nord (eds), *Handbook of Organization Studies*. London: Sage.

Alvesson, M. and Sköldberg, K. (1996), *Towards a Reflexive Methodology*. London: Sage.

Alvesson, M. and Willmott, H. (eds) (1992) *Critical Management Studies*. London: Sage.

Alvesson, M. and Willmott, H. (1995), 'Strategic Management as Domination and Emancipation: From Planning and Process to Communication and Praxis', in P. Shrivastava and C. Stubbart (eds), *Advances in Strategic Management*. vol. 11, Greenwich, CT; JAI Press.

Anderson, P.F. (1983), 'Marketing, Scientific Progress and Scientific Method', *Journal of Marketing*. 46: 18–31.

Anderson, P.F. (1986), 'On Method in Consumer Research: A Critical Relativist Perspective', *Journal of Consumer Research*. 13: 155–73.

Andersson, L. (1982), 'Konsumentintresset'. PhD Dissertation, Department of Business Administration, Lund University.

Anthony, P. (1977), *The Ideology of Work*. London: Tavistock.

Anthony, P. (1986), *The Foundation of Management*. London: Tavistock.

Argyris, C. (1952), *The Impact of Budgets upon People*. New York: Controllership Foundation.

Argyris, C. (1964), *Integrating the Individual and the Organization*. New York: Wiley.

Argyris, C. (1972), *The Applicability of Organizational Sociology*. Cambridge: Cambridge University Press.

Argyris, C. and Schon, D. (1978), *Organizational Learning*. Reading, MA: Addison-Wesley.

Armstrong, P. (1985), 'Competition between the Organizational Professions and the Evolution of Management Control Strategies', *Accounting, Organizations and Society*. 10, 2: 129–48.

Armstrong, P. (1986), 'Management Control Strategies and Inter-Professional Competition: The Cases of Accountancy and Personnel Management', in D. Knights and H.C. Willmott (eds), *Managing the Labour Process*. Aldershot: Gower.

Armstrong, P. (1987), 'The Rise of Accounting Controls in British Capitalist Enterprises', *Accounting, Organizations and Society*. 12: 415–36.

Armstrong, P. (1991), 'Contradiction and Social Dynamics in the Capitalist Agency Relationship', *Accounting, Organizations and Society*. 16, 1: 1–26.

Arndt, J. (1980), 'Perspectives for a Theory of Marketing', *Journal of Business Research*. 8: 389–402.

Arndt, J. (1985), 'On Making Marketing Science more Scientific: The Role of Observations, Paradigms, Metaphors and Puzzle Solving', *Journal of Marketing*. 49: 11–23.

Arnold, J. and Hope, T. (1983), *Accounting for Management Decisions*. London: Prentice Hall.

Arrington, C.E. and Francis, J.R. (1989), 'Letting the Chat out of the Bag: Deconstruction, Privilege and Accounting Research', *Accounting, Organizations and Society*. 14, 1: 1–28.

Arrington, C.E. and Puxty, A.G. (1991), 'Accounting, Interests and Rationality: A Communicative Relation', *Critical Perspectives on Accounting*. 2: 31–58.

Asplund, J. (1991), *Rivaler och syndabockar*. Göteborg: Bokförlaget Korpen.

Bagozzi, R. (1975), 'Marketing as Exchange', *Journal of Marketing*. 39: 32–9.

Bain, G. (1992), 'The Blackett Memorial Lecture: The Future of Management Education', *Journal of the Operational Research Society*. 43, 6: 557–61.

Baker, M.J. (1987), 'One More Time – What is Marketing?', in M.J. Baker (ed.), *The Marketing Book*. London: Heinemann in association with the British Institute of Marketing.

Bank, J. (1992), *The Essence of Total Quality Management*. London: Prentice Hall.

Bannon, L., Robinson, M. and Schmidt, K. (eds) (1991), *Proceedings of the Second European Conference on Computer-Supported Cooperative Work*, Amsterdam: Kluwer.

Baritz, L. (1960), *The Servants of Power*. Middletown: Wesleyan University Press.

Barley, S. and Kunda, G. (1992), 'Design and Devotion: Surges of Rational and Normative Ideologies of Control in Managerial Discourse', *Administrative Science Quarterly*. 37: 363–99.

Barnard, C. (1938), *The Functions of the Executive*. Cambridge, MA: Harvard University Press.

Bauman, Z. (1988), 'Is There a Postmodern Sociology?', *Theory, Culture & Society*. 5: 217–37.

Bauman, Z. (1989), *Modernity and the Holocaust*, Cambridge: Polity.

Bauman, Z. (1991), *Modernity and Ambivalence*. Cambridge: Polity.

Bedeian, A. (1989), 'Totems and Taboos: Undercurrents in the Management Discipline', *Academy of Management News*. 19, 4: 1–6.

Belk, R., Wallendorff, M. and Sherry, J. (1989), 'The Sacred and the Profane in Consumer Behaviour: Theodicy on the odyssey', *Journal of Consumer Research*. 16 (June): 1–38.

Bell, D. (1974), *The Coming of Post-Industrial Society*. London: Heinemann.

Bendix, R. (1956), *Work and Authority in Industry*. New York: Wiley.

Benhabib, S. (1986), *Critique, Norm and Utopia; A Study of the Foundations of Critical Theory*. New York: Columbia University Press.

Benhabib, S. (1992), *Situating the Self: Gender, Community and Postmodernism in Contemporary Ethics*. Cambridge: Polity Press.

Benhabib, S. and Cornell, D. (eds) (1987), *Feminism as Critique: Essays on the Politics of Gender in Late-Capitalist Societies.* Cambridge: Polity Press.

Benjamin, W. (1973), *Charles Baudelaire: A Lyric Poet in the Era of High Capitalism.* London: New Left Books.

Benson, J.K. (1977), 'Organizations: A Dialectical View', *Administrative Science Quarterly.* 22, 1: 1–21.

Benton, R. (1987), 'Work, Consumption, and the Joyless Consumer', in A.F. Firat, N. Dholakia and R.P. Bagozzi (eds), *Philosophical and Radical Thought in Marketing.* Lexington, MA: Lexington Books.

Berle, A. and Means, G. (1932), *The Modern Corporation and Private Property.* New York: Macmillan.

Bernstein, R.J. (1976), *The Restructuring of Social and Political Theory.* London: Methuen.

Bernstein, R.J. (ed.) (1985), *Habermas and Modernity.* Cambridge: Polity Press.

Billing, Y.D. and Alvesson, M. (1994), *Gender, Managers and Organizations.* Berlin/New York: de Gruyter.

Binns, D. (1993), 'Total Quality Management, Organization Theory and the New Right: A Contribution to the Critique of Bureaucratic Totalitarianism', Working Paper, East London University.

Bittner, E. (1965), 'The Concept of Organization', *Social Research.* 32: 230–55.

de Board, R. (1978), *The Psychoanalysis of Organizations.* London: Tavistock.

Boland, R.J. (1982), 'Phenomenology: A Preferred Approach to Research in Information Systems', in E. Mumford, R. Hirschheim, G. Fitzgerald and T. Wood-Harper (eds), *Research Methods in Information Systems.* North Holland: Amsterdam.

Boone, L.E. and Kurtz, D.L. (1981), *Principles of Management.* New York: Random House.

Bostrom, R.P. and Heinen, J.S. (1977), 'MIS Problems and Failures: A Socio-Technical Perspective', *MIS Quarterly.* 9: 17–32.

Bottomore, T. (1984), *The Frankfurt School.* London: Tavistock.

Bourdieu, P. (1984), *Distinction.* Cambridge, MA: Harvard University Press.

Bourgeois, L.J. (1984), 'Strategic Management and Determinism', *Academy of Management Review.* 9, 4: 586–96.

Bourgeois, L. and Brodwin, D. (1984), 'Strategic Implementation: Five Approaches to an Elusive Phenomenon', *Strategic Management Journal.* 5: 241–64.

Bowles, M.L. (1990), 'Recognizing Day Structures in Organizations', *Organization Studies.* 11, 3: 395–412.

Braverman, H. (1974), *Labor and Monopoly Capital.* New York: Monthly Review Press.

Braybrooke, D. and Lindblom, C.E. (1963), *A Strategy of Decision.* New York: Free Press.

Broadbent, J., Laughlin, R. and Read, S. (1991), 'Recent Financial and Administrative Changes in the NHS: A Critical Theory Analysis', *Critical Perspectives on Accounting.* 2, 1: 1–29.

Brown, L.D. and Tandon, R. (1983), 'Ideology and Political Economy in Inquiry: Action Research and Participatory Research', *Journal of Applied Behavioural Science.* 19: 277–94.

Brown, R H. (1976), 'Social Theory as Metaphor', *Theory and Society.* 3: 169–97.

Brown, S. (1993), 'Postmodern Marketing?', *European Journal of Marketing.* 27, 4: 19–34.

Brubaker, R. (1984), *The Limits of Rationality: An Essay on the Social and Moral Thought of Max Weber.* London: George Allen and Unwin.

Brunsson, N. (1985), *The Irrational Organization. Irrationality as a Basis for Organizational Action and Change.* New York: Wiley.

Burawoy, M. (1978), 'Contemporary Currents in Marxist Theory', *The American Sociologist.* 13: 50–64.

Burawoy, M. (1979), *Manufacturing Consent.* Chicago: University of California Press.

Burawoy, M. (1985), *The Politics of Production.* London: Verso.

Burchell, S., Clubb, C., Hopwood, A., Hughes, J. and Nahapiet, J. (1980), 'The Roles of Accounting in Organizations and Society', *Accounting, Organizations and Society.* 5, 1: 5–27.

Burgoyne, J. (1993), 'The Competence Movement: Issues, Stakeholders and Prospects', *Personnel Review.* 22, 6: 6–13.

Burgoyne, J.G. and Stuart, R. (1976), 'The Nature, Use and Acquisition of Managerial Skills and Other Attributes', *Personnel Review*. 5: 19–29.

Burnham, J. (1941), *The Managerial Revolution*. London: Pitman.

Burns, T. (1977), *The BBC: Public Institution and Private World*. London: Macmillan.

Burns, T. and Stalker, G.M. (1961), *The Management of Innovation*. London: Tavistock.

Burrell, G. (1980), 'Radical Organization Theory', in D. Dunkerley and G. Salaman (eds), *The International Yearbook of Organization Studies*. London: Routledge.

Burrell, G. (1984), 'Sex and Organizational Analysis', *Organization Studies*. 5: 97–118.

Burrell, G. (1992), 'The Organization of Pleasure', in M. Alvesson and H. Willmott (eds), *Critical Management Studies*. London: Sage.

Burrell, G. (1994), 'Modernism, Post Modernism and Organizational Analysis 4: The Contribution of Jürgen Habermas', *Organization Studies*. 15, 1: 1–19.

Burrell, G. and Morgan, G. (1979), *Sociological Paradigms and Organisational Analysis*. London: Heinemann.

Burris, B. (1993), *Technocracy at Work*. Albany, NY: State University of New York Press.

Calas, M. and Smircich, L. (1987), 'Is the Organizational Culture Literature Dominant but Dead?' Paper presented at the 3rd International Conference on Organizational Symbolism and Corporate Culture, Milan, June 1987.

Calas, M. and Smircich, L. (1991), 'Voicing Seduction to Silence Leadership', *Organization Studies*. 12, 4: 567–602.

Calas, M.B. and Smircich, L. (1992), 'Re-writing Gender into Organizational Theorizing: Directions from Feminist Perspectives', in M. Reed and M. Hughes (eds), *Re-thinking Organization: New Directions in Organizational Theory and Analysis*. London: Sage.

Calas, M. and Smircich, L. (1993), 'Dangerous Liaisons: The "Feminine-in-Management" Meets "Globalisation"', *Business Horizons*. March–April, 73–83.

Carter, P. and Jackson, N. (1987), 'Management, Myth, and Metatheory – from Scarcity to Postscarcity', *International Studies of Management and Organization*. 17, 3: 64–89.

Chandler, A.D. (1962), *Strategy and Structure*. Cambridge, MA: MIT Press.

Chandler, A.D. (1977), *The Visible Hand: The Managerial Revolution in American Business*. Cambridge, MA: Harvard University Press.

Checkland, P.B. (1981), *Systems Thinking, Systems Practice*. London: Wiley.

Checkland, P.B. (1983), 'O.R. and the Systems Movement: Mappings and Conflicts', *Journal of the Operational Research Society*. 34, 8: 661–75.

Child, J. (1969), *British Management Thought*. London: Allen and Unwin.

Child, J. (1972), 'Organizational Structure, Environment and Performance: The Role of Strategic Choice', *Sociology*. 6: 1–22.

Child, J. (1977), 'Management' in S.R. Parker, R.K. Brown, J. Child and M.A. Smith (eds), *The Sociology of Industry*, 3rd edition, London: George Allen and Unwin.

Child, J. (1984), *Organization: A Guide to Problems and Practice*, 2nd edition, London: Harper and Row.

Child, J., Fores, M., Glover, I. and Lawrence, P. (1983), 'A Price to Pay? Professionalism and Work Organization in Britain and West Germany', *Sociology*. 17, 1: 63–78.

Child, J. and Smith, C. (1987), 'The Context and Process of Organizational Transformation – Cadbury Limited and its Sector', *Journal of Management Studies*. 24, 6: 565–93.

Chua, W.F. (1986), 'Radical Developments in Accounting Thought', *The Accounting Review*. LXI, 4: 601–32.

Chua, W.F. (1988), 'Interpretive Sociology and Management Accounting Research – A Critical Review', *Accounting, Auditing and Accountability Journal*. 1, 2: 59–79

Chua, W.F., Lowe, T. and Puxty, T. (eds) (1989), *Critical Perspectives in Management Control*. London: Macmillan.

Cleaver, H. (1979), *Reading Capital Politically*. Brighton: Harvester.

Clegg, S. (1989), *Frameworks of Power*. London: Sage.

Clegg, S. (1990), *Modern Organizations: Organization Studies in the Postmodern World*. London: Sage.

Clegg, S. and Dunkerley, D. (1977), 'Introduction', in S. Clegg and D. Dunkerley (eds), *Critical Issues in Organizations*. London: Routledge and Kegan Paul.

Clegg, S. and Dunkerly, D. (1980), *Organization, Class and Control*. London: Routledge and Kegan Paul.

Cleverley, G. (1971), *Managers and Magic*. London: Longman.

Clifford, J. and Marcus, G.E. (eds) (1986), *Writing Culture*. Berkeley, CA: University of California Press.

Cohen, A.P. and Camaroff, J.L. (1976), 'The Management of Meaning: On the Phenomenology of Political Transactions', in B. Kapferer (ed.), *Transactions and Meaning: Directions in the Anthropology of Exchange and Symbolic Behaviour*. Philadelphia, PA: Institute for the Study of Human Issues.

Cohen, M.D., March, J.G. and Olsen, J.P. (1972), 'A Garbage Can Model of Organizational Choice', *Administrative Science Quarterly*. 19: 1–25.

Collinson, D. (1992), *Managing the Shopfloor*. Berlin/New York: de Gruyter.

Collinson, D. and Hearn, J. (1994), 'Naming men as men: implications for work, organization and management', *Gender, Work and Organization*. 1, 1: 2–22.

Collinson, D., Knights, D. and Collinson, M. (1990), *Managing to Discriminate*. London: Routledge.

Colville, I. (1981), 'Reconstructing "Behavioural" Accounting', *Accounting, Organizations and Society*. 6, 2: 119–32.

Comstock, D.E. (1982), 'A Method for Critical Research', in E. Bredo and W. Feinberg (eds), *Knowledge and Values in Social and Educational Research*. Philadelphia, PA: Temple University Press.

Connerton, P. (1976), *Critical Sociology*. Harmondsworth: Penguin.

Connerton, P. (1980), *The Tragedy of Enlightenment*. Cambridge: Cambridge University Press.

Cooper, D.E. (1990), *Existentialism: A Reconstruction*. Oxford: Basil Blackwell.

Cooper, D. and Hopper, T. (1990), *Critical Accounts: Reconstructing Accounting Research*. London: Macmillan.

Cooper, R. (1990), 'Organization/disorganization', in J. Hassard and D. Pym (eds), *The Theory and Philosophy of Organizations*. London: Routledge.

Cooper, R. and Burrell, G. (1988), 'Modernism, postmodernism and organizational analysis: An introduction', *Organization Studies*. 9, 1: 91–112.

Cooper, D.J., Puxty, T., Robson, K. and Willmott, H.C. (1994), 'The Ideology of Professional Regulation and the Markets for Accounting Labour: Three Episodes in the Recent History of the UK Accountancy Profession', *Accounting, Organizations and Society*. 19, 6: 527–53.

Coopey, J. (1995), 'The Learning Organization, Power, Politics and Ideology', *Management Learning*. 26, 2: 193–213.

Crook, S., Pakalski, J. and Waters, M. (1992), *Postmodernization: Change in Advanced Society*. London: Sage.

Cyert, R.M. and March, J.G. (1963), *A Behavioural Theory of the Firm*. Englewood-Cliffs, NJ: Prentice Hall.

Czarniawska-Joerges, B. (1992), *Exploring Complex Organizations*. London: Sage.

Daft, R. (1988), *Organization Theory and Design*. New York: West Publishing.

Dalton, M. (1959), *Men Who Manage*. New York: John Wiley

Dawe, A. (1979), 'Theories of social action', in T. Bottomore and R. Nisbet (eds), *A History of Sociological Analysis*. London: Heinemann.

Deal, T. and Kennedy, A. (1982), *Corporate Cultures; The Rites and Rituals of Corporate Life*. New York: Addison-Wesley.

Deetz, S. (1985), 'Ethical Considerations in Cultural Research in Organizations', in P. Frost, Moore, L., Louis, M.R., Lundberg, C. and Martin, J. (eds), *Organizational Culture*. Newbury Park, CA: Sage.

Deetz, S. (1992a), *Democracy in an Age of Corporate Colonization: Developments in Communication and the Politics of Everyday Life*. Albany, NY: State University of New York Press.

Deetz, S. (1992b), 'Disciplinary Power in the Modern Corporation', in M. Alvesson and H. Willmott (eds), *Critical Management Studies*. London: Sage.

Deetz, S. (1994), *Transforming Communication, Transforming Business: Building Responsive and Responsible Workplaces*. Cresskill, NJ: Hampton Press.

Deetz, S. and Kersten, S. (1983), 'Critical Models of Interpretive Research', in L. Putnam and M. Pacanowsky (eds), *Communication and Organizations*. Beverly Hills, CA: Sage.

Deetz, S. and Mumby, D. (1990), 'Power, Discourse, and the Workplace: Reclaiming the Critical Tradition in Communication Studies in Organizations', in J. Anderson (ed.), *Communication Yearbook. Vol 13*. Newbury Park, CA: Sage.

Dent, J. (1986a), 'Organizational Research in Accounting: Perspectives, Issues and a Commentary', in M. Bromwich and A. Hopwood (eds), *Research and Current Issues in Management Accounting*. London: Pitman.

Dent, J. (1986b), 'Accounting and Organizational Cultures; A Field Study of the Emergence of a New Organizational Reality', Unpublished Paper, London Business School.

Derry, R. (1989), 'An Empirical Study of Moral Reasoning Among Managers', *Journal of Business Ethics*. 8.

Dews, P. (ed.) (1986), *Habermas: Autonomy and Solidarity*. London: Verso.

Dickson, D. (1974), *Alternative Technology and the Politics of Technical Change*. London: Fontana.

Dietz, J.L. and Widdershoven, G.A.M. (1991), 'Speech Acts or Communicative Actions', in L.J. Bannon, M. Robinson and K. Schmidt (eds), *Proceedings of the Second European Conference on Computer-Supported Cooperative Work*, Amsterdam: Kluwer.

Dillard, J. (1991), 'Accounting as a Critical Social Science', *Accounting, Auditing and Accountability Journal*. 4, 1: 8–28.

Dillard, J. and Bricker, R. (1992), 'A Critique of Knowledge-Based Systems in Auditing: The Systematic Encroachment of Technical Consciousness', *Critical Perspectives on Accounting*. 3, 3: 205–24.

*Dragon* (1987), Special Issue on Community Operational Research at Hull University, 2, 2.

Dreitzel, H. (ed.) (1972), *Recent Sociology*. New York: Random House.

Dror, Y. and Romm, T. (1988), 'Politics in organizations and its perception within the organization', *Organization Studies*. 9, 2: 165–80.

Drucker, P. (1977), *Management*. London: Pan.

Earl, M. (1983), 'Management Information Systems and Management Accounting', in D.J. Cooper, R. Scapens and J. Arnold (eds), *Management Accounting Research and Practice*. London: Institute of Cost and Management Accountants.

Eccles, R.G. and Nohria, N. (1992), *Beyond the Hype: Rediscovering the Essence of Management*. Harvard, MA: Harvard Business School Press.

Eden, C. (1989), 'Operational Research as Negotiation' in M.C. Jackson, P. Keys and S.A. Cropper (eds), *Operational Research and the Social Sciences*. New York: Plenum Press

Edwards, R. (1979), *Contested Terrain*. London: Heinemann.

Elders, F. (ed.) (1974), *Reflexive Water: The Basic Concerns of Mankind*. London: Souvenir.

Eldridge, J., Cressey, P. and MacInnes, J. (1991), *Industrial Sociology and Economic Crisis*. Hemel Hempstead: Harvester Wheatsheaf.

Elkjaer, B., Flensberg, P., Mouritsen, J. and Willmott, H.C. (1992), 'The Commodification of Expertise: The Case of Systems Development Consulting', *Accounting, Management and Information Technology*. 1, 2: 139–56.

Emery, F. and Trist, E. (1960), 'Socio-Technical Systems', in Emery, F. (ed.), *Systems Thinking*. Harmondsworth: Penguin 1969.

Engeldorp Gastelaars, P., Magala, S. and Preuss, O. (eds) (1990), *Critical Theory and the Science of Management*. Rotterdam: University of Rotterdam Press.

Engwall, L. (1990), *Mercury Meets Minerva*. Oxford: Pergamon.

Enzensberger, H.M. (1974), *The Consciousness Industry*. New York: Seabury Press.

Esland, G., Salaman, G. and Speakman, M.A. (eds) (1975), *People and Work*. Edinburgh: Holmes McDougall.

Etzioni, A. (1988), *The Moral Dimension*. New York: Free Press.

Ezzamel, M. and Willmott, H.C. (1993), 'Corporate Governance and Financial Accountability: The New Public Sector', *Accounting, Auditing and Accountability Journal*. 6, 3: 109–32.

Fay, B. (1987), *Critical Social Science*. Cambridge: Polity Press.

Fayol, H. (1949), *General and Industrial Management*. London: Pitman.

Featherstone, M. (1991), *Consumer Culture and Postmodernism*. London: Sage.

Fenichel, O. (1945), *The Psychoanalytic Theory of Neurosis*. New York: Norton.

Ferguson, K.E. (1984), *The Feminist Case Against Bureaucracy*. Philadelphia, PA: Temple University Press.

Filby, I. and Willmott, H. (1988), 'Ideologies and contradictions in a public relations department: The seduction and impotence of living myth', *Organization Studies*. 9, 3: 335–49.

Firat, A.F. and Venkatesh, A. (1992), 'The making of postmodern consumption', in R.W. Belk and N. Dholakia (eds), *Consumption and Marketing: Macro Dimensions*. Boston, MA: PWS-Kent.

Firat, A.F., Dholakia, N. and Bagozzi, R.P. (eds) (1987), *Philosophical and Radical Thought in Marketing*. Lexington, MA: Lexington Books.

Fischer, F. (1984), 'Ideology and organization theory', in F. Fischer and C. Sarianni (eds), *Critical Studies in Organization and Bureaucracy*. Philadelphia, PA: Temple University Press.

Fischer, F. (1990), *Technocracy and the Politics of Expertise*. London: Sage.

Flax, J. (1987), 'Postmodernism and Gender Relations in Feminist Theory', *Signs*. 12: 621–43.

Flax, J. (1990a), *Thinking Fragments: Psychoanalysis, Feminism and Postmodernism in the Contemporary West*. Berkeley, CA: University of California Press.

Flax, J. (1990b), 'Postmodernism and Gender Relations in Feminist Theory', in L.J. Nicholson (ed.), *Feminism/Postmodernism*. London: Routledge.

Fletcher, C. (1974), 'The End of Management?' in J. Child (ed.), *Man and Organization*. London: Allen and Unwin.

Flood, R.L. (1990), 'Liberating Systems Theory', *Human Relations*. 43, 1: 49–76.

Flood, R.L. and Jackson, M.C. (1991a), *Critical Systems Thinking: Directed Readings*. Chichester: John Wiley.

Flood, R.L. and Jackson, M.C. (1991b), 'Critical Systems Heuristics: Application of an Emancipatory Approach for Police Strategy Toward the Carrying of Offensive Weapons', *Systems Practice*. 4, 4: 283–302.

Flood, R.L. and Jackson, M.C. (1992), *Creative Problem Solving: Total Systems Intervention*. London: John Wiley.

Forester, J. (1981), 'Questioning and Organizing Attention: Toward a Critical Theory of Planning and Administrative Practice', *Administration and Society*. 13, 2: 161–205.

Forester, J. (1982), 'A Critical Empirical Framework for the Analysis of Public Policy', *New Political Science*. 3, 1–2: 33–61.

Forester, J. (1983), 'Critical Theory and Organizational Analysis', in G. Morgan (ed.), *Beyond Method*. Beverly Hills, CA: Sage.

Forester, J. (ed.) (1985), *Critical Theory and Public Life*. Cambridge, MA: MIT Press.

Forester, J. (1988), 'The Contemporary Relevance of Critical Theory to Public Administration: Promises and Problems', Paper, Dept of City and Regional Planning, Cornell University.

Forester, J. (1989), *Planning in the Face of Power*. Berkeley, CA: University of California Press.

Forester, J. (1991), 'Questioning and Organizing Attention: Toward a Critical Theory of Planning and Administrative Practice', *Administration and Society*. 13, 2: 161–205.

Forester, J. (1992), 'Critical ethnography: On fieldwork in a Habermasian way', in M. Alvesson and H. Willmott (eds), *Critical Management Studies*. London: Sage.

Forester, J. (1993), *Critical Theory, Public Policy and Planning Practice: Toward a Critical Pragmation*. Albany, NY: State University of New York Press.

Foster, H. (ed.) (1985), *Postmodern Culture*. London: Pluto Press.

Foucault, M. (1977), *Discipline and Punish*. Harmondsworth: Penguin.

Foucault, M. (1980), *Power/Knowledge*. New York: Pantheon.

Foucault, M. (1982), 'The subject and power', *Critical Inquiry*. 8: 777–95.

Foucault, M. (1985), *The Use of Pleasure*. Harmondsworth: Penguin.

Foucault, M. (1986), *The Care of the Self*. Harmondsworth: Penguin.

Fox, A. (1974), *Beyond Contract: Work, Power and Trust Relations*. London: Faber and Faber.

Fox, S. (1994a), 'Debating Management Learning: I', *Management Learning*. 25, 1: 83–93.

Fox, S. (1994b), 'Debating Management Learning: II', *Management Learning*. 25, 4: 579–97.

Fox, R.W. and Lears, T.J. (1983), *The Culture of Consumption*. New York: Pantheon.

Frank, R.H., Gilovich, T. and Regan, D.T. (1993) 'Does Studying Economics Inhibit Cooperation?' *Journal of Economic Perspectives*. 7, 2: 159–71.

Fraser, N. (1987), 'What's Critical About Critical Theory?: The Case of Habermas and Gender', in S. Benhabib and D. Cornell (eds), *Feminism as Critique*. Cambridge: Polity Press.

Freely, M. (1995), *What About Us? An Open Letter to the Mothers Feminism Forgot*. London: Bloomsbury.

Freire, P. (1972), *Pedagogy of the Oppressed*. Harmondsworth: Penguin.

Freud, S. (1917), *Introductory Lectures in Psychoanalysis*. Harmondsworth: Penguin.

Freundlieb, D. (1989), 'Rationalism v Irrationalism? Habermas's Response to Foucault', *Inquiry*. 31: 171–92.

Friedman, A. (1977), *Industry and Labour*. London: Macmillan.

Friedman, G. (1981), *The Political Philosophy of the Frankfurt School*. Ithaca, NY: Cornell University Press.

Fromm, E. (1941), *Escape from Freedom*. New York: Holt, Rinehart and Winston.

Fromm, E. (1942), *Fear of Freedom*. London: Routledge and Kegan Paul.

Fromm, E. (1955), *The Sane Society*. London: Routledge and Kegan Paul.

Fromm, E. (1961), *Marx's Concept of Man*. New York: Frederick Unger.

Fromm, E. (1970), *The Crises of Psychoanalysis*. Harmondsworth: Penguin.

Fromm, E. (1976), *To Have or To Be?*. London: Abacus.

Frost, P. (1980), 'Toward a Radical Framework for Practicing Organizational Science' *Academy of Management Review*. 5, 4: 501–7.

Frost, P.J. (1987), 'Power, Politics and Influence', in F. Jablin, L. Putnam, K. Roberts and L. Porter (eds), *Handbook of Organizational Communication*. Newbury Park, CA: Sage.

Frost, P. and Egri, C. (1991), 'The Political Process of Innovation', *Research in Organizational Behaviour*. vol. 13: 229–95.

Frost, P., Moore, L., Louis, M.R., Lundberg, C. and Martin, J. (eds) (1985), *Organizational Culture*. Beverly Hills: Sage.

Frost, P., Moore, L., Louis, M.R., Lundberg, C. and Martin, J. (eds) (1991), *Reframing Organizational Culture*. Newbury Park, CA: Sage.

Galbraith, J.K. (1958), *The Affluent Society*. Harmondsworth: Penguin.

Galbraith, J.K. (1983), *The Anatomy of Power*. New York: Simon and Schuster.

Garfinkel, H. (1967), *Studies in Ethnomethodology*. Englewood Cliffs, NJ: Prentice Hall.

Garrett, D. (1987), 'The effectiveness of marketing policy boycotts: Environmental opposition to marketing', *Journal of Marketing*. 51 (April): 46–57.

du Gay, P. (1994), 'Colossal Immodesties and Hopeful Monsters: Pluralism and Organizational Conduct', *Organization*. 1, 1: 125–48.

du Gay, P. and Salaman, G. (1992), 'The Cult(ure) of the Customer', *Journal of Management Studies*. 29, 5: 615–33.

Geertz, C. (1973), *The Interpretation of Cultures*. New York: Basic Books.

Gephart, R.P. and Pitter, R. (1993), 'The Organizational Basis of Industrial Accidents in Canada', *Journal of Management Inquiry*. 2, 3: 238–52.

Geuss, R. (1981), *The Idea of Critical Theory: Habermas and the Frankfurt School*. Cambridge: Cambridge University Press.

Giddens, A. (1979), *Central Problems in Social Theory*. London: Macmillan.

Giddens, A. (1982), 'The Improbable Guru: Re-Reading Marcuse', in A. Giddens, *Profiles and Critiques in Social Theory*. London: Macmillan.

Giddens, A. (1989), 'Response to My Critics', in D. Held and J. Thompson (eds), *Social Theory of Modern Societies: Anthony Giddens and His Critics*. Cambridge: Cambridge University Press.

Giddens, A. (1991), *Modernity and Self-Identity: Self and Society in the Late Modern Age*. Cambridge: Polity.

Gilligan, C. (1982), *In a Different Voice: Psychological Theory and Woman's Development*. Cambridge, MA: Harvard University Press.

Goffman, E. (1959), *The Presentation of Self in Everyday Life*. Harmondsworth: Penguin.

Goldman, R. (1987), 'Marketing Fragrances: Advertising and the Production of Commodity Signs', *Theory, Culture and Society*. 4: 691–725.

Gore, J. (1992), 'What We Can Do For You! What *Can* "We" Do For "You"', in C. Luke and J. Gore (eds), *Critical Pedagogy*. London: Routledge.

Gortzen, R. (1982), *Jurgen Habermas: Eine Bibliographie seiner Schriften und der Sekundar-literatur*. Frankfurt: Suhrkamp.

Gouldner, A. (1973a), 'Anti-Minotaur: The Myth of a Value-Free Sociology', in A. Gouldner (ed.), *For Sociology: Renewal and Critique in Sociology Today*. London: Allen Lane.

Gouldner, A. (1973b), 'The Sociologist as Partisan', in A. Gouldner, *For Sociology: Renewal and Critique in Sociology Today*. London: Allen Lane.

Gowler, D. and Legge, K. (1983), 'The Meaning of Management and the Management of Meaning: A View from Social Anthropology', in M.J. Earl (ed.), *Perspectives in Management*. Oxford: Oxford University Press.

Gramsci, A. (1971), *Selections from the Prison Notebooks of Antonio Gramsci*. London: Lawrence and Wishart.

Granovetter, M. (1985), 'Economic Action and Social Structure: The Problem of Em-beddedness', *American Journal of Sociology*. 91: 481–510.

Grey, C., Knights, D. and Willmott, H.C. (1996), 'Is a Critical Pedagogy of Management Possible?', in R. French and C. Grey (eds), *New Perspectives on Management Education*. London: Sage

Grey, C. and Mitev, N. (1995a), 'Re-engineering Organizations: A Critical Appraisal', *Personnel Review*. 24, 1: 6–18.

Grey, C. and Mitev, N. (1995b), 'Management Education: A Polemic', *Management Learning*. 26, 1: 73–90.

Grimes, A. and Cornwall, D. (1987), 'The Disintegration of an Organization: A Dialectical Analysis', *Journal of Management*. 13, 1: 69–86.

Grint, K. (1994), 'Reengineering History: Social Resonances and Business Process Reengineering', *Organization*. 1, 1: 179–201.

Grinyer, P. and Spender, J.C. (1979), *Turnaround: Managerial Recipes for Strategic Success*. London: Associated Business Press.

Guba, E.S. and Lincoln, Y.S. (1989), *Fourth Generation Evaluation*. Newbury Park, CA: Sage.

Gustavsen, B. (1985), 'Workplace reform and democratic dialogue', *Economic and Industrial Democracy*. 6, 4: 761–80.

Habermas, J. (1970a), 'On Systematically Distorted Communication', *Inquiry*. 13: 205–8.

Habermas, J. (1970b), 'Towards a Theory of Communicative Competence', *Inquiry*. 13: 360–75.

Habermas, J. (1971), *Towards a Rational Society: Student Protest, Science and Politics*. London: Heinemann.

Habermas, J. (1972), *Knowledge and Human Interests*. London: Heinemann.

Habermas, J. (1973), *Legitimation Crisis*. Boston, MA: Beacon Press.

Habermas, J. (1974), *Theory and Practice*. London: Heinemann.

Habermas, J. (1975), 'A Postscript to *Knowledge and Human Interests*', *Philosophy of the Social Sciences*. 3: 157–89.

Habermas, J. (1976), 'A Positivistically Bisected Rationalism', in T.W. Adorno, H. Albert, R. Dahrendorf, J. Habermas, H. Pilot and K.R. Popper (eds), *The Positivist Dispute in German Sociology*. London: Heinemann.

Habermas, J. (1979), *Communication and the Evolution of Society*. London: Heinemann.

Habermas, J. (1982), 'A Reply to my Critics', in J. Thompson and D. Held (eds), *Habermas: Critical Debates*. London: Macmillan.

Habermas, J. (1984), *The Theory of Communicative Action Volume 1: Reason and the Rationalization of Society*. London: Heinemann.

Habermas, J. (1985), 'A Philosophico–Political Profile', *New Left Review*. 151: 75–105.

Habermas, J. (1986), *Autonomy and Solidarity* (ed. P. Dews), London: Verso.

Habermas, J. (1987a), *The Philosophical Discourse of Modernity*. Cambridge, MA: MIT Press.

Habermas, J. (1987b), *The Theory of Communicative Action Volume 2: Lifeworld and System: A Critique of Functionalist Reason*. London: Heinemann.

Habermas, J. (1988), *On The Logic of the Social Sciences*. Cambridge: Polity.

Habermas, J. (1989a), *The New Conservatism: Cultural Critique and the Historian's Debate*. Cambridge: Polity.

Habermas, J. (1989b), *The Structural Transformation of the Public Sphere*. Cambridge: Polity.

Habermas, J. (1991), 'A Reply', in A. Honneth and H. Joas (eds), *Communicative Action: Essays on Jürgen Habermas' The Theory of Communicative Action*. Cambridge, MA: MIT Press.

Habermas, J. (1992), *Postmetaphysical Thinking: Philosophical Essays*. Cambridge: Polity Press.

Habermas, J. (1994), *The Past as Future*. Cambridge: Polity Press.

Hales, C. (1993), *Managing Through Organization*. London: Routledge.

Hales, M. (1974), 'Management Science and the Second Industrial Revolution', *Radical Science Journal*. 1: 5–28.

Hales, M. (1980), *Living Thinkwork; Where Do Labour Processes Come From?*. London: CSE.

Hamel, G. and Prahalad, C.K. (1989) 'Strategic Intent', *Harvard Business Review*. 67: 63–76.

Hammer, M. (1994), 'Reengineering is *Not* Hocus-Pocus', *Across the Board*. September, 31, 8: 45–7.

Hammer, M. and Champy, J. (1993), *Reengineering the Corporation: A Manifesto for Business Revolution*. London: Nicholas Brealey.

Hannan, M.T. and Freeman, J. (1977), 'The Population Ecology of Organizations', *American Journal of Sociology*. 82: 929–64.

Harding, S. (1986), *The Science Question in Feminism*. Ithaca, NY: Cornell University Press.

Harms, J. and Kellner, D. (1991), 'Critical Theory and Advertising', in B. Agger (ed.), *Current Perspectives in Social Theory, Vol. 11*. Greenwich, CT: JAI Press.

Harris, R. (1987), *The Power and Powerlessness of Management*. London: Routledge and Kegan Paul.

Hartsock, N. (1984), *Money, Sex and Power: Toward a Feminist Historical Materialism*. Boston, MA: Northeast University Press.

Haug, W.F. (1986), *Critique of Commodity Aesthetics*. Minneapolis, MN: University of Minneapolis Press.

Hearn, J. and Parkin, W. (1983), 'Gender and organizations: A selective review and a critique of a neglected area', *Organization Studies*. 4: 219–42.

Hearn, J. and Parkin, W. (1986/87), 'Women, men and leadership: A critical review of assumptions, practices and change in the industrialized nations', *International Studies of Management and Organization*. 16: 3–4.

Hearn, J. and Parkin, W. (1987), *'Sex' at 'work': The Power and Paradox of Organisation Sexuality*. Brighton: Wheatsheaf Books Ltd.

Hearn, J., Sheppard, D.L., Tancred-Sheriff, P. and Burrell, G. (eds) (1989), *The Sexuality of Organization*. London: Sage.

Hedberg, B. and Jönsson, S. (1977), 'Strategy Formulation as a Discontinuous Process', *International Studies of Management and Organization*. 7, 2: 88–100.

Held, D. (1980), *Introduction to Critical Theory*. London: Hutchinson.

Herda, E.A. and Messerschmitt, D.S. (1991), 'From Words to Actions: Communication for Business Management', *Leadership and Organization Development Journal*. 12, 1: 23–7.

Heydebrand, W. (1977), 'Organizational Contradictions in a Public Bureaucracy: Toward a Marxian Theory of Organizations', *Sociological Quarterly*. 18, 1: 83–107.

Heydebrand, W. (1980), 'A Marxist Critique of Organization Theory', in W.M. Evan (ed.), *Frontiers in Organization and Management*. New York: Prager.

Heydebrand, W. (1985), 'The Technarchy and Neo-Corporatism: Toward a Theory of Organizational Change Under Advanced Capitalism and Early State Socialism', *Current Perspectives in Social Theory*. 6: 71–128.

Hines, R. (1988), 'Financial Accounting: In Communicating Reality, We Construct Reality', *Accounting, Organizations and Society*. 13, 3: 251–61.

Hird, C. (1983), *Challenging the Figures*. London: Pluto.

Hirsch, F. (1976), *Social Limits to Growth*. Cambridge, MA: Harvard University Press.

Hirschheim, R. and Klein, R. (1989), 'Four Paradigms of Information Systems Development', *Communications of the ACM*. 32, 10: 1199–216.

Hirschheim, R. and Klein, R. (1994), 'Realizing Emancipatory Principles in Information Systems Development: The Case of ETHICS', *MIS Quarterly*, March, 83–109.

Hirschman, E. (1990), 'Secular immortality and the American ideology of affluence', *Journal of Consumer Research* 17 (June): 31–42.

Hochschild, A.R. (1983), *The Managed Heart: Commercialization of Human Feelings*. Berkeley: University of California Press.

Hofstede, G., Neuijen, B., Ohayv, D. and Sanders, G. (1990), 'Measuring organizational cultures: A qualitative and quantitative study across twenty cases', *Administrative Science Quarterly*. 35: 286–316.

Holbrook, M.B. (1987), 'Mirror, Mirror, on the Wall, What's Unfair in the Reflections on Advertising?', *Journal of Marketing*. 51, (July): 95–103.

Hold, D. (1980), *Introduction to Critical Theory: Horkheimer to Habermas*. London: Hutchinson.

Hollway, W. (1984), 'Fitting Work: Psychological Assessment in Organization', in J. Henriques, C. Urwin, C. Kenn and V. Walkerdine (eds), *Changing the Subject: Psychology Social Regulation and Subjectivity*. London: Methuen.

Hollway, W. (1991), *Work Psychology and Organizational Behaviour*. London: Sage.

Holub, R. C. (1991), *Jurgen Habermas: Critic of the Public Sphere*. London: Routledge.

Honneth, A. (1987), 'Critical Theory', in A. Giddens and J.H. Turner (eds), *Social Theory Today*. Cambridge: Polity Press.

Honneth, A. (1991), *The Critique of Power: Reflective Stages in a Critical Social Theory*. Cambridge, MA: MIT Press.

Hopper, T. and Powell, A. (1985), 'Making Sense of Research into the Organizational and Social Aspects of Management Accounting: A Review of Its Underlying Assumptions', *Journal of Management Studies*. 22, 5: 429–65.

Hopper, T., Storey, J. and Willmott, H.C. (1987), 'Accounting for Accounting: Towards the Development of a Dialectical View', *Accounting, Organizations and Society*. 12, 5: 437–56.

Hopwood, A.G. (1972), 'An Empirical Study of the Role of Accounting Data in Performance Evaluation', *Journal of Accounting Research*. 10, 1: 156–82.

Hopwood, A.G. (1987), 'The Archaeology of Accounting Systems', *Accounting, Organizations and Society*. 12, 3: 207–34.

Horkheimer, M. (1937), 'Traditional and Critical Theory', in P. Connerton (ed.), *Critical Sociology*. Harmondsworth: Penguin (1976).

Horkheimer, M. (1972), *Critical Theory; Selected Essays*. New York: Herder and Herder.

Horkheimer, M. and Adorno, T. (1947a), *The Dialectics of Enlightenment*. London: Verso (1979).

Horkheimer, M and Adorno, T. (1947b), *Eclipse of Reason*. New York: Oxford University Press.

Hoy, D. (ed.) (1986), *Foucault: A Critical Reader*. Oxford: Basil Blackwell.

Huczynski, A.A. (1993), *Management Gurus: What Makes Them and How to Become One*. London: Routledge.

Huff, A.S. (1982), 'Industry Influences on Strategic Reformulation', *Strategic Management Journal*. 3: 119–31.

Hunt, S. (1976), 'The nature and scope of marketing', *Journal of Marketing*. 40 (July): 17–28.

Hunt, S.D. (1990), 'Truth in Marketing Theory and Research', *Journal of Marketing*. 40: 17–28.

Hyman, R. (1975), *Social Values and Industrial Relations*. Oxford: Blackwell.

Hyman, R. (1987), 'Strategy or Structure? Capital, Labour and Control', *Work, Employment and Society*. 1, 1: 25–55.

Illich, I. (1973), *Tools for Conviviality*. London: Fontana/Collins.

Ingersoll, V.H. and Adams, G.B. (1992), *The Tacit Organization*. Greenwich, CT: JAI Press.

Ingram, D. (1987), *Habermas and the Dialectic of Reason*. New Haven, CT: University of Yale Press.

Jackall, R. (1988), *Moral Mazes; The World of Corporate Managers*. New York: Oxford University Press.

Jackson, M.C. (1982), 'The Nature of Soft Systems Thinking: The Work of Churchman, Ackott and Checkland', *Journal of Applied Systems Analysis*. 9: 17–29.

Jackson, M.C. (1985), 'Social Systems Theory and Practice: The Need for a Critical Approach', *International Journal of General Systems*. 10: 135–51.

Jackson, M.C. (1990), 'Beyond a System of System Methodologies', *Journal of the Operational Research Society*. 41, 8: 657–68.

Jackson, M.C. (1992), 'An Integrated Programme for Critical Thinking in Information Systems Research', *Journal of Information Systems*. 2: 83–95.

Jackson, M.C. and Flood, R.L. (1991a), *Critical Systems Thinking: Directed Readings*. Chichester: John Wiley.

Jackson, M.C. and Flood, R.L. (1991b), 'Critical Systems Heuristics: Application of an Emancipatory Approach for Police Strategy Toward the Carrying of Offensive Weapons', *Systems Practice*. 4, 4: 283–302.

Jackson, N. and Carter, P. (1991), 'In Defence of Paradigm Incommensurability', *Organization Studies*. 12, 1: 109–27.

Jackson, N. and Willmott, H.C. (1986), 'Beyond Epistemology and Reflective Conversation – Towards Human Relations', *Human Relations*. 40, 6: 361–80.

Jaggar, A. and Bordo, S. (1989), *Gender/Body/Knowledge: Feminist Reconstructions of Being and Knowing*. New Brunswick, NJ: Rutgers University Press.

Jay, M. (1973), *The Dialectical Imagination: A History of the Frankfurt School and the Institute of Social Research 1923–50*. Berkeley: University of California Press.

Jeffcutt, P. (1993), 'From interpretation to representation', in J. Hassard and M. Parker (eds), *Postmodernism and Organizations*. London: Sage.

Jermier, J.M. (1981), 'Infusion of Critical Theory into Organizational Analysis: Implications for Studies of Work Adjustment', in *International Yearbook of Organizational Studies*. 2: 195–211.

Jermier, J. (1985), 'When the Sleeper wakes: A Short Story Extending Themes in Radical Organization Theory', *Journal of Management*. 11, 2: 67–80.

Johnson, G. (1987), *Strategic Change and the Management Process*. Oxford: Basil Blackwell.

Jonsson, E. (1979), *Konsten att lura konsumenten*. Stockholm: Rabén and Sjögren.

Jonsson, S. and Lundin, R.A. (1977), 'Myths and Wishful Thinking as Management Tools', in P.C. Nystrom and W.H. Starbuck (eds), *Prescriptive Models of Organization*. Amsterdam: North-Holland.

Kakabadse, A. (1983), *The Politics of Management*. Aldershot: Gower.

Kalgaard, R. (1993), 'ASAP Interview with Michael Hammer', *Forbes*. September 13: 69–75.

Kanter, R.M. (1983), *The Change Masters. Innovations for Productivity in the American Corporation*. New York: Simon and Schuster.

Kanter, R.M. (1989), *When Giants Learn to Dance*. London: Routledge.

Keat, R. (1981), *The Politics of Social Theory: Habermas, Freud and the Critique of Positivism*. Oxford: Blackwell.

Keenoy, T. and Anthony, P. (1992), 'HRM: Meaning, Metaphor and Morality', in P. Blyton and P. Turnbull (eds), *Reassessing Human Resource Management*. London: Sage.

Kellner, D. (1988), 'Postmodernism as Social Theory: Some Challenges and Problems', *Theory, Culture & Society*. 5: 239–69.

Kellner, D. (1989), *Critical Theory, Marxism and Modernity*. Cambridge: Polity Press.

Kelly, J. (1985), 'Management's Redesign of Work: Labour Process, Labour Markets and Product Markets', in D. Knights, H. Willmott and D. Collinson (eds), *Job Redesign*. Aldershot: Gower.

Kerfoot, D. and Knights, D. (1994), 'Empowering the "Quality" Worker: The Seduction and

Contradiction of the Total Quality Phenomenon', in A. Wilkinson and H.C. Willmott (eds), *Making Quality Critical*. London: Routledge.

Kets de Vries, M. and Miller, D. (1984), *The Neurotic Organization*. San Francisco, CA: Jossey-Bass.

Kilmann, R.H., Saxton, M.J. and Serpa, R. (1985), *Gaining Control of the Corporate Culture*. San Francisco, CA: Jossey-Bass.

Kjonstad, B. and Willmott, H.C. (1995) 'Business Ethics: Restrictive or Empowering?' *Journal of Business Ethics*. 13: 1–20.

Klatt, L.A., Murdick, R.G. and Schuster, F.E. (1985), *Human Resource Management*. London: Charles Merrill.

Klein, H. (1986), 'Organizational Implications of Office Systems: Towards a Critical Social Action Perspective', in A. Verrijn-Stuart and R. Hirschheim (eds), *Office Information Systems*. Amsterdam: North Holland.

Klein, H. and Hirschheim, R. (1985), 'Fundamental Issues of Decision-Support Systems: A Consequentialist Perspective', *Decision Support Systems*. 1, 1: 5–24.

Klein, H.J. and Lyytinen, K. (1985), 'The Poverty of Scientism in Information Systems' in E. Mumford, R. Hischheim, G. Fitzgerald and T. Wood-Harper (eds), *Research Methods in Information Systems*. Amsterdam: North Holland.

Knights, D. (1992), 'Changing Spaces: The Disruptive Impact of a New Epistemological Location for the Study of Management', *Academy of Management Review*. 17: 514–36.

Knights, D. and Collinson, D. (1987), 'Disciplining the Shopfloor: A Comparison of the Disciplinary Effects of Managerial Psychology and Financial Accounting', *Accounting, Organization and Society*. 12: 457–77.

Knights, D. and Morgan, G. (1991), 'Corporate Strategy, Organizations, and Subjectivity: A Critique', *Organization Studies*. 12: 251–73.

Knights, D. and Murray, F. (1992), 'Politics and Pain in Managing Information Technology: A Case Study from Insurance', *Organization Studies*. 13, 2: 211–28.

Knights, D. and Murray, F. (1994) *Managers Divided: Organisation Politics and Information Technology Management*. Chichester: John Wiley.

Knights, D. and Willmott, H.C. (1974/5), 'Humanistic Social Science and the Theory of Needs', *Interpersonal Development*. 5, 4: 213–23.

Knights, D. and Willmott, H.C. (1987), 'Organizational Culture as Corporate Strategy', *International Studies of Management and Organization*. 17, 3: 40–63.

Knights, D. and Willmott, H.C. (1988), 'The Executive Fix: Strategic Decision Making in the Financial Services Industry', in J. McGoldrick (ed.), *Business Case File on Behavioural Science Students*. Wokingham: Van Nostrand Reinhold.

Knights, D. and Willmott, H.C. (1989), 'Power and Subjectivity at Work: From Degradation to Subjugation in Social Relations', *Sociology*. 23, 4: 535–58.

Knights, D. and Willmott, H. (eds) (1990), *Labour Process Theory*. London: Macmillan.

Knights, D. and Willmott, H.C. (1997), 'The Hype and Hope of Interdisciplinary Management Studies', *British Journal of Management*, forthcoming.

Knights, D., Willmott, H. and Collinson, D. (eds) (1985), *Job Redesign*. Aldershot: Gower.

Knights, D., Morgan, G. and Murray, F. (1991), 'Strategic Management, Financial Services and Information Technology', Paper presented at the 10th EGOS Colloquium, Vienna.

Knights, D., Murray, F. and Willmott, H.C. (1993), 'Networking as Knowledge Work: A Study of Strategic Interorganizational Development in the Financial Services Industry', *Journal of Management Studies*. 30, 6: 975–95.

Kohn, M. (1980), 'Job Complexity and Adult Personality', in N. Smelser and E.H. Erikson (eds), *Themes of Work and Love in Adulthood*. Cambridge, MA: Harvard University Press.

Kortian, G. (1980), *Metacritique: The Philosophical Argument of Jürgen Habermas*. Cambridge: Cambridge University Press.

Kotler, P. (1976), *Marketing Management*, 3rd edition. Englewood Cliffs, NJ: Prentice Hall.

Kotter, J. (1979), *Power in Management*. New York: Amacon.

Kotter, J.P. (1982), *The General Managers*. New York: Free Press.

Kouzmin, A. (1980), 'Control in Organizational Analysis: The Lost Politics', in D. Dunkerley and G. Salaman (eds), *The International Yearbook of Organization Studies*. London: Routledge.

Kuhn, T.S. (1962), *The Structure of Scientific Revolutions*. Chicago, IL: University of Chicago Press.

Kunda, G. (1991), 'Ritual and the management of corporate culture: A critical perspective', Paper presented at the 8th International Conference on Organizational Symbolism, Copenhagen.

Kunda, G. (1992), *Engineering Culture. Control and Commitment in a High-Tech Corporation*. Philadelphia, PA: Temple University Press.

Lakoff, G. and Johnson, M. (1980), *Metaphors We Live By*. Chicago, IL: University of Chicago Press.

Lammers, C. J. and Hickson, C.J. (eds) (1979), *Organizations Alike and Unalike: International and Inter-Institutional Studies in the Sociology of Organizations*. London: Routledge and Kegan Paul.

Lane, C. (1989), *Management and Labour in Europe*. Aldershot: Edward Elgar.

Lane, R E. (1978), 'Markets and the satisfaction of human wants', *Journal of Economic Issues*. XIL (December).

Lasch, C. (1979), *The Culture of Narcissism*. New York: Norton.

Lasch, C. (1984), *The Minimal Self*. London: Picador.

Laughlin, R. (1987), 'Accounting Systems in Organizational Contexts: A Case for Critical Theory', *Accounting, Organizations and Society*. 12, 5: 472–502.

Laughlin, R. (1988), 'Accounting in its Social Context: An Analysis of the Accounting Systems of the Church of England', *Accounting, Auditing and Accountability Journal*. 1, 2: 19–42.

Laughlin, R. (1991), 'Environmental Disturbances and Organizational Change Pathways', *Organization Studies*. 12: 209–32.

Laughlin, R. and Broadbent, P.J. (1993), 'Accounting and Law: Partners in the Juridification of the Public Sector in the UK?', *Critical Perspectives on Accounting*. 4, 4: 337–68.

Laughlin, R. and Broadbent, J. (1994), 'Beyond Accountability: An Evaluation Model for the Public Sector Reforms in the UK', Working Paper, Sheffield Business School.

Laughlin, R. and Gray, R. (1988), *Financial Accounting; Method and Meaning*. London: Van Nostrand Reinhold.

Laughlin, R. and Puxty, A.G. (1983), 'Accounting Regulation: An Alternative Perspective', *Journal of Business Finance and Accounting*. 10, 3: 451–79.

Laughlin, R. and Puxty, A.G. (1984), 'Accounting Regulation: A Reply', *Journal of Business Finance and Accounting*. 11, 4: 593–96.

Legge, K. (1989), 'Human Resource Management: A Critical Analysis', in J. Storey (ed.), *New Perspectives on Human Resource Management*. London: Routledge.

Legge, K. (1995), *Human Resource Management: Rhetorics and Realities*. London: Macmillan.

Lehman, C. (1992), *Accounting's Changing Roles in Social Conflict*. New York: Markus Wiener.

Leigh, A. (1994), 'How to Reengineer Hearts and Minds', *Management Consultancy*, May, 51–4.

Leiss, W. (1976), *The Limits to Satisfaction*. Toronto: University of Toronto Press.

Leiss, W. (1983), 'The icons of the marketplace', *Theory, Culture & Society*. 1, 3: 10–21.

Leiss, W., Kline, S. and Jhally, S. (1986), *Social Communication in Advertising: Persons, Products and Images of Well-being*, New York: Methuen.

Letiche, H. and Van Hattem, R. (1994), 'Fractalization of the Knowlege Worker'. Paper presented at Knowledge, Work, Managerial Roles and European Competitiveness Workshop, ESC, Lyon, 30 November–3 December 1994.

Levine, D.N. (1985), 'Rationality and Freedom: Weber and Beyond', *Sociological Inquiry*. 51, 5: 5–25.

Lindblom, C.E. (1959), 'The Science of Muddling Through', *Public Administration Review*. XIX, 2: 79–88.

Lipietz, A. (1992), *Towards a New Economic Order: Postfordism, Ecology and Democracy*. Cambridge: Polity Press.

Littler, C. (1982), *The Development of the Labour Process in Capitalist Societies*. London: Heinemann.

Littler, C.R. and Salaman, E. (1982), 'Bravermania and Beyond: Recent Theories of the Labour Process', *Sociology*, 16, 2: 251–69.

Locke, R. (1989), *Management and Higher Education Since 1940*. Cambridge: Cambridge University Press

Lowe, E.A. and Shaw, R.W. (1968), 'An Analysis of Managerial Biasing: Evidence from a Company's Budgeting Process', *Journal of Management Studies*. 5, 3: 304–15.

Luke, C. and Gore, J. (eds) (1992), *Feminism and Critical Pedagogy*. London: Routledge.

Luhmann, N. (1982), *The Differentiation of Society*. New York: Columbia University Press.

Lukacs, G. (1971), *History and Class Consciousness*. London: Merlin.

Luke, T.W. and White, S.K. (1985), 'Critical Theory, Information Revolution, and an Ecological Path to Modernity', in J. Forester (ed.), *Critical Theory and Public Life*. Cambridge, MA: MIT Press.

Lukes, S. (1982), 'Of Gods and Demons: Habermas and Practical Reason', in J.B. Thompson and D. Held (eds), *Habermas. Critical Debates*. London: Macmillan.

Lupton, T. (1971), *Management and the Social Sciences*. Harmondsworth: Penguin.

Lyotard, J.-F. (1984), *The Postmodern Condition: A Report on Knowledge*. Manchester: Manchester University Press.

Lyytinen, K. (1987), 'Different Perspectives on Information Systems: Problems and Solutions, *Computing Surveys*. 19, 1: 5–42.

Lyytinen, K. (1992), 'Information Systems and Critical Theory', in M. Alvesson and H.C. Willmott (eds), *Critical Management Studies*. London: Sage.

Lyytinen, K. and Hirschheim, R. (1988), 'Information Systems as Rational Discourse; An Application of Habermas' Theory of Communicative Action', *Scandinavian Journal of Management Studies*. 4, 1/2: 19–30.

Lyytinen, K. and Klein, H. (1985), 'The Critical Theory of Jurgen Habermas as a Basis for a Theory of Information Systems', in E. Mumford, R. Hirschheim, G. Fitzgerald and T. Wood-Harper (eds), *Research Methods in Information Systems*. Amsterdam: North Holland.

Maccoby, M. (1976), *The Gamesman*. New York: Secker and Warburg.

MacIntyre, A.E. (1981), *After Virtue; A Study of Moral Theory*. London: Duckworth.

March, J.G. and. Olsen, J.P. (1976), *Ambiguity and Choice in Organizations*. Bergen: Universitetsforlaget.

March, J. and Simon, H. (1958), *Organizations*. New York: John Wiley.

Marcus, G. & Fischer, M. (1986), *Anthropology as Cultural Critique*. Chicago, IL: University of Chicago Press.

Marcuse, H. (1955), *Eros and Civilization*. Boston, MA: Beacon Press.

Marcuse, H. (1964), *One-Dimensional Man; Studies in the Ideology of Advanced Industrial Society*. Boston, MA: Beacon Press.

Marcuse, H. (1969), *An Essay on Liberation*. Boston, MA: Beacon Press.

Marcuse, H. (1978), *The Aesthetic Dimension: Towards a Critique of Marxist Aesthetics*. Boston, MA: Beacon Press.

Marshall, J. (1984), *Women Managers. Travellers in a Male World*. Chichester: Wiley.

Marshall, J. (1993), 'Viewing Organizational Communication from a Feminist Perspective: A Critique and Some Offerings', in S. Deetz (ed.), *Communication Yearbook*. Vol. 16, Newbury Park, CA: Sage.

Martin, J. (1990), 'Deconstructing organizational taboos: The suppression of gender conflict in organizations', *Organization Science*. 1: 339–59.

Martin, J. (1992), *The Culture of Organizations. Three Perspectives*. New York: Oxford University Press.

Marx, K. (1975), *Early Writings*. Harmondsworth: Penguin.

Marx, K. (1976), *Capital*. vol. 1, Harmondsworth: Penguin.

Mason, R.O. and Mitroff, I. (1981), *Challenging Strategic Planning Assumptions*. New York: John Wiley.

Mayo, E. (1949), 'Hawthorne and the Western Electric Company', in D. Pugh (ed.), *Organization Theory*. Harmondsworth: Penguin (1977).

McCarthy, T. (1978), *The Critical Theory of Jurgen Habermas*. London: Hutchison.

McGregor, D. (1960), *The Human Side of Enterprise*. New York: McGraw-Hill.

McIntosh, D. (1994), 'Language, Self and Lifeworld in Habermas' *Theory of Communicative Action'*. *Theory and Society*. 23: 1–33.

McKenna, R. (1991), 'Marketing is everything', *Harvard Business Review*. Jan–Feb 1991: 65–79.

McLaughlin, H. and Thorpe, R. (1993), 'Action Learning – A Paradigm in Emergence: The Problems Facing a Challenge to Traditional Management Education and Development', *British Journal of Management*. 4, 1: 19–27.

Meisenhelder, T. (1989), 'Habermas and Feminism. The Future of Critical Theory', in R.A. Wallace (ed.), *Feminism and Sociological Theory*. Newbury Park, CA: Sage.

Merchant, C. (1980), *Ecological Revolutions: Nature, Gender and Science in New England*. Chapel Hill, NC: University of North Carolina Press.

Meyer, J. and Rowan, B. (1977), 'Institutionalized Organizations: Formal Structure as Myth and Ceremony', *American Journal of Sociology*. 83: 340–63.

Miles, R.E. and Snow, C.C. (1978), *Organizational Strategy, Structure and Process*. New York: McGraw-Hill.

Miller, D. (1986), 'Configurations of Strategy and Structure: Toward a Synthesis', *Strategic Management Journal*. 7: 233–49.

Miller, P. and O'Leary, T. (1987), 'Accounting and the Construction of the Governable Person', *Accounting, Organizations and Society*. 12, 3: 235–61.

Mills, A. (1988), 'Organization, Gender and Culture', *Organization Studies*. 9, 3: 351–70.

Mills, A. and Tancred, P. (eds) (1992), *Gendering Organizational Analysis*. London: Sage.

Mingers, J. (1980), 'Towards an Appropriate Theory for Applied Systems Thinking: Critical Theory and Soft Systems Methodology', *Journal of Applied Systems Analysis*. 7: 41–9.

Mingers, J. (1984), 'Subjectivism and Soft Systems Methodology – A Critique', *Journal of Applied Systems Analysis*. 11: 85–103.

Mingers, J. (1991), 'The Content of OR Courses: Results of a Questionnaire to OR Groups', *Journal of the Operational Research Society*. 42: 375–82.

Mingers, J. (1992a), 'Technical, Practical and Critical OR – Past, Present and Future?', in M. Alvesson and H.C. Willmott (eds), *Critical Management Studies*. London: Sage.

Mingers, J. (1992b), 'What are Real Friends For? A Reply to Mike Jackson', *Journal of the Operational Research Society*. 43, 7: 732–5.

Mingers, J. (1992c), 'Recent Developments in Critical Management Science', *Journal of the Operational Research Society*. 43, 1: 1–10.

Mintzberg, H. (1973), *The Nature of Managerial Work*. New York: Harper and Row.

Mintzberg, H. (1975), 'The Manager's Job: Folklore and Fact', *Harvard Business Review*. July–Aug.: 49–61.

Mintzberg, H. (1987), 'Crafting Strategy', *Harvard Business Review*. July–Aug.: 66–75.

Mintzberg, H. (1990), 'The Design School: Reconsidering the Basic Premises of Strategic Management', *Strategic Management Journal*. 11: 171–95.

Mintzberg, H. and Waters, J.A. (1985), 'Of Strategies, Deliberate and Emergent', *Strategic Management Journal*. 6: 257–72.

Mintzberg, H., Raisinghani, D. and Theoret, A. (1976), 'The Structure of "Unstructured" Decision Processes', *Administrative Science Quarterly*. 21: 246–75.

Moore, D.C. (1991), 'Accounting on Trial: The Critical Legal Studies Movement and Its Lessons for Radical Accounting', *Accounting, Organizations and Society*. 16, 8: 763–93.

Morgan, Gareth (1980), 'Paradigms, metaphors and puzzle solving in organization theory', *Administrative Science Quarterly*. 25: 605–22.

Morgan, Gareth (1986), *Images of Organizations*. Newbury Park, CA: Sage.

Morgan, Glenn (1990), *Organizations and Society*. London: Macmillan.

Morgan, Glenn (1992), 'Marketing Discourse and Practice: Towards a Critical Analysis', in M. Alvesson and H. Willmott (eds), *Critical Management Studies*. London: Sage.

Morgan, Glenn and Willmott, H.C. (1993), 'The 'New Accounting Research: On Making Accounting More Visible', *Accounting, Auditing and Accountability Journal.* 6, 4: 3–36.

Mumby, D. (1988), *Communication and Power in Organizations: Discourse, Ideology and Domination.* Norwood, NJ: Ablex.

Mumby, D.K. and Putnam, L.L. (1992), 'The Politics of Emotion: A Feminist Reading of Bounded Rationality', *Academy of Management Review.* 17, 3: 465–86.

Mumford, E. (1983), 'Designing Human Systems for New Technology – The ETHICS Method', Manchester: Manchester Business School.

Muncy, J.A. and Fisk, R.P. (1987), 'Cognitive Relativism and the Practice of Marketing Science', *Journal of Marketing.* 51: 20–33.

Murray, F. and Knights, D. (1990), 'Inter-Managerial Competition and Capital Accumulation: IT Specialists, Accountants and Executive Control', *Critical Perspectives on Accounting.* 1, 2: 167–90.

Murray, J.B. and Ozanne, J.L. (1991), 'The critical imagination: Emancipatory interests in consumer research', *Journal of Consumer Research* 18: 129–44.

Murray, F. and Willmott, H.C. (1993), 'The Communication Problem in Information Systems Development', in P. Quintas (ed.), *Social Dimensions of Systems Engineering.* London: Ellis Horwood.

Naess, A. and Rothenberg, D. (1991), *Ecology, Community and Lifestyle.* Cambridge: Cambridge University Press.

Neimark, M. (1991), 'The King is Dead. Long Live the King!', *Critical Perspectives on Accounting.* 1, 1: 103–14.

Nichols, T. (1969), *Ownership, Control, and Ideology.* London: Allen and Unwin.

Nichols, T. and Beynon, H. (1977), *Living with Capitalism; Class Relations and the Modern Factory.* London: Routledge and Kegan Paul.

Nicholson, L.J. (ed.) (1990), *Feminism/Postmodernism.* London: Routledge.

Nord, W. (1983), 'The Political Economic Perspective On Organizational Effectiveness', in K. Cameron and D. Whetton (eds), *Organizational Effectiveness.* New York: Academic Press.

Nord, W. and Jermier, J. (1992), 'Critical social science for managers? Promising and perverse possibilities', in M. Alvesson and H. Willmott (eds), *Critical Management Studies.* London: Sage.

Nordquist, J. (1986), *Jurgen Habermas: A Bibliography.* Santa Cruz University, Reference and Research Services.

Oakland, J. (1989), *Total Quality Management.* London: Heinemann.

O'Connor, J. (1973), *The Fiscal Crisis of the State.* New York: St Martins Press.

O'Connor, M. (1994), *Is Capitalism Sustainable: Political Economy and the Politics of Ecology.* New York: Guilford Press.

Offe, C. and Wiesenthal, H. (1980), 'Two logics of collective action: Theoretical notes on social class and organizational form', in M. Zeitlin (ed.), *Political Power and Social Theory. Vol. 1*, Greenwich, CT: JAI Press.

Ogbonna, E. and Wilkinson, B. (1990), 'Corporate Strategy and Corporate Culture: The View from the Checkout', *Personnel Review.* 19, 4: 9–15.

Oliga, J.C. (1988), 'Methodological Foundations of Systems Methodologies', *Systems Practice.* 1, 1: 113–24.

Orlikowski, W. and Baroudi, J.J. (1989), 'IS Research Paradigms: Methods versus Substance', *Information Systems Research.* 2, 1: 1–28.

Otley, D. (1980), 'The Contingency Theory of Management Accounting: Achievements and Prognosis', *Accounting, Organizations and Society.* 5, 4: 413–28.

Ouchi, W. (1981), *Theory Z: How American Business Can Meet the Japanese Challenge.* New York: Addison-Wesley.

Pahl, R. and Winkler, J.T. (1974), 'The Economic Elite: Theory and Practice', in P. Stanworth and A. Giddens (eds), *Elites and Power in British Society.* Cambridge: Cambridge University Press.

Parry, R. and Mingers, J. (forthcoming), 'Community Operational Research: Its Context and Its Future', *Omega.*

Pascale, R.T. (1982), 'A Curious Addition to Corporate Grant Strategy', *Fortune*. 25 January: 115–16.

Pascale, R.T. (1984), 'Perspectives on Strategy: The Real Story Behind Honda's Success', *California Management Review*. 16: 47–73.

Pascale, R.T. (1992), *Managing on the Edge: How Successful Companies Use Conflict to Stay Ahead*. Penguin: Harmondsworth.

Pascale, R.T. and Athos, A.G. (1982), *The Art of Japanese Management*. Harmondsworth: Penguin.

Payne, S.L. (1991), 'A Proposal for Corporate Ethical Reform', *Business and Professional Ethics Journal*. 10, 1: 67–88.

Payne, S.L. (1992), 'Critical Systems Thinking: A Challenge or Dilemma in Its Practice', *Systems Practice*. 5, 3: 237–49.

Pendergrast, M. (1993), *For God, Country and Coca-Cola*. London: George Weidenfeld and Nicolson.

Perrow, C. (1986) *Complex Organizations. A Critical Essay*. 3rd edn, New York: Random House.

Peter, J.P. (1992), 'Realism and Relativism in Marketing Theory and Research: A Comment on Hunt's Scientific Realism', *Journal of Marketing*. 56: 72–9.

Peter, J.P. and Olson, J.C. (1983), 'Is Science Marketing?', *Journal of Marketing*. 47: 111–25.

Peters, T.J. (1984), 'Strategy Follows Structure: Developing Distinctive Skills', in G. Carroll and D. Vogel (eds), *Strategy and Organization: A West Coast Perspective*. Mansfield, MA: Pitman.

Peters, T.J. (1988), *Thriving on Chaos; Handbook for a Management Revolution*. London: Macmillan

Peters, T.J. (1992), *Liberation Management: Necessary Disorganization for the Nanosecond Nineties*. London: Macmillan.

Peters, T.J and Waterman, R.H. (1982), *In Search of Excellence; Lessons from America's Best-Run Companies*. New York: Harper and Row.

Pettigrew, A. (1973), *The Politics of Organizational Decision-Making*. London: Tavistock.

Pettigrew, A. (1975), 'Strategic Aspects of the Management of Specialist Activity', *Personnel Review*. 4: 5–13.

Pettigrew, A. (1985a), *The Awakening Giant; Continuity and Change at ICI*. Oxford: Blackwell.

Pettigrew, A. (1985b), 'Examining Change in the Long-Term Context of Culture and Politics', in J.M. Pennings (ed.), *Organizational Strategy and Change*. San Francisco, CA: Jossey-Bass.

Pettigrew, A. (1988), 'Longitudinal Field Research on Change: Theory and Practice', Paper presented to the National Science Foundation Conference on Longitudinal Research Methods in Organizations, Austin, Texas.

Pfeffer, J. (1978), 'The Micropolitics of Organizations', in M.W. Meyer (ed.), *Environment and Organizations*. New York: Jossey-Bass.

Pfeffer, J. (1981a), *Power in Organizations*. Boston, MA: Pitman.

Pfeffer, J. (1981b), 'Management as Symbolic Action; The Creation and Maintenance of Organizational Paradigms', in L.L. Cummings and B.M. Staw (eds), *Research in Organizational Behaviour*. 3: 1–52.

Pfeffer, J. (1993), 'Barriers to the Advance of Organizational Science: Paradigm Development as a Dependent Variable', *Academy of Management Review*. 18, 4: 599–620.

Pfeffer, J. and Salancik, G.R. (1978), *The External Control of Organizations: A Resource Dependency Perspective*. New York: Harper and Row.

Pine, B.J. (1993), *Mass Customization: The New Frontier in Business Competition*. Boston, MA: Harvard Business School Press.

Pollard, S. (1965), *The Genesis of Modern Management*. London: Edward Arnold.

Pollay, R.W. (1986), 'The Distorted Mirror: Reflections on the Unintended Consequences of Advertising', *Journal of Marketing*. 50 (April): 18–36.

Pollay, R. W. (1987), 'On the Value of Reflections on the Values in "The Distorted Mirror"', *Journal of Marketing*. 51 (July): 104–9.

Pondy, L.R. (1983), 'The Role of Metaphors and Myths in Organization and in the Facilitation of Change', in L.R. Pondy, P.J. Frost, G. Morgan and T.C. Dandridge (eds), *Organizational Symbolism*. Greenwich, CT: JAI Press.

Porter, M.E. (1980), *Competitive Strategy: Techniques for Analysing Industries and Competitors*. New York: Free Press.

Porter, M.E. (1985), *Competitive Advantage: Creating and Sustaining Superior Performance*. New York: Free Press.

Poster, M. (1989), *Critical Theory and Poststructuralism: In Search of a Context*. Ithaca, NY: Cornell University Press.

Power, M. (1990), 'Modernism, Postmodernism and Organizations', in J. Hassard and D. Pym (eds), *The Theory and Philosophy of Organizations: Critical Issues and New Perspectives*. London: Routledge.

Power, M.K. (1991), 'Educating Accountants: Towards a Critical Ethnography', *Accounting Organizations and Society*. 16, 4: 333–53.

Power, M. and Laughlin, R. (1992), 'Critical Theory and Accounting', in M. Alvesson and H. Willmott (eds), *Critical Management Studies*. London: Sage.

Prichard, C. and Willmott, H.C. (1997), 'Just How Managed is the McUniversity?', *Organization Studies*, forthcoming.

Pringle, R. (1988), *Secretaries Talk*. London: Verso.

Pusey, M. (1987), *Jurgen Habermas*. London: Tavistock.

Putnam, L., Bantz, C., Deetz, S., Mumby, D. and Van Maanen, J. (1993), 'Ethnography Versus Critical Theory: Debating Organizational Research', *Journal of Management Inquiry*. 2, 3: 221–35.

Puxty, A.G. (1991), 'Social Accountability and Universal Pragmatics', *Advances in Public Interest Accounting*. 4: 35–45

Puxty, A. (1993), *The Social and Organizational Context of Management Accounting*. London: Academic Press.

Quinn, J.B. (1980), *Strategies for Change: Logical Incrementalism*. Homewood, IL: Irwin.

Rabinow, P. (ed.) (1986), *The Foucault Reader*. Harmondsworth: Penguin.

Rasmussen, D. (1990), *Reading Habermas*. Oxford: Blackwell.

Raspa, R. (1986), 'Creating Fiction in the Committee: The Emergence of the Saturn Corporation at the General Motors', *Dragon*. 4: 7–22.

Ray, L.J. (1993), *Rethinking Critical Theory; Emancipation in the Age of Global Social Movements*. London: Sage.

Reed, M. (1985), *Redirections in Organizational Analysis*. London: Tavistock.

Reed, M. (1989), *The Sociology of Management*. London: Harvester Wheatsheaf.

Reed, M. (1990), 'From Paradigms to Images: The Paradigm Warrior Turns Post-modern Guru', *Personnel Review*. 19, 3: 35–40.

Reed, M. (1992), *The Sociology of Organizations: Themes, Perspectives and Prospects*. London: Harvester/Wheatsheaf.

Reed, M. and Anthony, P. (1992), 'Professionalizing Management and Managing Professionalization: British Management in the 1980s', *Journal of Management Studies*. 29, 5: 591–613.

Riesman, D. (1950), *The Lonely Crowd*. New Haven, CT: Yale University Press.

Ritzer, G. (1993), *The McDonaldization of Society*, Newbury Park, CA: Pine Forge.

Robbins, S. P. (1983), *Organization Theory. The Structure and Design of Organizations*. Englewood Cliffs, NJ: Prentice Hall.

Roberts, J. (1984), 'The Moral Character of Management Practice', *Journal of Management Studies*. 21, 3: 296–302.

Robey, D. and Farrow, D. (1982), 'User Involvement in Information Systems Development: A Conflict Model and Empirical Test', *Management Science*. 28, 1: 73–85.

Rockmore, T. (1989), *Habermas on Historical Materialism*. Bloomington, IN: University of Indiana Press.

Roderick, R. (1986), *Habermas and the Foundations of Critical Theory*. London: Macmillan.

Rorty, R. (1985), 'Habermas and Lyotard on Postmodernity', in R.J. Bernstein (ed.), *Habermas and Modernity*. Cambridge: Polity.

Rorty, R. (1989), *Contingency, Irony and Solidarity*. Cambridge: Cambridge University Press.

Rose, D. (1993), 'Private Rhetoric for the Public Sphere', Paper presented to the 11th EGOS Colloquium, Paris, July 1993.

Rose, N. (1990), *Governing the Soul: The Shaping of the Private Self*. London: Routledge.

Rosen, M. (1985), 'Breakfast at Spiro's: Dramaturgy and dominance', *Journal of Management*. 11, 2: 31–48.

Rosen, M. (1987), 'Critical Administrative Scholarship, Praxis and the Academic Workplace', *Journal of Management*. 13: 573–86.

Rosen, M. (1991), 'Coming to Terms with the Field: Understanding and Doing Organizational Ethnography', *Journal of Management Studies*. 28: 1–24.

Rosenberg, D., Tomkins, C. and Day, P. (1982), 'A Work Role Perspective on Accountants in Local Government Service Departments', *Accounting, Organizations and Society*. 7, 2: 123–37.

Rosenhead, J. (1989), 'O.R.: Social Science or Barbarism?' in M.C. Jackson, P. Keys and S.A. Cropper (eds), *Operational Research and the Social Sciences*. New York: Plenum Press.

Rosenhead, J. and Thunhurst, C. (1982), 'A Materialist Analysis of Operational Research', *Journal of the Operational Research Society*. 33: 111–22.

Roslender, R. (1990), 'Sociology and Management Accounting Research', *British Accounting Review*. 22: 351–72.

Roslender, R. (1992), *Sociological Perspectives on Modern Accountancy*. London: Routledge.

Roth, G. and Schluchter, W. (1979), *Max Weber's Vision of History: Ethics and Methods*. Berkeley, CA: University of California Press.

Sabia, D.R. and Wallukis, J. (eds) (1983), *Changing Social Science: Critical Theory and Other Critical Perspectives*. Albany, NY: State University of New York Press.

Sahlins, M. (1976), *Culture and Practical Reason*. Chicago, IL: University of Chicago Press.

Salaman, G. (1981), *Class and the Corporation*. Glasgow: Fontana.

Salaman, G. (ed.) (1992), *Strategic Human Resource Management*. London: Sage.

Sampson, E. (1989), 'The Deconstruction of Self', in J. Shotter and K. Gergen (eds), *Texts of Identity*. London: Sage.

Sandberg, Å. (ed.) (1981), *Forskning för förändring* (Research for Change), Stockholm: Centre for Working Life.

Schroyer, T. (1973), *The Critique of Domination: The Origins and Development of Critical Theory*. New York: George Braziller.

Schumacher, E.F. (1974), *Small is Beautiful*. London: Abacus.

Schwartz, H. (1987), 'Anti-Social Actions of Committed Organizational Participants', *Organization Studies*. 8, 4: 327–40.

Schwartz, H. (1990), *Narcissistic Process and Corporate Decay*. Albany, NY: State University of New York Press.

Scitovsky, T. (1976), *The Joyless Economy*. Oxford: Oxford University Press.

Scott, W.G. and Hart, D.K. (1989), *Organizational Values in America*. New Brunswick, NJ: Transaction.

Sculley, J. (with J.A. Byrne) (1988), *Odyssey: Pepsi to Apple . . . A Journey of Adventure, Ideas, and the Future*. New York: Harper and Row.

Sennett, R. (1980), *Authority*. New York: Vintage Books.

Shrivastava, P. (1986), 'Is Strategic Management Ideological?', *Journal of Management*. 12, 3: 363–77.

Shrivastava, P. (1987), *Bhopal: Anatomy of A Crisis*. Cambridge, MA: Ballinger.

Shrivastava, P. (1993), 'Management Paradigm for a Risk Society: Ecocentric Management in Industrial Ecosystems', Working Paper, Bucknell University, Lewisburg.

Shrivastava, P. (1994a), 'CASTRATED Environment: GREENING Organizational Studies', *Organization Studies*. 15, 5: 705–26.

Shrivastava, P. (1994b), 'Greening Business Education', *Journal of Management Inquiry*. 3, 3: 235–43.

Sievers, B. (1986), 'Beyond the Surrogate of Motivation', *Organization Studies*. 7, 4: 335–51.

Sikka, P. and Willmott, H.C. (1995) The Power of "Independence": Defending and Extending the Jurisdiction of Accounting in the UK , *Accounting, Organizations and Society*. 20, 6: 547–81.

Silverman, D. (1970), *The Theory of Organizations*. London: Heinemann.

Sloterdijk, P. (1980), *Critique of Cynical Reason*. London: Verso.

Sloterdijk, P. (1984), 'Cynicism – The Twilight of False Consciousness', *New German Critique*. 11, 3.

Smircich, L. (1983a), 'Organizations as Shared Meanings', in L.R. Pondy, P.J. Frost, G. Morgan and T.C. Dandridge (eds), *Organizational Symbolism*. Greenwich, CT: JAI Press.

Smircich, L. (1983b), 'Concepts of Culture and Organizational Analysis', *Administrative Science Quarterly*. 28: 339–58.

Smircich, L. (1985), 'Is Organizational Culture a Paradigm for Understanding Organizations and Ourselves?', in P.J. Frost, L.F. Moore, M.R. Louis, C.C. Lundberg and J. Martin (ed.), *Organizational Culture*. Beverly Hills, CA: Sage.

Smircich, L. (1986), 'Can a Radical Humanist Find Happiness Working in a Business School?' Paper presented to Academy of Management Meeting, August 1986.

Smircich, L. and G. Morgan (1982), 'Leadership: The Management of Meaning', *The Journal of Applied Behavioural Science*. 18, 3: 257–73.

Smircich, L. and Stubbart, C. (1985), 'Strategic Management in an Enacted World', *Academy of Management Review*. 10, 4: 724–36.

Smith, T. (1992), *Accounting for Growth*. London: Century Business.

Smith, V. (1990), *Managing in the Corporate Interest: Control and Resistance in an American Bank*. Berkeley, CA: University of California Press.

Snow, C.C. and Hrebiniak, L.G. (1980), 'Strategy, Distinctive Competence, and Organizational Performance', *Administrative Science Quarterly*. 25: 317–36.

Soeters, J. (1986), 'Excellent Companies as Social Movements', *Journal of Management Studies*. 23: 299–312.

Stablein, R. and Nord, W. (1985), 'Practical and Emancipatory Interests in Organizational Symbolism: A Review and Evaluation', *Journal of Management*. 11, 2: 13–28.

Stark, D. (1980), 'Class Struggle and the Transformation of the Labor Process: A Relational Approach', *Theory and Society*. 9: 89–130.

Stead, E. and Stead, J.G. (1992), *Management for a Small Planet*. Newbury Park, CA: Sage.

Steffy, B.D. and Grimes, A.J. (1986), 'A Critical Theory of Organizational Science', *Academy of Management Review*. 11, 2: 322–36.

Steffy, B.D. and Grimes, A.J. (1992), 'Personnel/Organization Psychology: A Critique of the Discipline', in M. Alvesson and H. Willmott (eds), *Critical Management Studies*. London: Sage.

Stirner, M. (1907), *The Ego and His Own*. London: Libertarian Book Club.

Storey, J. (1983), *Managerial Prerogative and the Question of Control*. London: Routledge and Kegan Paul.

Storey, J. (1985), 'Management control as a bridging concept', *Journal of Management Studies*. 22: 269–91.

Stubbart, C.I. (1989), 'Managerial Cognition: A Missing Link in Strategic Management Research', *Journal of Management Studies*. 26, 4: 325–47.

Susman, G. and Evered, R. (1978), 'An Assessment of the Scientific Merits of Action Research', *Administrative Science Quarterly*. 23: 582–608.

Tar, Z. (1977), *The Frankfurt School: The Critical Theories of Max Horkheimer and Theodor W. Adorno*. New York: John Wiley.

Taylor, F.W. (1911), *Principles of Scientific Management*. New York: Harper and Row.

Taylor, F.W. (1947), *Scientific Management*. London: Harper and Row.

Taylor, J.A. and Williams, H. (1994), 'The "Transformation Game": Information Systems and Process Innovation in Organizations', *New Technology, Work and Employment*. 9, 1: 54–65.

Therborn, G. (1980), *The Power of Ideology and the Ideology of Power*. London: Verso.

Thomas, A. (1980), 'Management and Education: Rationalization and Reproduction in British Business', *International Studies in Management and Organization*. X, 1–2: 71–109.

Thomas, A. (1993), *Controversies in Management*. London: Routledge.

Thompson, J. and Held, D. (eds) (1982), *Habermas: Critical Debates*. London: Macmillan.

Thompson, P. (1989), *The Nature of Work*. 2nd edition, London: Macmillan.

Thompson, P. and McHugh, D. (1990), *Work Organizations: A Critical Introduction*. London: Macmillan.

Thompson, P. and McHugh, D. (1995), *Work Organizations: A Critical Introduction*. 2nd edn, London: Macmillan.

Tinker, A.M. (1980), 'Towards a Political Economy of Accounting', *Accounting, Organizations and Society*. 5, 1: 147–60.

Tinker, A.M. (1985), *Paper Prophets; A Social Critique of Accounting*. Eastbourne: Holt Saunders.

Tinker, A.M. (1986), 'Metaphor or Reification: Are Radical Humanists Really Libertarian Anarchists?', *Journal of Management Studies*. 24, 3: 367–82.

Tinker, A.M. and Lowe, E.A. (1982), 'The Management Science of the Management Sciences', *Human Relations*. 35, 4: 331–47.

Tinker, A.M. and Lowe, E.A. (1984), 'One-Dimensional Management Science: The Making of Technocratic Consciousness', *Interfaces*. 14, 2: 40–56.

Tinker, A.M., Merino, B. and Neimark, M. (1982), 'The Normative Origins of Positive Theories', *Accounting, Organizations and Society*. 7, 2: 167–200.

Townley, B. (1993), 'Foucault, Power/Knowledge and its Relevance for Human Resource Management', *Academy of Management Review*. 18, 3: 518–45.

Townley, B. (1994), *Reframing Human Resource Management*. London: Sage.

Tsoukas, H. (1992), 'Panoptic Reason and the Search for Totality: A Critical Assessment of the Critical Systems Perspective', *Human Relations*. 45, 7: 637–57.

Tsoukas, H. (1993), 'Analogical reasoning and knowledge generation in organisation theory', *Organization Studies*. 14: 323–46.

Ulrich, W. (1983), *Critical Heuristics of Social Planning*. Berne: Werner-Haupt.

Ulrich, W. (1986), 'Critical Heuristics of Social Systems Design', Working Paper 10, Dept. of Management Science and Systems, University of Hull.

Ulrich, W. (1988), 'Systems Thinking, Systems Practice and Systems Philosophy: A Program of Research', *Systems Practice*. 1, 2: 137–63.

Van Maanen, J. (1991), 'The Smile Factory', in P.J. Frost, L.F. Moore, M.R. Louis, C.C. Lundberg and J. Martin (eds), *Reframing Organizational Culture*. Newbury Park, CA: Sage.

Veblen, T. (1953), *The Theory of the Leisure Class*. New York: New American Library

Wachtel, P. (1983), *The Poverty of Affluence: A Psychological Portrait of the American Way of Life*. New York: Free Press.

Walby, S. (1986), *Patriarchy at Work*. Cambridge: Polity.

Walsham, G. (1993), *Interpreting Information Systems in Organizations*. London: Wiley.

Watson, T. (1977), *The Personnel Managers*. London: Routledge.

Watson, T. (1994), *In Search of Management*. London: Routledge

Weber, M. (1948), *From Max Weber: Essays in Sociology*. London: Routledge and Kegan Paul.

Weber, M. (1949), *The Methodology of the Social Sciences*. New York: Free Press.

Weber, M. (1968), *Economy and Society; An Outline of Interpretive Sociology*. New York: Bedminster Press.

Weber, M (1978), *Economy and Society*. 3 vols, New York: Bedminster Press.

Weedon, C. (1988), *Feminist Practice and Poststructuralist Theory*. Oxford: Basil Blackwell.

Weick, K. (1969), *The Social Psychology of Organizing*. Reading, MA: Addison-Wesley.

Weick, K.E. (1979), *The Social Psychology of Organizing*. 2nd edition, Reading, MA: Addison-Wesley.

Weick, K.E. (1987), 'Theorizing About Organizational Communication', in F. Jablin, L. Putnam, K. Roberts and L. Porter (eds), *Handbook of Organizational Communication*. Newbury Park, CA: Sage.

Weisbord, M. (1987), *Productive Workplaces*. San Francisco, CA: Jossey-Bass.

Weizenbaum, J. (1976), *Computer Power and Human Reason – From Judgement to Calculation*. New York: Freeman.

Wensley, R. (1987), 'Marketing Strategy', in M.J. Baker (ed.), *The Marketing Book*. London: Heinemann in association with the British Institute of Marketing.

Westley, F. (1990), 'Middle Managers and Strategy: Microdynamics of Inclusion', *Strategic Management Journal*. 11: 337–51.

Wexler, P. (ed.) (1991), *Critical Theory Now*. London: The Falmer Press.

White, S. (1988), *The Recent Work of Jürgen Habermas*. Cambridge: Cambridge University Press.

White, S.K. (1986), 'Foucault's Challenge to Critical Theory', *American Political Science Review*. 80, 2: 419–32.

Whitebrook, J. (1984), 'Reason and Happiness: Some Psychoanalytic Themes in Critical Theory', *Praxis International*. 4, 1: 15–31.

Whitley, R. (1984a), 'The Fragmented State of Management Studies', *Journal of Management Studies*. 21, 3: 21–48.

Whitley, R. (1984b), 'The Scientific Status of Management Research as a Practically-Oriented Social Science', *Journal of Management Studies*. 21, 4: 369–90.

Whitley, R. (1988), 'The Management Sciences and Managerial Skills', *Organization Studies*. 9, 1: 47–68.

Whitley, R. (1989), 'On the Nature of Managerial Tasks and Skills: Their Distinguishing Characteristics and Organization', *Journal of Management Studies*. 20, 3: 209–24.

Whitley, R. (1990), 'East Asian Enterprise Structures and the Comparative Analysis of Forms of Business Organization', *Organization Studies*. 11, 1: 47–74.

Whitley, R. (ed.) (1992), *Business Systems in East Asia*. London: Sage.

Whittington, R. (1989), *Corporate Strategies in Recession and Recovery: Social Structure and Strategic Choice*. London: Unwin Hyman.

Whittington, R. (1992), 'Putting Giddens into Action: Social Systems and Managerial Agency', *Journal of Management Studies*. 29, 6: 693–712.

Whittington, R. (1993), *What is Strategy – and Does it Matter?*. London: Routledge.

Wiggerhaus, R. (1994), *The Frankfurt School: Its History, Theories and Political Significance*. Cambridge: Polity.

Wildavsky, A. (1968), *The Politics of the Budgeting Process*. Boston, MA: Little Brown.

Wilkinson, A. (1993), 'Managing Human Resources for Quality', in B.G. Dale (ed.), *Managing Quality*. 2nd edition, London: Prentice Hall.

Wilkinson, A. and Willmott, H.C. (eds) (1995a), *Making Quality Critical*. London: Routledge.

Wilkinson, A. and Willmott, H.C. (1995b) 'Introduction', in Wilkinson and H. C. Willmott (eds), *Making Quality Critical*. London: Routledge.

Willmott, H.C. (1983), 'Paradigms of Accounting Research', *Accounting, Organizations and Society*. 8, 4: 389–405.

Willmott, H.C. (1984a), 'Images and Ideals of Managerial Work: A Critical Examination of Conceptual and Empirical Accounts', *Journal of Management Studies*. 21, 3: 349–68.

Willmott, H.C. (1984b), 'Accounting Regulation: An Alternative Perspective', *Journal of Business Finance and Accounting*. 11, 4: 585–91.

Willmott, H.C. (1986), 'Organizing the Profession: A Theoretical and Historical Examination of the Development of the Major Accounting Bodies in the UK', *Accounting, Organizations and Society*. 11, 6: 555–80.

Willmott, H.C. (1987), 'Studying Managerial Work: A Critique and a Proposal', *Journal of Management Studies*. 24, 3: 249–70.

Willmott, H.C. (1989), 'OR as a Problem Situation: From Soft Systems Methodology to Critical Science', in M.C. Jackson, P. Keys and S.A. Cropper (eds), *Operational Research in the Social Sciences*. New York: Plenum Press.

Willmott, H.C. (1990), 'Beyond Paradigmatic Closure in Organizational Enquiry', in J. Hassard and D. Pym (eds), *The Theory and Philosophy of Organizations: Critical Issues and New Perspectives*. London: Routledge.

Willmott, H.C. (1992), 'Postmodernism and Excellence: The De-differentation of Economy and Culture', *The Journal of Organizational Change Management*. 5, 1: 58–68.

Willmott, H.C. (1993a), 'Strength is Ignorance; Slavery is Freedom: Managing Culture in Modern Organizations', *Journal of Management Studies*. 30, 4: 515–52.

Willmott, H.C. (1993b), 'Breaking the Paradigm Mentality', *Organization Studies*. 14, 5: 681–720.

Willmott, H.C. (1994a), 'Theorising Human Agency, Responding to the Crisis of (Post) Modernity', in J. Hassard and M. Parker (eds), *Towards a New Theory of Organizations*. London: Routledge.

Willmott, H.C. (1994b), 'Management Education: Provocations to a Debate', *Management Learning*. 25, 1: 105–36.

Willmott, H.C. (1994c), 'Business Process Reeingineering and Human Resource Management', *Personnel Review*. 23, 3, 34–46.

Willmott, H.C. (1995a), 'Managing the Academics: Commodification and Control in the Development of University Education in the UK', *Human Relations*. 48, 9: 993–1028.

Willmott, H.C. (1995b), 'Management as Science? Methodologies of Change Management in Critical Perspective', Working Paper, Manchester School of Management.

Willmott, H.C. (1995c) 'Death. So What? Sociology and Sequestration', Mimeo, Manchester School of Management, UMIST.

Willmott, H.C. (1995d), 'The Odd Couple: Reengineering Business Processes, Managing Human Resources', *New Technology, Work and Employment*. 10, 2: 89–98.

Willmott, H.C. (1996a), 'On the Idolization of Markets and the Denigration of Marketers: Some Critical Reflections on a Professional Paradox', in D. Brownlie, M. Saren, R. Wensley and R. Whittington (eds), *Rethinking Marketing*. London: Sage.

Willmott, H.C. (1996b), 'Re-cognizing "The Other": Reflections on a New Sensibility in Social and Organization Studies', in R. Chia (ed.), *In the Realm of Organization: Essays for Robert Cooper*. London: Routledge.

Willmott, H.C. (1996c), 'A Metatheory of Management: Omniscience or Obfuscation?', *British Journal of Management*. In press.

Willmott, H.C. and Knights, D. (1982), 'The Problem of Freedom: Fromm's Contribution to a Critical Theory of Work Organization', *Praxis International*. 2, 2: 204–25.

Willmott, H.C. and Wray-Bliss, E. (1996), 'Process Reengineering, Information Technology and the Transformation of Accountability', in W.J. Orlikowski, G. Walsham, M.R. Jones and J.I. DeGross (eds), *Information Technology and Changes in Organizational Work*. London: Chapman and Hall.

Wilson, D. (1982), 'Electricity and Resistance: A Case Study of Innovation and Politics', *Organization Studies*. 3, 2: 119–40.

Wilson, R.M.S. and Chua, W.F. (1988), *Managerial Accounting; Method and Meaning*. London: Van Nostrand Reinhold.

Winograd, T. and Flores, F. (1986), *Computers and Cognition: A New Foundation for Computer System Design*. New York: Ablex.

Wood, S. (1980), 'Corporate Strategy and Organizational Studies', in D. Dunkerley and G. Salaman (eds), *International Yearbook of Organization Studies*. London: Routledge and Kegan Paul.

Wood, S. (ed.) (1982), *The Degradation of Work?*. London: Hutchinson.

Wood, S. and Kelly, J. (1978), 'Towards a Critical Management Science', *Journal of Management Studies*. February, 1–24.

Yates, D. (1985), *The Politics of Management*. San Francisco, CA: Jossey-Bass.

Zeitlin, M. (1974), 'Corporate Ownership and Control: The Large Corporation and the Capitalist Class', *American Journal of Sociology*. 79, 5, 1073–119.

# Index